viaBooks, a PennDesign Publication, Volume 2

Edited by
Megan Born, Helene Furján, and Lily Jencks,
with Phillip M. Crosby

Book design by
K.T. Anthony Chan

Published by
PennDesign and The MIT Press
Philadelphia, Pennsylvania; Cambridge, Massachusetts; London, England

First published 2012 by
viaBooks, a PennDesign Publication
University of Pennsylvania
Philadelphia, PA 19104
http://design.upenn.edu/via

The MIT Press
Massachusetts Institute of Technology
Cambridge, Massachusetts 02142
http://mitpress.mit.edu

©2012 Trustees of the University of Pennsylvania
All rights reserved. No part of this publication may be reproduced, stored in a retrieval system, or transmitted in any form or by any means including and not limited to electronic, mechanical, photocopying, recording or otherwise without the prior permission in writing from the publishers, except in the context of reviews.

Typeset in Alte Haas Grotesk, Distro, Garamond Premier Pro, and Helvetica Neue.
Printed and bound in Hong Kong.

Library of Congress
cataloging-in-publication information:
Dirt / edited by Megan Born, Helene Furján,
Lily Jencks, with Phillip M. Crosby.
    p.   cm. — (Viabooks ; v. 2)
Includes bibliographical references and index.
ISBN 978-0-262-51692-1 (pbk. : alk. paper)
1. Design. I. Born, Megan. II. Furján, Helene Mary,
1966– III. Jencks, Lily. IV. Crosby, Phillip M.
NK1525.D56   2012
720—dc23
2011026454

MIT Press books may be purchased at special quantity discounts for business or sales promotional use. For information, please email: special_sales@mitpress.mit.edu

Or write to:
Special Sales Department
The MIT Press
55 Hayward Street
Cambridge, MA 02142

Send editorial correspondence to:
viaBooks
Meyerson Hall
University of Pennsylvania, School of Design
Philadelphia, PA 19104

Disclaimer
The views expressed in this volume do not necessarily represent the views of viaBooks, PennDesign, or the University of Pennsylvania. Contributors are solely responsible for securing copyrights and/or licensing for their respective content. In making Dirt, we have used a small number of images for which copyright holders could not be identified. In these cases, it has been our assumption that such images belong to the public domain. If you claim ownership of any the images presented here, and have not been properly identified, please notify viaBooks and we will be happy to make a formal acknowledgment in all future editions. All images used under a Creative Commons license have been credited as such. The Editors have made every effort to contact copyright holders for material in this volume. Please contact viaBooks in case of error or omission.

via Logo:
Designed by K.T. Anthony Chan for viaBooks

viaBooks, a PennDesign Publication
Marilyn Jordan Taylor
Dean

David Leatherbarrow
Associate Dean of Aacademic Affairs

Helene Furján
Series Editor and Assistant Professor

Cathryn Dwyre
Managing Editor

Megan Schmidgal
Director of Communications

Christopher Cataldo
Director of Finance

Dirt
viaBooks Volume 2

Megan Born, Helene Furján, and Lily Jencks
Editors

Phillip M. Crosby
Associate Editor

Cathryn Dwyre
Assistant Editor

K.T. Anthony Chan
Designer

Tzu-Ching Lai
Layout Editor

Susan Crosby
Copy Editor and Layout Editor

Gabriela Sarhos
Copy Editor

Susannah Brewster with Lisa Schwert
Cover Illustration

Editorial Staff
Leslie Billhymer, Deb Hoy, Aroussiak Gabrielian, and Sarah Peck

Staff
Jared Bledsoe, Jason DeMarco, Joshua Freese, Kristi Loui, Virginia Melnyk, and Daniel Whipple
with Ana Blomeier, Gregory Hurcomb, Alex Lee, Ginna Nguyen, Margaux Schindler, and Jenny Trumble

viaBooks is generously supported by
American Institute of Architects
New York Chapter

Center for Architecture
New York

Graduate and Professional Student Assembly
University of Pennsylvania

Graham Foundation for
the Advancement of the Arts
Chicago, Illinois

School of Design
University of Pennsylvania

Contents

6 **Acknowledgements**

8 **Editorial**

Story Lines

18 **Flashes of Brilliance**
Sylvia Lavin in conversation

24 **Autonomous Worlds**
The Work of Larissa Fassler
Helene Furján

30 **Rumor**
Keller Easterling

36 **The Gleaming Toys**
Mark Campbell

40 **6 Ways of Being a Stranger**
Lindsay Bremner

Fertile Minds

56 **Robert Le Ricolais**
And the Search for Automorphic Structure
Richard Wesley

64 **Things Themselves Are Lying, and So Are Their Images**
Robert Le Ricolais

74 **At the Boundaries of Practice**
The Remaking of Spiral Jetty
Ruth Erickson

78 **Skull / Kidney / Skin**
Kim Brickley

84 **On Duration**
Frank Matero

94 **So Close You Can Touch It**
Helene Furján

Process Work

114 **Orbigraphia**
Rhett Russo

130 **Branching Morphogenesis**
A Tale of Imagination, Translation and Visualization
Sabin+Jones LabStudio,
Essay by Annette Fierro

136 **Secret Pact of Parts**
Of Plants and Parametrics
Ferda Kolatan

142 **Live Models**
Jason Kelly Johnson and Nataly Gattegno, Future Cities Lab

148 **Tickle the Shitstem**
Phoebe Washburn in conversation

154 **Between Line and Shadow**
Marion Weiss in conversation

Active Agents

174 Rising Currents:
Contemporary Design Discourse

Barry Bergdoll

180 The Suburbs are Dead, Long Live the Suburbs!

John D. Landis

186 Pathos and Irony
Industrial Still-Life in Japan

Tetsugo Hyakutake

194 Dirty Cities, Dirtier Policies
The Philadelphia Office of Sustainability

Mark Alan Hughes and William W. Braham in conversation

206 FLUXscape
Remapping Philadelphia's Post-Industrial Terrain

Andrea Hansen

218 Holey Urbanisms

Phillip M. Crosby

Rich Ground

232 Root WordsW

Megan Born

238 Ecology, for the Evolution of Planning and Design

Ian McHarg

252 A New Systemic Nature
For Mussolini's Landscape Urbanism

Alan Berger and Case Brown

262 Surface In-Depth
Between Landscape and Architecture

Anita Berrizbeitia, William Braham, James Corner, Phu Hoang, Keith Kaseman, Cathrine Veikos, and Marion Weiss

272 Waste and Dirt
Notes on the Architecture of Compost

William W. Braham

276 Hydrophile
Hydrodynamic Green Roof

Marcelyn Gow and Ulrika Karlsson, Servo

284 Not Garden

Karen M'Closkey and Keith VanDerSys

290 An Ornament of Sustainability, or, How Do I Keep This Damn Orchid Alive?

Lily Jencks

302 Contributors

308 Credits

310 Image Credits

314 viaBooks

316 Words from the pages of *Dirt*

Illustration by Jake Levine

The Editors of Dirt would like to thank Barry Bergdoll, William Braham, Eugenie Birch, Roger Conover, James Corner, Gary Hack, Simon Kim, John Landis, David Leatherbarrow, Randall Mason, Frank Matero, Karen M'Closkey, Detlef Mertins (*in memoriam*), Joshua Mosely, Marion Weiss, Richard Wesley, and Patricia Woldar, for their continued support and guidance of viaBooks; William Whitacker and Nancy Thorne of the Architectural Archives of the University of Pennsylvania, for their invaluable assistance; Nancy Levinson, Sarah Herda and the Graham Foundation, Erin McClosky and the AIA New York Chapter, and the GAPSA of the University of Pennsylvania for their support and recognition of viaBooks; Luke Bulman and Jessica Young of Thumb Design, Rhett Russo, David Ruy, and Brent Wahl, for their valuable interest and insight; Tonya Markiewicz and Morgan Martinson, for their experience and generosity; Kristine Allouchery, Catherine C. DiBonaventura, Clark L. Erickson, Rick Haverkamp, Chris Howie, Staci Kaplan, Stacy Lutner, Nysia Petrakis, Diane Pringle, Christine Reid, Julianna Siracusa, and Karl M. Wellman for their support; Faris Al-Shathir, Jonathan Asher, Alex Bevk, Gregory Hurcomb, Nadine Kashlan, Douglas Meehan, Alex Gabriel Muller, John Sands, Samir Shah, Kristen Smith, and Sarah Zimmer, for their energy, enthusiasm and contributions; Susan Crosby, Aaron Jezzi, Jeremy Leman, Jason Santa Maria, Scott Mitchell, Chris Perry, and Anne Reeve, for patience, encouragement and insight; Tammy Poon, for her generosity and support; and Freya Rozie Furján, for enlivening meetings and eating dirt.

Finally, we would like to thank Marilyn Jordan Taylor for her enthusiastic support of the project, and for her invaluable guidance, advice and input, at all levels of the production of Dirt.

Dirt is not messy.
Dirt is not 'dirty.'
Dirt is teeming with life, and rich with possibility.

Nothing would give up life; Even the dirt kept breathing a small breath.
Theodore Roethke, "Root Cellar" (1948)

You don't get anything clean without getting something else dirty.
Cecil Baxter

Dirt comes from a position at the intersection of landscape and architecture and presents a selection of work that shares dirty attitudes. A landscape architect's understanding of dirt—a fertile medium—overturns the term's negative connotations to understand it as explicitly productive. Rooted in the study of ecology, landscape architecture sees dirt as a highly-complex system, dynamic, adaptive, and able to accommodate great difference while maintaining a cohesive structure. This productive definition of dirt collides with the historical view of dirt: that which is unclean, out of place, or morally corrupt. Dirt is less that by which we are repulsed than that which is endlessly giving and fertile. Organisms grow, thrive, and evolve amidst dirt. Dirt is thus a matrix capable of emergent behaviors, nurturing growth, spawning development, and igniting change.

Dirt is interested in the noise in the system, the irritant that forces productive mutations and adaptations. Dirt is the stuff that makes a system jump. As a catalyst, dirt challenges its cohesive, totalizing logic to provoke evolution into a sophisticated, more complexly-structured system. Applied to social linkages, working processes, and urban networks, dirt is not always visible or easily understood, but its effects are tangible and productive.

Dirt can be a modifier, causing effect and change. It can also be the modified material itself. This tension between—illustrated via the verb *to dirty* and noun *dirt*—is visible in an attitude towards process and material. These two terms are the point and counterpoint of this volume of *viaBooks*.

Layered together, these meanings of dirt define a metaphor robust enough to apply to social linkages, working processes, imaginative ideas, physical substrates, and urban networks. Here, dirt leaves behind the moral baggage given by modernists and is freed to new perceptions and potentials. *Dirt* investigates, evaluates, critiques, and celebrates dirt in five chapters. Story Lines, Fertile Minds, Process Work, Active Agents, and Rich Ground collect the work in a matrix, organizing a diverse collection of essays, observations, interviews, and art and design projects.

Story Lines
Narratives of all kinds—stories, tales, and rumors—are the stuff of ideas—concepts and hypotheses—and the stuffing of history. Stories and tales take on their own life, passed on virally in networks and tribes of readers or listeners. Fast and efficient, tales spread quickly and easily through families, social networks, and professional cohorts.

Without a known author, gossip is the pinnacle of narrative influence: illogical, unpredictable, and ever changing. These yet-to-be-proven facts (laced with fictions) are packaged in between the lines of stories, and dispersed in hushed voices over cocktails, in off-the-record conversations, on blogs, in tweets, through friends. This dirty mode of communication propagates trends, ideas, and movements, and is crucial to the evolution of critical discourse.

Fertile Minds

Brilliant projects do not follow straight lines, but rather meander through metaphor, hopscotch across a plethora of mediums, and dodge logistic, financial, and temporal bullets. Innovation is born out of a dirty mash-up of fact, experience, technique, intuition, and imagination. Illogical leaps are made from what is known to what could potentially be. Materials and processes that were once considered out of place are reshaped, repositioned, recontextualized, and reappropriated for new productive ends. By exploring possibilities and potentials through imagination, experiment, and proposition, what was once unwanted becomes productive and desired.

Process Work

Elegant and useful things are born out of complex, redundant, and excessive methods of production. False starts, brilliant failures, and the distractions from the periphery help to spawn unexpected results and fuel unpredictable realizations. The relationship between a designer and their creative products is intimate and complex. The accumulation of multiple techniques, media, and/or fields of study generate unexpected connections that spark novel ideas and lead to innovative artifacts. A fertile creative process is also a dirty one.

Active Agents

Cities are dirty. They are made of recognized systems and organizations such as infrastructural frameworks, bureaucratic hierarchies, economic markets, municipal plans, and street grids, as well as informal networks and constructions that are neither planned nor sanctioned at-large. These informal systems and adaptive forms work outside political and geographic boundaries to fill infrastructural gaps and redirect urban flows. The tension and collaboration of the formal with the informal creates productive urban life.

Rich Ground

The material that is dirt is not 'matter out of place,' but rather a fertile medium. Soil and earth, as well as dust, debris, waste and compost, are often unseen, unrecognized, and disliked, yet provide critical structure and nourishment to encourage growth, harvest change, and record time.

Dirt is designed. It is uniquely composed, site specific, and innately intelligent. The matter is constantly shifting, changing, and evolving to become a more intelligent, efficient, and productive medium. Dirt is a design tool. Collecting and composing dirty matter is a fruitful foundation for the creation of spaces, artifacts, and atmospheres.

We aspire to *Dirt* being robust enough to accommodate a heterogeneous mix of disciplines—architecture, landscape architecture, urban planning and design, historic preservation, fine arts, and art history. We are not presenting a totalized argument, but rather revealing the variety that can be created and collected with a shared attitude and rigorous but divergent processes. The structural matrix of dirt is neither oppositional nor hierarchical, and, while it is not pure, it is consistent and potent. *Dirt* does not aim to define dirt, but to bring the collected essays, projects, interviews, and debates into conversation to reveal a contemporary attitude that is rich for consideration.

Editors

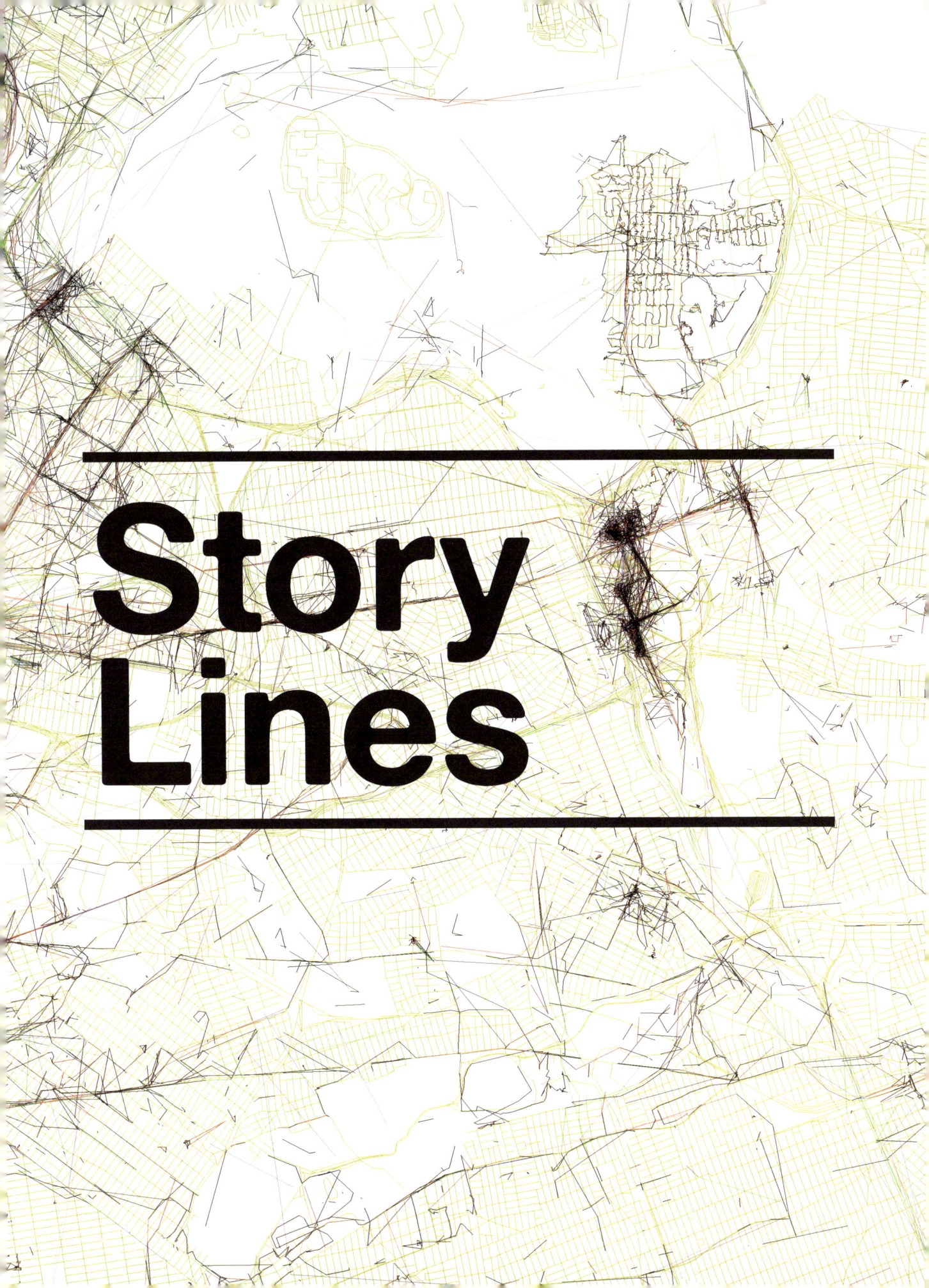

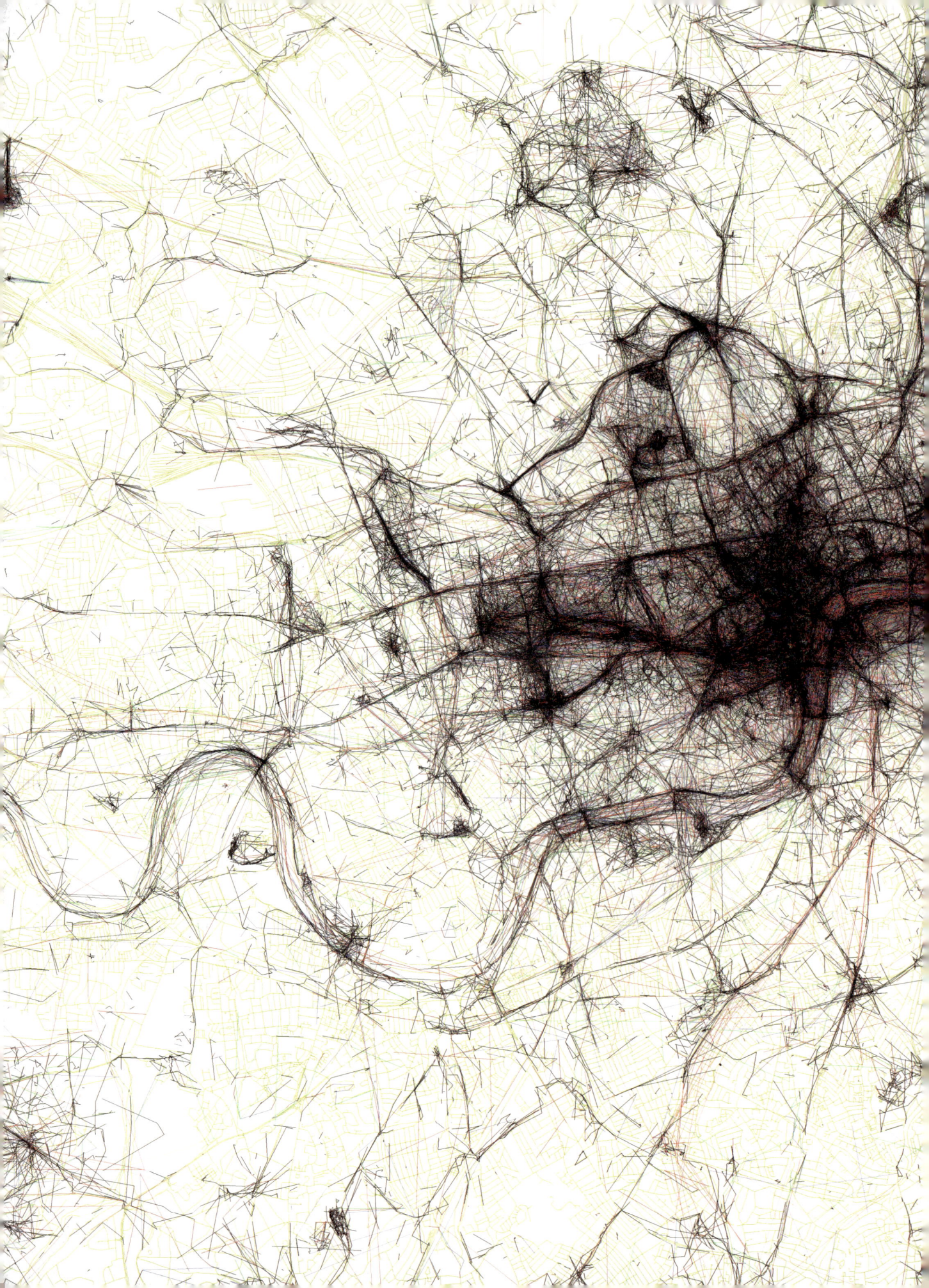

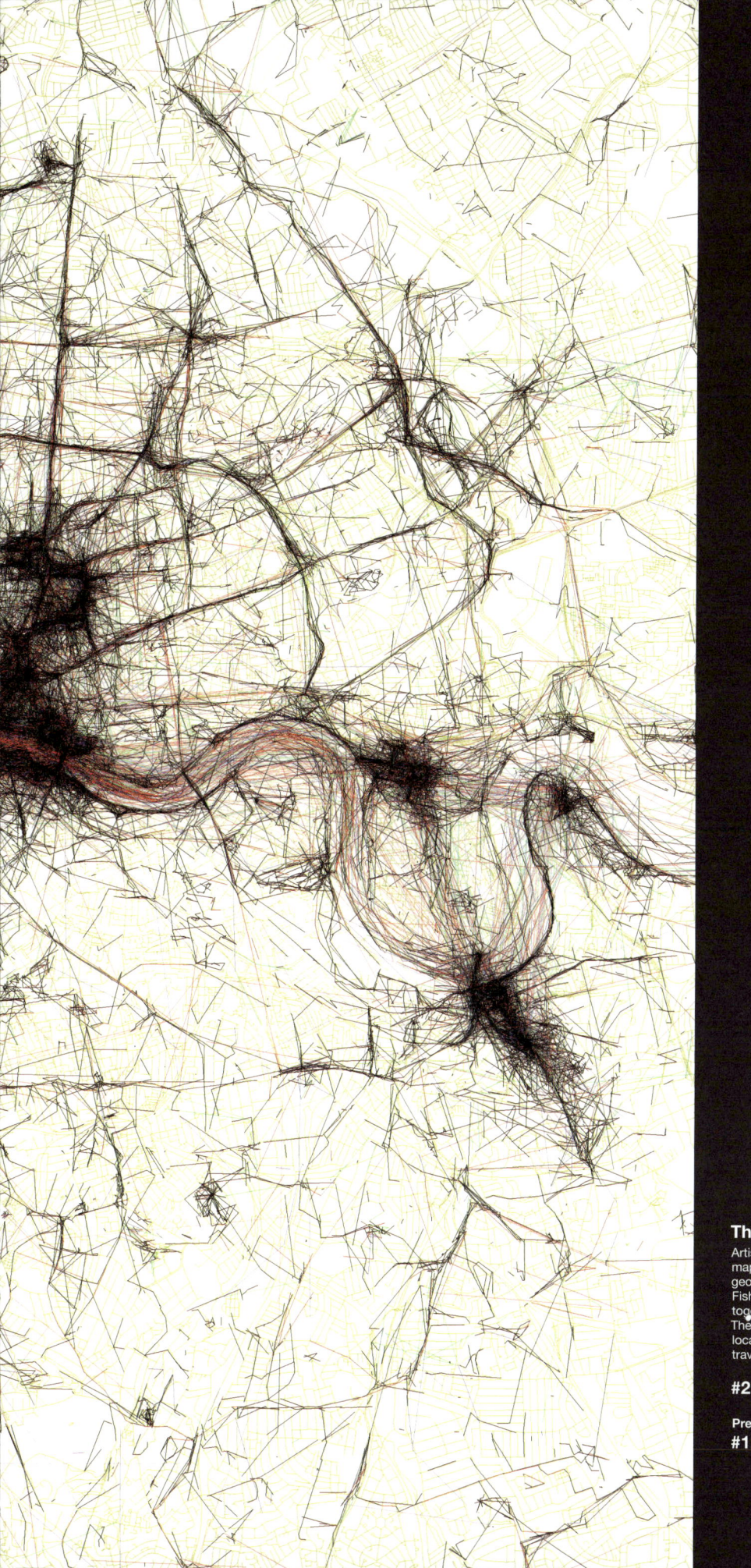

The Geotaggers' World Atlas
Artist and digital cartographer Eric Fischer created maps of 50 cities through the accumulation of geotags on photos uploaded to Flickr and Picasa. Fisher converted the geotags into points, which together amass into recognizable urban forms. The layering of color (red for tourists, blue for locals) makes visible areas of cities populated by travelers versus dwellers.

#2: London

Previous Spread
#1: New York

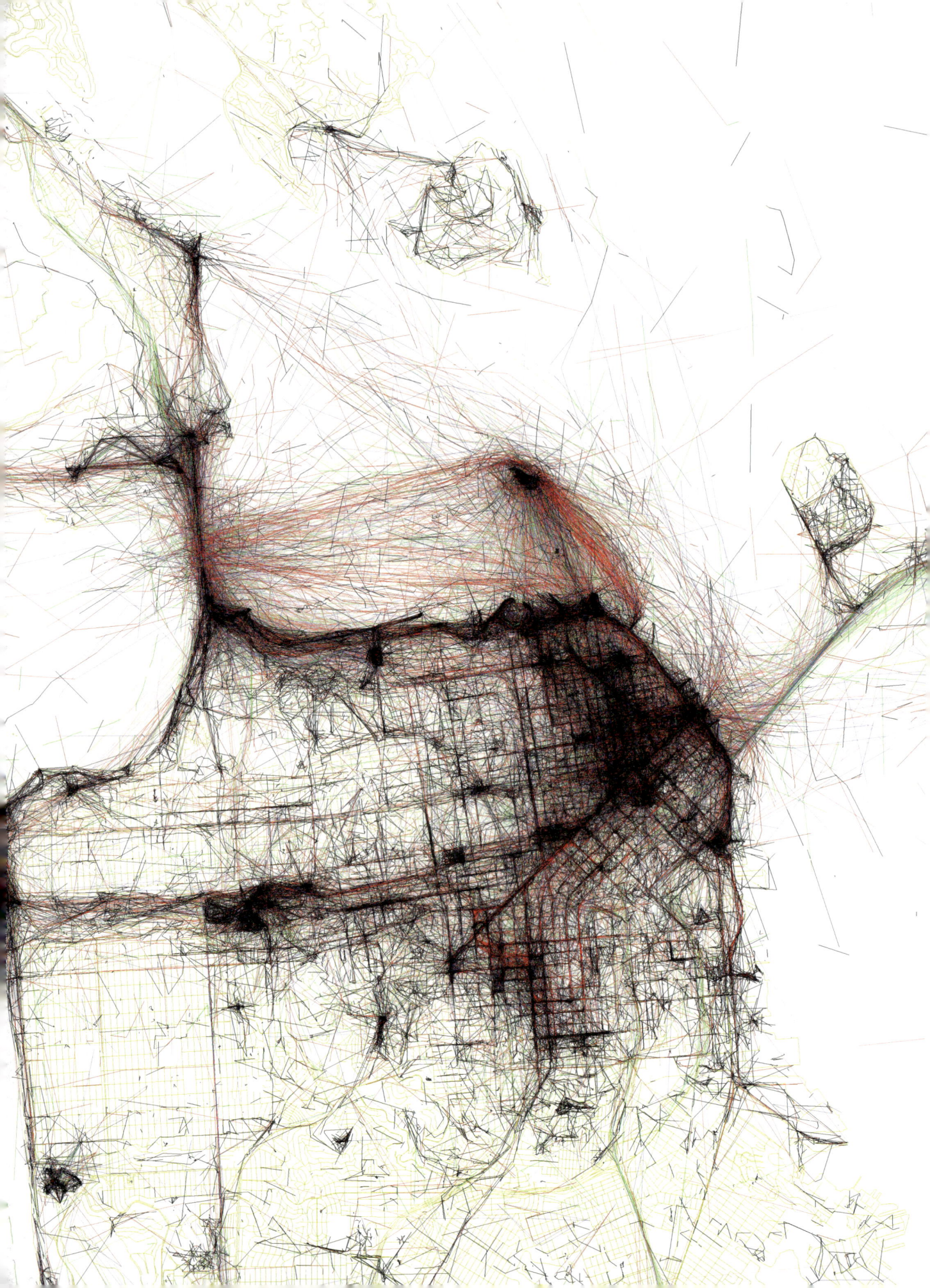

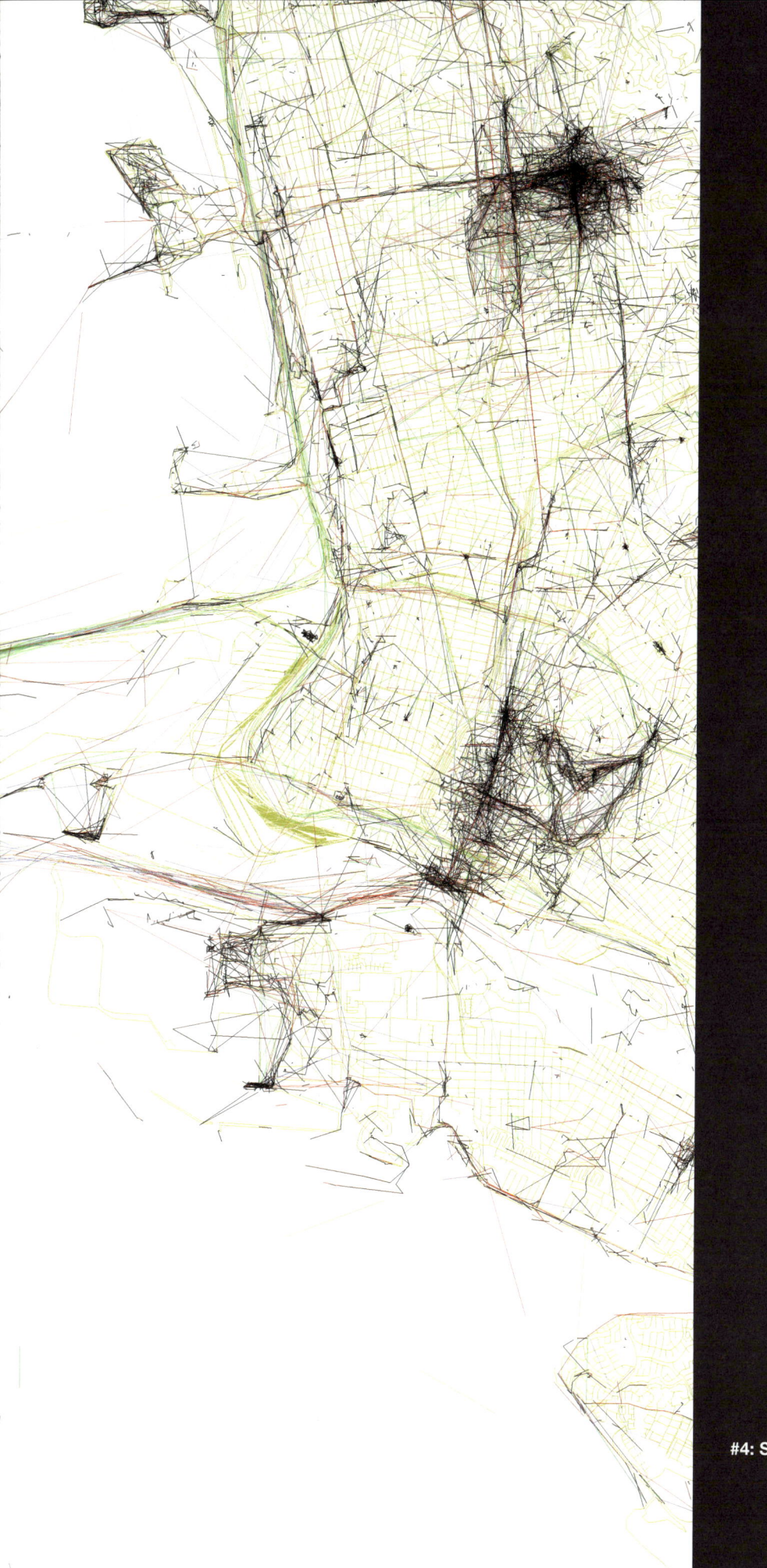

#4: San Francisco

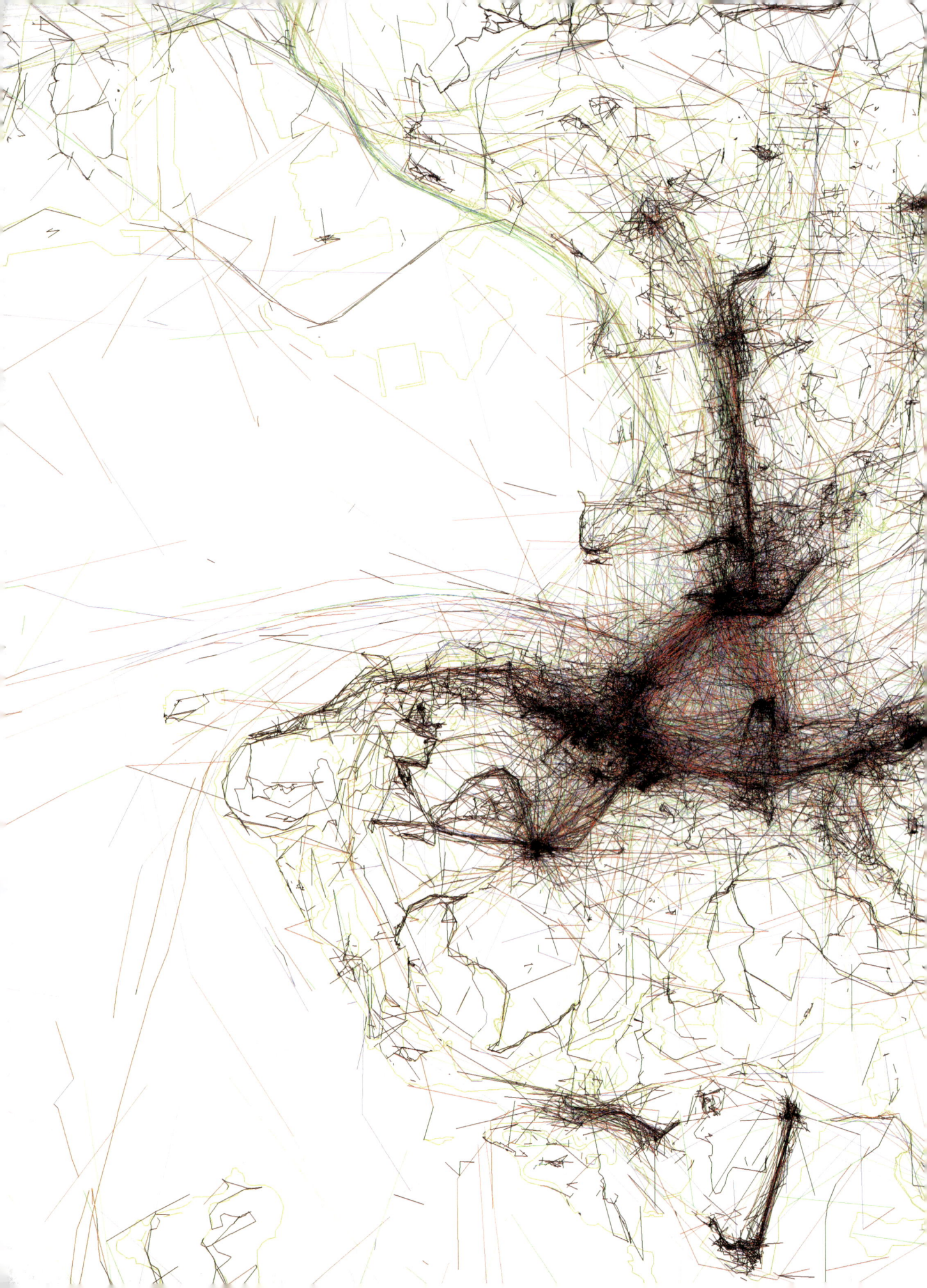

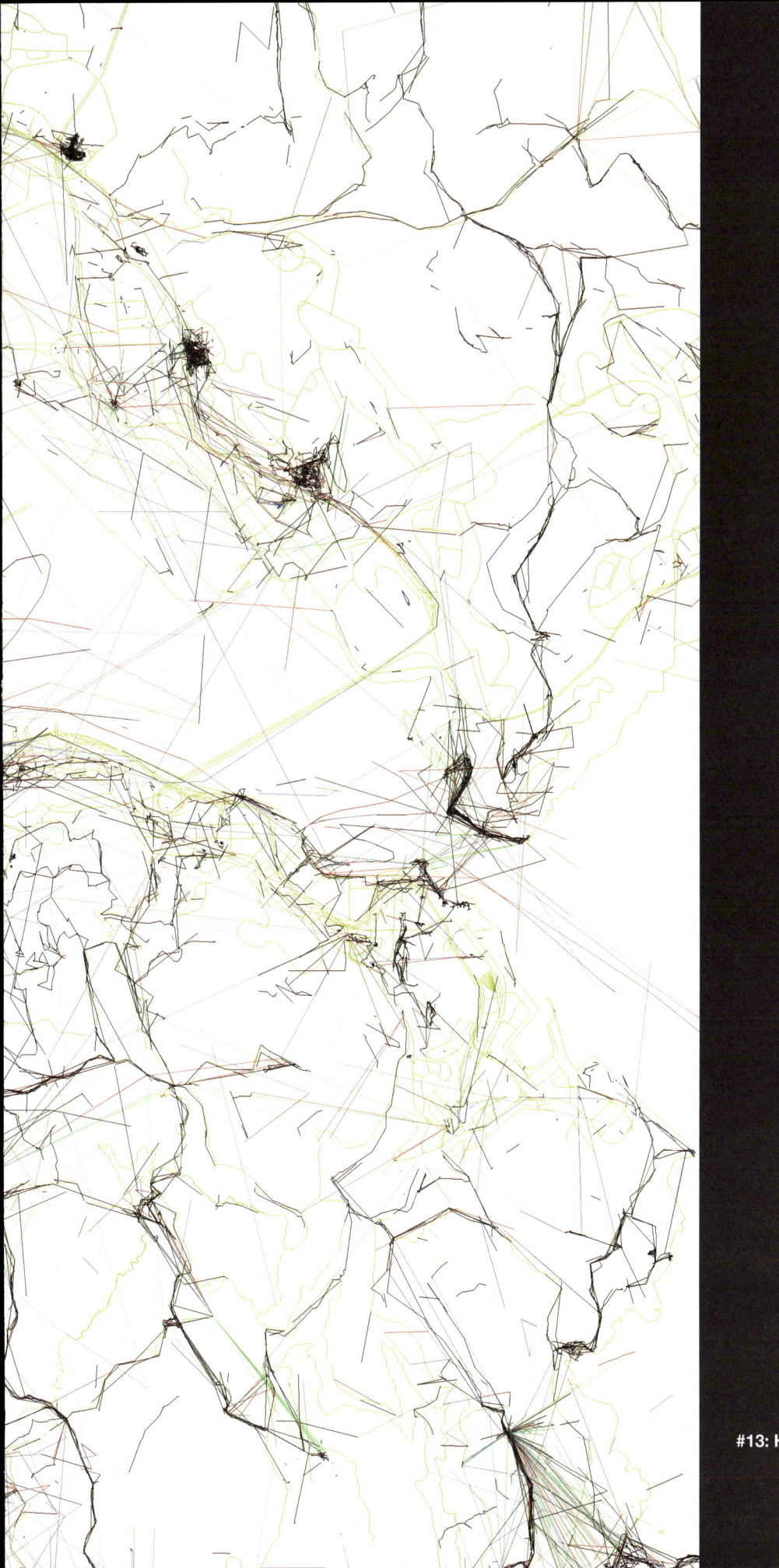

#13: Hong Kong

Flashes of Brilliance
Sylvia Lavin in conversation

Dirt Editors Helene Furján and Lily Jencks recently spoke with Sylvia Lavin about contemporary architecture theory and practice.

Dirty Practices

Dirt
We are interested in how the idea of "dirt" might operate methodologically: could rumor, for instance, operate as a method of criticism? Michel Serres has talked about the central importance of noise or interruption in a system as a catalytic agent: we see rumor as dirt in the system that forces the logic of the system to change. Could rumor and informal conversation become productive means of exploring and disseminating research?

Sylvia Lavin
I am extremely interested in rhetorical practices. One could either talk about dirt as a rhetorical gambit, or one could understand the question in broader terms: what is the role of rhetoric regardless of its particular context?

Rumor was once perfectly official. Rumor is thus of less interest to me in terms of the comparison between the official and the unofficial than in the way that it shapes, and is situated within, an understanding of how language operates. Demarcations between high and low, or official and unofficial, give stature and clarity to distinctions that are no longer useful. They also don't reflect the degree to which those distinctions are eroded in a contemporary political sense.

In the era of Cicero, the form of rhetoric that had the contemporary as its temporal terrain was considered to be the highest form of political oratory because it was the thing that was understood to potentially change behavior the most. It had its own rules. It had its own temporal and verbal structure. This category of the rhetorical deals with producing impressions in the present; in other words, it neither legislates potential futures nor adjudicates events of the past, but rather produces effects in the present. Although it isn't intrinsically oral, we think of rumor as oral: it is disseminated for the immediacy of its impact rather than for its utopian or historical value. In other words, it simply doesn't traffic in the notions of truth or projective regulation.

The role of text messaging in Barack Obama's campaign suggests that how one would begin to classify what constitutes formal political discourse is not so clear. A million people getting an informal text message from Obama is an interesting development: it isn't quite rumor, but it is certainly a rhetorically significant aspect of his campaign. His use of instant messaging as a campaign strategy has generally been talked about in terms of his technological savvy, but it is also a capacity to understand and exploit multiple forms of expression in order to have more than one rhetorical regime operating at the same time that are all official.

I'm not trying to offer a comprehensive account of the functions and nature of rumor, and I certainly wouldn't

The London Underground
Vestiges of layers of advertisement posters, Central Line Tunnel.

always think that rumors are a good thing. There are figures in our own contemporary architectural circle, for instance, that are famous for deliberately starting rumors, often maliciously, and I have no interest in supporting such a project. It is more interesting to view rumor's effectiveness in abstract terms. One can start a rumor, for instance, that so-and-so is going to win a project, which then begins to shape the territory of the reception of the competition, and may even have some effect on the outcome of the competition. As a member of a competition jury, part of your job description is to field such rumor and innuendo. Rumor, or rumoring, and discourses on "the cool" have certain similarities in the sense that their coinage involves a certain designation of insider versus outsider. One of the hostilities toward rumor is thus the degree to which you have to be part of an inner circle to hear the rumor when it is fresh.

Dirt
You collapse historian and critic, with theorist sandwiched between: a literary form of criticism, off the cuff, and op-ed based. You are an extremely skilled writer, making your texts a pleasure to read. How does (prose) style operate as a methodology?

Sylvia Lavin
As an academic I believe that you have to practice with the knowledge and erudition of a historian, the suspicious, analytic mind of a theorist, and the

impassioned attachment of a critic. There has been a recent history of writing in our field: Tafuri and the writers of the early twentieth century—people like Giedion and Pevsner—were *writers*. They were many things, but they also practiced as literary figures. The craft of writing was important to them. I would also consider all of those people to have been critics in some way. They did things that later historians despise so much, like leave out futurism. It isn't that these people didn't know that futurism happened; they deliberately left it out! This links them to Diderot and the tradition of criticism. In its rhetorical flexibility, criticism permits one to actualize the restructuring of narrative, and the sense of play that comes out of what we loosely call theory. But I do also believe that to perform that kind of looseness, you have to know more than anyone else in the room about your subject. You have to have the self-knowledge of the weight of your choices as a critic, and you have to execute them with passion.

Recently I've become interested in Nicholas Pevsner, who has become everybody's *bête noir* since Reyner Banham. Banham has become the person who is easy to love, but I'm currently more interested in the people that he hated, and the key figure was Pevsner. I was astonished to see that the many guide-books to English architecture that Pevsner produced—those apparently narrow minded, preservationist, myopic focuses on chintz and national character—are constantly being updated. The new one for Birmingham is going to have a giant picture of Future Systems' new *Selfridges Department Store* on the cover. So, Pevsner, in his own secret way, is continuing to be the discursive bedrock with which contemporary architecture is entering mass culture.

In the 1950s Pevsner did a series of radio broadcasts for the BBC because he felt that architectural history had not only an inadequate distinction from art history, but also inadequate public appeal. When you listen to these radio broadcasts, the High-Anglican Englishness of his speech is mind-boggling: this is a man who erased every feature of his German Jewish origin. Clearly this was somebody who was acutely sensitive to how a manner of speaking could betray all kinds of things about him. It would thus be interesting to go back and read Pevsner again on the hunt for the traces of what he was repressing. Not to out him as a German Jew, but to demonstrate the degree of attention that he placed on the way that he spoke, and to attempt to see whether that attention is part of the secret survival-rate of Pevsner.

Dirt

In "What Good is a Bad Object," you critique a position within architectural theory and history—one might say within history over theory—that developed in the post-1968 period, grew up in the 1980s when Marxist post-structuralist thought dominated theory in the English speaking world, and is surprisingly still prevalent: one that privileges a certain form of "radical practice" that is necessarily a resistance to the forces of capitalism. In this view, protests and guerilla tactics are good; while building at all is generally bad, the latter a complicity with capitalism that is unconscionable. As you succinctly put it, architecture is almost always the bad guy—the target of opposition in such practices. We could view the proponents of this position as the most vehement opposition to what they have labeled the "post-critical." Is this fight in the end over the life or death of architecture—whether it is possible to build or not—and over the relation between critical thought and practice—no longer the argument over whether critical thought is a form of practice, but whether it can be productive for practice, or simply writes very clever epitaphs?

Sylvia Lavin

I think that it is fair to say that one of the longest standing ways of defining architecture is that it is a field that always asks itself, "What am I?" I don't think that is the case with painting, for example. Painting has had moments of tremendous self-confidence about what it is.

In the late 1960s, as architecture and adjacent fields came to be increasingly anatomically isomorphic with one another, the psychoanalytic definition of the relations between objects—not the material relations between objects but the psychologically structuring role of the relationship between objects—came to be a significant feature. The definition of mediums as culturally, rather than materially, determined started to become prevalent. That prevalence permitted things to get really close and cozy. As a result, getting close to things that looked like they were close to power was very complicated. Thus, architecture started to play a structural role in the development of other fields of criticism that have generally had much more cultural power than architectural criticism; it was enormously successful as a cultural "bad object." Architects, in their perpetual state of anxiety about being inferior, found being a "bad object" to be the best ticket to gaining importance: "Look how important I am! Everything that is bad resides in me!" I think that a self-flagellating pleasure became part of the milieu of the field. It is not a question of whether to practice or not to practice, rather it is how to practice, I suppose.

While the immediate argument about "critical" versus "post-critical" is over, "post" is an important term because the development of new forms of agency is often used as an excuse to return to old forms of positivism and practice. I would not go as far as some of my colleagues have in claiming that nothing has political value unless it is actualized in real world terms because there is a significant risk of anti-intellectualism. There has been tremendous and enthusiastic interest in tearing down the ivory tower, engaging the political realm, and criticizing the legacy of autonomy. While you never want to go backwards, I'm extremely concerned that we're returning to the naive anti-intellectualism that required the very theoretical turn that we're trying to move beyond to develop in the first place.

Dirt
You have used the term "the productivity of pollution" to define a hybridized form of working. How does what you define as "pollution" challenge disciplinary and methodological boundaries? In other words, how do design fields both "confuse disciplinarity as such as well as catalyze it," and how might this meander be productive? How does a "productive pollution" operate in practice? You've noted that the most interesting of contemporary architectures is the product of contamination and we'd like to expand upon that.

Sylvia Lavin
We can have the same conversation about pollution as we would about dirt because I wouldn't want to succeed in sanitizing pollution on the one hand, and there is pollution that I would be happy to get rid of on the other. But you could say of the discipline of architecture that the territory of knowledge and set of vocabularies has always been constituted by self-questioning, and by borrowing, cribbing, plagiarizing, or sampling things from outside. This is one of the ways architecture is interesting to me, though not everyone would share this view. Architecture is an almost empty vessel that is meaningful insofar as it absorbs things around it to produce itself, and I find this endlessly fascinating.

At certain moments I have increasingly been interested in exploring the effects of, "What happens if we call 'X' architecture?" Take Andy Warhol for example: if we call him an architect something presumably happens to Andy Warhol. Warhol tried on every conceivable media around him, so why wouldn't he also try on architecture? What does it mean that his boyfriend of many years was an interior decorator? What does it mean that one of his most famous projects was an architectural installation? Why can't it be called architecture? Calling Andy Warhol an architect, or Richard Neutra a bad analyst, reverberates in ways that change the field because the field is constituted by those very questions.

The Low-Down and Dirty
Dirt
We are interested in what you refer to as "false scientific justification." With the huge emphasis on science—especially biology—as once again the inspiration for, and imprimatur of, contemporary practice, we are in a moment where, as you put it, "the law of nature" is used "to lure [architecture] toward ever more variety." But, as you warn, "biodiversity produces flora and fauna of unprecedented brilliance; excessive architectural chromophilia, on the other hand, can produce dead ends, lost generations, architecture designed by absorbing color without commitment or concept." Is there a place for research in practice in your view? What forms are productive? Is there a way that research can operate as a "productive pollution" rather than simply instrumentally?

Sylvia Lavin
At UCLA, I was responsible for getting rid of thesis and substituting something that we called "the research studio." So, I am in part responsible for the research craze. As this thing called "research" has now taken over the world, and we can see how it has unfolded, as so often happens with experimentation, nine-tenths should probably go

Selfridges Department Store
Future Systems, 2003

back in the box. I'm talking not as a scholar, but rather as a witness to what gets called research in the culture of design schools, and how that culture is permeating the younger generation of professional practice. Research, or what one would say is generally referred to as research, has, I think, largely become a visualization problem, where broad spectrums of data or code get formalized and re-represented in design. Here I would go back to the initial question about rhetoric: Why would you call that research as opposed to design process?

The word research suggests design practice as a forward intellectual commitment, a practice aimed at eradicating outmoded attachments to notions of authorship, or fetishistic attachments to handcraft and the workshop. I am one hundred percent for that. That was work that the word "research" had to do. It had to align architecture with the world of thought rather than with the cult of the artist. The shift in the term from "thesis" to "research" was meant to do that, and I think that in some cases it did.

The turn to research did most of the work that it needed to do. The question now is: "Is it still doing that work? If not, what other kinds of work is it doing now? Or, what excuses for backsliding is it providing?" I think that your question is not about what the potential for research is, but rather: "How is it being used in ways that don't have very much to do with that notion of research? What is it covering over?" For instance, I thought that Nature and God were killed in the eighteenth century. I don't understand how they are coming back everywhere. I'm too much of a historian to not firmly believe that if they've been dead for two hundred years and they're coming back to life, at least they have to be zombies. Something must have happened to them over the course of those two hundred years. Some acknowledgement that it is a return with a transformation is due. Part of what I find irritating is the lack of that acknowledgement. When biology and nature are simply used as self-justifying systems, then they are no longer part of an intellectual practice and therefore don't belong to the word research. If you call them something else it is a whole other matter.

As I flip through the syllabi of my architectural theory classes in my mind, Viollet-le-Duc has been ousted by someone like Deleuze. So I would not hold anybody to the standard of historical knowledge that I myself do not feel obligated to provide. On the other hand, I do hold them obligated to the field of knowledge that they enter. If you're going to use science, then, you have to know something about science. If you know anything at all about theories of science, then certainly one of the most readily accessible and interesting developments in the sociology of science is the notion that the very distinction between inside and outside no longer exists. The distinction on which research is predicated—that it happened inside a laboratory, a space of controlled experiment that is categorically, epistemologically, socially, and politically different from the real world as a place of experience—has been rendered moot by developments in thinking about science. You don't have to become an expert historian of the history of science in architecture, but you can't go naively to science.

Dirt

You define a form of "dirty practice" that we might frame, in your words, through "the aberrant and spectacular": "techniques of cunning, scenography, special effects, spectacle and liveness." We are interested in the ways in which you tie all these "tricks of the trade" to performance, defined as "the quick, furtive, provisional" rather than the "pseudo-positivistically measurable achievements" so much in circulation today. In a recent essay on Coop Himmelb(l)au, you called for the need "to shift architecture into the contemporary, to make architecture operate like a shifter." The idea of the shifter—even a "shape-shifter"—or of shiftiness in general, is the kind of dirty practice we would also consider to be contemporary. Could you talk more about this kind of practice? And if we are somewhere between the fox's cunning and the down-right foxy, how do you define the flash—and the flashiness—that for you marks contemporaneity?

Sylvia Lavin
I am less interested in defining contemporaneity, which would lead to shutting it down, than I am in mobilizing it as a problem and making it permissible to think and speak about the question again.

The very possibility of novelty and newness has been intrinsic to definitions of modernity since the Renaissance, even if that newness could only be measured in relation to forms of oldness. The irony of the modern period is that it begins its cult of the new with a look at the old. But we've had six hundred years to get over our fascination with that oxymoron; that is just the way that it works. However, one of the achievements—in all senses of the word—of the turn to theory and then to history was to eliminate the capacity to think the new. Under postmodernism, notions of the new not only became suspect but they were actually prohibited. One of the reasons is that it is in the character of theory to be ahistorical. That is what makes theory closer to philosophy than to history. Some capacity for historical thinking must be present, if only as a metric for producing the effect of the new. In a kind of irony I suppose, I wanted to give the question of the new back to the larger project of modernity.

The things that I want to describe as contemporary are the things that helped make the contemporary emerge today as a problem. Invoking Banham at a certain point, for instance, had tremendous contemporary effects. For some amount of time, it produced a surprise gust of air in a conversation that had a very limited number of people at the table. So, I invited Banham to the dinner table and it made such a difference that my dinner with Banham went on and on and on. But then I looked up and Banham was at the head of the table, and the subject of the most boring, positivistic analyses of historicism. And the work that Banham could do by being invited to the table had been done. Now it seems more productive of contemporary effects to invite someone else.

There is a way to think of dirt and pollution as a bad thing that you're trying to make look good. And when you think of the literal dirt in the ground, it encroaches on something stable. What I'm saying about the notion of the contemporary is that it lacks exactly that stability: there is no elemental or genetic make up to it. It just depends upon what is going on around it. This is also true of shape-shifters. The blob, for instance, is a shape-shifter that has some quality of materials or matter that is able to change its shape—such as the T-1000 in *Terminator 2*. But a shifter in the linguistic sense is something that has absolutely no shape except in the moment of its use.

I would describe the contemporary as a conceptual version of the linguistic category of the shifter: one that is sensitive to its context, that is revealed in a structuralist sense by virtue of its contrast with the things around it, or by virtue of the effects that it has on the things that are around it. I was trying to turn Wolf Prix's phrase "Architecture must burn!" into a shifter or something that articulated the ethics of the 1960s, which was an ethic of truth. Even though it wasn't said in 1968, when it is put in the context of 1968 it succeeds in expressing that ethical culture of the period. However, it was said in the 1980s and in that context it was totally false, and therefore timely in that sense. It isn't true any more, but its falseness is in step with both the ethics of post-structuralist notions of representation that all is false, and with the development of late-capitalism. Yet, there is clearly some other effect of that statement, "Architecture must burn!," when thought about today. It activates a fantasy of potential that is reemerging. That's what I meant. Thinking about that phrase was an effort to take something and both know its history, and abuse its history, to make it operate as a shifter.

Autonomous Worlds
The Work of Larissa Fassler
Helene Furján

"It is only in the manner of immense parentheses that non-places daily receive increasing numbers of individuals...The non-place is the opposite of utopia: it exists, and it does not contain any organic society."

Marc Augé, *Non-Places* (1995)

Larissa Fassler's work maps the quotidian spaces of the modern city. Fassler focuses on the most banal—and the most sterile and unimaginative—aspects of the city traversed everyday by its inhabitants: the underground pedestrian-ways and train networks, and the squares, streets, and residential complexes they connect to, spaces that are the product of bureaucratic problem-solving rather than design or social sensitivity.

Fassler's work is only ostensibly about the spatial forms of Berlin's "non-places." While she uses the conventions of architectural representation—maquettes (scale models), plans, sections, elevations, projections—to map these spaces, she is interested in an entirely different agenda: the practices of everyday life that animate—and critique, or rather, undermine—these spaces. We could think of the projects of the 1960s and 1970s that accomplished similar aims through drawings and mapping in architecture: for instance, British architectural couple, Peter and Alison Smithson's interest in elevating everyday space, and in particular the conjunction of concrete and steel banality with the neon-lit, billboard-scaled world of advertising that now makes the city ubiquitous.

The Smithsons passed this interest on to Robert Venturi and Denise Scott-Brown in the US, whose seminal book produced with Steven Izenour, *Learning From Las Vegas* (1972), was first developed as a research studio at Yale and involved mapping the Las Vegas Strip of the 1970s. Signage, the density and intensity of lighting, program, uses of words, images, and icons, were among the elements mapped, set out on plan or elevation drawings, and abstracted into diagrams. But the research also focused on the user's perspective, mapping the entire strip, for instance, as two sets of photographs: one taken from the windscreen of a car moving down the strip; the second taken out the side window and mapping the strip on either side as a continuous elevation. In the generation following them, Archigram used the trappings of media culture and advertising to develop "instant cities" and events that both celebrated pop culture and subverted the tired urban and entertainment spaces of 1970s Britain.

But most significant to Fassler's project are the famous psychogeographic maps that document the dérives of the French Situationist International, that counted chief amongst its members Guy Debord. Fassler undermines the rationality of architectural measure and representation by a tactical re-working of unit and data: length and distance is measured in number of footsteps, height as "me + arm + hand" or "me + arm + hand + hand"; site

Facing Page
Kotti
(2008) Archival C-Print
Dimensions: 160 x 157 cm

Following Spread
Kotti
Detail at 1:1 scale

Story Lines 25

notes include the number of people who cross the bridge, number of bikes, the weather, where punks sit, where people pee, where the Vietnamese illegal cigarette seller stashes his wares, when police cars arrived, how much a sausage and beer cost, train arrival and departure times, bikes, signs, plaques, regulations, billboards, posters, graffiti and stickers, photos of historic events that took place on the site, newspaper articles, cost projections for redevelopment of the sites, municipal reports, crime reports, and even novels. The Situationists' maps followed their intoxicated ramblings around Paris, reworking the traditional totalizing map of the city into a new system of connections and networks that traced relationships rather than geographical location: topological layered over topographical information.

Fassler's techniques of documentation and representation are, like the Situationists' maps before them, tactical: they map a dense multiplicity of fragmentary and incommensurable effects. More interested in "the public" than in "public space" or even "public art," Fassler's work over-rights the technocratic rationality of the measured drawing with the minutiae of context and occupation. Fassler sees media, architecture and body as inseparably linked. Her urban world is phenomenal, a realm in which spatial organization, sensation, and corporeal existence

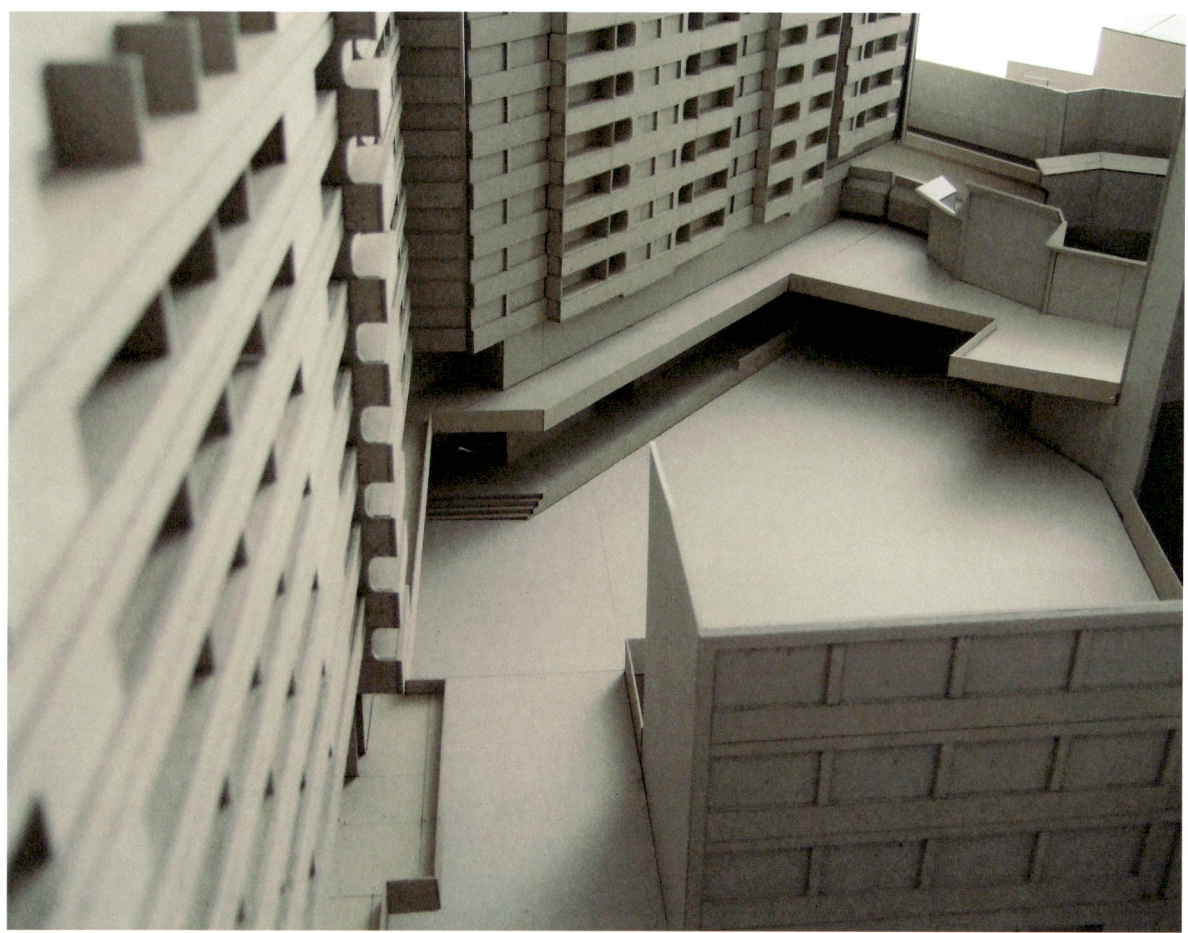

Above and Facing Page
Kotti
(2008) Grey Cardboard and Glue
Approximate scale: 1 footstep = 3 cm cardboard
Dimensions: 300 x 300 x 135 cm

Kotti is a model representation of the publicly accessible areas of the Zentrum Kreuzberg (ZK) housing estate and its surroundings. Starting once again with the act of walking I have measured this concrete housing estate as well as its front plaza and underground access tunnels in order to construct a third model-like structure that questions the impact of urban planning on communities, and conversely, the impact of communities on planning.

merge and contaminate each other. Kantian biologist and fore-runner of Phenomenology, Jakob von Uexküll, defined the concept of the "Umwelt," the subjective environment, an "environment-world" or the spatio-temporal context of an organism. Martin Heidegger both followed this thinking, distinguishing between measured, rational space (that of the architect, builder, or engineer) and experienced space—the situational, contextual present of the sensing, perceiving body in space. This optical-tactile experiencing of space is one in which the real and virtual collapse—a space in which imagination, fantasy, hallucination, affect, fiction, mingle with the material, the visual, the sensory[1]. This is Fassler's world.

Notes
A longer version of this essay was included in Fassler's catalogue, "Larrisa Fassler: Walking in Place," produced for Splendid Isolation—Goldrausch 2009 at the Kunstraum Kreuzberg/Bethanien, Berlin.

Endnotes
[1] "The distracted mass absorbs the work of art. This is most obvious with regard to buildings. Architecture has always represented the prototype of a work of art the reception of which is consummated by a collectivity in a state of distraction." Walter Benjamin, "The Work of Art in the Age of its Mechanical Reproduction," in Illuminations, trans. Harry Zohn (New York: Schocken, 1968): 239. On the question of delirious effects, see Rem Koolhaas, Delirious New York: A Retroactive Manifesto for New York (New York: Monacelli Press, 1994 (1978).

Rumor

Keller Easterling

Gossip is perhaps the most familiar and elementary form of disguised popular aggression...Gossip might be seen as the linguistic equivalent and forerunner of witchcraft...Rumor is the second cousin of gossip and magical aggression.

James C. Scott, *Domination and the Arts of Resistance: Hidden Transcripts* (1990)

[There is] no great idea that stupidity could not put to its own uses; it can move in all directions, and put on all the guises of truth. The truth, by comparison, has only one appearance and only one path, and is always at a disadvantage.

Robert Musil, *The Man Without Qualities* (1995)

And because these daft and dewy-eyed dopes keep building up impossible hopes, impossible things are happening every day!

Lyrics to Rogers and Hammerstein's "Impossible," from the musical *Cinderella*

Certain American fireflies have become specialized in mimicking the mating signals of others for the purpose of preying on them. These aggressive mimics are a major factor in the survival and reproduction of the prey and vice versa and certainly are the prime movers of the extraordinary system of deceptive and counterdeceptive behaviors that characterize this group.

James E. Lloyd, "Firefly Communication and Deception: 'Oh, What a Tangled Web,'" in *Deception, perspective on human and nonhuman deceit* (1986)

Facing Page
Some True Stories
Storefront for Art and Architecture, 2008

In *Domination and the Arts of Resistance,* James C. Scott identifies gossip and rumor as one of the chief forms of aggression among the powerless.[1] The servant gossips about the master. The underlings can, with anonymity, stir public opinion about the boss. Gossip never started anywhere. It cannot be attributed to anyone. Scott writes about the way in which it is invisibly multiplied and about the apparent magic of this viral movement. Rumor is perhaps considered to be witchcraft because it can be invisible, venomously destructive, and impossible to contain. Moreover, gossip and rumor are universal tools. While they are available to the powerless, they are also used by the most powerful. Rumor fuels the mischief of micro-salons while also being a practical technique of markets and governments: special interest groups, for instance, created a hoax that global warming was a hoax to delay support for green policies. Hoax and spin are the raw material of politics. Mixtures of fact and fantasy are very ordinary ingredients in any confidence game to popularize and capitalize change. The most official communiqué and the most hard-boiled business plan marshal "facts" in a pliable reality suited to the success of specific intentions and profits.

Design also vividly anticipates and materializes change, using tools found in many forms of cultural persuasion. Yet a strange instinct within the profession sometimes veers away from hoax and rumor—the dirtier forms of projection—in favor of the visionary or utopian. Here, in what is somehow regarded as a more elevated form, the future is closer to a perfect afterlife where dimensional

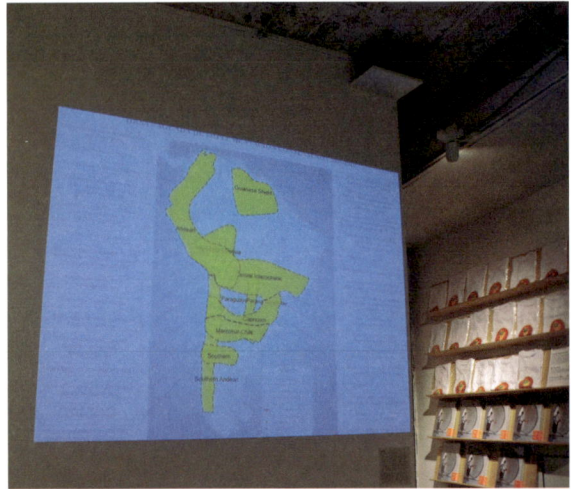

Amazone
Carol Ruiz & Santiago del Hierro

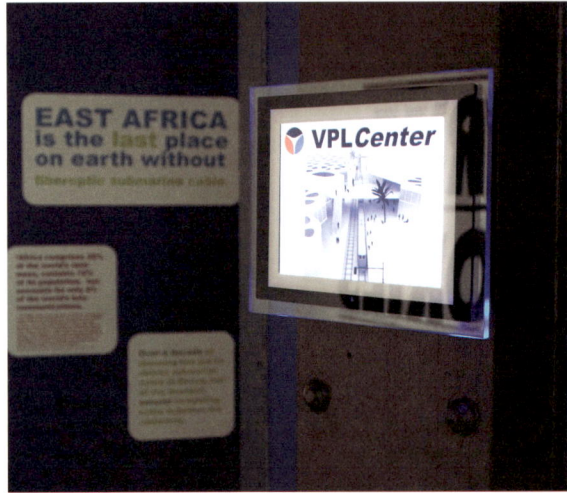

VPL
Rustam Metha & Thom Moran

VPL
Rustam Metha & Thom Moran

worlds are reconciled into a single compatible format. The always-unattainable vision may also be tragic, producing what Jacques Rancière has called "the pleasure of declaring it insoluble."[2] These worlds can remain perfect and intact—the story that ought to unfold or the remedy that should, but never does, occur.

While the utopian and visionary might be associated with the rationalizing consensus or reasonable, even righteous, reform, less resolute but rumored news might be more contagious. Moreover, the powers of the often nasty and pernicious rumor may be turned towards more productive intent.

Illogics

While we often expect political stories to follow familiar epic or tragic plot lines, no really good rumor attempts to communicate logical plans and outcomes. The rumor mongers know very well most of what happens in the world might be considered to be part of the wrong story—the things that are not supposed to happen. Rumors, on the one hand, are best when they appear unreasonable. Yet perhaps we are also attracted to them because we know they are somehow more representative of the naturally-occurring and unpredictable phenomena of our lives. They represent the common occurrence made magic because it is side-lined in relation to more dominant logics. We train ourselves to understand and anticipate the "right story" even when the real turn of events rarely follows our accustomed logics—even when it is rumor, hoax, unreasonable innovations, and hyperbolic situations that actually rule the world. Many political events exist as outlying evidence and category leftovers—the butterflies that do not get pinned to the board because they do not reinforce expectations. They exceed prevailing logics or conventional wisdom and reset our accustomed narratives. If they inspire incredulity, perhaps it is because the instrumentality and logic of these non-stories is simply underexplored. Many such phantom turning points and fulcrums are not easily taxonomized or moralized by the left or the right. Yet however invisible to our political orthodoxies, such events may be the real cause of shifts in sentiment, changes in economic fortune, the escalation or suspension of violence, and swift epidemic or watershed

to change. The wrong story may not be sanctioned by a recognized form of polity, but rather presides over a more extensive parallel polity with fickle or unexpressed logics. Everyday we work within a large field of seemingly illogical, rumor-worthy, and yet common occurrences. As examples, we could cite the following:

» The politically conservative and seemingly immovable "red states" in the US, have suddenly and quickly shifted their economy. Although they are supporters of big-oil politicians, they grow ethanol. Their megachurches sign the Kyoto protocol, and their oil pirates have begun to steal old cooking oil from US fast-food restaurants to fuel cars.

» Running counter to the automobile and aeronautic research conducted and deployed in the major superpowers, post-World War II Japan pursued high-speed trains and now lends that technology to countries in the Middle East, at the epicenter of oil. Transportation rivals like airlines and trains that used to be pitted against each other in a war of obsolescence and replacement are now absorbing and mimicking each other.

» While the US gun and tobacco lobbies might seem equally matched in power, it is quite easy to buy a gun one day and kill someone the next while it is now impossible to smoke a cigarette after dinner in a restaurant.

» Contrary to all the avowed necessities of the US Department of Defense, interrogators like Deuce Martinez in US offsite prisons extract more information with long empathetic conversations rather than coercive aggression.[3]

» In the middle of a fuel crisis, the US Department of Transportation experienced a shortfall due to decreased driving and gas tax revenues. Thinking that this probably meant increased revenues for public transit, the department's first plan for remedying the situation was to borrow the money from the public transit fund.[4]

» The current US mortgage fiasco was initially lubricated with rhetoric about making homeownership more available to those in a lower income bracket. Many of the lending products were targeted at minorities and others who had not yet become part of the national banking system. While this population may have meant greater volumes of banking customers, it has also meant greater volumes of loss and a flood of housing product. In an inverted version of the American dream as initially expressed, some economic analysts are advocating the demolition of many unwanted homes in foreclosure to prevent them souring the larger housing market.[5]

» Wal-Mart, a fabled offender with regard to health care, is getting into the health care business. The possibility that a service might be marketed to a large population entices the retailers.[6]

» Oil money in Abu Dhabi is investing in Daimler Chrysler with a view to developing electric cars and new automotive materials.[7]

Surely architecture should be considered within a list of rumored events that are not supposed to happen. We have developed a fatigue for expressing incredulity at the booms of building in China and the Middle East. We are often ready with another swaggering tale of hyperbolic building in Dubai, Qatar, Kuwait, Chongqing, Astana, or Moscow. Architecture is accustomed to telling itself that it is not invited to weigh in on official policy and so cannot bear any real responsibility for it. But within the parameters of the wrong story, the less official political field seems more vast and consequential.

Multipliers

For rumor, the world is a penetrable place, a vast soft underbelly. Far from being deterred by verifiable facts or unreasonable expectations, the confidence game thrives on these apparent obstacles. Since it is very easy to demonstrate that Barack Obama is Christian, for instance, saying that he is Muslim is a very effective rumor—the rumor can be kept alive even longer and repeated twice as much, in fact, first to spread the falsehood and then to refute it.

If one wants to spread a rumor, it is crucial to find an agent that will virally multiply the tale. Entrepreneurs understand the power of multipliers—how to play market networks with the viral dissemination of both objects and aesthetic regimes. Rumor relies on the relational population thinking and 'unreasonable' solutions common in most entrepreneurial formulations. More than just a customer base for sales or a management style, multipliers build the network environment within which companies reside and the global populations with which they communicate. While it may seem unreasonable to attempt to influence a hermetic and isometric corporation like Wal-mart, the company's sheer size multiplies any detail that is introduced into the organization. For instance, however perverse it may seem, selling green consciousness to Wal-mart (compact fluorescents, marketing products in daylighting, etc.) is powerful because it is multiplied by millions of SKUs and square feet.

Mecca
Ashima Chitre & Mustapha Jundi

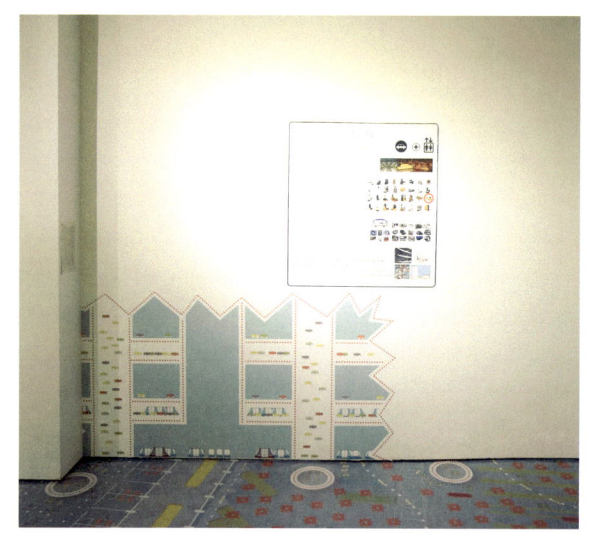

Cable
Keller Easterling & Mwangi Gathinji

Section 27-751
Gaby Brainard & Jacob Reidel

A multiplier is a contagion or germ in the market that compounds exponentially. Inventors and entrepreneurs are often considered to be 'unreasonable,' just as practical and theoretical are often considered to be opposing concepts. For the entrepreneur, the theoretical must feed the practical. The entrepreneur will be most successful if their innovations renovate what is considered to be practical. They are so practical that they understand and anticipate the successes of as yet un-theorized events—the stories that are not supposed to happen. Entrepreneurs, unlike architects, do not value or author the enduring masterpiece; they author change and reactivity. They do not wish to stabilize, but rather to send more and more innovations and products into a market. Consequently, they often find fertile territory in an inversion. As in the case of Barack Obama's religion, denials and nay-saying may make the trend more contagious. Social entrepreneurs like Muhammad Yunus, founder of Grameen Bank and inventor of micro-credit, ironically expanded capital by investing in a much larger population who were considered to be in poverty. Recognizing that the world builds bubbles of confidence on its most recent fictions, rumor is an essential tool of production. An emerging market prematurely signals to the world that it is ready to trade to support that eventuality.

Design is Rumor

When design is manipulated within the palette of rumor and hoax, the magic of its techniques might be tuned to empower other intentions and political goals. Within this craft, unlikely political events excite feelings of resourcefulness. The most obdurate urban problems that continually manage to resist intelligence may be especially attractive and inspiring. In research that is reset to allow non-conforming information, improbability becomes the raw material, and when it does, the territory of operations is expanded.

Relational aesthetics and active population thinking are under-rehearsed techniques in architecture repertoires. Population thinking has influenced sophisticated techniques with regard to *objective* form. Still architecture is less comfortable with relational or *active forms* that distribute spatial changes within heterogeneous populations—that do not create a singularly authored object form. The arts now more readily experiment with networked practices, performance, and relational aesthetics rather than exclusively tutoring an appreciation of the singularly authored object. While architecture is composed of repeatable components and recipes, the profession is often structured to support singular creations as enclosures or master plans. An architect of rumor might understand the power of these components to alter localized or globally disseminated environments.

Rumor is more powerful than it is pure. For instance, architectural components may find economies of scale in response to luxurious desires so that they might later be transposed and made available for more urgent needs. Most inventions travel a very unlikely path through market expectations. Learning to surf these twists and turns is essential to effective intervention. These tools may be the only ones powerful enough to address the truly unsavory challenges that the most powerful global forces introduce as they look for means to expand that power. New objects of practice and entrepreneurialism, redefined in a relational register, potentially reflect the network's ability to amplify structural shifts or smaller moves in the back channels of global infrastructure.

Crucial to the success of the architectural rumor is an apparent hyperbole and implausibility. Hoax is design. Trends do not proceed logically, but rather snag or accelerate on stray desires and obstacles that make their own peculiar sense. While our researchers train us to anticipate echoes of precedent within our own society they do not train an imagination that participates in global changes and innovations. The world's impure uncertainties are better things to study. Its backstage, behind-the-hand fictions and fake displays will contain the material necessary for ingenuity. In this larger field of operations, it is easier to see what the world will believe and what it can be taken for.

Architects can happily swim in the dirty waters occupied by all the shills, butlers, and go-betweens looking for new points of leverage within the fictions and persuasions that expel utopian prescriptions in favor of agility, ricochet, "faction," and cultural contagion. We can be attracted to spatial entrepreneurialism, unreasonable innovation, impure ethical struggles, and obdurate problems that continually resist intelligence. We can hope to spread

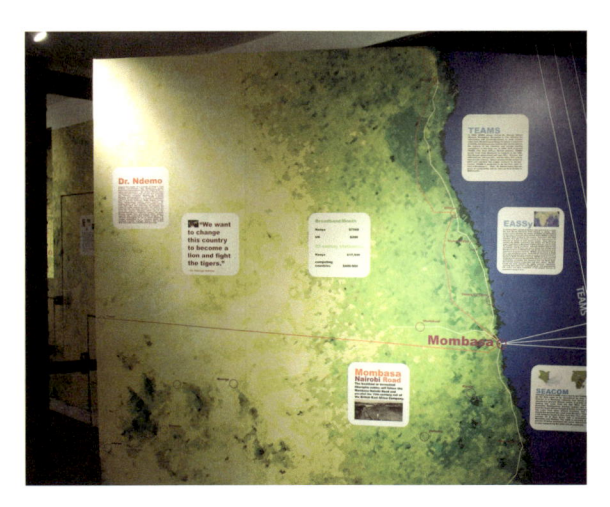

Floor
Keller Easterling

rumors that the world has changed—operating with all the guises and none of the disadvantages of truth.

If the world spins around the actions of discrepant characters, architects, as classic facilitators of power, have long had a seat at the table. But since most spatial environments do not respond to the earnest prescriptions of architects and planners, our work might be more about agility, ricochet, and cultural contagion. Architecture and urbanism contribute many wrong stories to the mix as they move headlong into the world, propagating forms of polity faster than proper political channels can legislate them. Architecture has always been an instrument to willfully alter the world, or to spread the rumor that an architect has altered the world. The counterfeiting process can be ingenuity. Rumor tutors spatial entrepreneurialism, impure ethical struggles and a new species of spatio-political activism.

Endnotes

1 See James C. Scott, *Domination and the Arts of Resistance: Hidden Transcripts* (New Haven; Yale University Press, 1990).
2 Jacques Rancière in "Art of the possible: Fulvia Carnevale and John Kelsey in conversation with Jacques Rancière" *Artforum International* 45.7 (March 2007): p. 256.
3 Scott Shane, "Inside a 9/11 Mastermind's Interrogation," *New York Times*, 22 June 2008, A1.
4 Matthew L. Wald, "Drop in Miles Driven Is Depleting Highway Fund; Loan From Mass Transit Is Urged," *New York Times*, 29 July 2008.
5 Holman W. Jenkins, Jr., "How to Shake Off the Mortgage Mess," *Wall Street Journal*, 30 July 2008, A13.
6 Steve Lohr, "Wal-Mart Plans to Market Digital Health Records System," *New York Times*, 10 March 2010, B1.
7 David Jolly, "Daimler to Sell Stake of Almost 2 Billion Euros to Abu Dhabi," *New York Times*, 23 March 2009.

The Gleaming Toys
Mark Campbell

Like a well-balanced tire iron, or an overly familiar TV remote, a good anecdote can prove especially useful in trying circumstances. In contrast to the blunt necessity of fixing a tire, or the casual resignation of changing channels, a favored anecdote patching over an uncomfortable silence in conversation can often seem ungainly, cheap even, with the recycling of that story suggesting an intellectual laziness and a self-conscious complicity that borders on parody. However, anecdotes are an inherently social form, which grow and develop rather than dissipate in influence or comedic value with each retelling. That polyvalence is evident in the fact that although anecdotes ostensibly refer to biographic episodes, they are strangely autonomous, reflecting a proclivity that not only allows for an attribution to different historic figures, but also permits a new set of connections with each narrative recasting. The more implausible each anecdote becomes, the more effective it seems.

Winston Churchill, who had more than his fair share of biographers, famously referred to anecdotes as "the gleaming toys of history," a quip that duly reflects the fascinating, trivial, and playful character of the form. History is full of such gleaming toys. And while anecdotes might offer a kind of base currency for biographers (who duly consider them superfluous to serious biography), it should not be forgotten that the term has its etymological origins in classical Greek, where it referred to "things not given out"—to what ought to remain unpublished, or which is best left out of print, if only because anecdotes, like confessions or dreams, are best relayed in person, where their distortions and exaggerations grow in response to the immediacy of conversation.

It would be restating an obvious cliché to suggest that the majority of architects—with a few notable exceptions, the most prominent being Rem Koolhaas and the most obvious being Le Corbusier—are lousy writers; either too cowed by language to venture beyond mere description, or too unbowed to appreciate that language has structures that should rightly be considered rhetorical, not architectural. Instead, I think that architects in general, and those who can afford it in particular, fully appreciate the value of language; like drawing, language is essential to the discipline, and the words we use to speak or write of architecture constitute a system—a network of exchanges and correspondences—like drawing or architecture itself, that we inhabit.

In the introduction to his recent book, *Words and Buildings*, Adrian Forty has convincingly argued that those words we use to consider a building are no less a part of its architecture than the ideas that drove the design. "Why does Architecture utter architecture so abundantly?," he asks (paraphrasing Roland Barthes). "Why does it interpose, between the object and its user, such a luxury of words, such a network of meaning?"[1] It is such a persuasive network, moreover, that it supposes the ability to accommodate both immediate needs and distant contingencies. As several critics have noted, this network was initially woven by the architects of the 'First Machine

Age,' as Reyner Banham famously described them—such as Le Corbusier and Walter Gropius, together with contemporaneous historians like Sigfried Giedion—who saw no need in distinguishing between the mechanical and rhetorical production of buildings.

However, beyond that apparent convergence laid a more complicated distrust with modernism's suspicion of language, reflecting a concern that Forty traces back to Immanuel Kant's reconceptualization of aesthetics as subjective experience rather than objective description— the notion that experience could only ever lie outside of language. (Which, in turn, partially explains why modern architecture was largely conceived through visual metaphor, deferring to such emerging optical modes as the close-up, enlargement, crop, fragment, and, most crucially, montage.) If modernist architecture depended on maintaining a network of plausibility, then that system was haunted, in turn, by what remained implausible: by those discrepancies between words and meaning which not only generated a luxury of words, but also alluded to a promiscuity of meaning; a malleability that anecdotes, with their elasticized ability to piece together even the most disjointed of narratives, provides the most obvious, which is to say the least convincing, form of evidence.

Needless to say, it was an extremely strange experience being paid to write as someone else. From the beginning of 2004 until late-2006 I ghosted the various articles, forewords, speeches, opinions, newsworthy quotes, and, on rare occasions, even the private correspondence of one of the world's most famous architects. All written anonymously, drafted without a trace, like a benevolent ghost.

Although my employment with a 'starchitect' supplied me with a readymade collection of anecdotes, the majority of which are either potentially libelous—such as anything that occurred in the 1980s—or genuinely libelous—such as anything more recent—what this collection really pointed to was not so much the obvious conceit of the 'signature architect's' singular genius, but the indelible anonymity of much of the signature architecture it produced. With a few notable exceptions, the firm's projects seemed to evince an architecture that simply existed, illustrating the complicated mechanics of capital exchange, commercial procurement, and technical delivery, rather than any latent architectural genius. Following this logic, the firm seemed to have perfected a form of systemic anonymity, in which each component was substitutable or endlessly replicable, and the buildings manifested a kind of architectural Esperanto, in which the language's synthetic quality scarcely masked the banality of the message it conveyed.

Facilitating that anonymity entailed a kind of textual erasure and what lingered in my mind were captions and afterimages. A perpetual slow learner, I came to realize that I had actually been employed to write captions: captions to remarks, opinions, questions, or images of architecture that had yet to be built, were in the process of being built, had recently been built, or, in many cases, would never be built. (Or, on several other trying occasions, had yet to even be conceived). These heavily vetted labels were reassuringly descriptive, quantitative, formulaic, and duly expressive of both an architecture, and an experience of that architecture, which was reassuringly anonymous; or, if you prefer, assuredly 'democratic' in the sense that it conflated all difference within the singular statement.

In my opinion, captions should be a form of deductive reasoning, a type of detective work that doesn't attempt to come to any real or definitive conclusion because its only motive rests in the attempt to investigate something, with the discovery of one clue only referring to the presence of another. (In that sense, captions are not so much whodunits, as whydunits.) As any editor will tell you, good captions are difficult to write. And the satisfaction of producing those captions tingled with the knowledge that, after the frustrations of wresting the pertinent information out of distracted hands, whatever you do write never actually corresponds to the image anyway; there is always something missing, something you have chosen not to add, something you have neglected to mention. Yet it is precisely that omission, whether professionally negligent or amateurishly convenient, which reaffirms the disparity between the caption and what it purportedly describes, freeing up a dialogue between the two.

By contrast, the closed captions I wrote were meant to describe an "immediate future," not in the sense that Banham—who rightly considered himself a "historian of the immediate future"—thought would allow new possibilities, but in the sense of an immanent, foreclosed, future. Ironically, Banham's uniquely intuitive belief in "events in the future" led him to overestimate the potential of certain technologies and architects; a tendency which further led him to argue, wrongly in my opinion, that the architects of the 'Second Machine Age,' one of whom I was employed by, saw 'functionalism' in "severely qualified" terms, with none of the "wide-eyed innocence" of their predecessors. Contrary to Banham's view, it could be argued that this act of qualification was more governed by commercial, rather than intellectual, imperatives.

In retrospect, it was Banham's friend and contemporary, the architect Cedric Price, who offered the simplest rebuttal to such hi-tech opportunism when he stated, or simply restated—following the early modernists—that architecture should be considered as both a form and means of communication; one which remains intellectually engaging, nuanced, complicated, and, above all in its humanist implications, amusing. Price recognized the empty vicissitudes toward which much of 1990s British modernism aspired and he not only believed that should such architectural conversations engage, fascinate, frustrate, and, ultimately, charm its participants, but that they would remain incomplete by nature. In that sense, Price—who is the subject of a legion of posthumous anecdotes—exemplified the value of a continuing ongoing discussion that need not be recalled in its entirety, but only glimpsed in fragments.

Price not only knew how to talk, he also knew how to write, and he certainly knew how to draw, producing deceptively simple sketches that displayed the same fierce intelligence and conversational generosity he exhibited in person. (Here I should add the obvious confession: Price and I shared a very drunken lunch shortly before he died, leaving me with a blinding hangover and the accompanying memory of his wit and intellectual generosity.) But most of all, Price knew how to think. And to think as an architect who recognized the polyvalent relationships between writing, talking, and drawing architecture: relationships that generated still more sketches, conversations, and arguments. Within such an inexhaustible system of exchanges, interactions and divergences, "the recognition of space," Price noted, would "be achieved through trust."

Interestingly, Price made this statement in reference to the 'organizational matrix,' a work that reflected the contemporaneous cultural fascination with complex systems, whether architectural or not, which many other theorists, such as Gilles Deleuze, read with a corresponding degree of distrust, arguing that our internment within these matrices enacted an existential division. A keen cybernetician, and an innate optimist, Price considered our negotiation of those systems a form of 'play' and his trusting—if not wilfully naïve—belief in the positivism of that engagement can be traced back to the *Fun Palace*, the "university of the streets" he designed along the principles of flexibility, non-conformity, uncertainty, and "delight in the unknown." In part, the *Palace* envisaged a perpetual architectural happening in which every participant could, in the most sixties way imaginable, go to lose themselves in order to find themselves again amongst the mirage of performance art, theatre, circus, rock n' roll, drugs, and, presumably, sexual experience.

Suspended within that ever-changing network, the participant was less divisible than narcotically pliant, and, considered in this way, the trust that Price spoke of might also refer to the anecdotal; to those elasticized points of reconnection, perhaps even of understanding, through which we recognize—or, more appropriately, we forget—our existential expatriation. A truly British confection, Price's *Fun Palace* was a kind of eccentric and inefficient machine, one whose dysfunctional-functionality not only fostered a multitude of stories, but also celebrated the childish delight of catching our reflections in such a gleaming toy. Yet, as many subsequent happenings, such as the '14-hour Technicolor Dream' held at London's Alexandra Palace in 1967, demonstrated, at its basest this engagement was decidedly less reliant on a hallucinatory architectural, than it was on a narcotically potent hallucinogen.

In a sense, this vague architectural indeterminacy was only indicative of the extent to which we all, to varying degrees, ghostwrite our lives, recasting our surroundings and the events within them as we recall them through narrative. "We tell ourselves stories in order to live," the Californian writer Joan Didion once noted. An emblematic figure of the sixties (like Price and Banham), Didion not only represented a generation who was not supposed to be able to remember that decade, but also the anxieties associated with an early-seventies comedown in which she began "to doubt the premise of all of the stories I had told myself." Needless to say, we all doubt the veracity of those stories we tell ourselves and, in that deeply suspicious context, it would be remiss of me to conclude without offering a final anecdote; one that not only illustrates the ghostwriter's dubious position, but is also justly famous, always worth repeating, and entirely without libelous consequence, concerning, as it does, not a famous contemporary architect, but three celebrated figures from a redundant age.

Within six months of arriving in Paris, Sigfried Giedion had already established himself at the center of avant-garde circles and befriended a number of luminaries, including Le Corbusier and James Joyce. Mindful of their respective geniuses, Giedion waited patiently for an appropriate opportunity to bring the pair together, which he found, appropriately enough, by seating them next to one another at a supper party. The only problem lay with his wife's large and extremely expensive parrot, whose vocabulary almost entirely consisted of ribald curses and sea shanties, many of which it could deliver with multilingual flair. Clearly the bird was worth every franc and Madame Giedion was understandably reluctant to secret away such a treasure. After a couple of hours listening to one of the bird's finest monologues, Joyce finally leaned over to Le Corbusier, prompting the other guests to lower their voices expectantly, only to utter his sole words to the great architect: "The Giedions have a truly remarkable parrot," he noted, to which Le Corbusier replied, "They do."

While almost entirely superfluous in its significance, only the harshest of critics would dispute that this anecdote affords—beyond all else—a true 'luxury of words.' A wealth that both Le Corbusier and Joyce, who were as acquainted with each other's work as they were strangers to humility, acknowledged with their concession to a maledictive and multi-lingual parrot. (Of course, not all architects are as acquiescent toward language, leaving their ghosts to squawk petulant obscenities from a neglected corner.) Yet what could be more profanely illuminating than that seemingly trivial moment at the Giedion's supper party? A moment in which history proved to be as irreverent as it is unremitting, allowing that the words we use to speak of architecture can be as mundane, or profane, as the buildings they describe, while also granting that the pleasure inherent to such anecdotes not only lies in their spurious character, but also in recognizing that they are best left unfinished.

Endnotes
1   Adrian Forty, Words and Buildings: A Vocabulary of Modern Architecture (London: Thames & Hudson, 2000), 12.w

Six Ways of Being a Stranger
Lindsay Bremner

In today's fluid, rhizomic world, more and more people pass through places as strangers, without long histories or memories of the spaces they inhabit. They throw into question place-bound identities and singular conceptions of space and time that until recently have underpinned spatial and architectural practice. For those of us involved in thinking about the nature of such practice this raises important questions about the kinds of spatial and temporal landscapes strangers produce, about how landscapes are configured and shaped by the practices of strangers, and about how places need to adjust to the permanence of strangers in them.

This short essay, inspired by Georg Simmel's essay "The Stranger," as well as Mary Douglas' book *Purity and Danger*, aligns ideas about dirt with ideas about the stranger.[1] In his characterization of the stranger, Simmel makes the important distinction between the wanderer—who "comes today and goes tomorrow"—and the stranger—who "comes today and stays tomorrow."[2] The stranger is a figure who permanently unsettles and alters social and spatial relationships through a particular configuration of nearness and remoteness, attachment and detachedness. S/he is a figure of anomaly, ambiguity, and disorder. "The distance in this relation indicates that one who is close by is remote, but his strangeness indicates that one who is remote is near."[3] The stranger is inside, here, part of a group, place, or community, and at the same time outside, confronting, them, and there. Although the stranger has gone no further now, s/he remains—dangerously—always a potential wanderer. The presence of strangers calibrates anxiety, desire, fascination, and repulsion.

Dirt symbolizes the creative formlessness of the stranger and the fears and potentialities s/he configures. For Mary Douglas, dirt is "matter out of place."[4] Shoes are not dirty in themselves, but they are so when placed on a dining room table; food is not dirty in itself, but it is dirty to leave cooking utensils in the bedroom. Similarly, a person becomes a stranger when s/he is out of place. Reactions to the stranger are thus no different from the reactions of society to other forms of dirt—regarded as objectionable and brushed away. The stranger is brought under control through theories of attendant harm, contamination, or pollution by mobilizing taboos and theories of hygiene that re-establish boundaries, margins, and internal structures, and so restore order. The alternative is to risk the dangers of affirming the stranger as a figure of potentiality, as representative of "those vulnerable margins and those attacking forces" that, while threatening to destroy good order also ensure life, fertility, and growth.[5] Purity is poor and barren. Dirt is dangerous and potent.

In the contemporary world, ideas of dwelling alongside strangers have become increasingly unwelcome.[6] Diversity is seen as dangerous: revived discourses of national culture, identity, and xenophobia are being mobilized against immigrants and strangers, making the idea of a multi-cultural ethics and politics unimaginable. This politics of un-conviviality has a long history. One

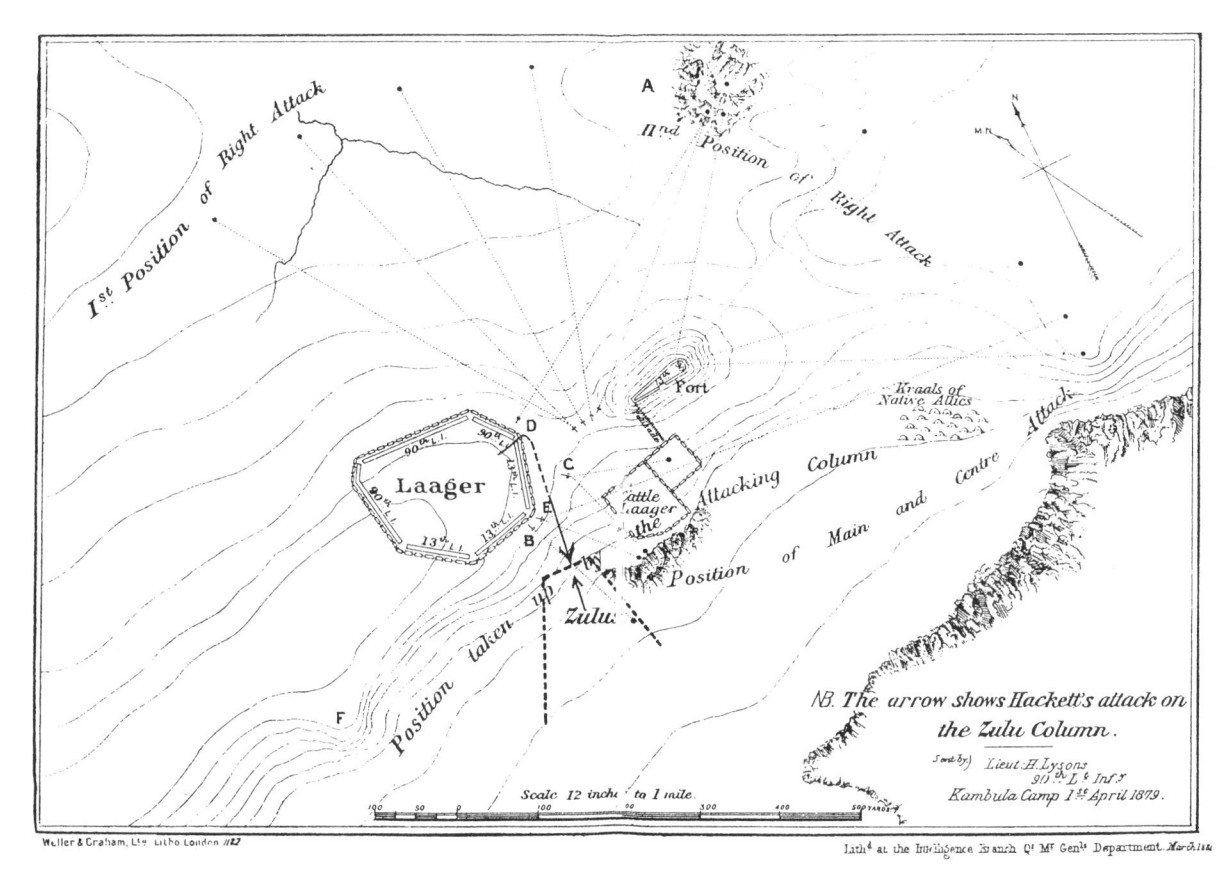

Figure 1
Attack on Colonel Wood's Camp, 1879

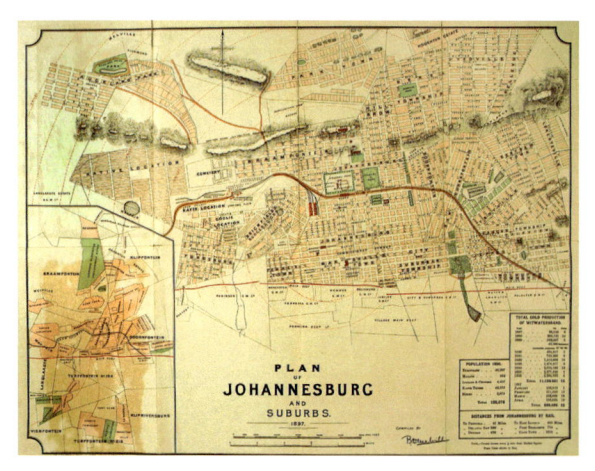

Figure 2
Plan of Johannesburg and Suburbs, 1897

Figure 3
Langlaagte Deep 'Native Compound'

of its genealogies was the "ruthless and practical racism" practiced by Boer settlers at the Cape of Good Hope from the 1650s onwards.[7] This provided the model, not only for patterns of colonial organization, but also for future forms of racism in South Africa. The history of South Africa can be read as a failure to live together as strangers—of a failure to develop dirt-affirming rituals, arising from this initial colonial act. Activated by fantasies of moral superiority, contamination, impotence, and impending invasion, colonists dealt with their anxieties by refusing to acknowledge the humanity of the colonized and by shaping relations of domination and subjugation through the deployment of boundaries, margins, and internal segregations. Permanent relations of violence and intimate estrangement were institutionalized. Out of this, a number of ways of being (strangers) evolved. In this essay, I put six of these to work, suggesting that they continue to haunt, not only the delicate postcolonial project in South Africa, but also, more generally, today's globalized world.

1. The Colonist

The city was still really a camp in the middle of Africa ringed by hostile tribes and the bush.

R. Jurgens, *The Many Houses of Exile* (2000)

An impatient public never anticipated how much time must elapse before the finished conditions of an English town would be reproduced in one of these raw communities.

L. Curtis, "Report of the Local Government Branch of the Colonial Secretary's Office." *Annual Reports for the Year Ended 30th June*," Transvaal (1904)

Colonial relations in South Africa brought together two fantasies for the colonist: the fantasy of being surrounded, born down upon, by a hostile and less than human native (Fig. 1); and the fantasy that, through mimicry, the colonial homeland could be reproduced (Fig. 2). In the first, the relation took the shape Simmel describes between Greek and barbarian, "in which the general characteristics one takes as peculiarly and merely human are disallowed to the other," or, in Paul Gilroy's words, displaying the "inability of the colonizer's humanitarianism to accommodate the humanity of the colonized."[8] In fact, the whole epistemology of colonialism was based on a simple equation that, between the native principle and the animal principle, there was hardly a difference.[9] To assert him or herself as human, the colonizer relegated the native to the status of an animal. Forced into intimacy by mutual dependency, however, this non-relation was codified in spatialities which domesticated, regulated, and set the native apart. A dual urban imaginary constructed the white city as a pastoral urban forest, while the black city was nothing more than temporary warehousing for black bodies forced into permanent migration between the city and the bush.

2. The Migrant Worker

My brother's death has been the only thing to bring me home in seven years. His coffin stands in the front room, its polished handles bronzed and gleaming in the mid-morning sun. Tomorrow we will put him to earth.

Morabo Morojele, How We Buried Puso (2006)

The industrialization of South Africa began with the discovery of gold. Its extraction demanded vast reserves of labor, setting in motion flows of migrant workers circulating between their place of origin and the mines. Most were forced into this out of economic necessity. Deprived of access to land and water by white settlement, their labor was all migrant workers had to sell. Recruited in their place of origin for short term contracts (six to eighteen months), workers lived in tightly controlled single-sex barracks (Fig. 3), often up to twenty to a room, surrounded by high fences and covered by wire mesh. Food, clothing, and medical treatment were available only within the barracks compound. Identity documents known as 'passes' controlled movement beyond its perimeter. This space of exception that converted a labor contract into a period of imprisonment with hard labor was the modern city's mirror image.[10] Each city and town in South Africa had one or more of these out of sight, unmapped doubles, each territory its Bantustan. Here a form of bio-power calibrated dependency with contempt to produce territorial fragmentation and fractured, transient, precarious lives constantly on the move between compounds, townships, and native reserves. Compounded by apartheid-era forced removals, workers became vagrants without citizenship, whose only idea of home was the place where they would one day return to be buried.

3. The Exile

The city was a staging post, a waiting room. They were all troubled by a longing to be somewhere else.

Connie Braam, Operation Vula (2004)

After the Soweto uprising of 1976, thousands of South Africans left the country for education or military training (Fig. 4) and lived in political exile, collectively a nation in waiting, until 1990. The majority lived in African National Congress (ANC) military camps, schools, headquarters, or diplomatic missions. They paid no heed to the place they were in and assumed the identity of outsiders, living inside their dreams "of some place in South Africa, in the township of their youth, where everything was more beautiful, warmer and greener…than anywhere else on earth."[11] Memories of the reality of poverty or brutality had to be deeply repressed, so as not to cloud this yearning for an idealized home.

The geography of this exile life covered a vast transcontinental network of dispersed but interconnected sites, isolated and disengaged from their surroundings. (Fig. 5) In the case of the South African exile of 1960 to 1990, such locales were governed—not unlike today's foreign military bases or humanitarian camps—not by the laws of their host countries but by the constitution of the ANC, overseen by its internal structures, including its own military police. Connected by routes and corridors that allowed continuous flows of information, ideology, weapons, and supplies, relations were only forged with adjacent populations out of reluctant necessity.

4. The Underground Operative

The friend who told me he was coming made me close the windows and curtains, and my contact slipped in so quickly through the back door that I didn't hear a thing. A tall shabbily dressed man in a very baggy brown suit, very polite with no fuss…

In the beginning there we were, my housemate and me, sitting sizing each other up in that empty house with no electricity. It felt strange to be living with someone I didn't know. Mostly he just sat in the living room with piles of paper, reading and writing…I didn't ask about them…I made double curtains, so that nobody outside could see shadows…He had a strict routine. During the day he never

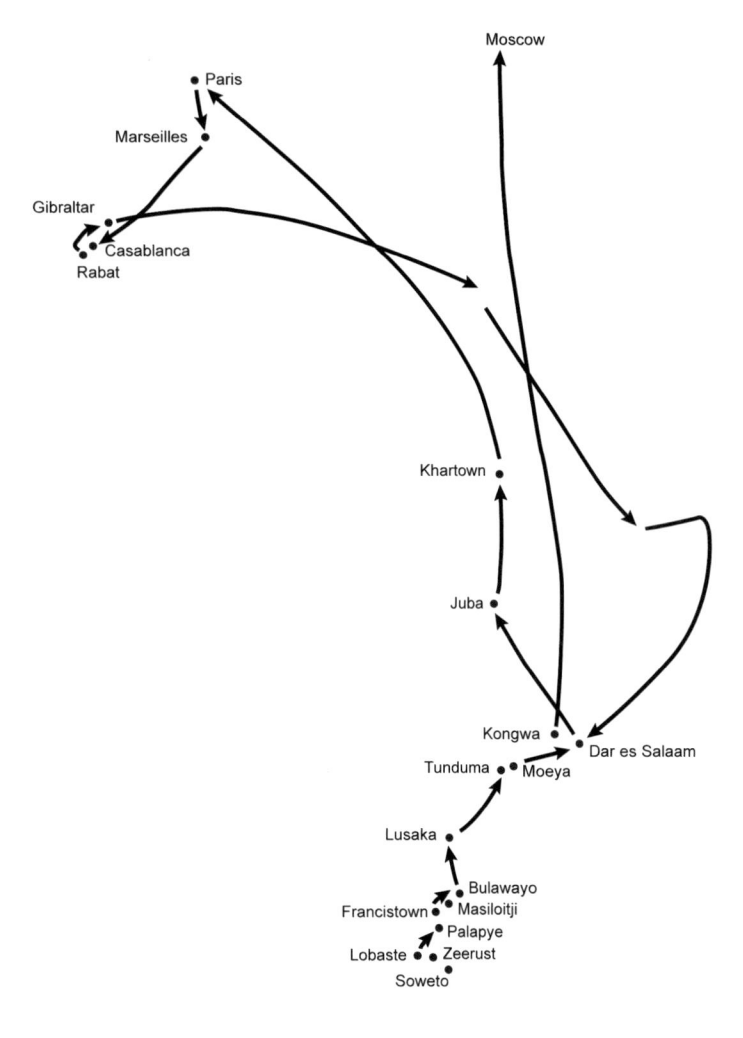

Figure 4
African National Congress Route Into Exile, 1960 – 1970

went out; only in the evening when it was really dark, then he'd be away until well after midnight.

Connie Braam, *Operation Vula* (2004)

Connie Braam, the leader of the anti-apartheid group Anti-Apartheidsbeweging Nederland (AABN), offers a vivid portrayal of the life of underground operatives deployed on secret missions by the ANC in the 1990s. She describes a group of five who lived together in a house for nine months, without once going outside; a Dutch woman in a house in Lusaka who had no idea where she was, having nothing more than a vague memory of the route from the airport to the house; an operative living in a safe house in the Netherlands in near complete darkness with blinds rolled down, heating cranked up, and the television constantly on in the middle of summer; or a group on a mission inside South Africa whose base was a disused gold mine ten meters underground, which they left only in darkness until it collapsed on their heads.

These were shadow lives, stealthy, disciplined, invisible, and silent. Alone or in small groups, operatives lived in darkness, camouflage, or disguise between safe houses, dead letter boxes, dug-outs, border crossings, ruses, and missions. (Fig. 6) Their lives produced a shifting geography of secret, silent, dislocated spaces that offered them invisibility and the ability to live as if they were not there.

5. The Mercenary

Infiltration would be long and arduous, moving mostly at night, conducting anti-tracking, lying up in hides in the day, avoiding all enemy forces and local population—all the while carrying this killing weight, navigating accurately through the bush or through mountains, crossing crocodile-infested, deep and fast-flowing rivers (not by bridge), coming across lions and other dangerous animals, eating and drinking hardly anything to conserve rations, tolerating all weather conditions from freezing to frying and from tropical rain to no water at all, never speaking, never cooking, never making noise, always doing anti-tracking, always alert—all the while aware that if you were compromised, you were on your own, and however far you were in—so far you would have to get out—without any help, and with the full and mighty force of the enemy hunting you.

Special Forces Operator

Between 1957 and 1989, South Africa fought a clandestine, proxy war on behalf of the world's super-powers on the border of South West Africa (now Namibia) and Angola. (Fig. 7) Operating in secret, deep in enemy territory, its operatives were answerable to no rules or conventions of war and loyal only to each other.[12] After the war ended, with the independence of Namibia, these so-called special force units were disbanded, but not debriefed. Many of their former officers continued their operations by setting up private military companies, often collaborating with their former enemies and contracting throughout Africa. (Fig. 8) By the late 1990s, this had resulted in a corporate maze of companies with innocuous names like Executive Outcomes, Alpha 5, Stabilco, Corporate Tracking International, etc., designed to obscure the relations between soldiering companies, unstable governments, and mineral and oil concessions.[13]

This was the beginning of today's private military-security industry. Executive Outcomes was dissolved in 1999 when mercenary activity was declared illegal by the South African government, but it transferred key personnel to the United Kingdom-based company Sandline International, many of whom have been absorbed into Aegis Defence Services, on contract to the United States in Iraq. Today, South Africans comprise the fourth largest contingent of security contractors (known alternatively as defense or supply contractors) in Iraq, ostensibly employed to provide security to government, military or reconstruction efforts, and personnel.[14] They are in fact private military operators, engaged in the business of war, answerable to no one but their shareholders, working with and training Iraqi civilians for security operations. Frequently engaged in combat, they are classified as mercenaries or unlawful combatants under the Third Geneva Convention of 1949 and have no right to prisoner of war status.

Mercenaries are the predators of today's post-ideological, post-human grey zones. In them, alliances are made expediently and allegiances shift fluidly, secretively and unaccountably, and moral and ethical questions of life and death, friendship and enmity, war and peace are reduced to matters of pure exchange.

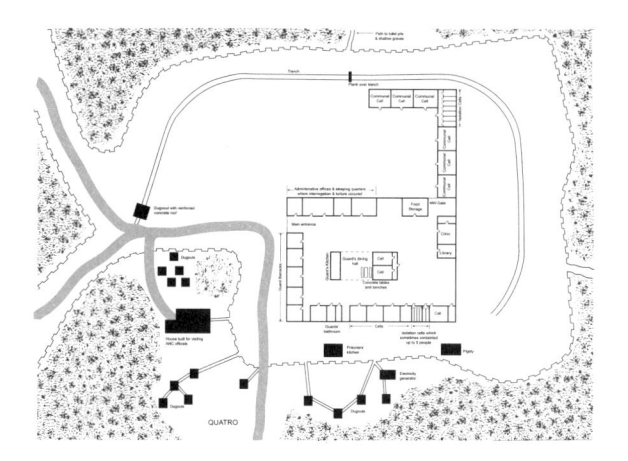

Figure 5
Plan of Quatro

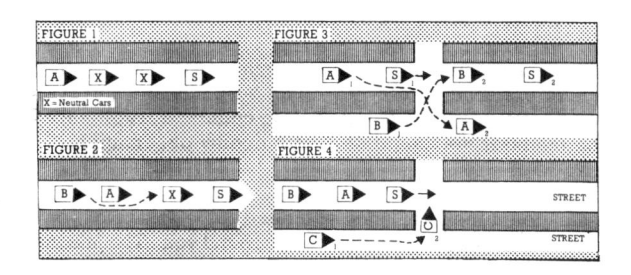

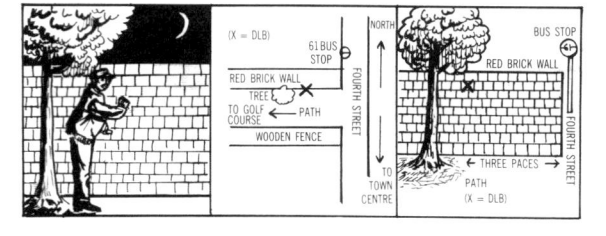

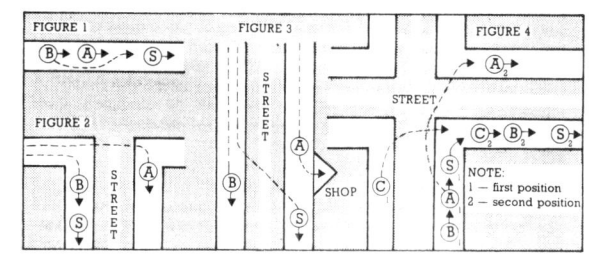

Figure 6
Diagrams of How to Master Secret Work

Story Lines 45

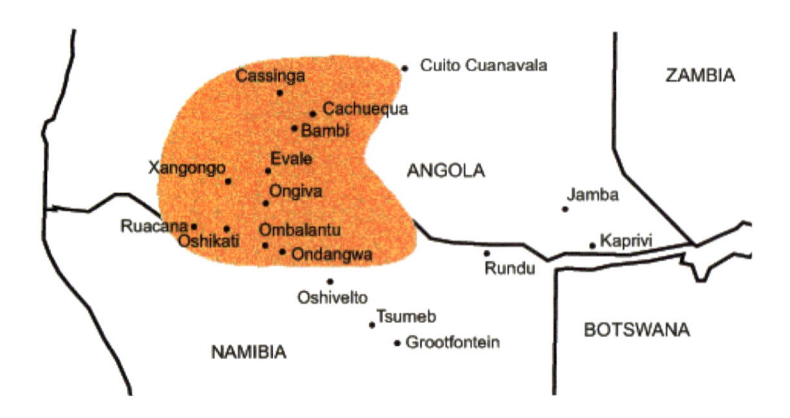

Figure 7
South African Defense Force Operational Area
The South African Border War, 1957-1989

6. The Expat

The golden rule is to get used to being a nobody with no history who no one cares about, and being regarded as a loser. Then you can move on and succeed and become a Mr. Somebody again. Assimilate and don't hang around with an all-South African, whenwe ghetto mentality. It takes about three years to settle and feel semi-human again.

>   Trevor, CEO, Auckland, from *The Expat Confessions* (2006)

The Expat Confessions describes the lives of five hundred South Africans who have left the country since 1990, mostly living in the United Kingdom, Australia, or the United States, but as far a field as Taiwan, the Sudan, and Canada.[15] Giving a range of reasons for having left South Africa—crime, racism, frustration, discrimination, or just wanting to live a different life—most are united by contradictory resentments against and yearnings for home. The expat is someone whose identity is defined by the place they have left behind. Even the term 'expat', like 'ex-wife' or 'ex-partner', signifies a life lived in deference to a past place and time. A Somali living in Johannesburg in the mid 1990s in a tightly knit Somali enclave told me that he lived Johannesburg through a sandy lens:

"I walk the streets of Johannesburg with camels in my head," he said. In the case of the South African expat, the relationship with home is maintained through a number of channels—the numerous web and blog sites through which expats communicate with one another and shape an idea of a community, either of fellow South Africans living abroad or of expats in general;[16] through clubs, pubs, restaurants, churches, and synagogues; through memorabilia—flags, African beadwork, wall hangings, wooden giraffes, calendars, etc.; through food—Mrs. Balls Chutney, Ouma's Rusks, Five Roses Tea, Nando's sauces, Rooibos Tea, Pronutro, biltong, droewors (dried sausage), Castel Lager, Meerlust wine, or The African Hut: South African Food Store; through sport and web-based television channels. These preserve and protect a selective, metonymic construct of home, no longer as lived experience, but as a collection of products, brands, and rituals in which longing can be contained. (Fig. 9)

These six ways of failing to live together as strangers or, alternatively, of failing to engage the fertility of dirt, all deploy ideas of the other as polluted, contaminated, formless, or dangerous, and invent ways of restoring

Figure 8
Star Security
Johannesburg (1995)

Figure 9
Expat Favorites

order through the erection of boundaries of one sort or another. They not only persist, but have been given new life, amplified in today's anxious post-colonial, globalized world. Today, boundaries are not merely lines, walls and buffer zones, but also funnels, pipes, folds, sponges, phantom limbs, and, most of all, enclosures.[17] As the world has globalized, the unresolved potentiality, both potent and dangerous, of the stranger/dirt, has meant that the camp has displaced the city as the primary imaginary and spatio-political instrument of modern life.[18]

Endnotes

1   Georg Simmel, "The Stranger, " in *Georg Simmel: On Individuality and Social Forms*, ed. D .N. Levine (Chicago: University of Chicago Press, 1971), pp. 143-149; Mary Douglas, *Purity and Danger: An analysis of the Concepts of Pollution and Taboo* (London: Routledge, 1966).
2   Simmel, *On Individuality*, p. 143.
3   Simmel, *On Individuality*, p. 143.
4   Douglas, *Purity and Danger*, p. 44.
5   Douglas, *Purity and Danger*, p. 199.
6   Paul Gilroy, *Postcolonial Melancholia* (New York: Columbia University Press, 2005).
7   Gilroy, *Postcolonial Melancholia*, p. 15. See also Hannah Arendt, *The Origins of Totalitarianism* (Germany: Schocken, 1951).
8   Simmel, *On Individuality*, p. 148; Gilroy, *Postcolonial Melancholia*, p. 16.
9   Gilroy, *Postcolonial Melancholia*, and Achille Mbembe, "Aesthetics of Superfluity," *Public Culture* 16:3 (2004): pp. 373–405.

10   Mbembe, "Aesthetics of Superfluity".
11   Connie Braam, *Operation Vula* (Johannesburg: Jacana, 2004), p.17.
12   The Special Forces, 2007. Retrieved December 9, 2008, from http://www.nationmaster.com/encyclopedia/South-African-Border-War
13   *The War Business*, Journeymanpictures (1997), accessed 1Dec. 2007 at <http://www.youtube.com/watch?v=Y4wGNCB0PJ8>.
14   *The Business of War: Iraq*, Journeymanpictures (October 2004), accessed 1 Dec. 2007 at <http://www.youtube.com/watch?v=pwA07kID85w>.
15   Ted Botha and Jenni Baxter *The Expat Confessions* (Sydney: Jented Publishing, 2005).
16   Sites such as http://www.kuduklub.com, http://www.boereworsexpress.com, http://www.mammaafrica.com, http://www.rsa-overseas.com, http://www.SAReunited.com, http://www.expat-blog, http://www.blogspot.com, accessed 1 Dec. 2007.
17   *Making Things Public: Atmospheres of Democracy*, eds. Bruno Latour and Peter Weibel (Cambridge, MA: MIT Press, 2005).
18   Giorgio Agamben, *State of Exception*, trans. Kevin Attell (Chicago: University of Chicago Press, 2005); and also Gilroy, *Postcolonial Melancholia*, p.8.

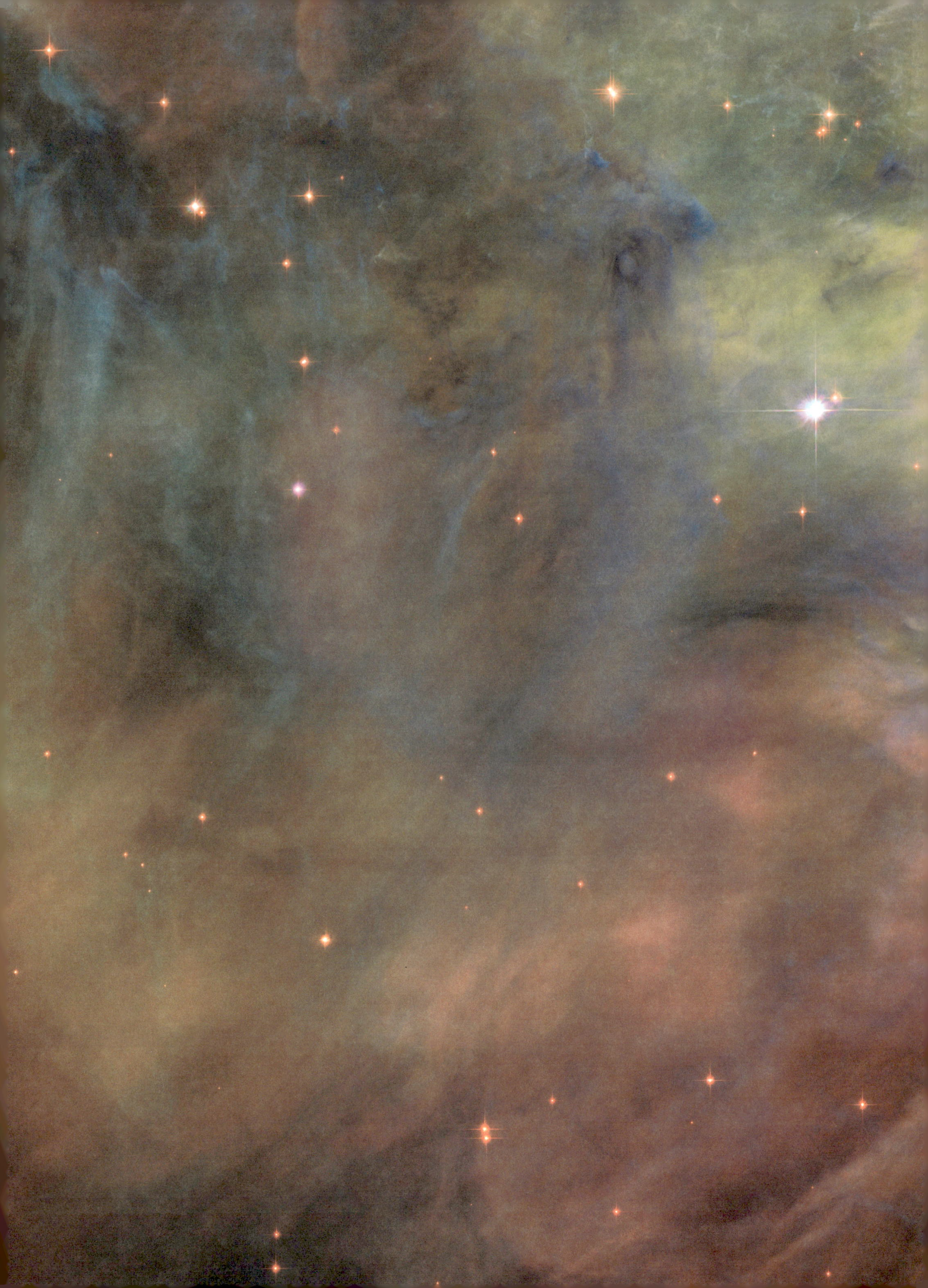

Fertile Minds

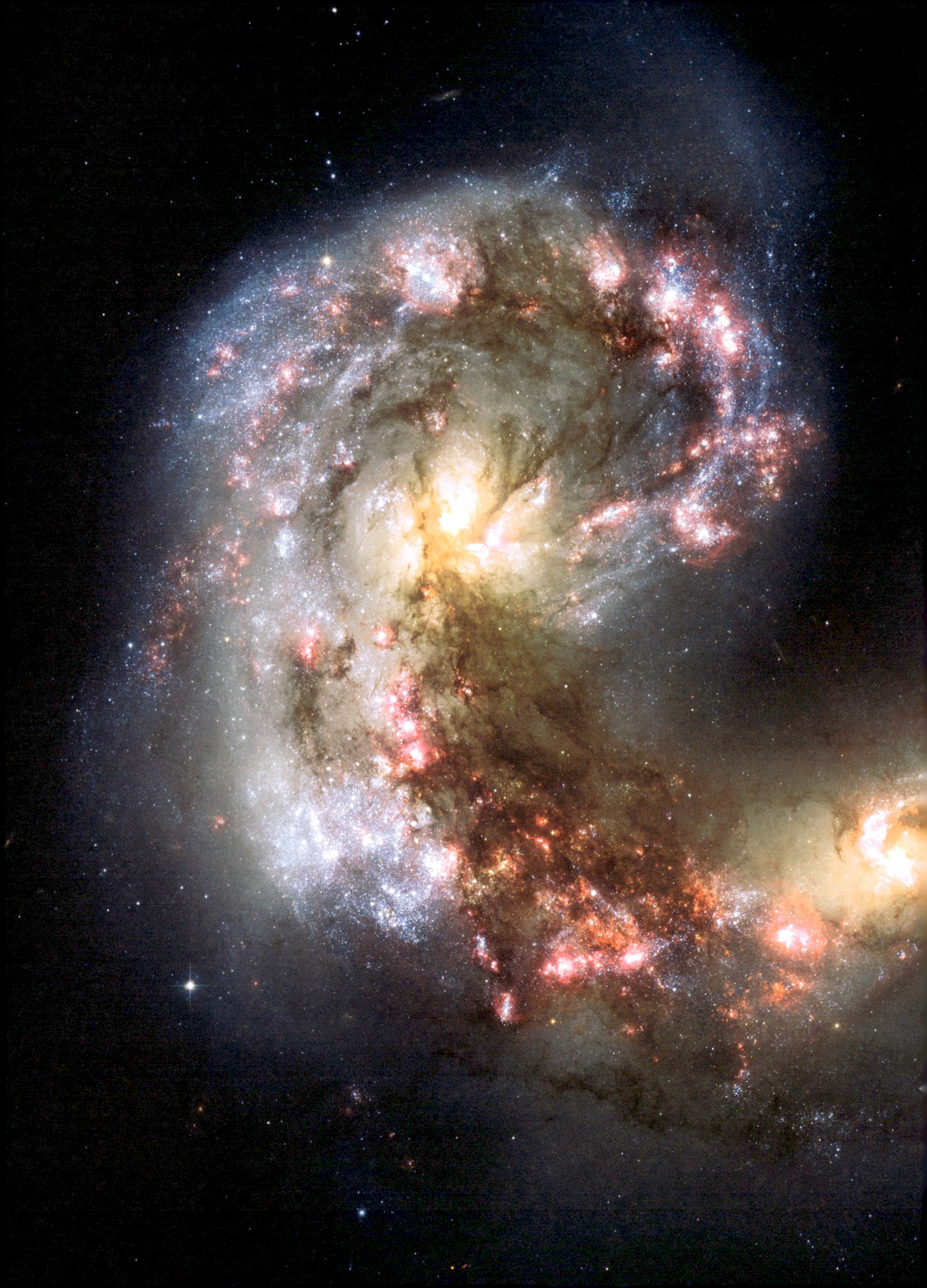

The Antennae Galaxies
Drawn together by gravity, the Antennae are a pair of colliding galaxies. They began interacting a few hundred million years ago and were observed here by the Hubble Space Telescope in 2006. During the course of this collision billions of stars will be formed.

Previous Spread
The Orion Nebula
Captured by the Hubble Space Telescope in 2006, the Orion Nebula is a nearby, rich star-forming region. It appears as intensely contrasting areas of light and dark blending with a rich palette of colors made of gases, dust, and particulate.

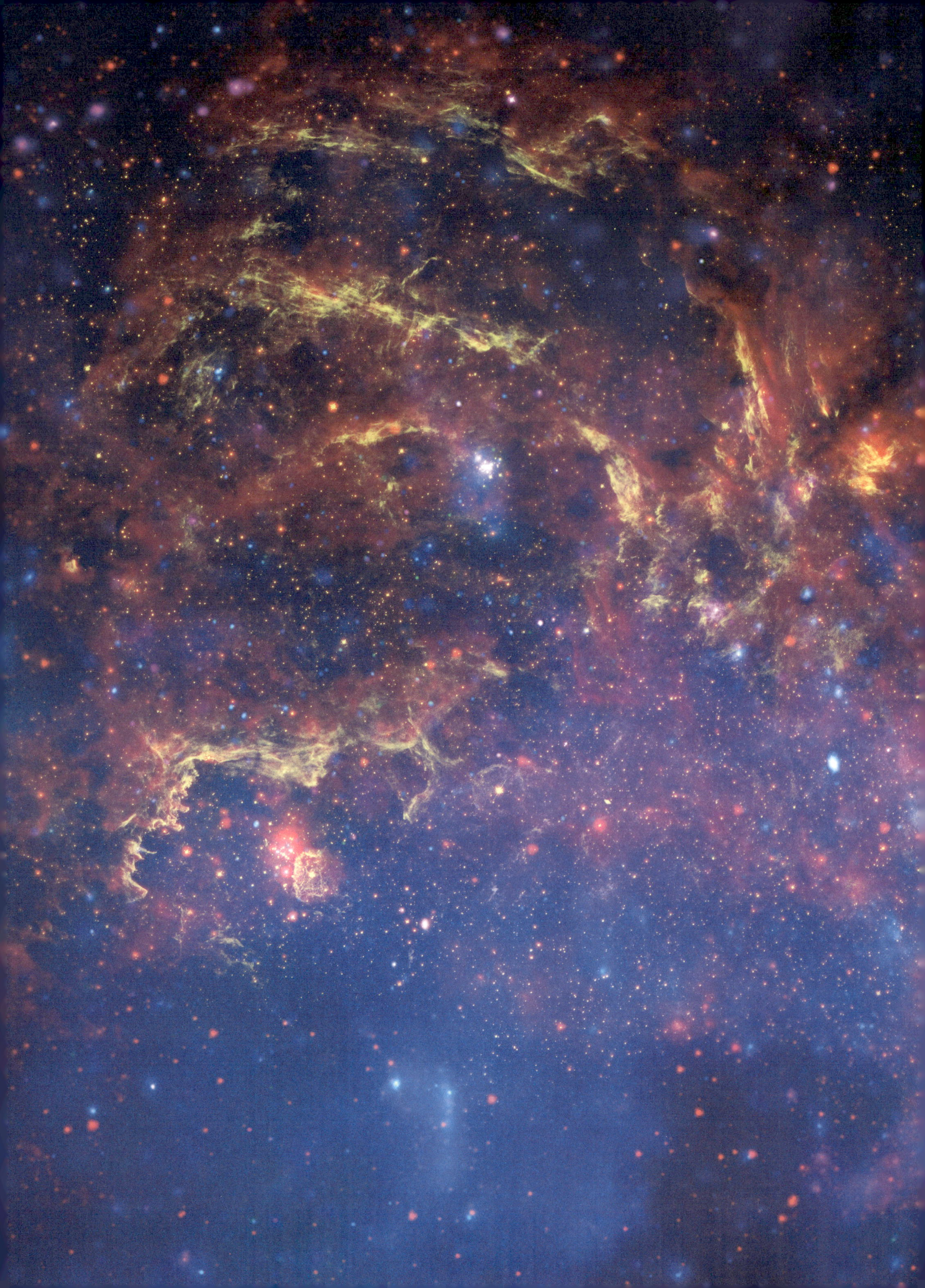

Center Region of the Milky Way

The center of our Milky Way Galaxy is seen here, a bright white spot surrounded by the intense activity of star creation and evolution. This image is a composite from the combined observations of three telescopes—the Hubble Space Telescope, the Spitzer Space Telescope, and the Chandra X-Ray Observatory—each illuminating specific areas in the light spectrum from x-ray to infrared.

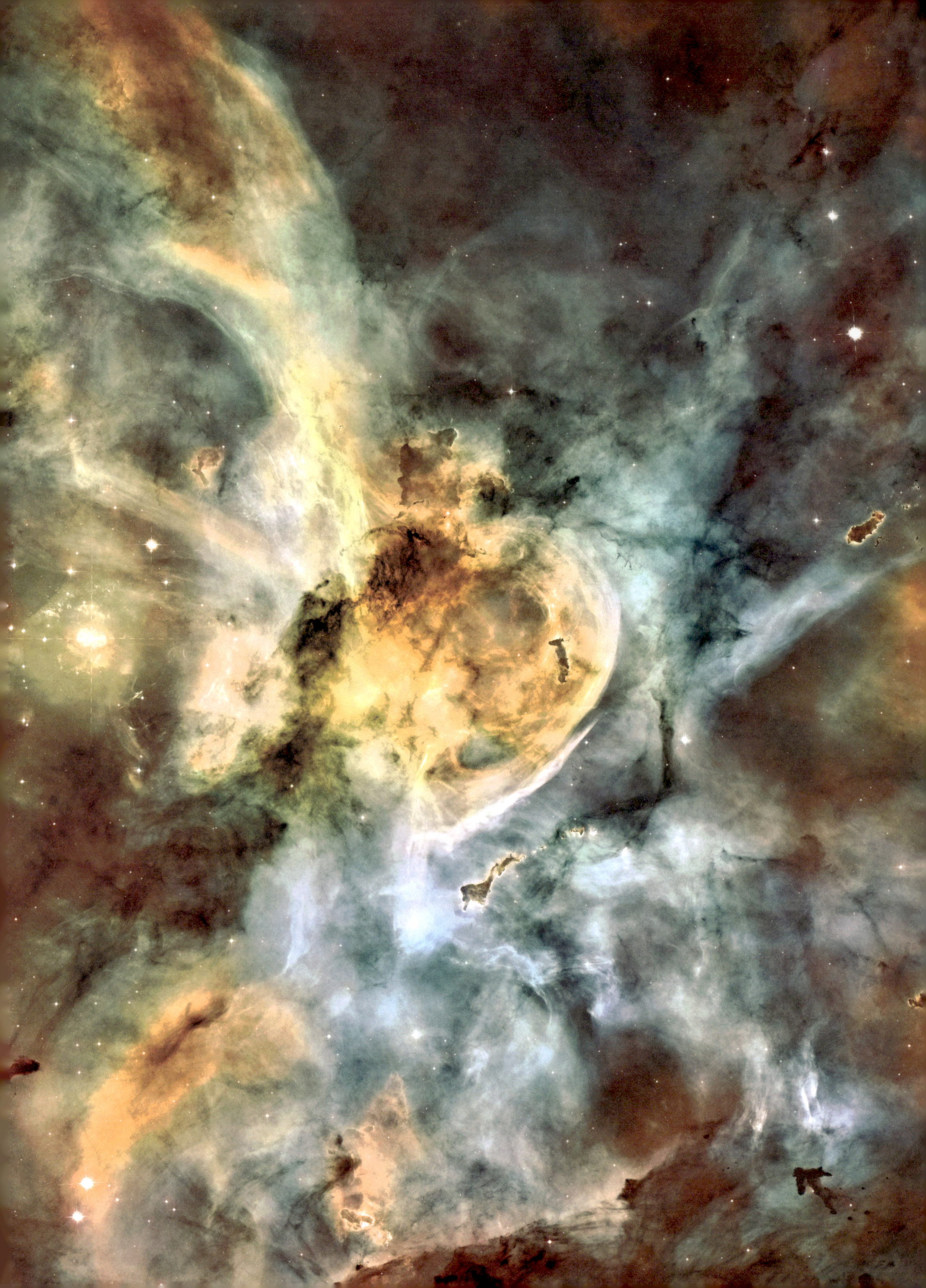

The Carina Nebula

This 50-light-year wide panoramic image of the central region of the Carina Nebula captures the birth and death of multiple stars, each 50–100 times more massive than our sun. Our solar system was likely born out of a similar nebula 4.6 billion years ago.

Robert Le Ricolais
And the Search for Automorphic Structure
Richard Wesley

Lightness for me goes with precision and determination, not with vagueness and the haphazard.

-Italo Calvino, *Six Memos for the Next Millenium* (1988)

Il faut être léger comme l'oiseau, et non comme la plume. (One should be light like a bird and not like a feather.)

-Paul Valéry, *Choses Tues* (1930)

Recent interest in biomorphic form is leading a new generation of architects to reconsider the work of the structural engineer Robert Le Ricolais (Fig. 1). The most extensive publication of Le Ricolais's work to date appeared in an interview in *VIA 2: Structures Implicit and Explicit* (1973) along with essays by Claude Levi Stauss, Umberto Eco, Roland Barthes, and others.[1] The interview was published in two parts. In the first part Le Ricolais explained the nature of his research and teaching at the University of Pennsylvania, while in the second part he commented on his own work. Running parallel to and interwoven with the text of the interview were numerous photographs of students' structural models interspersed with freehand sketches, diagrams, and projects by Le Ricolais. Also included were a photograph of a one-armed human skeleton, a microphotograph of bone, and drawings of radiolaria by Ernst Haeckel. Because a number of the images had lengthy explanatory captions, the interview unfolded as a dual narrative—one narrative following the text of the interview itself, the other following the text of the captions. The interview was enigmatic and sometimes rambling, ranging from comments on faculty meetings and personality traits, to explanations of image diagrams and physical models. The title of the interview was "Things Themselves Are Lying, and So Are Their Images," which Le Ricolais attributed to a Chinese proverb.

To disentangle Le Ricolais's thought from these texts and images, it might be useful to begin with the last image published in the interview, a photograph of a human skeleton (Fig. 2). "There was a good joke played by my students," said Le Ricolais. "They put a skeleton next to one of the models we had built, to illustrate how abstract and inhuman my structures were."[2] Being abstract, in the sense of employing mathematics and geometry, was fundamental to Le Ricolais's research into structural form; but for him mathematics and geometry were seen less as tools for engineering calculation, and more as conceptual frameworks to move one's thinking about structure beyond anthropomorphism. "It's an enormous reservoir of unexploited forms, mathematics and its symbols. These abstract concepts, which may be devised purely for the support of thought, enable our mind to escape the anthropomorphic attitude and confront an unknown universe."[3] Being abstract and being inhuman (an antonym of anthropomorphic) were equally important to Le Ricolais's research.

Anthropomorphism, as understood by him, represented the embodiment of orthogonal space and biaxial symmetry inappropriately overlaid by architects on the problem of structural form. One of the most compelling

Fertile Minds

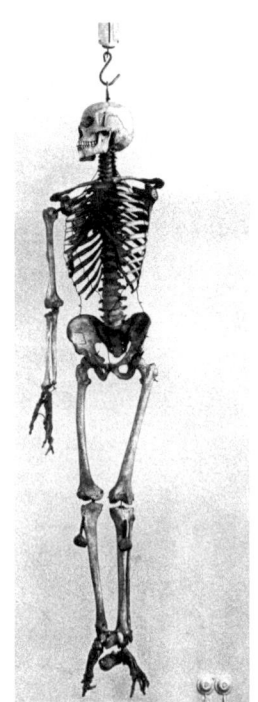

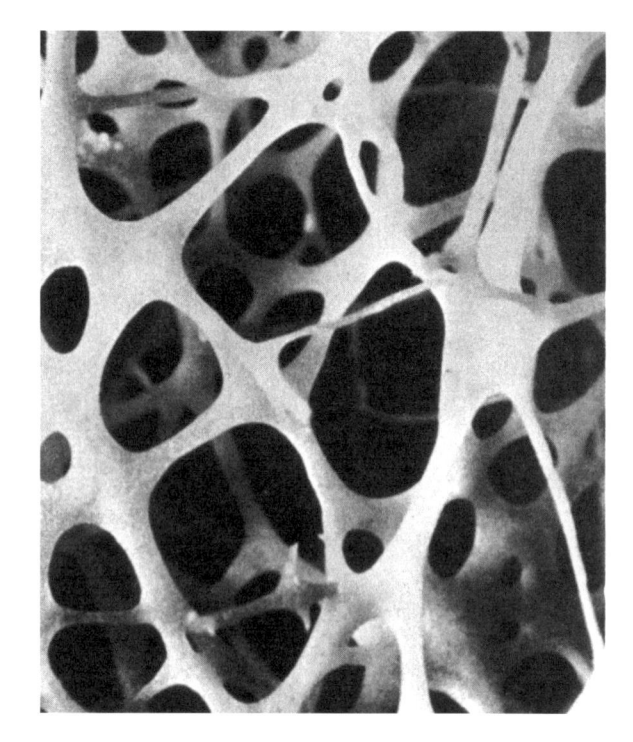

From Right
Figure 2
A "memento" hung by students "next to one of the models we had built to illustrate how abstract and inhuman my structures were."

Figure 3
Microphotograph of bone. "But the answer came with a photo of the bone itself."

Previous Page
Figure 1
George Robert Le Ricolais (1894-1977)

descriptions of anthropomorphic space can be found in Le Corbusier's *Le Poeme de l'angle droit*, (1955).[4] The images and accompanying text in Le Poeme celebrate the orthogonal within the human body co-joined with the horizon of the landscape and the vertical of gravity. Despite the celebration of the right angle in *Le Poeme*, Le Corbusier understood nature's geometries as being far more complex than the orthogonal. After all, the Fibonacci series laid the foundation for Le Corbusier's quest for *l'espace indicible* and the dynamic spiral of the Moduloric scales. While the abstraction of geometry and mathematics underlying Le Corbusier's *Notre-Dame-du-Haut* (1955) and the *Philips Pavilion* (1958) may have revealed the potential of non-orthogonal architectural space at mid-century, Le Ricolais research into the nature of structure from the mid-1950s to the mid-1970s moved the exploration of structural form beyond the anthropomorphic.

For Le Ricolais, anthropomorphism's orthogonal geometry and bilateral symmetry had little to do with structures found in nature, including the human skeleton. Given the skeleton by his students, Le Ricolais's first action was to subject it to a structural analysis. "It made me feel rather humble, but we took it to the lab and made some experiments. For example, we weighed it. Result: eleven pounds, a fairly light weight considering the man of one hundred fifty pounds that it had to carry plus many superimposed loads...little weight, yet great structural solidity. At first sight this is an incomprehensible accomplishment of nature, since even with our special steels, very good materials compared to bone, we don't achieve comparable results."[5] For Le Ricolais nothing in the skeleton's structure had to do with the orthogonal and no mathematical calculation could explain its structural efficiency. "But the answer," said Le Ricolais, "came with a photo of the bone texture (Fig. 3). The complexity of this structure was laughing at us. Not one element was the same.

We read an astonishing three-dimensional network, whose geometry is practically impossible to resolve statistically."[6] Moreover, Le Ricolais concluded, the strength of bone had less to do with solids and more to do with voids. "But if you think about the voids instead of working with the solid elements, the truth appears. The structure is composed of holes, all different in dimension and distribution, but with an unmistakable purpose in their occurrence. So we arrive at an apparently paradoxical conclusion, that the art of structure is how and where to put holes. It's a good concept for building, to build with holes, to use things which are hollow, things which have no weight, which have strength but no weight...It takes

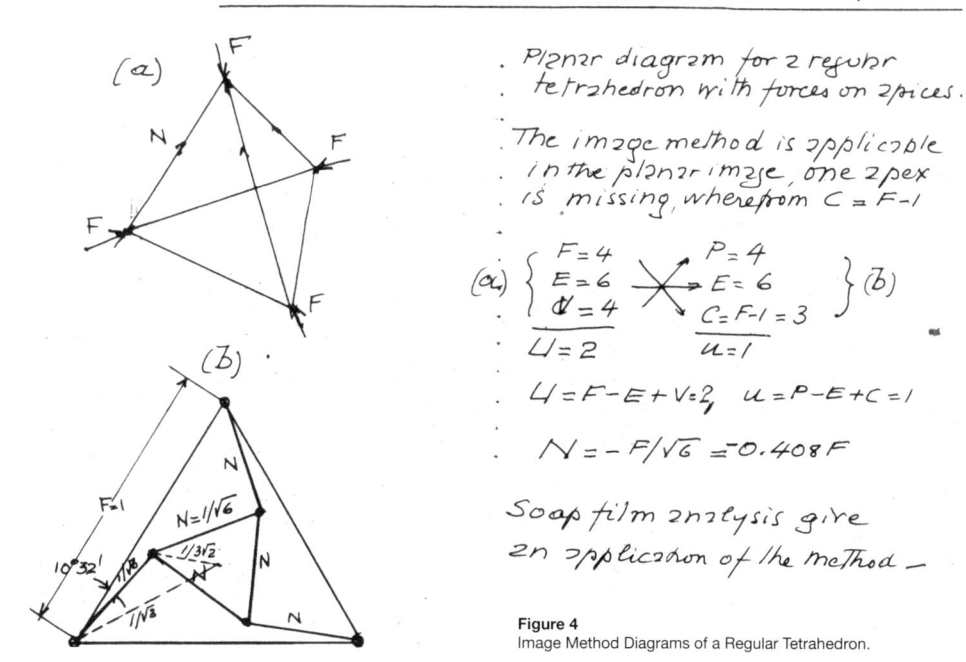

Figure 4
Image Method Diagrams of a Regular Tetrahedron.

time to build up your mind for this."[7] Perhaps this is what Le Ricolais meant by "things themselves are lying"—but what about "their images"?

To the extent that a structural configuration is the reciprocal diagram of its load pattern and vice versa, structural engineers deal primarily with enantiomorphs, non-identical mirror images.[8] This duality enables an engineer to determine visible structure from the invisible loads, or the reverse, to intuit the invisible loads from the visible structure. Le Ricolais's search for alternative techniques for generating structural configurations outside of anthropomorphism and calculations led him to James Clark Maxwell's research in two-dimensional and three-dimensional graphic statics. Maxwell studied rod-and-joint structures, similar to those found in early iron bridges, as examples of triangulated frameworks. In his research into the theory of triangulated frameworks, he used simple two-dimensional graphic statics to derive a precise relation between the number of structural members and joints necessary for a framework to remain rigid under imposed loads. According to Maxwell's criterion, a structure would be stiff or statically determinate only if the removal of any structural member would result in mechanical motion and failure, and, conversely, only if the addition of one or more members would render the framework overly-stiff and statically indeterminate causing self-strain and failure.[9]

Le Ricolais's image method, derived in part from Maxwell's research, is based on the principle of duality and the definition of spatial invariance found in Leonhard Euler's formula for simple polyhedra: F - E + V = 2 where F is the number of faces, E is the number of edges, and V is the number of vertices (Fig. 4).[10]

These image diagrams allowed Le Ricolais to graphically represent the forces in structural members, once the reactions at the boundaries had been determined. "Le Ricolais formulates two major hypotheses, which say that structural form is measurably influenced by: first, the rapport between forms and their mirror images (with its vocabulary of dual image, enantiomorph, and bimorph); and second, by the distribution of material in space (with its vocabulary of inertia, directionality, dimensionality, and isotropy). His interest not only extends the notions of (topological) connectivity and repetitive form (i.e. sinusoidal corrugations)...but also finds some kind of hybrid system between stressed skin and triangulation. Thus, from a natural form he abstracts an analogue and its isomorph, and finds a rapport between the derived alternative forms that yields a hybrid or some connective relationship."[11]

Fertile Minds

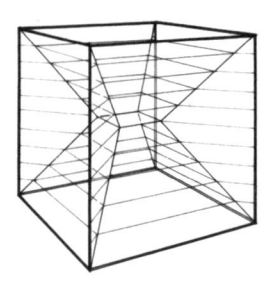

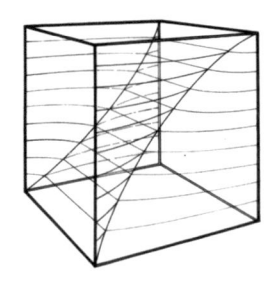

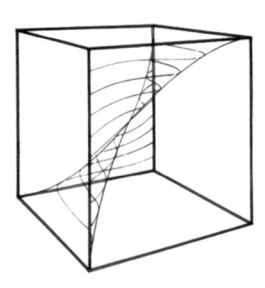

Figure 5 (Above)
Cubic wire frames and soap film configurations used to generate a "monkey saddle" structure.

Figure 6 (Facing Page)
A "monkey saddle" structure, 180 inches between points of support, made of steel tubes of 1 5/8-inch diameter and rods of 3/8-inch diameter, welded, for the frame and aircraft cable of 3/16-inch diameter, strung on Bakelite aircraft-pulleys, for the tension network, 1959-60.

In addition to the image method, Le Ricolais's research relied heavily on the fabrication of physical models. In one instance students dipped several geometric wire frames into a soap solution and then punctured certain faces of the soap film occurring within the frame (Fig. 5). The result was a representation in soap film of complex surfaces otherwise difficult to demonstrate or visualize in an abstract way. Based on the soap film surfaces the students fabricated a physical model of a "monkey saddle" structure made of welded steel tubes and aircraft cable. (Fig. 6) Like most of the models produced by Le Ricolais's students, the monkey saddle structure was never intended to be a final form so much as a necessary stage in ongoing research. "It may be naïve," wrote Le Ricolais, "but I believe these elementary models should be built, so that they can be experienced and contemplated. They should speak to us, or help us in some way to see what might be done with them."[12] While it isn't possible to describe a uniform approach, Le Ricolais's research often began with an observation of certain phenomenon, e.g. soap bubbles, radiolaria, spider webs, etc., followed by the identification of a geometrical pattern. An alternative structural configuration would then be proposed based on a mechanical principle derived from the geometrical pattern. Physical models of the structural configuration would then be fabricated and weights or forces applied to the models in order to test alternatives and achieve what Le Ricolais called the "beauty of failure."

One topic of investigation, the concept of an automorphic tube, led to a series of structural configurations. "Among the possible motifs for such a partition of space, it was natural that some automorphic system like those we had seen many times comes to mind. I'm sure you've seen this kind of thing before, when during the course of a telephone conversation, for example, your hand mechanically draws triangles inscribed in triangles. These elementary diagrams are intriguing in that they express very well a phenomenon of discontinuous growth related to a continuous curve, that is, the logarithmic spiral. More precisely, a configuration is said to be automorphic when it reproduces itself by a permutation of lines and points in such as way that no incidence is lost and no new incidence gained; we should also note that, for unbounded configurations, an automorphism of structure will correspond to an automorphic diagram of forces."[13]

The automorphic tubes were based on a reversal of Le Ricolais's research into the funicular polygon of revolution (FPR), a kind of horizontal "hollow rope" that treated the structural dissymmetry between compression and tension by configuring a structure into to two groups of members brought into equilibrium through tension. (Fig. 7, 8, and See p. 66 for Fig. 1) As a counterpart to the investigation of the tension networks in the FPR, Le Ricolais's research on automorphic tubes sought the optimum form for an axial compression member of minimum weight. Over many years of research numerous automorphic tube models were fabricated with varying numbers and positions of vertical bars and horizontal nodes. (See p. 64, Fig. 2) The automorphic tubes were then tested in order to determine the pattern of failure under the axial compressive forces of a hydraulic jack. (See p. 64, Fig. 3) In the instance of the T-12 automorphic tube, for example, "the buckling length was broken into its harmonics, with a wavelength of 9 inches, or twice the distance between nodes. (See p. 65, Fig. 4) The inner bundle of tubes tended toward a convex curvature while the outer one took a concave curvature of greater axis, showing that for an even distribution of stresses between the two layers their neutral axis should be slightly displaced toward the periphery."[14]

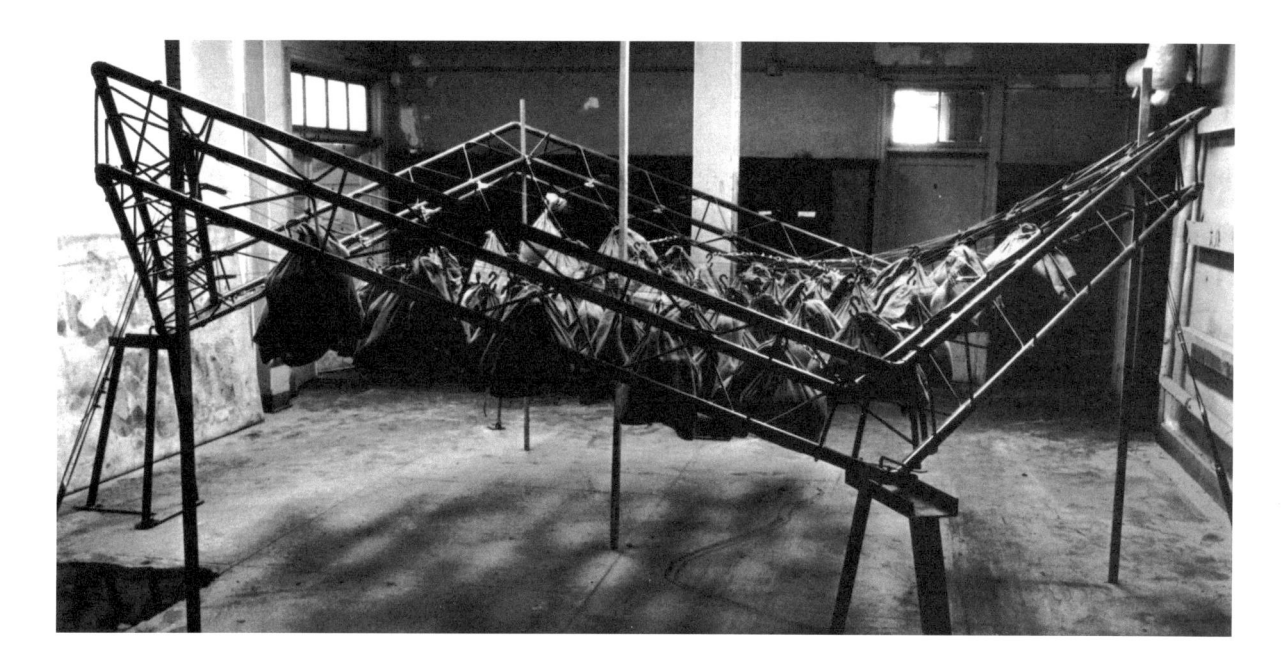

Le Ricolais's fascination with bi-triangulated automorphic form led to the study of radiolaria, marine amoeboid protozoa consisting of an inner siliceous skeletal core with radiating spicules joined to an outer membrane.[15] For Ernst Haeckel the elegance and complexities of the pattern and structure of these microscopic sea creatures embodied the unity of science and art. In classifying over four thousand known species of radiolaria Haeckel sought the key to the creative power of nature. What Haekel discovered in many of the skeletons of the radiolaria were a series of concentric, radial shells connected in a single crystal web. For Le Ricolais certain radiolaria could be interpreted as structural configurations consisting of an external skin in tension and an internal skeletal core of three-directional hexagonal configurations in compression. In the aggregation of the pyramids in the skeleton of the radiolarian Sagoscena, for example, Le Ricolais found the properties of both stressed-skin and triangulated structures. (See p. 65, Fig. 5) Moreover, to Le Ricolais's delight, one face of each of the pyramids within the structure was bi-triangulated and the bases were faceted into three triangular planes. In certain other radiolaria, Le Ricolais found automorphism, a geometric assemblage of structural elements that go into one another, repeating themselves. In the radiolaria Actinomma and Pityomma, for example, Le Ricolais saw "a ball inside a ball inside another ball."[16] (See p. 66, Fig. 6) For him the presence of these principles of automorphism in other natural forms, e.g. the curves of the *spira mirabilis*, the Nautilus shell, confirmed the results of his research on automorphic structural form. A sketch of the shell appeared on a page from Le Ricolais's notebook published in the *VIA* interview (See p. 70, Fig. 7). Below the shell Le Ricolais wrote "eadem mutata resurgo," which he translated as "always reborn into itself." The Latin phrase, perhaps better translated as "I arise again the same though changed," was first known to be used by Swiss mathematician Jakob Bernoulli (1654-1705), and appears on his tombstone in Basel. Like Le Ricolais, Bernoulli was referring to the logarithmic spiral in nature.

Of all the radiolaria studied by him, the *Auloscena* was perhaps the most significant and relevant to Le Ricolais's research. (See p. 69, Fig. 8) In the radiolarian *Auloscena* Le

Fertile Minds

Ricolais found both automorphism, the self-adjustment of form toward an optimum equilibrium, and bimorphism, the combination of a form with its dual. "We can associate cyclic forms to cyclic patterns of re-formation," Le Ricolais wrote, "such as those found in structures submitted to vibrations, a self-adjustment of form tending toward an optimum equilibrium condition. The radiolarian *Auloscena*...shows this cyclic organization ruled by automorphism in a truly admirable way: the inner sphere radiates spicules which are reinforced by a peripheral wall reproducing the initial form, this being repeated a number of times. With the geometric differentiation between open configurations, typical of the growth of crystals and found in natural forms, and closed configurations, which are their duals, organized for stability and permanence, we are thus led to the notion of 'bimorphism', or the combination of a form with its dual."[17] To illustrate the principles of automorphism and bimorphism Le Ricolais drew a diagram of dimetral section. (See p. 68, Fig. 9) The most profound manifestation of the principles of automorphism and bimorphism in Le Ricolais's work can be seen in a axial view photograph of the 65-foot *Octen* tower, a geometric assemblage of structural elements that go into one another, repeating themselves, much like "a ball inside a ball inside another ball." (See p. 70, Fig. 10)

Le Ricolais was introduced to Louis Kahn by mail in 1953 and began teaching at the University of Pennsylvania in 1954. "I find Le R. of particular sensitivity and by far the purer engineer and philosopher," wrote Louis Kahn to Anne Tyng. "His study of Topology is the reason for his advanced position and his preoccupation with geometry *per se* is another. He has a thick notebook of diagrams and formulas (of his own)...based on Topological formulae. It is precisely the scientific knowledge which an architect needs if he is at all interested in forms and plan and intends to work in the 3-D field."[18] Although Le Ricolais was an engineer, his teaching with Kahn had ramifications beyond engineering. "Le Ricolais, Tyng, and Fuller associated space frames with a progressive social agenda in two ways. The first was their proposition, familiar to supporters of the modern movement, that technology properly used would create a better world. The second was more mystical. Space frames, in their reliance on nature's geometries, revealed that underneath the apparent chaos and randomness of structures and forms was an order of almost mystical simplicity."[19] The definition of engineering, as the application of scientific principles to design or develop structures, machines, or manufacturing processes—all as respects an intended function, economics of operation and safety to life and property—did not fit the engineer Le Ricolais very well. In a 1972 interview Kahn didn't mention Le Ricolais by name, but he did say "It's the discovery of nature's powers, that's all – that's what anyone does who's a real engineer."[20]

What Le Ricolais discovered in nature's powers were dualities and paradoxes. "The book of nature is so big," he wrote, "that sometimes you find the answer to a question you had not even asked yourself. The phenomenon of

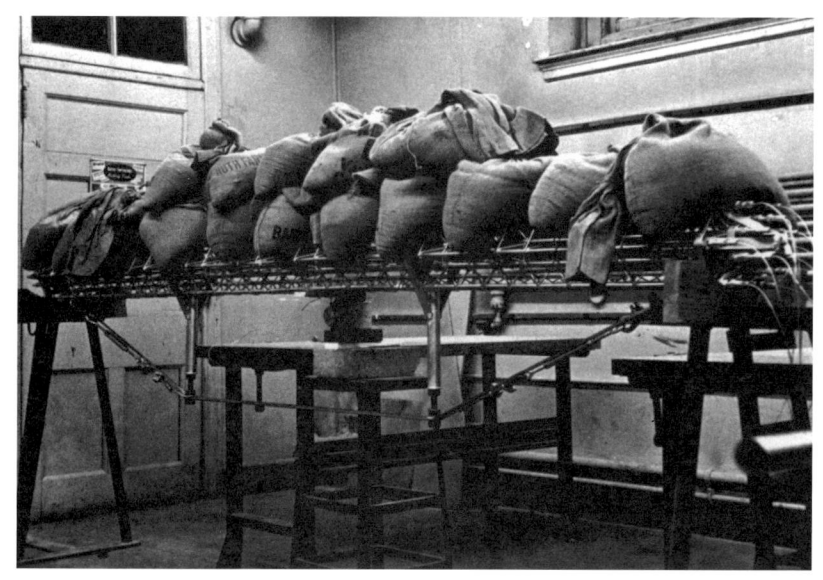

Figure 7 (Facing Page)
Model of an FPR (funicular polygon of revolution) bridge for the Skyrail, 1961-62.

Figure 8 (Left)
A prestressed T-12 Automorphic tube with queen posts, 1961-62.

the eggshell is a revelation, putting forward this kind of contradiction of a form which is extremely strong yet locally very fragile."[21] From nature as a point of departure, Le Ricolais's research entered into the realm of dualities—between forms and stresses, between compression and tension, between matter and holes. He described the ultimate goal of his research—"zero weight, infinite span"—as being derived "from a principle which may seem paradoxical at first glance…i.e. contradiction, whereby the contrary of any evoked principle is also acceptable."[22] Le Ricolais, the real engineer, had an analogical mind coupled with a fascination for dualities and paradoxes, for self-contradictory or counter-intuitive statements and structural arguments. As a teacher of structures he incited future architects to think beyond the habitual anthropomorphic and orthogonal domain of architectural space. Much like the concept of automorphic structure, his students' analogical and rhetorical models sought a difficult and delicate balance. "Habit," Le Ricolais wrote, "has desensitized us to the miracle of the phenomenon of solids and the paradox between molecular chaos and the stability of a body which is actually a diagram of forces in equilibrium."[23]

Endnotes

1 *VIA 2* (1973) also included a photo essay, "Matieres," with text by Le Ricolais and photographs by Henriette Grindat, (1923-1986) known for photographs with connections to writers and poets. George Robert Le Ricolais (1894-1977) was born at La Roche sur Yon, France. He taught at the University of Pennsylvania from 1954-1975.
2 Le Ricolais, "Things Themselves are Lying, and So Are Their Images," *VIA: Structures Implicit and Explicit, Vol. 2* (1973): p. 88.
3 Le Ricolais, "Things Themselves are Lying, and So Are Their Images": p. 87.
4 Le Corbusier, *Le Poeme d'angle droit* (Paris, Vevre, 1955)
5 Le Ricolais, "Things Themselves are Lying, and So Are Their Images": p. 88.
6 Le Ricolais, "Things Themselves are Lying, and So Are Their Images": p. 88.
7 Le Ricolais, "Things Themselves are Lying, and So Are Their Images": p. 88.
8 "Two asymmetric figures, each the mirror image of the other, are said to be enantiomorphs. Each is enantiomorphic to the other." Martin Gardner, *The New Ambidextrous Universe: Symmetry and Assymetry from Mirror Reflections to Superstrings* (New York: Freeman, 1990); pp. 16.
9 T.M. Charlton, "An Extension of Maxwell's Theory of Pin-Jointed Frameworks by M.W. Crofton," *Notes and Records of the Royal Society of London* (January 1989): p. 53-56.
10 Mathematician and physicist Leonhard Euler (1707-1783) discovered the formula $V - E + F = 2$ relating the number of vertices, edges, and faces of a convex polyhedron in the form of a planar graph.
11 Peter McCleary, "Robert Le Ricolais' Search for the 'Indestructible Idea,'" *Lotus International 99* (2000): p. 105.
12 Le Ricolais, "Things Themselves are Lying, and So Are Their Images": p. 83
13 Le Ricolais, "Things Themselves are Lying, and So Are Their Images": p. 103
14 Le Ricolais, "Things Themselves are Lying, and So Are Their Images": p. 103
15 Radiolaria are protozoa distinguished by segregation of their soft anatomy into the central capsule, containing the endoplasm and the surrounding ectoplasm, and by their siliceous skeletons. Radiolarians have existed since the beginning of the Paleozoic era, producing an astonishing diversity of intricate shapes during their 600 million year history. Radiolarians take their name from the radial symmetry, often marked by radial skeletal spines; however, skeletal elements of radiolarians, do not actually meet at the center of the organism.
16 Le Ricolais, "Things Themselves are Lying, and So Are Their Images": p. 91.
17 Le Ricolais, "Things Themselves are Lying, and So Are Their Images": p. 89.
18 Anne Griswold Tyng, *Louis Kahn to Anne Tyng: The Rome Letters 1953-1954* (New York: Rizzoli, 1997); p. 146.
19 Sarah Williams Goldhagen, *Louis Kahn's Situated Modernism* (New Haven: Yale University Press, 2001); p. 70.
20 Louis Kahn, "How'm I Doing Corbusier?," *The Pennsylvania Gazette 71* (December 1972): pp. 18-26.
21 Le Ricolais, "Things Themselves are Lying, and So Are Their Images": p. 88.
22 Le Ricolais, "Things Themselves are Lying, and So Are Their Images": p. 81
23 Le Ricolais quoted in René Motro, "Robert Le Ricolais (1894-1977) Father of Spatial Structures." *International Journal of Space Structures* (December 2007): p. 236.

Things Themselves Are Lying, and So Are Their Images

Robert Le Ricolais

Fundamentally, my attitude—I should not say this to a student—is that I'm fantastically hedonistic, and you know by hedonistic I mean the search for my own pleasure. It's not at all the desire to be sensational. You know what we are, we have limits. Sometimes it's absolutely silly, some little analogies which are really infantile are enough to keep me going for quite a while. These analogies may be pure fancy, maybe very stupid things, but sometimes they illustrate in an amusing way things which are very difficult to comprehend. And even if the analogy by itself isn't right, there is something there: it's the almighty power of an idea, as an incentive. I mean I'm obliged to admit that a fine work of engineering is okay, a standard of excellence which is visible, but the idea behind it may be more exciting. Because a building is a unique thing, and I have the feeling that the idea can give solutions for different sorts of things.

Look how wrong some thinking can be: it was a great mistake, which I realized a good many years later, to say that the art of building is to build with matchsticks, that if you want to build light structures you must use light members because if you use light members a group of light members will be light. It took me quite a long time to see that it was just the opposite; it's the art of making a light structure with big, heavy members. A paradox.

You see, some people have got a sense of order, a privative sense of things being symmetrical, which I have not. I think it's a pseudo-order, because neither in nature nor in art do you find this kind of total repetition that puts you to sleep; there are many more relations between things than their being simply contiguous, bing-bing-bing in a row, which is what you see in many planning projects—one would die of monotony living in such nice, clean arrangements. On the other hand, you know it's been made by a great architect when you see one of those Islamic walls where the symmetry is always broken with some kind of little detail. The patterns look fantastically well organized, but all of a sudden you see something surprising and out of context, which upsets the symmetry in a very discreet way. As you know, they avoided the presence of man, because representations of man were considered unholy, but in following these arabesques of geometric and naturalistic motifs you see that you can lose yourself in the delicate variation of details. This was not just to stun you. They wanted you to go into the play of the whole and the detail, which could become all-absorbing, a high without drugs. It's most impressive... So I don't think one can find valid criteria in the sense of beauty by itself. It exists, no question about that, but everyone has his own coordinates; what may be beautiful to you may not be beautiful to me, unless perhaps you explain. I don't think it's innate. You see how your point of view is modified by a certain amount of culture.

But at least we know that the work of the engineer and the architect has to do with materials and matter, and when you want to devise some new structure, you have to have a clear enough idea of the orders of magnitude involved to know that the thing can exist…Of course architects are people who automatically make a drawing,

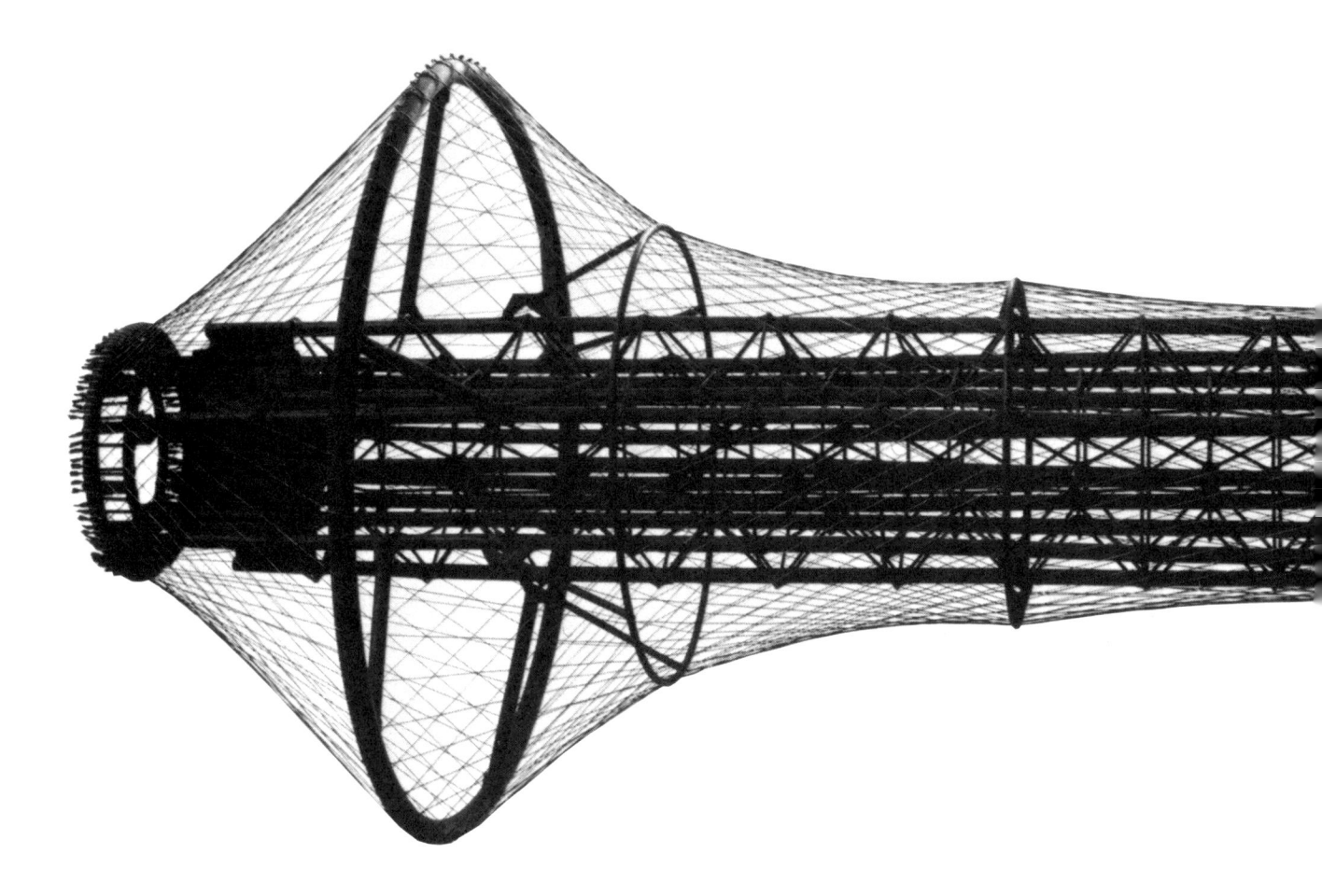

Figure 1
Detail of a model of a FPR (funicular polygon of revolution) bridge for the Skyrail showing automorphic tube 132 inches in length with a diameter varying from 8 1/2 inches to 24 inches (scale, 1:100), made of steel tubes of 1/2-inch diameter and rods of 1/8-inch diameter for the axial compression member, tubes of 1/4-inch, 1/2-inch, and 3/4-inch diameters for the diaphragm rings, and aircraft cable of 1/32-inch diameter for the tension network, 1961-62.

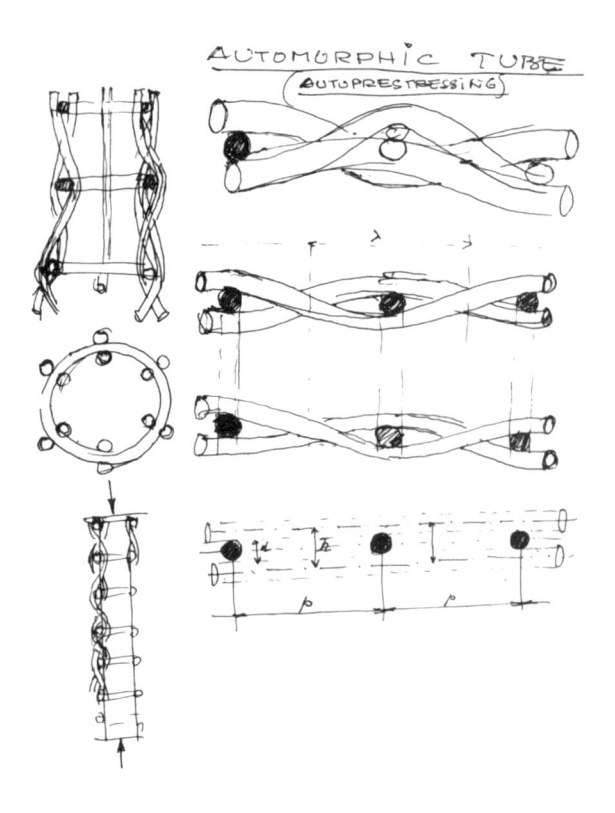

Figure 2
Sketch of an Automorphic tube, 1966.

Figure 3
T-12 Automorphic tube, 9 inches in diameter, made of steel tubes of 1/2-inch diameter and 1/32-inch wall thickness and rods of 1/8-inch diameter, 1961–62.

always making some abstraction, which is easy, because you do it in a void. Even if these are very simple, they can give you a completely imperfect notion of what the thing is. So in a way I kind of deplore the idea of image…And yet I think it would be stupid to say that our abstractions have no use, because there are a lot of things we may be doing which appear to be totally impractical but which indeed have some light to shed on serious problems. So the other sequence would be quite good too: trying, from pure abstraction or a pure spatial concept, to find some correlation with things which exist, in which there could be an analogy. I won't say this should lead to application, because application has always some kind of sordid side— but analogy, I think that's right. It's a two-way system: we go from the concrete to the abstract, going there, going back, back and forth, and that's perpetually what I think any man has to do. Getting lost in pure theoretical consideration isn't good. It starts you, but you get dry and just say, 'So what?'

There's a question of rapport, you see, this very fascinating thing between reality and symbols. Think of the mathematical models for moment, deflection, and so forth; even moment of inertia is a symbol, and quite a powerful one when you use it. But the question is whether we are playing with symbols—maybe symbols play some funny farce on us too. We become addicted to the symbol, even if many times we use it in the wrong way.

It's an enormous reservoir of unexploited forms, mathematics and its symbols. These abstract concepts, which may be devised purely for the support of thought, enable our mind to escape the anthropomorphic attitude and confront an unknown universe. Probably magic and poetry in ancient times had the same power. But sometimes I wish we could have a physical model or apparatus that would show us the reality of, say, Euler's formula for polyhedra, $F - E + V = 2$, so that these things which are supremely abstract could be conveyed in a direct way. We can't live too well—at least I can't live too well—in such a rarefied atmosphere. Sometimes you need to see things, or experience them, where your eyes can help your mind. For example, I know that if I draw before you what we know is a rhombohedron, you would not be

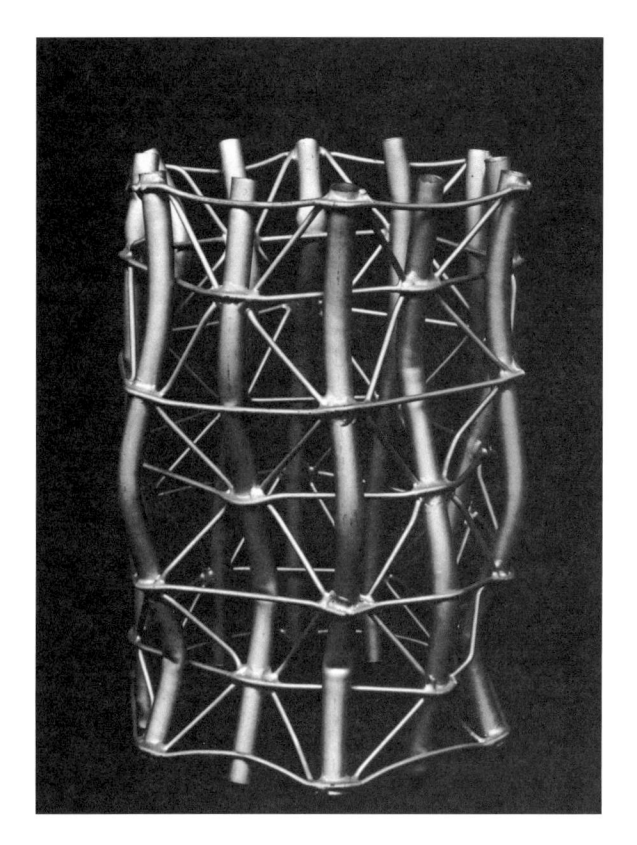

Figure 4
T-12 Automorphic tube, 9 inches in diameter, made of steel tubes of 1/2-inch diameter and 1/32-inch wall thickness and rods of 1/8-inch diameter, 1961-66.

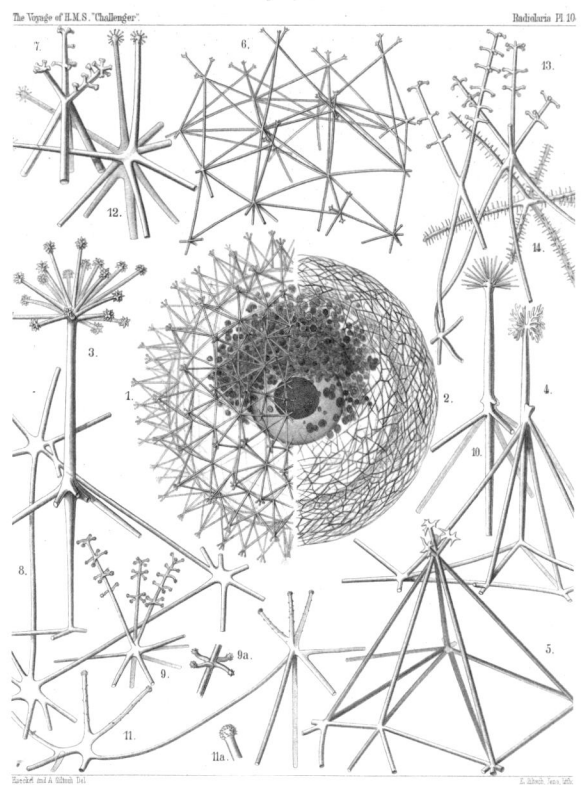

Figure 5
Drawing by Ernst Haeckel of a radiolarian *Sagoscena*; center: shell cut in half; top center: piece of shell with eight pyramids; bottom right: single eight-sided pyramid.

satisfied at all; it doesn't speak to your senses. Whereas as soon as you get the damn thing in your hand, you know what you're talking about. We are really maimed, you see. This need for representation, this need to make some kind of physical model as soon as a concept comes to us, proves how infantile our mind is. But it's a support. Our mind is not powerful enough to tell us what the angle is here when we have sixty degrees over there; it doesn't jump into your mind. So the contact with things is full of meaning: you know where you are, you have something that exists, that you can put your teeth into

Therefore I feel one has to start on the concrete and slowly converge with the abstract, but always keeping your eye on how the symbolism works with the fact. I would fight against too much symbolism—people relying too much on formulas and bookish things until they're just like ambulating textbooks, people eating symbols all the day, forgetting, you know, reality. That's my trouble: I may know very well what sort of symbolism should be applied, I know the rule, but going from the symbolism to some kind of particular solution is a difficult trick. I can do it for myself, but I can't always explain it to others. It's still an art, and anyone looking at the problem with a certain attention should be able to do at least as well as we do.

The fact that we rely on a safety coefficient which varies from 2 to 3, sometimes more than that, tells you a great story about our inability to get high precision in the difficult art of building. This makes it very interesting to consider the problem of the beehive, the economy made by the bee with his trihedral lid. It was a great problem in the seventeenth century. I think it was an astronomer that started the damn thing—it's funny to see astronomers measuring the fantastic angle the bees use. Maraldi finally found it, something like one hundred nine degrees. And the saving in material is about two percent. Why should the bee do that, working on two percent while we work on two hundred percent? It tells you how far we have to go compared to the way of nature, the puzzling notion of the beehive. You know, at one time it was proposed to take the dimension of the bee's cell as the unit of length instead of the meter, because it has been observed that this is practically constant. It's

Fertile Minds

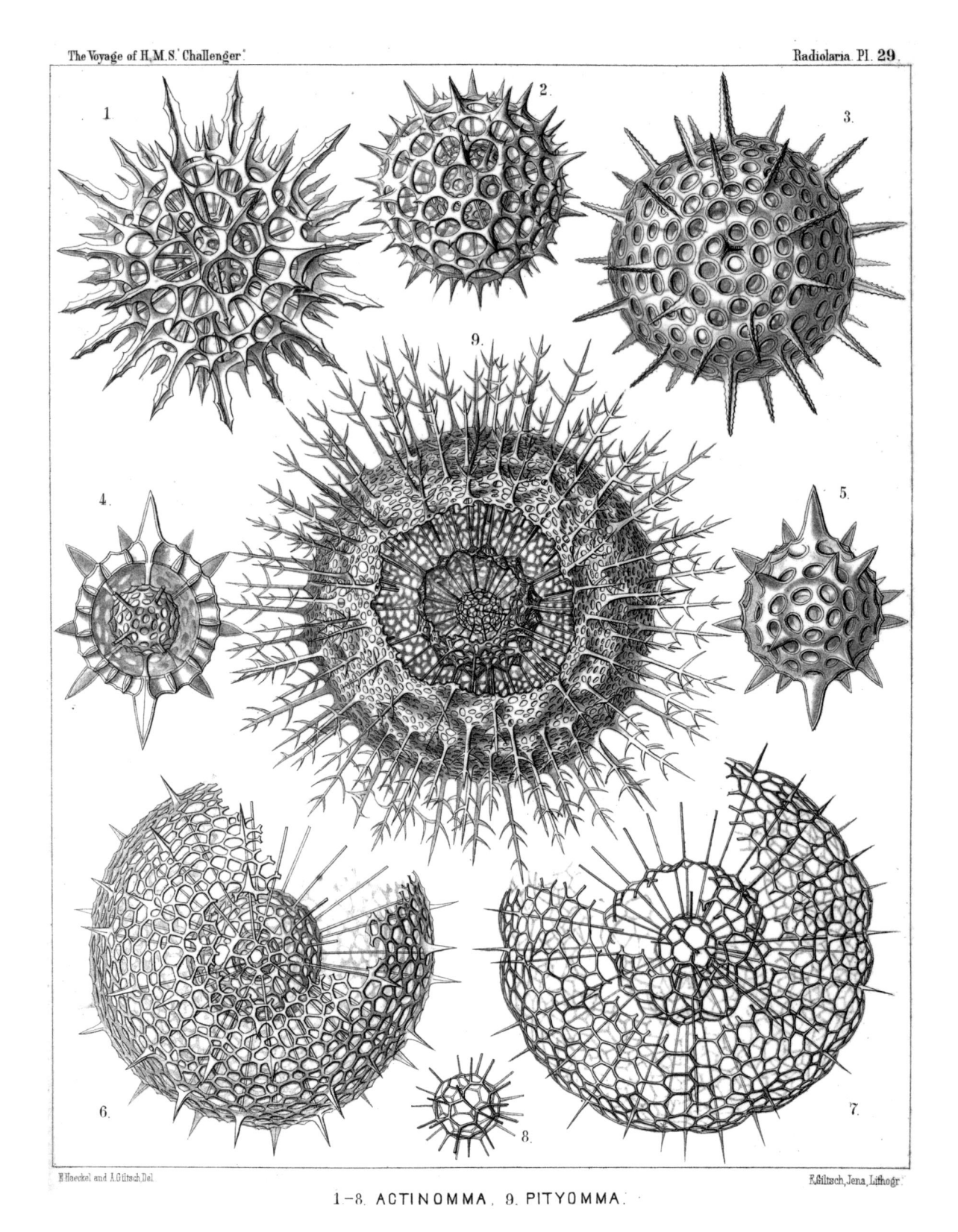

Figure 6
Drawing by Ernst Haeckel of radiolaria *Actinomma* and *Pityomma*; "ball inside a ball inside a ball."

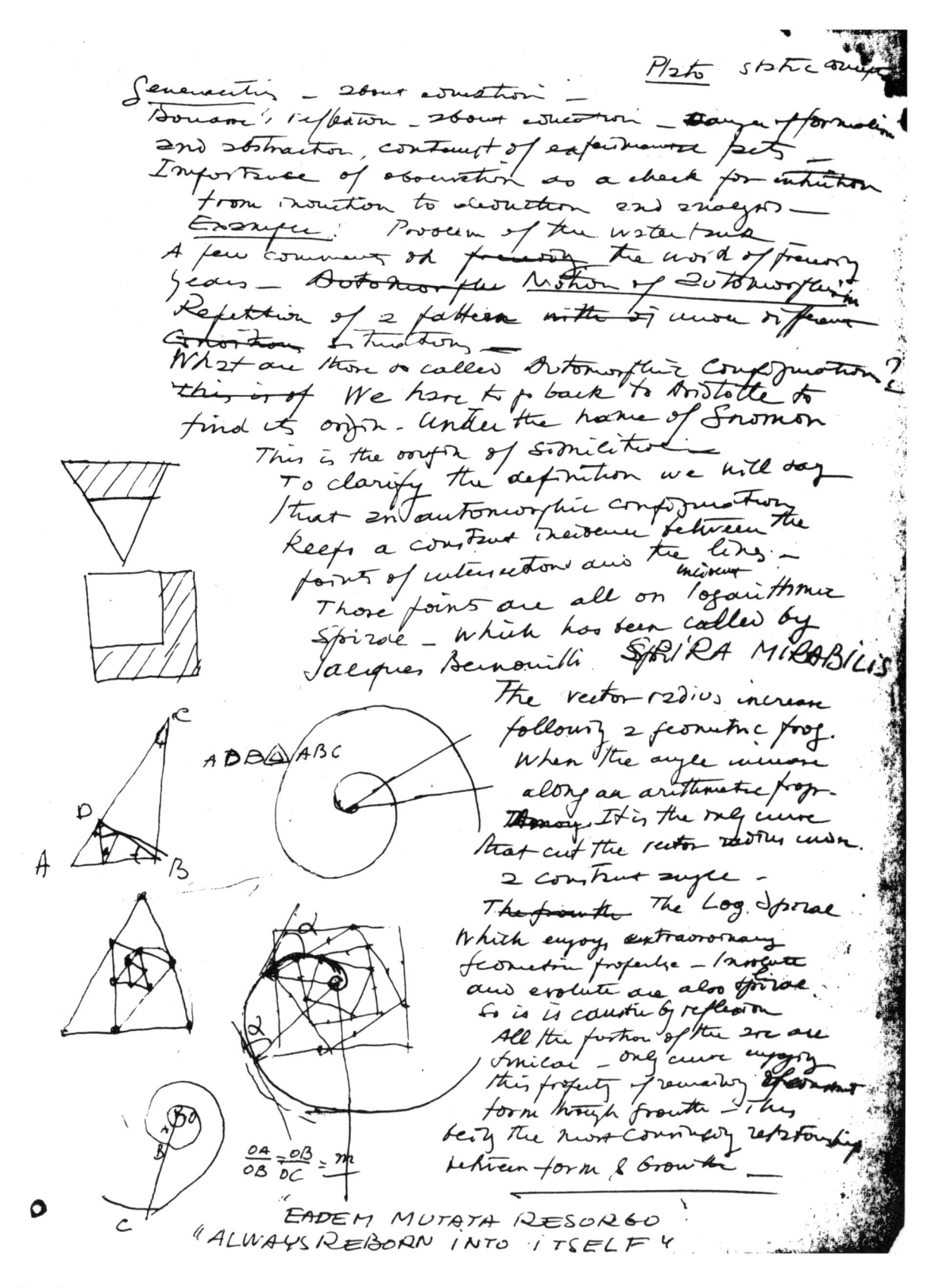

Figure 7
Page from Le Ricolais's notebook with a sketch of the *spira mirabilis* and a translation of "eadem mutata resurgo."

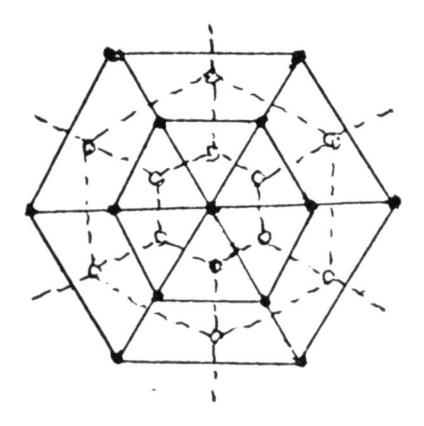

Figure 8 (Left)
Drawing by Ernst Haeckel of a radiolarian *Auloscena*; center: complete shell composed of equal hexagonal pyramids with a radial tube atop each pyramid; upper left: a single tentshaped six-sided pyramid with a radial tube.

Figure 9 (Above)
Diagram of dimetral section illustrating automorphism and bimorphism.

very hard to find things which remain constant with evolution and time...

I must admit that everything dealing with mathematics was entirely confusing in my mind when I was your age; I was absolutely horrified by anything mathematical. I hated that attitude, and that's why I wasted so gloriously so many years of doing painting. You see the opposition? In painting you just do away with all this comparing, this fastidious way of mathematics. In mathematics, it's always precision; you have to know a few definitions, you have to compare, to measure, you have to deduct. When you do painting, you have this wonderful feeling of the unknown—especially since I really had no discipline. I came very late to this, so I didn't know how to paint; but I made the best out of ignoring how to paint. And as soon as I got to know a little more about it, I was not so amused. Really what was prodigiously amusing for me were my mistakes. Maybe some well-known operator would have just said, 'Well, this character, this guy doesn't know anything about the job of painting. There's a technique. There's a way of doing things.' This I would ignore fantastically, and many times that's probably the way I did my best painting. I was naturally very incompetent with my hands and could not draw—yet I had this eye for fairly exact definition of form. That's why I used the airbrush. I made some kind of stencil of cardboard, so you had a very wonderful definition of black and white. But why all this? It's because I was not sure of my hand to make the transition between black and gray and white. You see it comes to this notion of compensation: at some point you come to enjoy the thing you are lacking.

It looks like a cheap homily, what I'm saying, but honestly I believe that we do many things by compensation. We have some limitation, and well, all of a sudden you start to take it seriously, as a challenge to yourself. This plays very often—people who go through some kind of conversion, just reversing the trend. It's a challenge. Maybe it will take you a week more to understand something, but you go through it. Besides, things that come to be too easy are no fun. Things must be too difficult, you know...I mean we have to be careful, even with the little models that we try to make, using soap films and things like this. We go very near phenomena many times that look complicated and are simple, but more often it's not as simple as it looks. At every moment one has to question himself. Indeed, you know the amusing story about bubbles is that they don't exist; we speak of a film, but really there's no film, only a phenomenon of attraction of molecules which are always moving. The fact is that we can't simulate this in any other physical or chemical way; you need the liquid, so the bubble is unstable and just dries up. There we are again, there is some kind of mirage in the image. One can be fooled so easily by the appearance of things and not see what is behind...

Oriental wisdom has codified the problem in the proverb saying, 'Things themselves are lying, and so are their images.' So I think a certain self-analysis is needed, in order to determine our own coefficient of error. For instance, the frequency of a vibrating string to someone with well-trained ears is almost as precise as that given by computation; and you know there are engravers who can incise a steel plate to a measured accuracy of one-hundredth of a millimeter. This self-imposed discipline has some cathartic virtue in helping us to realize the discrepancy between what we really are and what we think we are, between the known and the unknown; it refines the meaning of experience. Because when you express yourself in this work, it's not a romance. When you're dealing with exact things, or things that are supposed to be pretty exact, you have to know what you're talking about—you can't misname things and make confusion. I don't take myself for a scientist, not in the least, but I know well that nothing in this domain of form is that arbitrary. It's not the arbitrariness of the historian, of the literary approach, of the art approach, although these have fascinated our imagination since the beginning of time. Deductions and propositions have to prove themselves, and not by seduction or good intentions; they have to come to facts.

I've found no better discipline in this unpredictable problem of form than to observe the prodigies created by nature. I mean you've got to have an eye, but the world is full of marvelous little things; their beauty and rigor is an amazing incentive.

So we arrive at an apparently paradoxical conclusion, that the art of structure is how and where to put holes. It's a good concept for building, to build with holes, to use things which are hollow, things which have no weight, which have strength but no weight. The phenomenon of the eggshell is also a revelation, putting forward this kind of contradiction of a form which is extremely strong and yet locally very fragile. You can say that an egg is really very strong when you submit it to something like hydrostatic pressure, but when you exert a puncture load, when you squeeze it with two fingers, it's gone. It takes time to build up your mind for this. I was thirty when I came to ask myself about this notion of strength and fragility; before, the two were incompatible in my thinking.

You see, it's always the convergence of certain ideas. There's some dilettantism in this attitude, but I think I would take it as a hobby which may be more than a hobby. I mean you may have a significant contribution to make here, because there's always some kind of no-man's-land between ideas, or between, say, strength of materials and biology. This is strange, but you can feel it very easily: there's some bridge to make between things. For instance, we speak of stressed-skin structures, which aircraft has developed a great deal, and of triangulated structures—here we are immediately facing two technologies, which belong to extremely different worlds...Why should only a zoologist look at *Radiolaria*? That's a shame. I found in some magazine an interesting article about spiders and even communicated with one man about it. I don't think he understood exactly what I had in mind; I mean we were probably miles apart. You see, usually the spiders make indeterminate structures—there are always many connections—except one kind, with a funny name, who knows how to make strictly determinate structures. She has not gotten to the top class, remaining behind in the Maxwell diagrams. That's fun really, some kind of stimulation we need. And of course in terms of strength-to-weight, spiders are amazing, much better than we can do. The point is that the book of nature is so big that sometimes you find an answer to a question you have never formulated yourself.

So there is this rather exciting point between ideas, finding what is different, what is common, to what limit one system can go with another. Maybe you'll find some connection between the two which could lead you toward a solution. As you can see in some of the *Radiolaria*, there are forms that encompass the properties of both stressed-skin and triangulated structures. They are just in-between: configurations with multiple holes, a

Figure 10
An Octen tower (axial view), 65 feet in height with a diameter of 23 inches, made of steel rods of 3/8-inch diameter, welded, and aircraft cable of 1/4-inch diameter for the six axial cables and three stays, 1965-66.

perforated membrane in tension working together with a triangulated frame. And this may give an analogy, based on a few topological notions of the arrangement and number of holes, that could bridge the gap between two kinds of structures and, possibly, the two technologies.

I don't think these *Radiolaria* should be ignored. They are more than mere curiosities, and we should study them carefully as highly elaborate pieces of work. The collection is of a fantastic vastitude. I think there are about four thousand different types, and you could spend days and days looking at the wonderful illustrations by Haeckel, dating from the 1870s, when he sailed with the Challenger around the world. But one peculiar species, which was fascinating to me, is the one looking very much like the little Chinese ivory things you find in antique shops—where you have a ball inside a ball inside another ball. It's probably cheap labor involved here, because it must take some guy all his life to make one, unless they have a machine now. But it's kind of a prodigy, to see in a sphere another sphere and so forth. I mean there is something that really puzzles you. We are confronted with something full of meaning. Why should there be this kind of recurrence of form? It may be too obvious, but after all this may be the way standardization started, the importance of repeating something. And this principle is what in our jargon we call automorphism: some kind of geometric assemblage of forms which go into one another, repeating themselves. Of course nature does not simply repeat herself, and we have to be careful not to confuse the little object which we see and can touch or hold in our hands with form; as Eddington said, there can be no confusion between natural and man-made objects, because what man makes is usually single-purposed, whereas nature is capable of fulfilling many requirements, not always clear to our mind.

Whatever it is, when you look at these things, it's very hard for me to explain, but you see some kind of coherence and a purity of design which is amazing, which is frightening. From the point of view of the *Radiolarian*, the geodesic dome is three hundred million years old. We have been speaking about space frames for twenty-five or thirty years, and nature has been there for three hundred million. So what? Well, it's not by chance, and I'm glad that I saw the *Radiolaria* before I saw Mr. Fuller's dome.

So I started to play around with these things, during the years counting the number of bars, counting the angles, and so forth. There's delight in this. You learn something. Even if you learn that what you think is not true, even if you make the wrong conclusion, the landscape that has been before your eyes is great. Of course you can't just convert these things into building structures, but there is much to admire and understand. You know, there is something rather tragic and sordid in man—as soon as he puts his fingers on something, he wants to take it. We should fight against this kind of possessive behavior. Why should the *Radiolaria* help us to make money? They don't care. Hell, they are not our servants. Yet there's always this tendency for people to jump into some kind of trick, a quick way to success and reputation. No-no-no, you have to be patient to understand, infinite patience. And besides as soon as you use things, they cease to be art things. They become a little vulgar, tools.

But well, it's a little of both. You see, I'm not that pragmatic. I enjoy its mystery too. Maybe the *Radiolaria* will give you some analogy to help you resolve some particular problem, but I think it's not so important to arrive at a particular solution as it is to get some general view of the whole damn thing, which leaves you guessing.

Notes

This essay is an excerpt from Robert Le Ricolais, "Things Themselves Are Lying, and So Are Their Images," *VIA* 2 (1973): 80-109.

At the Boundaries of Practice:
The Remaking of Spiral Jetty
Ruth Erickson

During one of innumerable scouting missions to the Southwestern United States, the prominent "Land" or "Earth" artists Michael Heizer and Walter De Maria sent a telegram to New York art dealer Richard Bellamy in April 1968: "LAND PROJECT POSITIVE... DON'T UNDERESTIMATE DIRT."[1] Excavated or amassed in distant locales to create artworks, dirt/earth/soil became a central medium for so-called "Earth artists" in the late 1960s and early 1970s. Susan Boettger describes the societal mood of the period as "the broad rejection of tradition in all forms of art and social mores," and dirt posed a seductively subversive medium for artists.[2] Practically, dirt offered an inexpensive material that could accommodate large-scale works, but these artists' use of dirt doubles as a polemic, a conscious material decision with political, economic, aesthetic, and conceptual implications. To not "underestimate dirt," we must assess these agendas underlying its use. While artistic skill and material worth have provided two key markers for the valuation of art, the Earth artists established their practices in contradistinction to this rubric; they sought to get outside of art through dirt. Thirty years later, the contemporary photographer Vik Muniz built and photographed "re-creations of famous Earthworks at table-top scale" in his Brooklyn studio.[3] This series, entitled *Brooklyn, NY*, 1997, marks a transition from dirt as a material of subversion to dirt as a modality of practice. Starting from the premise that in contemporary culture everything is taken from something else, Muniz draws on the by-products of an advanced media culture, creating images of objects based on images of other objects. This strategy of appropriation triggers questions regarding the status of the real in an era of excess, offering yet another conception of dirt.

Earth artists such as Nancy Holt, Robert Smithson, Heizer, and De Maria challenged traditional art practices through their use of unrefined as opposed to valuable materials; of industrial machinery, such as bulldozers, in lieu of brushes; and of distant sites instead of New York galleries, thereby fundamentally changing art's production, experience, and distribution. In conversation with Smithson and Dennis Oppenheim in a 1970 issue of *Avalanche*, Heizer explains his hope to transcend the commercial system: "Art usually becomes another commodity. One of the implications of earth art might be to remove completely the commodity-status of a work of art and to allow a return to the idea of art as...I guess I'd like to see art become more of a religion." While the remoteness and physical form of much Earth art made its commodification difficult, the proliferation of documentation ultimately led to its re-absorption into the gallery system through the exhibition and sale of models and photographs.[4] Smithson, for instance, documented his *Spiral Jetty*, 1970, probably the most famous of all Earth works, in preliminary drawings, photographs, a short film, and also an essay. To create the work, Smithson leased property on the Great Salt Lake in Utah and hired professional excavators, a backhoe, and a pair of dump trucks to displace 6,650 tons of basalt rocks and earth into the water in the shape of a spiral.[5] The spiral has a diameter of three hundred feet and extends over five hundred feet from the bank of the lake. On account of *Spiral Jetty*'s location and rapid immersion due to a rising water level, Smithson's documentation of the work constituted the only means of access for many years.[6] Muniz traces his initial interest in Earth art to his experience of its photographic documentation, already once removed from the physical matter: "The first time I saw a picture of Smithson's *Spiral Jetty*, my immediate reaction was—'Wow! What this guy had to go through to end up with a photograph!'"[7] Smithson, in Muniz's words, "did not just build a form in a remote salt lake in Utah; he built a monument *in our minds*."[8] In other words, the mental monument is as important, if not more so, than the actual displaced dirt, a monumentality built on information, representation, repetition, and even lore. Muniz's somewhat sarcastic remark about the immense labor and cost endured by Smithson to create what most people experience as a photograph engenders the question, "Why bother with the original?" The studio recreation of *Spiral Jetty* by Muniz begs this question while also participating in the collective invention of the work's monumentality.

Against a fabricated backdrop of low, barren mountains, Muniz traces a spiral in dirt on the blank surface of a table. He is not rebuilding *Spiral Jetty* but instead recreating the photographs of it. In Muniz's model, the salt-encrusted rocky edges of Smithson's *Spiral Jetty* become smooth, monochromatic, and more tightly coiled, but it shares the tractor marks leading to the spiral as well as the hazy horizon line visible in most photographs of Smithson's work. Muniz's image, therefore, recollects the familiar photographs while hinting at the artificiality of *this* spiral jetty. The grey photograph "works" on account of *Spiral Jetty*'s iconic status as well as photography's claim to reality. Furthermore, photography tends to distort scale, and Muniz relies on the medium to equalize the divergent sizes of the miniature model and the immense real thing. Artificiality and the contingency of scale are also conceptual concerns of Smithson. In a manner prescient of Muniz's recreation, Smithson writes, "[My work] is not involved with nature, in the classical sense. [. . .] I'm more interested in denaturalization or in artifice than I am in any kind of naturalism."[9] Smithson intervenes in the landscape, and his modifications to nature rather than nature itself comprise his artistic output. In his 1972 essay "The Spiral Jetty," Smithson associates the uncertainty

Spiral Jetty
Robert Smithson, 1970

Fertile Minds 75

of scale with art: "The scale of the Spiral Jetty tends to fluctuate depending on where the viewer happens to be. Size determines an object, but scale determines art. [...] For me scale operates by uncertainty."[10] While the dialectics of nature/artifice and of scale/size interest both Smithson and Muniz, the generation of these conceptual concerns diverges significantly for the two artists, a distinction most apparent in how the two artists discuss dirt.

In the ecstatic and even quasi-religious tone of "The Spiral Jetty," Smithson writes, "Following the spiral steps we return to our origins, back to some pulpy protoplasm, a floating eye adrift in an antediluvian ocean."[11] The phrase "return to origins" appears in a number of Smithson's essays and becomes an important component in his theorization of site as "a return to the origins of material, sort of a dematerialization of refined matter."[12] *Spiral Jetty*'s evocative form itself recalls the microscopic spiraling lattice of the lake's salt crystals, and the dirt, stone, and elemental substances associated with most of Smithson's remote sites offered for him a point of origin. If origin marks the point of creation, the original is that singular, initial creation, and originality is the quality of being the first. For Muniz, these terms no longer resonate with contemporary culture, a culture of copies. In an essay suggestively titled "The Aura Can't Be Found Because the Original Is in the Garbage," Muniz asserts his "firm belief in the nonrevolutionary pattern of creativity," advocating the productive and essential use of prior art.[13] Drawing on the well-known theory of Jean Baudrillard and Walter Benjamin, Muniz reiterates the loss of the original, arguing that originality persists only as a "kind of by-product of the copy."[14] Muniz's description of the original as "in the garbage" and as a "by-product" immediately connotes dirt, and his process of sampling and working with pre-digested forms typifies a modality of practice dominant in contemporary culture as well as the unifying character of his diverse output. Whether recreating Piranesi's famous engravings out of string or the *Mona Lisa* with peanut butter and jelly, Muniz engages a ricochet of correspondences: "Things look like things, they are embodied in the transience of each other's meaning; a thing looks like a thing, which looks like another thing, or another."[15] His final photographs—"the worst possible illusion," in Muniz's words—are entirely referential *and* artificial; they declare their status as derivative outright. Unlike artists such as Sherrie Levine or Richard Prince, who generally practice "straight" appropriation, Muniz photographs a newly created material reality based on reproductions, thereby using the copy as a kind of origin. He fixes the obsolescence of his fugitive materials—dust, sugar, dirt, and chocolate syrup—with the significance of his images and use of photography. The anthropologist Mary Douglas defines "dirt" as a "matter out of place": "the by-product of a systematic ordering and classification of matter in so far as ordering involved rejecting inappropriate elements."[16] For the 1960s avant-garde, dirt provided access to a privileged realm, maybe mythical or religious, which assured sincerity on account of the material's exteriority to the commercial art world. Muniz questions this material strategy by taking the by-product not just as an object but also as a method of creative production. Artists, curators, historians, and cultural theorists have obsessively sought the vanguard at the boundaries of the proscribed taxonomy, and so, we must consider dirt as a site and a means for innovative practice today.

Endnotes

1 Susan Boettger, *Earthworks: Art and the Landscape of the Sixties* (Berkley: University of California Press, 2002); p. 116.
2 Boettger, *Earthworks: Art and the Landscape of the Sixties*; p. 51.
3 Vik Muniz, *Reflex A Vik Muniz Primer*, ed. Lesley A. Martin (New York: Aperture, 2004); p. 157.
4 The first major exhibition, titled "Earth Works," at Dwan Gallery, New York, in October 1968, brought the movement and artists wide public acknowledgement.
5 For Smithson's sketches, extensive photographs, and statistics, see, Lynne Cooke and Karen Kelly, eds. *Robert Smithson Spiral Jetty* (New York: Dia Art Foundation, 2005); pp. 14-50, 53, 189.
6 Between 1971 and 2002, the *Spiral Jetty* was submerged under water, visible as a shadowy form from above. However, since 2002, intermittent drops in the water level have revealed the rocks and earth.
7 Muniz, *Reflex A Vik Muniz Primer*, p. 155.
8 Muniz, *Reflex A Vik Muniz Primer*, p. 157.
9 "Discussions with Heizer, Oppenheim, Smithson," *Avalanche* 1 (Fall 1970); p. 67.
10 Robert Smithson, "The Spiral Jetty (1972)," in *The Collected Writings*, ed. Jack Flam (Berkley: University of California Press, 1996); p. 147. Originally written for *Arts of the Environment*, ed. Gyorgy Kepes (1972).
11 "Fragments of an Interview with P.A. [Patsy] Norvell (1969)," *The Collected Writings*, ed. Jack Flam, p. 148.
12 "Fragments of an Interview with P.A. [Patsy] Norvell (1969)," p. 192.
13 Muniz, *Reflex A Vik Muniz Primer*, pp. 90-91.
14 Muniz, *Reflex A Vik Muniz Primer*, pp. 90, 92.
15 Thomas Zummer, "The Commutability of Traces," accessed 16 Apr. 2010 at http://www.vikmuniz.net/www/doctools/printable.php?pg=articleZummer.
16 Frazer Ward, "Foreign and Familiar Bodies," in *Dirt & Domesticity: Constructions of the Feminine: June 12 – August 14, 1992* (New York: Whitney Museum of American Art, 1992); p. 9. Also quoted in Ann Reynolds, *Robert Smithson: Learning from New Jersey and Elsewhere* (Cambridge, MA: MIT Press, 2003); p. 193.

Spiral Jetty After Robert Smithson
Vik Muniz, Brooklyn, New York, 1997

Skull / Kidney / Skin

Kim Brickley

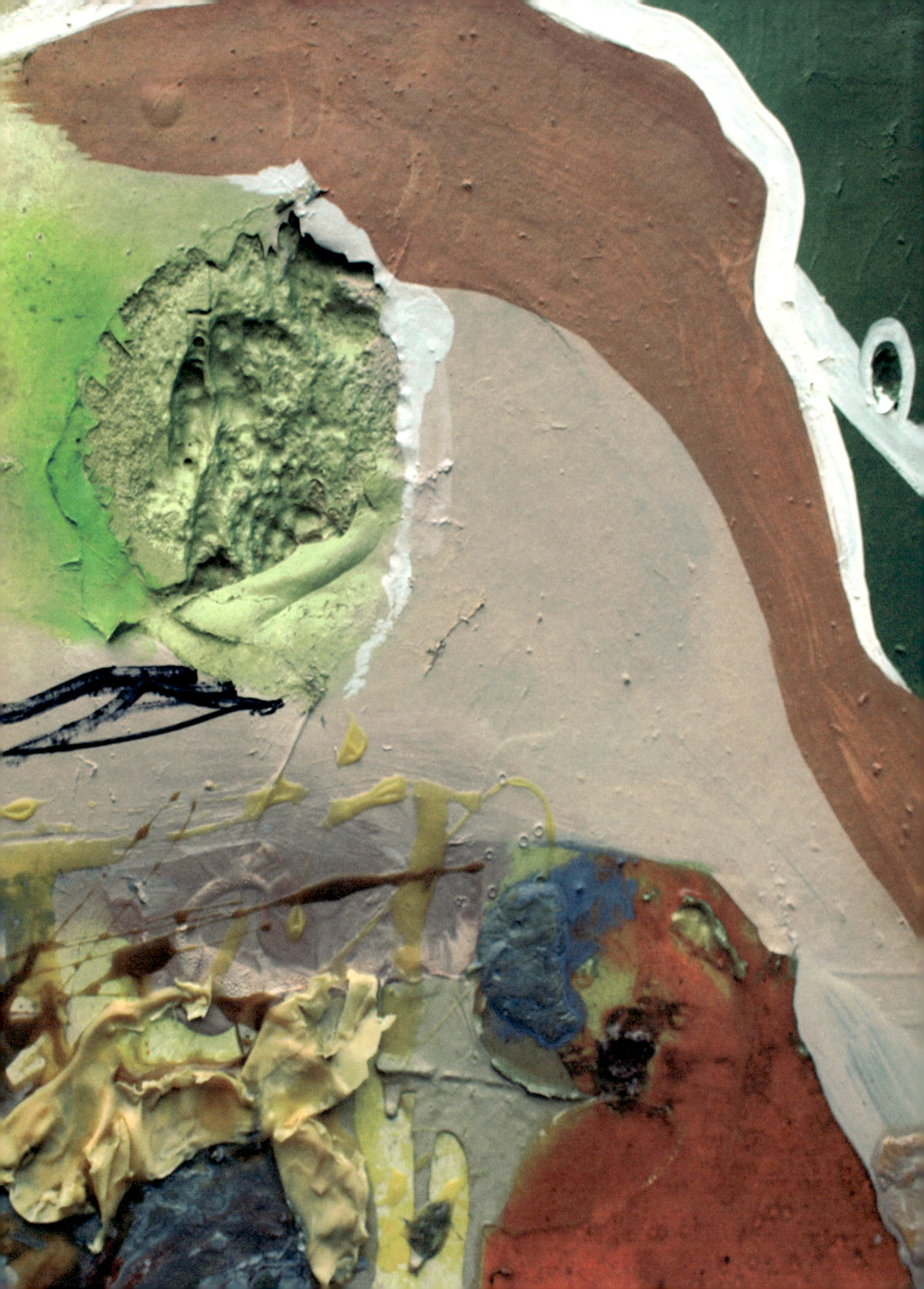

Left
Kidney
63 by 24 in. mixed media on Styrofoam, 2009.

Facing Page
Kidney (detail)

Previous Spread, Left
Skull
48 by 48 in. Tyvek mounted on Styrofoam, mixed media, 2009.

Previous Spread, Right
Skull (detail)

Skull / Kidney / Skin Kim Brickley

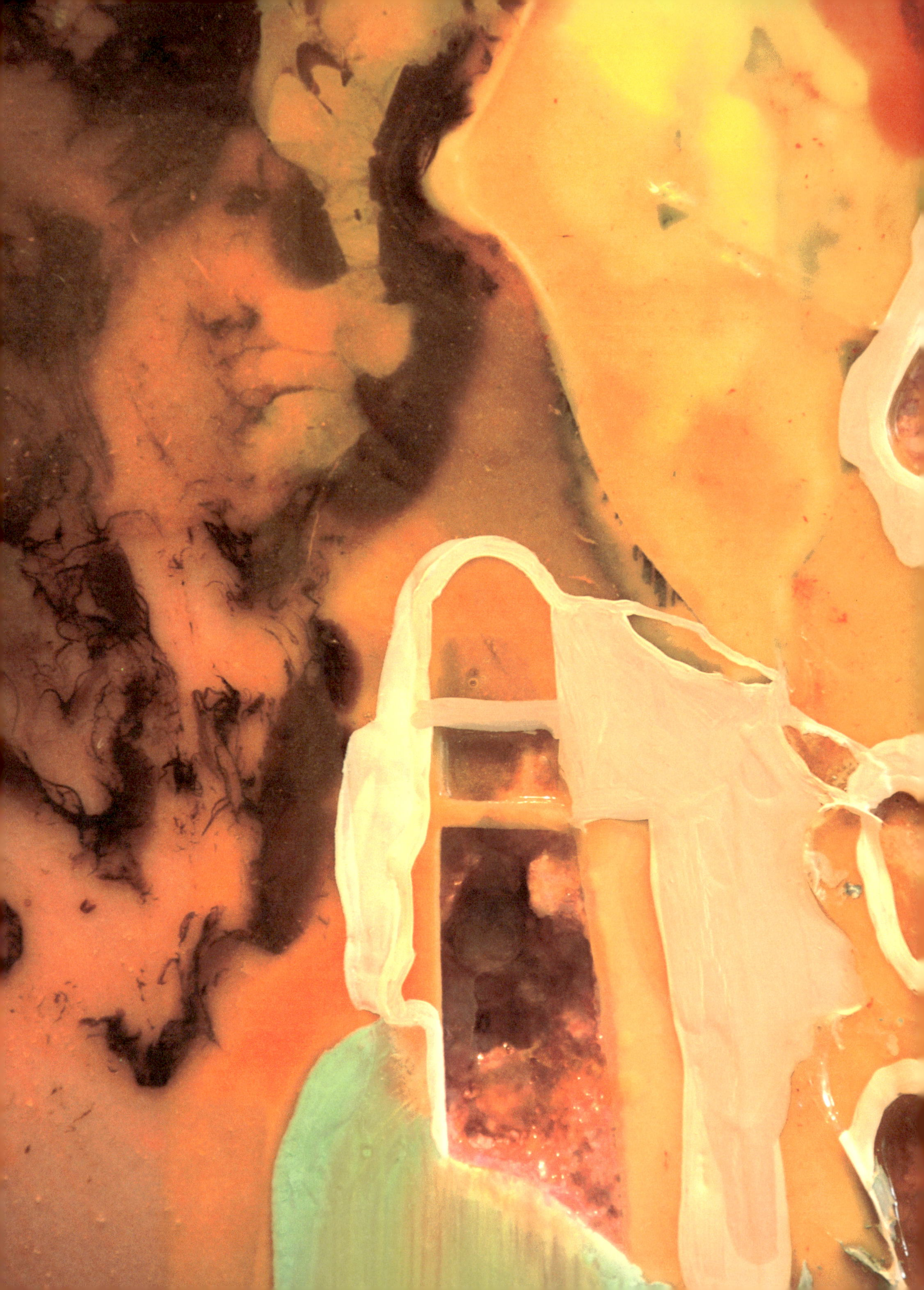

Left
Skin
50 by 24 in. wood glue and mixed media on Styrofoam, 2009.

Facing Page
Skin (detail)

82 **Skull / Kidney / Skin** Kim Brickley

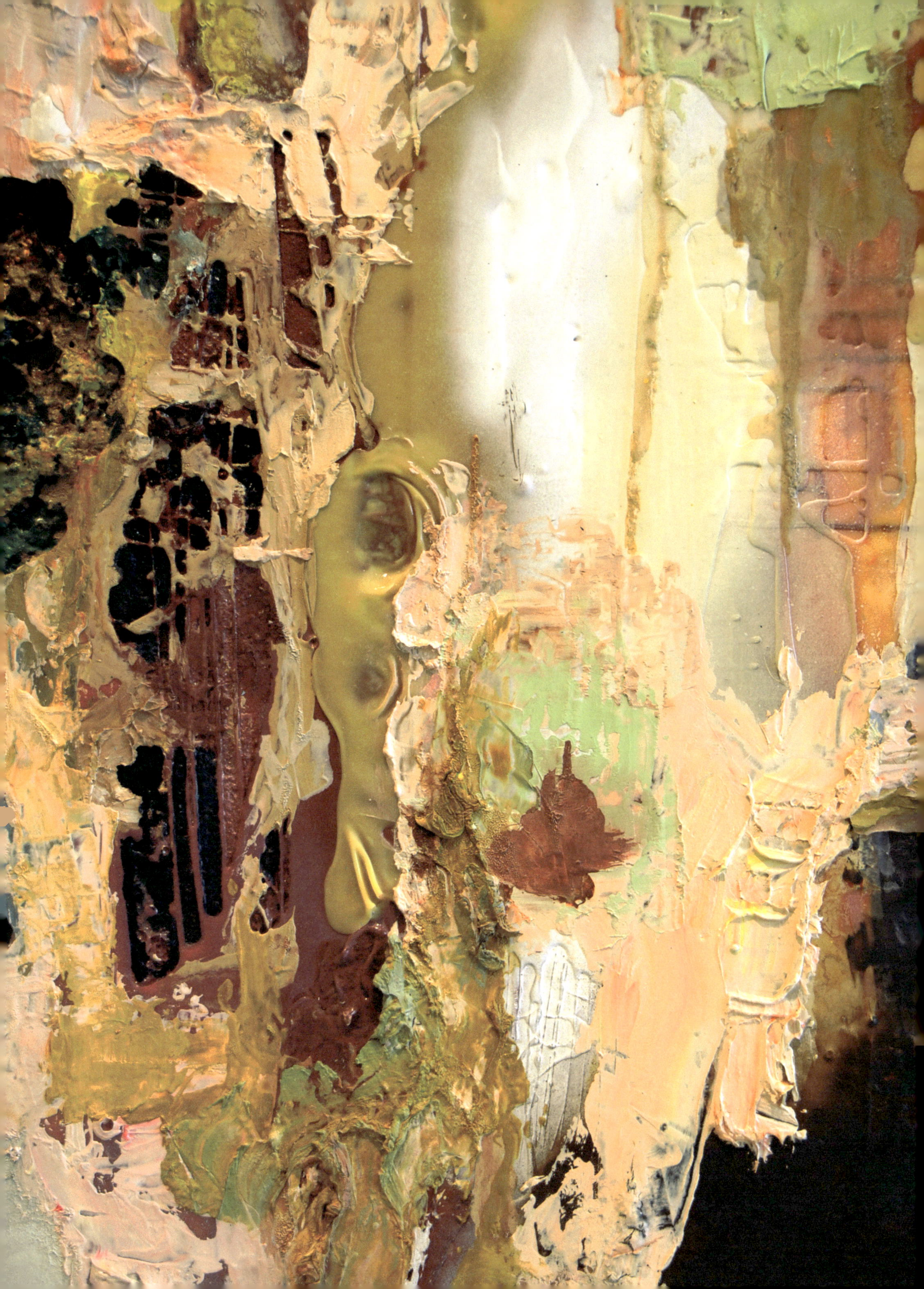

On Duration

Frank Matero

> What is Duration, but the persevering of a thing in its existence?
> Gale *Crt. Gentiles* IV. 287(1677)

Time, like space, is all around us. Its evidence is visible in the natural world as physical change. In our own physical works, time exerts its presence through the tell-tale signs of material degradation and stylistic anachronism. (Fig. 1) It is through these indicators that we confront time indirectly and attempt to position a thing or place in relation to the present. Time is therefore both qualifier and quantitative measure for the historian, scientist, and conservator who attempt to define and interpret it through words, images, calculations, and physical interventions.

With few exceptions, all human works pass through time. That passage, regardless of its length (not coincidently expressed in spatial terms as observed by Heidegger) is duration, the time during which a thing, action, or state continues to exist. In our efforts to relate to any creative work from the past, we use time as the primary measure from the present. As time affords a measure of change, both time and change are critical components shaping the arrival and survival of any work to the present. How historic and artistic works are received by each generation then depends on the specific conditions of time and change.

The visual arts—be they a painting, sculpture, tapestry, or building—reflect the individual and collective sensibilities of their maker(s) and in turn, their *zeitgeist*. Certainly much scholarly work has been dedicated to this proposition. The primary arguments for preserving cultural heritage are values-based, beginning with the fundamental assumption that as material culture, creative works embody various forms of knowledge, e.g. aesthetic, technical, cultural, social, religious, and scientific. This belief owes its origins in part to the great knowledge accumulation projects of the Enlightenment. Of equal interest in the current discourse on cultural heritage is the ability of a thing or place to present the everyday human experience of lived time. Here we can trace such concerns to earlier arguments raised in the nineteenth century by John Ruskin on the visible age of creative works and especially architecture, as a reflection of the fullness of life.

Conservation has always been about duration, about transmission and reception. What survives, what is forgotten, what is cared for or destroyed, describes the lives that creative works can take. Such trajectories are dependent on many diverse factors. However, once consciously examined, all creative works come under consideration for their ability to communicate to us; to have relevance in ways consistent or new to their original authorship and to contemporary society. In this capacity they go beyond mere existence; they persevere. Since time is not reversible and history cannot be undone (only rewritten), conservation is a true historical event; a critical human action that is one of the ways in which we remember and how a work and its values are transmitted to the future.

Fertile Minds 85

Figure 2
Triadic Model of the Modalities of Tangible Cultural Heritage

Figure 3 (Facing Page)
Finis–or, The Tail Piece–The Bathos, &c
William Hogarth, 1794
Hogarth's satirical view of the end of all things. According to Timbs's *Anecdote Lives* (1881), Hogarth dedicated this plate to "the dealers in dark pictures," a reference to his disapproval of and irritation at the high value ascribed to antique paintings due to their aged appearance rather than true artistic merit.

Figure 1 (Previous Page)
New York State Pavilion
Built for the 1964-5 Worlds Fair by Philip Johnson, shown in its current state, 2011, Flushing Meadows Park, Queens, New York. Decay and the promise of futurism combine to make a forceful and poignant post-modern ruin.

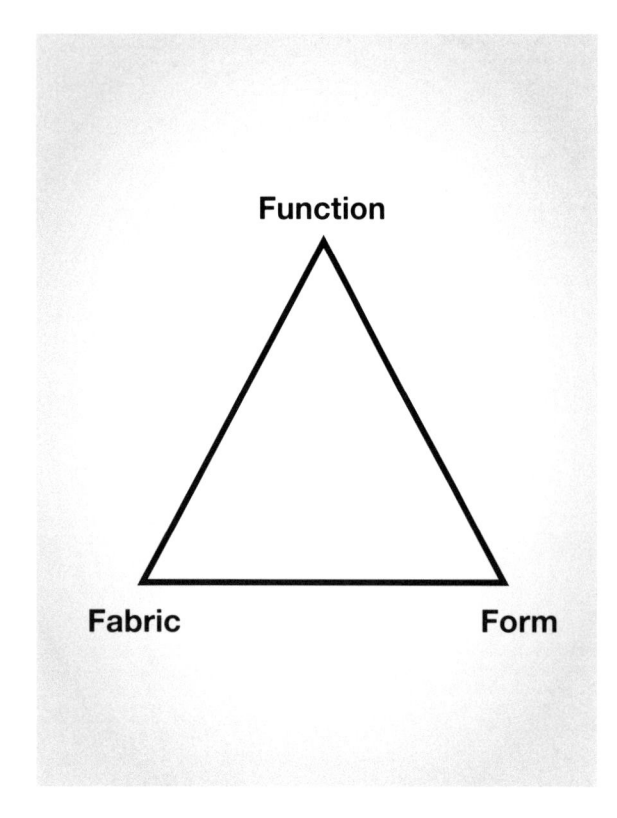

If we accept the most basic definition of conservation as the protection of cultural works from loss and damage, then conservation of all cultural heritage—tangible and intangible—addresses and contributes to memory, itself basic to all human existence. Conservation as an intellectual pursuit is predicated on the belief that knowledge, memory, and experience are tied to cultural production, and especially to material culture. Conservation helps extend these places and things into the present, and establishes a form of mediation critical to the interpretive process that reinforces these aspects of human existence. The fundamental objectives of conservation also concern ways of evaluating and interpreting cultural heritage for its safeguarding now and for the future. In this last respect, conservation itself becomes a way of extending and reifying cultural identities and historical narratives over time through valorization and interpretation of an identified heritage at any given moment.[1]

As central as tradition is to the concept of cultural identity, it is also dynamic, manufactured, and reformulated by each generation through personal and collective interpretations of the past. This recycling and reassigning of value through memory over time will eventually result in a transformation of cultural form and meaning.[2] As a modern concept existing self-consciously outside tradition, conservation views history as continuous change, thus seeking to make the past relevant through critical distance and empathetic engagement.

Weathering Change

At different times and in different ways, conservation, in its theoretical development and practice, has concerned itself with three basic constructs or modalities: *form, fabric*, and *function*, the latter being the intangible beliefs, uses, and traditions associated with the material correlates of form and fabric. (Fig. 2) Implicit in all three constructs is the notion of maintaining contact with the past through the identification, transmission, and protection of that which is considered valuable and relevant in the present.

For the traditional visual arts, the idea of the work is closely tied to its materiality through form and fabric, and—certainly in the case of immovable heritage—its function through context. Conservation directly engages the former (materiality) and when possible the latter (function), assuming both are recoverable. Contemporary conservation theories argue that value and significance are based in part in physical materiality and its effect on the perception of the viewer/user, and, in the case of the visual arts, have been categorized as artistic- and historical-values, age-value, and use-value.[3] Originality and authenticity have traditionally been defined by these qualities; however, as we have come to discover in recent years, this is not nor has ever been universal.

Weathering, as a natural entropic process, always results in a transformation of materials through physical, mechanical, and chemical alteration. Weathering indicates the passage of time as visible aging. It occurs during the life of the work, and its occurrence is predictable, if not immediately apparent. Depending on the material fabric and the form, such alterations have been viewed over time in different ways. Whereas structural degradation has generally been held as a decidedly negative aspect of weathering, except in the unique case of ruins and some contemporary art, some types of surface alteration have enjoyed varying degrees of acceptance depending on the time, place, material, and subject. (Fig. 3) This is perhaps best observed in our taste for preserving archaic "old-fashioned" things as aged or incomplete whereas no imperfection is tolerated for works of the recent past.[4] As early as 1903 the Austrian art historian, Alois Riegl observed that the twentieth century viewer was as disturbed by "signs of decay [premature aging] in new works...as much as signs of new production [conspicuous restorations] in old works, and particularly enjoy(ed)...the purely natural cycle of growth and decay."[5]

Implicit in the underlying principles of conservation is the notion that degradation is generally considered destructive or a negative condition that is detrimental to the visual and structural integrity of the work. Such concerns, related to conservation's interest in the aesthetic and intellectual legibility of the work, are the legacy of the mid-twentieth century theorist Cesare Brandi who considered "the reestablishment of the potential unity of the work" critical to conservation's mission.[6] Intervention addresses degradation by reducing the tension to the formal whole created by material damage and loss and involves reconciling conscious (original or subsequent) aesthetic values with historical values. This concern with safeguarding the artistic as well as documentary values of the work, especially as they relate to incompleteness of form and meaning, draws its inspiration from philological models. (Fig. 4)

Fertile Minds

The term *patina* has been used since the seventeenth century to describe acceptable entropic changes that are considered intrinsic to the material due to the natural weathering of that material under normal circumstances.[7] This is in contradistinction to excessive alteration resulting from decay and the obfuscation of the surface from soiling, crusts, and deterioration.[8] (Fig. 5) This suggests an acceptance of alteration that is judged or measured to have little physical effect on the durability or performance of the material, or imparts an acceptable or desired visual aesthetic, as well as those changes that more or less preserve the historical appearance of the form. This latter point is significant for there is often confusion on the difference between original and historical appearance. Original appearance, usually linked to artistic intent (with the exception of time-based media), is a transient condition that exists only briefly, if at all, after completion or delivery of the work. The notion is a false one, however, as few materials are truly inert or stable for long, and many works continue to evolve and change over time as part of their natural life. While entropic change is inevitable for all material things, decay has not always been considered the negation of creation, as in the case of certain twentieth-century design ideologies or native people's belief systems.

The indicators and qualities of age, defined most directly by weathering (in architecture), patina (in works of art) and style (in both), became major issues in eighteenth and nineteenth century aesthetic theory, art history, and restoration philosophy, linking the worlds of new art and architecture with historic buildings, monuments, and works of art.[9] Weathering, as time and nature's finishing touches to human works, was a major element in the aesthetic principles of the Picturesque. However, it was John Ruskin who gave a moral voice to weathering in his definition of historical monuments and their preservation, a concept later reworked by Reigl who developed a values-based approach to the definition and treatment of unintentional monuments as those works that serve to commemorate past human activity through their aged appearance.

For Ruskin, the greatest expression of truthfulness was to be found in weathered and patinated surfaces and accumulated accretions. In *The Seven Lamps of*

From Left
Figure 4
Ayyubid Wall, Cairo, 2009
Cairo, Egypt. Intervention interpreting all the diachronic alterations to an original 12th century arrow slit remodeled during the Ottoman period into a residential opening, then broken, and now stabilized providing access into the new Museum of the Ayyubid Wall.

Figure 5
Metropolitan Club, New York
Masonry cleaning tests revealing complex surface alterations including overpaint, intrinsic ferrous staining, and an aged exposed stone surface below.

Figure 6
Plate VIII, *The Seven Lamps of Architecture*
John Ruskin, 1855
Ruskin's careful rendering of the Gothic carving reveals both the intrinsic asymmetry of handmade work and the effects of time on the surface.

Architecture (1848)—perhaps his most famous work, and one that had a great influence on nineteenth and twentieth century aesthetic theory—he wrote, "The greatest glory of a building is not in its stones nor its gold, but in its age."[10] Through age, architecture embodied memory—"we cannot remember without her."[11] And this memory was reflected in its physical appearance.[12] (Fig. 6) In *The Lamp of Memory*, he wrote:

> [I]t is in that golden stain of time, that we are to look for the real light, and color, and preciousness of architecture; and it is not until a building has assumed this character, till it has been entrusted with the fame, and hallowed by the deeds of men, till its walls have been witnesses of suffering, and its pillars rise out of the shadows of death, that its existence, more lasting as it is than that of the natural objects of the world around it, can be gifted with even so much as these possess of language and of life.[13]

Thus it was through weathering that the fullness of life was recorded and architecture, paintings, and sculpture gained nobility or, in his own words, "accumulated voicefulness." Ruskin attributed beauty to age, combining and promoting documentary and aesthetic values over original appearance.[14]

It is to Ruskin, then, that we must attribute the idea that weathering records and allows the recollection of earlier stages in the history of a work, and the human lives associated with it. It is for these reasons that Ruskin so passionately argued for the *preservation* as opposed to the *restoration* of art and historic buildings, which removed the face of time in an attempt to offer "fresh readings."[15] This is summarized in his often-quoted Article 18 of *The Lamp of Memory*:

> [Restoration] means the most total destruction which a building can suffer…a destruction accompanied with false description of the thing destroyed…that spirit which is given only by the hand and eye of the workman, can never be recalled…What copying can there be of surfaces that have been worn half an inch down?…How is the new work better than the old? There was yet in the old some life, some mysterious suggestion of what it had been, and of what it

Fertile Minds

Figure 7
Plate from "The Art of Restoring"
Louis Sullivan, 1877

Figure 8 (Facing Page)
Extreme Formal Restoration
Restoration involving anastylosis and fragment reassembly in combination with structural infill.

had lost; some sweetness in the gentle lines which rain and sun had wrought.¹⁶

Ruskin voiced a similar negative view toward the restoration of paintings, stating that "...cleaning, which is incipient destruction, and...restoring, that is, painting over, which is of course total destruction...[Those paintings] however fragmentary, however ruinous, however obscured and defiled, [are] almost always the real thing..."¹⁷ Riegl also remarked on the failure of restoration in its conflation of newness-value with artistic value, the latter in support of recapturing and displaying the architect's original intent.

Yet age is not the only consequential factor in determining value and significance. The older something is, the more powerful it is to elicit an emotional response, yet this is incidental to real historical significance.¹⁸ Historical appearance acknowledges time as an essential component of works from the past. It is time that distinguishes and separates such works from the present, and it is time that continues to shape and define them through weathering. However the concept of *patina* implies benign change over time, which acknowledges the natural processes of weathering we find acceptable or appealing. For many works of the twentieth century, weathering and age were ignored or incompatible with the ideological concerns of modernity. But for centuries, weathering was accommodated or in the original selection of materials and the design of construction counteracted with a desire for permanence.

Viollet-le-Duc's equally famous definition of restoration from his encyclopedic *Dictionnaire raisonné* (1854) stands in complete contrast to Ruskin's preservation philosophy, and offers an argument now often invoked by post-modern attitudes towards preservation of modernist architecture:

> To restore an edifice means neither to maintain it, nor to repair it, nor to rebuild it; it means to re-establish it in a finished state, which may in fact never have actually existed at any given time.¹⁹

Since their first publication, these two statements have come to represent the dominant opposing positions on the subject. However both men expressed far more complex views. In the *Dictionnaire*, Viollet-le-Duc posed the problem of restoration as one of choice through rational deduction based not on blind adherence to one position or another but rather case by case, determined by a building's physical integrity:

> Should the unity of style simply be restored without taking into account the late modifications? Or should the edifice be restored exactly as it was, that is, with an original style and later modifications? It is in fact imperative not to adopt either of these two courses of action in any absolute fashion; the action taken should depend instead upon the particular circumstances....We hold that an edifice ought to be restored in a manner suitable to its own integrity....We must scrupulously respect all traces or indications that show additions or modifications to a structure.[20]

Like Ruskin, Viollet-le-Duc rejected imitation as being equal to the original. However, unlike Ruskin, he believed that the integrity of the whole work and the artistic spirit or intent behind it could be understood and should be re-established through "the new analytic method" of restoration. Restoration was a rational process of information recovery, not unlike the new sciences of geology, comparative anatomy, ethnology, or archaeology of his day. By moving beyond sheer imitation of forms to the ideas behind them, Viollet-le-Duc saw restoration as a creative process no different than contemporary architectural design whose primary task was the manifestation of ideals based on principles. Viollet-le-Duc's search for functional explanations in the forms of Romanesque and Gothic buildings was the objective, and restoration was an exercise toward exploring and proving that concern. His insistence on style at the expense of the individuality of a building—in an age when the sum knowledge was as yet very incomplete, the chronology of reference works inexact, and the number of publications limited—could only lead to simplifications which have been justly denounced.[21] (Fig. 7)

Reconciling History and Intent

Any attempt to situate duration within the larger conservation discourse must acknowledge the three basic constructs of *form*, *fabric*, and *function*. All are tied together in defining works of art and architecture; however, depending on the situation, we can choose any number of strategies that either privilege one over the other or attempt to present all three in balance. For example,

Ruskinian preservation favored the fabric and its age-value above all else in contrast with the formalistic concerns of stylistic restoration. Content as value or meaning was associative and different in each case. The balance of these modalities in the conservation project is, of course, dependent on a great many factors: cultural, social, technical, economic, and visual, to name a few. The scale and type of work—whether it is a building or a miniature, of primary historic or artistic value, or intentionally permanent or ephemeral—will dictate options.

Contemporary practice is no less polarized despite a greater theoretical embrace of both aesthetic and historical values. Despite the prevalence of "schools" of conservation that owe their practices partly to inherited traditions based on place or medium, the prevailing practice of identifying authenticity in the material fabric has given rise in its most extreme expression to embalming, which has developed an entire kit of scientific procedures and aesthetic tricks to sustain and present compromised fabric. (See p. 91, Fig. 8) This, in turn, has prompted critical responses toward the "fetishizing" of the materiality of the work over other modalities. The result has been at times to reassert the dominance of form and function by repositioning conservation as an act whose authenticities reside in process and artistic tradition instead.[22]

By approaching all visual works through their modalities of form, fabric, and function this simple model offers a means of assessing the immediate outcome and long-term effects of any intervention decision. As each modality is governed by one or more of the various disciplines associated with preserving cultural heritage, critical issues relevant to the work, and the professional input required, can be better placed in perspective to both develop and critique proposed interventions and predict their outcome. (Fig. 9)

Contemporary conservation must strive to seek a middle ground by acknowledging both process and product whereby knowledge and experience are tied together. Its primary obligation is to extend the whole life of the work, which in addition to the creative energies of original and subsequent artistic intent, must also embrace the equally long and complex history of its reception over time. As a modern practice, conservation is a scientific activity where its aims and methods are involved, and at the same time it has humanistic goals. As such, contemporary practice now requires input from various specialists, as well as public stakeholders, each bringing their insight to the problem. However conservation begins and ends with the work, and its ultimate responsibility depends on the conservator. All conservation is a product of its time and as such is an act of critical interpretation. We restore with intention, and it is that intention that needs to be continually re-examined as much as the creative work itself.

Figure 9 (Facing Page)
Bab al Maruq, Cairo
An alternative approach to Figure 8 that reinstates the architectonic integrity of one of Cairo's city gates without literally completing the form while at the same time displaying and structurally supporting the remaining elements.

Endnotes

1 The term heritage is used here specifically to mean constructed history that is intentionally biased toward a particular group or issue. See David Lowenthal, *The Heritage Crusade and the Spoils of History* (London: Viking Press, 1997).

2 Marshall Sahlins has described the process of traditional and ethnic memory as "what began as reproduction ends as transformation," so that in the process of remembering, a reinterpretation or "cultural reordering" occurs. In this way tradition is neither static nor anti-modern. Quoted in Michael W. Meister, "Sweetmeats of Corpses?," *Art History and Ethnohistory Res.* 27 (1995); p. 120.

3 A rational classification of heritage values was first developed by A. Riegl, "The Modern Cult of Monuments: Its Character and its Origin,"(1903) in *Historical and Philosophical Issues in the Conservation of Cultural Heritage*, eds. N. Stanley Price, M. Kirby Talley, Jr. and A. Mellucco Vaccaro (Los Angeles: Getty Conservation Institute, 1996); pp. 69-83. More recent efforts of The Getty Conservation Institute on values and cultural heritage can be found in *The Getty Conservation Institute, Values and Heritage Conservation* (Los Angeles: The J. Paul Getty Trust, 2000).

4 At the Science Museum in London, this distinction was observed where visitors were disturbed to see expensive old motorcars looking shabby, whereas when the Museum of London opened its stores to the public, the old looking horse-drawn carriages were preferred to the newly restored ones.

5 Riegl, "The Modern Cult of Monuments".

6 Cesare Brandi, "Theory of Restoration," (1963) in *Historical and Philosophical Issues in the Conservation of Cultural Heritage*, eds. N. Stanley Price, M. Kirby Talley, Jr. and A. Mellucco Vaccaro (Los Angeles: Getty Conservation Institute, 1996); pp. 230-235. Axiom 2: Restoration must aim to reestablish the potential unity of the work; as long as this is possible without producing an artistic or historical forgery and without erasing every trace of the passage of time. The concept of "unity": a fragmented work will continue to exist as a potential whole in each of its fragments. The form of each work of art is indivisible. Therefore *lacunae* or interruptions, be they visual (aesthetic) or structural, must be reintegrated to reestablish the image-related or material unity of the work. The reintegration must be recognizable yet reestablish unity of the work.

7 Patina is the imperceptible muting placed on the materials that are compelled to remain subdues within the image. Patina is age value and the face of time and preserves the unity and equilibrium of the work. "For restoration to be a legitimate operation it cannot presume that time is reversible or that history can be abolished" (232)..."It must allow itself to be emphasized as a true historical event..." (233). Brandi, "Theory of Restoration," pp. 232-233.

8 Beginning in the mid-19th century, the destructive effects of pollution from industrialization began to be observed and distinguished from natural weathering processes thus prompting the entry of science into building and monument conservation.

9 Paul Philippot, "Restoration from the Perspective of the Humanities," in *Historical and Philosophical Issues in the Conservation of Cultural Heritage*, eds. N. Stanley Price, M. Kirby Talley, Jr. and A. Mellucco Vaccaro (Los Angeles: Getty Conservation Institute, 1996); p. 217.

10 John Ruskin, *The Seven Lamps of Architecture* (unabridged reproduction of second edition, 1880, (New York: Farrar, Straus and Giroux, 1988); pp.233-234.

11 Ruskin, *Seven Lamps*, p.168.

12 Ruskin challenged and extended Vitruvius's primary requirements of firmness, commodity and delight in his *Seven Lamps* to include sacrifice, truth, power, beauty, life, memory, and obedience.

13 Ruskin, *Seven Lamps*, p.177.

14 A fascination with ruins was common throughout the late 18th and 19th centuries and appears in painting, literature, aesthetics and architecture. The dilemma Ruskin clearly articulates is the contradiction between age or weathering with what he terms "original or true character..." (183). "For though, hitherto, we have been speaking of the sentiment of age only, there is an actually beauty in the marks of it..." (178). Ruskin, *Seven Lamps*.

15 John Ruskin, *Stones of Venice*, edited and abridged by J. G. Links (New York: Da Capo Press, 1960), Vol. II, Ch. VIII, Articles 135-8.

16 Ruskin, *Seven Lamps*, p.184.

17 Ruskin, *Stones of Venice* (1960), Vol. II, Ch. VIII, Articles 135-8.

18 Richard Longstreth, "The Significance of the Recent Past." *APT Bulletin* 22 (1991); p.17. It is important to note that there is no age criteria for inclusion of cultural properties in the World Heritage List.

19 Eugène-Emmanuel Viollet-le-Duc, *Restoration in the Foundations of Architecture: Selections from the Dictionnaire Raisonne*, trans. Kenneth D. Whitehead (New York : G. Braziller, c1990).

20 Viollet-le-Duc, *Restoration*, pp. 210-213.

21 Francoise Bercé and Bruno Foucart, *Viollet-le-Duc: Architect, Artist, Master of Historic Preservation*, exhibition catalog (Washington, DC: The Trust for Museum Exhibitions, 1987); pp. 15-16.

22 For recent criticism see Paolo Marconi, *Materia e significato: La questione del restauro architettonico*, 2nd ed. (Bari-Roma: Laterza, 2003).

So Close You Can Touch It
Helene Furján

Spectacularity has had a presence in architecture throughout much of its history, more recently becoming "post-spectacle," the dissolution of the city into electronic fields and digital virtualities. But throughout this history runs a counter-history interested in experience, space, and effect over image and spectacle, which seeks to engage the user in a more active fashion: bodily, sensorially, emotively.

It is in the late 1960s and early 1970s that the experience of modernity becomes a fully spectacular one. As news media evolve into corporations and advertising becomes a global industry, images (print and electronic) begin to saturate the visual field. Television explodes throughout the domestic universe, spreading like a virus. Movies begin to experiment with the structure of the medium itself (editing and effect over narrative). The nascent germs of the computer age begin to take seed. The contemporary city is no longer that of the old urbanity, dense with history, matter; but the new city of light (a pure medium): Times Square and Las Vegas, seedy, neon-crazy, and above all devoted to the spectacular, are exemplary. It is at this moment, tellingly, and thanks to theorists like Marshall McLuhan, that media becomes an object of study in its own right. And it is at this moment that the medium, already, becomes more significant than what it mediates: the medium becomes the message, the massage.[1] And everyone from theorists to artists and novelists begins to speculate on the implications of this new modernity.

Image Mazes

J. G. Ballard's early novel, *The Atrocity Exhibition* (written between 1966 and 1970), presents a spectacular landscape of overwhelming fragmentation and disarticulation, already figuring the over-proximate and overexposed "crisis of the spectacle" that Jean Baudrillard and Paul Virilio warn of in later decades. In Jonathan Crary's terms, an undecipherable terrain of "fractured zones in which sheer contiguity replaces syntax, and which extend only in terms of the ceaseless conjugation of bodies, architecture, and images that briefly abut, then detach to make new connections," the novel presents the modern landscape as a psychotic space "in which relations of proximity and resemblance are hopelessly convoluted onto a single plane."[2]

The novel fixates on conjunctions. The city, a technological sublime, is an intersection of concrete landscapes—overpasses, parking structures, plazas, and the geometries of highrise balconies, many in ruin—and the mediatic effects of curtain walls, giant billboards, hoardings, radioscopes, antennae, and satellite dishes. This urban landscape merges with the media landscapes of flickering television screens and multiple projection screens that dissolve architecture into the filmic imagery of war zones and car crashes—the Zapruder film of J. F. K.'s assassination and images of the Vietnam War endlessly repeated and magnified. The interior conjunction of walls and floor planes are somehow linked to the geometries and molecular structures of photographic landscapes of intense magnification—the

The Comcast Experience
Comcast Center, Philadelphia, winter garden/lobby; world's largest HD LED video display.

blowup or the zoom—oversized images that repeat and overwhelm or collections of close-ups, x-rays, images from physics and astrophysics, landscapes of contour and media images, placed together as hieroglyphic lists devoid of the possibility of order or decipherment. Recorded by a helicopter film crew that marks the omnipresence of media's "tele-surveillance," these couplings and contiguities form a complex intertwining of media surfaces, technological apparatuses, and vectors of speed and transmission, together forming moduli for the structures of event, matter and consciousness.

Spectacular Space

At the same time, in 1967, Guy Debord publishes his manifesto of spectacular modernity, *The Society of the Spectacle*, in which spectacular space operates as a form of distraction and illusion, a space dominated by advertising spectacles and media flows. Debord argues that by the late 1960s social relationships between people are mediated by images and subject to a logic of "Spectacle" (in a limited sense, the excesses of the mass media):

> The whole life of those societies in which modern conditions of production prevail presents itself

Las Vegas Advertising

Las Vegas Strip

as an immense accumulation of spectacles... The spectacle is capital accumulated to the point where it becomes image.[3]

He updates Karl Marx and Georg Lukács' theory of reification, confirmed by Walter Benjamin, whereby social relations between people are mediated by commodities and objectified through their labor—itself a commodity—under capitalist methods of production and consumption.

The spectacle is auto-generational and autonomous, a stream of images, "the medium of all commodities,"[4] that transforms the world into a zone of mediation and a space of appearances (the space of publicity), offered up to a passive contemplation. Themes similar to Ballard's pervade Debord's writing: mass media effects, advertising, media stars (the personification of the spectacle of politics as well as the spectacle of consumption), J. F. K., abstraction, and above all, contemporary modernity as the experience of an exposure to the saturation of image that is simultaneously an estrangement: "Spectators are linked only by a one-way relationship to the very center that maintains their isolation from one another. The spectacle thus unites what is separate, but it unites it only in its separateness."[5]

Phantasmagorias

The city has already become "the city of spectacles" by the early nineteenth century, the streets themselves now a space for seeing and being seen rather than acting out roles, and a space of ephemeral impressions and distractions.[6] In 1805, London is for William Wordsworth already a spectacular milieu, an overwhelming constellation of spectacles and scenes—the city fabric itself, the crowds, theatre (including what he calls "pantomimic scenes"), shows (including wax-works and mechanical theatres), circuses, exhibitions, pleasure gardens, even the courts and parliament.[7] For Wordsworth, the Londoner of the early nineteenth century consumes "a proliferating range of optical and sensory experiences," and "an expanding chaos of images, commodities, and stimulation."[8] The city-spectacle encompasses a radical heterogeneity. Wordsworth's London is a dazzling variety of differing and competing spaces, technologies, and effects, a concatenation of myriad micro-spectacles. The public self now participates at a remove, a *spectator* of the world rather than an actor on its stage. This is the modern observer: silent, atomized, and increasingly passive, the product of "the rebuilding of an observer fitted for the tasks of 'spectacular' consumption."[9]

Entertainment, museological and commodity spectacles combine with new technologies of vision to form an

Store Window Display
The Museum of Modern Art

Helios House
Office dA and Johnston Marklee, Los Angeles. Green BP gas station.

exhibitionary complex that enables disciplinary and power relations to form a new "public" within relations of sight and vision. This "society of the spectacle" is already the realm in which "the commodity contemplates itself in a world of its own making."[10] Reaching its apotheosis in the Crystal Palace—in which national exhibition combines department store, museum, panorama, and panopticon—the "exhibitionary complex" orders objects and a newly formed citizenry alike under the principles of transparency: "the power to command and arrange things and bodies for display" allows "the people, and *en masse* rather than individually, to know rather than be known, to become the *subjects* rather than the objects of knowledge."[11] A power that regulates through organization utilizes the Crystal Palace to produce a place for the people in relation to that power, one that works through the principle of incorporation: drawn into the spectacle, the crowd interiorizes its gaze and its principles as a form of "self-surveillance and, hence, self-regulation."[12] On the other, they are machines for the production of the seductive allure of what Walter Benjamin has termed the "phantasmagoria" of the commodity spectacle.

Optical Zoom

But for Debord, it is not the nineteenth century in which the Society of the Spectacle develops its full potential, it is the twentieth, in particular the emergence of electronic transmission technology. Two distinct forms of the spectacle characterize the early twentieth century, the concentrated spectacle of dictatorial states and the diffuse spectacle of capitalism, posited by Debord as "the Americanization of the world"[13]: "The diffuse form of the spectacle is associated with the abundance of commodities, with the undisturbed development of modern capitalism."[14] With new electronic media technologies the spectacular reproduction and dissemination of commodities not only explodes in growth but reaches new markets—fashion, media, advertising, information, and communications technologies penetrating into, and appropriating, every aspect of daily life.

By the late 1980s, electronic technologies, television in particular, have become the primary vehicle of spectacular saturation, the flows of advertising and media images, particularly news and documentary footage of war and disaster, accelerating the de-realization and fragmentation of modernity. The penetration of media and communications technologies is for Debord the defining effect of late Capitalism, heralding a new form of spectacle: the integrated. Both product and means of globalization, this manifestation of spectacle merges the concentrated and diffuse, spreading itself "to the point where it now permeates all

Fertile Minds

Times Square
New York, New York

McCormick Tribune Campus Center
OMA/Rem Koolhaas, Illinois Institute of Technology, Chicago.

reality": "the harsh logic of the spectacle controls the abundant diversity of media extravagances."[15]

This new globalized spectacle combines an incessant drive towards technological renewal with an endless saturation of media flows forming an "eternal present": "When social significance is attributed only to what is immediate, and to what will be immediate immediately afterwards, always replacing another, identical, immediacy, it can be seen that the uses of the media guarantee a kind of eternity of noisy insignificance."[16] This kind of "noise" is also linked to the opacity of control systems, to the merging of state and economy, in which what is at stake is not representation—the "content" in the words of Marshall McLuhan—but "distribution and regulation"[17]—the operations of the medium—the spectacular already shifting from representation to transmission and pure surface, to the formal organization of images. In the hum and blur of electronic static lies hidden a truth: "secrecy dominates this world, and first and foremost as the secret of domination."[18] In both cases is "a dissolution of legibility generated by the very efficacy and supremacy of the spectacle."[19]

Cybercity

In the 1990s Beatriz Colomina claims that "the mass media…are the true site within which modern architecture is produced and with which it directly engages."[20] At the same time, the city—Times Square and Las Vegas remain iconic—undergoes a morphing or hybridization that sees urban form dissolved into electronic fields and virtualities, the city overcome by the electronic and digital image-streams that are the relentless outpouring of capitalism endlessly reconfiguring itself as spectacular flow. "The space of flows" for Manuel Castells now operates "on the basis of exchanges between electronic circuits linking up information systems in distant locations": "In the network society, a fundamental form of social domination is the prevalence of the logic of the space of flows over the space of places… These electronic circuits do not operate in the territorial vacuum" but "link up territorially based complexes of production, management and information."[21]

Paul Virilio identifies the "overexposed city" in which "constructed space now occurs within an electronic topology": While the topical City was once constructed around the 'gate' and the 'port,' the teletopical metacity is now constructed around the 'window' and the teleport, that is to say, around the screen and the time slot."[22] As "public space yields to public image,"[23] traditional urbanism yields to an urbanization of time that is also "the urbanization of one's own body plugged into various interfaces":

McCormick Tribune Campus Center
OMA/Rem Koolhaas, Illinois Institute of Technology, Chicago.

Cloud Gate
Anish Kapoor, AT&T Plaza, Millennium Park, Chicago, 2006.

> The staking out of the territory with heavy infrastructure (roads, railroads) is now giving way to control of the immaterial, or practically immaterial, environment (satellites, fibre-optic cables), ending in the body terminal of man, of that interactive being who is both transmitter and receiver.[24]

The city is exposed—overexposed—by optoelectronic signals, the speed of transmission of "teletopic technologies," a "dromospheric contamination" which erases extension, compressing geophysical space and duration into an arrival without departure, the "generalized arrival of data" that is the logic of instantaneous transmission and teleaction: telepresence, teleoperation, televiewing, telecommunication, teleconferencing, or telesurveillance.

Digital Zoom

Design discourse proposes that the city is no longer an outmoded and decaying landscape penetrated by new systems of communication and information,[25] but a fully networked field inseparable from the circuits that weave through its fabric. In the last year of the twentieth century, Alex Wall declares that the urban landscape is a "field," a responsive "functioning matrix of connective tissue that organizes not only objects and spaces but also the dynamic processes and events that move through them."[26] Around the same moment, Michael Hays claims architecture becomes "a multimedia fusion," the "digitized, energized, emulsified surface" of information and effect.[27] Architecture is now interface—"smart" buildings or media surfaces.[28] The urban is organized between the long-term "architectonic interval (the building)" and the hyper-short "teletopical interval (the network)," a light interval, the interface of telecommunications technologies.

Already in the early 1980s, Jean Baudrillard argues for an *Ecstasy of Communication* in which the dominance of the spectacle has given way to its modes of operation: to networks and interfaces, the space of "the smooth operational surface of communication"[29]:

> The medium itself is no longer identifiable as such, and the merging of the medium and the message (McLuhan) is the first great formula of this new age. There is no longer any medium in the literal sense: it is now intangible, diffuse and diffracted by the real, and it can no longer even be said that the latter is distorted by it.[30]

Advertising, the primary goal of these new circuitries, invades everything, monopolizing public space: "It is our only architecture today: great screens on which are

Fertile Minds

Inauguration of President Barack Obama
22 January 2009. Washington, DC.

reflected atoms, particles, molecules in motion. Not a public scene or true public space but gigantic spaces of circulation, ventilation and ephemeral connections."[31]

White Noise

This "viral, endemic, chronic, alarming presence of the medium," is the violence of a "hyper-reality," a simulated electronic production that presents itself as the Real in an epidemic multiplication. Excessive to the point of obscenity, it is an over-proximity that obliterates the distance between receiver and transmitter necessary to the constitution of spectator or spectacle:

> Obscenity begins precisely when there is no more spectacle, no more scene, when all becomes transparence and immediate visibility, when everything is exposed to the harsh and inexorable light of information and communication... Thus at bottom the message already no longer exists; it is the medium that imposes in its pure circulation.[32]

A year after Baudrillard, Jonathan Crary declares "the spectacular consumption of the commodity" is dissolved into "binarized pulses of light or electricity that unhinges the fictive unity of spectacular representation. Figurative images lose their transparence and are consumed as simply one more code" in the continuous stream of transmission.[33]

"Overexposure" is akin in its perceptual effects to transmission errors or interference. Noise in a system creates a resistance to its own circuitries of control as much as it marks illegibility for the spectator—the channels that circulate visual, auditory, computational, or communications information are less and less totalizable, hyper-diversified and multiplied, and prey to breaks, discontinuities, errors, malfunctions, duplications, hackings, and so on. Castells points out, the cultural realm is increasingly "enclosed in or shaped by [the] world of electronic media. But the new media system is not characterized by the one-way, undifferentiated messages through a limited number of channels that constituted the world of mass media. And it is not a global village."[34]

In 1960s, Michel Serres states that noise is part of communication; it cannot be eliminated from the system. There is no communication without medium, channel or context; but there is no channel without noise—it is the presence of the medium itself, the trace of its effects left on the message. Filtering noise only adds other kinds of noise. Communication is thus always prey to "background noise, jamming, static, cut-offs, hyteresis, various interruptions."[35] Noise is dirty, it is extra-linguistic, pure medium; but it is also fertile, a space for translation, decipherment, misreading, mutation. Noise is always in the system; noise *is* the system. Noise is also the message of the crowd, the

The Light Inside
James Turrell, Museum of Fine Arts (MFAH), Houston, 1999.

multitude: "noise is born in the square, it swells, ripples, rise, fills the forum, slips in everywhere, seizes the city. It accompanies the multiple and it is the multiple."[36]

Multitudes

In 2000, Michael Hardt and Antonio Negri redefine the "multitude" as networks, flows, swarms—dynamic complexes of circulation, always re-aligning, always re-configuring:

> The movements of the multitude designate new spaces, and its journeys establish new residences. Autonomous movement is what defines the place proper to the multitude…The cities of the earth will become at once great deposits of cooperating humanity and locomotives for circulation, temporary residences and networks of the mass distribution of living humanity.[37]

A year earlier, Stan Allen defines the city that will accommodate this multitude: open-ended field conditions.[38] Within this logic, the concept of "noise" is used to maintain heterogeneity, flux, and uncertainty, privileging a tactical operationality.

In 1980, Michel de Certeau identifies tactics with the multitude: tactics are the operational modalities of users, consumers, those subjected to regimes of power. Strategies are the operational modality or power; they are interested in circumscribing the space of institutions of power in order to determine—and control—relations with exteriors distinct from them. Tactics do no not rely on the established borders or on recognizing the "enemy" as a visible totality—the tactic is always localized, always "on the watch for opportunities that must be seized 'on the wing.'"[39] Tactics introduce a Brownian movement or "swerve" into the system that causes potential mutations and variations. Their operations and results are unpredictable: they are noisy, dirty.

Distractions

Tactics map a dense and complex terrain through urban vectors, data-scapes and image fields in relation to which the spectator is no longer detached but incorporated into a multiplicity of fragmentary and incommensurable effects no longer reducible to a totality but nevertheless forming an undecidable map of the contemporary world. It is hypertextual, distractive. In the 1950s the hypertext is already, for Charles Eames, a distracted mode of reception crucial to maximum information absorption, transforming the image into an imaging system. It demands an absorption that pushes perception to its limits: a distracted concentration, or a concentrated distraction.[40] In 1953, Charles and George Nelson stage a "Sample Lesson for a Hypothetical Course," an attempt to reconfigure pedagogical method through the audiovisual (and olfactory) presentation of

The Weather Project
Olafur Eliasson, Tate Modern, London, 2003.

information using high-speed techniques and multiple formats. The goal is to increase awareness of relationships (including a "decompartmentalization" of curricula) through distractive techniques, using a formatting methodology—a "rigorous theory of presentation," as Barry Katz will term it—developed for World War II military intelligence by designers that include Raymond Loewy, Oliver Lundqusit and Eero Saarinen.[41]

Like the Eameses, Marshall McLuhan believes a distractive and immersive relation to information provides for the most absorption. In the 1960s McLuhan gives texts an "acoustic" or tactile dimension, "writing" through a hybridization of epigrammic sound bytes, images, and formatting. The city—like the book—is henceforth not about representation, but a sensory awareness of the whole field (peripheral or subliminal), one that leads to "involvement in depth."[42] A distracted attention cannot focus on any one piece of information; it is required to actively engage with the matrix of information. The sound-byte is low on resolution (a "cool" medium): it does not spell out its intent but provides cryptic allusions that have to be reconstructed by the reader.[43] It is an engine of speculation, experimentation, generation whose operation centers on the trans-coding of information. It is what Edward Tufte in the 1990s calls "envisioning information."[44]

Already by 1935, Walter Benjamin has ascribed a synaesthesic mode of perception to both cinema and architecture in his celebrated essay, "The Work of Art in the Age of its Technical Reproducibility." Distinguishing between an absorbed concentration—the demand of "art," in which the viewing subject *is absorbed by* the object—and a distracted attention, in which the viewing subject *absorbs* the object, Benjamin links the latter to the multitude, its object of attention not a work of art but the city.[45]

The distracted absorption of the built environment, particularly the urban environment, is for Benjamin a visuality that becomes "tactile"—an unconscious absorption akin to "feeling one's way" distinguished from the tourist's concentrated contemplation of a famous building.[46] This distracted attention is part of Benjamin's theory of the decline of aura. The "withering" of the aura of the artwork is the direct result of the development of technologies of mass production or "technical reproducibility"—Hugo's "this will kill that" model of the impact of the Gutenberg press on written media extended generally to human creativity. Linked to the urban "masses"

National Rifle Association (NRA) Convention
Welcome banner

is a massification of media. But, as Sam Weber points out in 1994, the mass media do not so much destroy aura as shift its functioning.[47] Weber links the tactile-tactical unconsciousness of habit—a collapsing of distance and close proximity—to "massmediaura": "auratic flashes and shadows that *are* themselves media."[48]

Again in the 1990s, Ben van Berkel and Caroline Bos describe a particular category of architectural effect that they liken to walking through a painting: "your gaze swerves and orients you through color, shininess, light, figuration, and sensation."[49] For Gilles Deleuze the experience of encountering such effects is similar to Benjamin's model of distracted attention:

> An ideal optical space that nonetheless maintains virtual references to tactility (depth, contour, relief)… [Haptic space] implies a type of seeing that is distinct from the optical, a close-up viewing in which 'the sense of sight behaves just like touch.'[50]

This optical-tactile experiencing of space is one in which the real and virtual collapse—a space in which imagination, fantasy, hallucination, and affect mingle with the material, the visual, the sensory.[51]

Delirious Immersions

The distractive and immersive realities of the post-spectacular metropolis engage an inhabitant that finds itself in constant oscillation between an authorized subject position (qua spectator), and its dissolution into a fragmented and multiplied flux in which a mastering gaze is impossible. But overexposure paradoxically allows the very distraction, repetition, compression, and concatenation that characterize the hybridity of spectacles and flows to drag the spectator into animation, and away from the very possibility of remaining a spectator as such. Contemporary space is about hyper-effects, about the production of atmosphere—a field of effects, a generalized "mood." Already in 1964, McLuhan notes, "Concern with effect rather than meaning is a basic change of our electric time, for effect involves the total situation, and not a single level of information movement."[52]

Spectacular spatial practices now create environments in which the body as a whole is engaged, wrapping the body in immersive atmospheres. At the very moment of Debord's work on the spectacle, Constant's *New Babylon* already provides this kind of resistance, an interactive space of effect, atmosphere, and mood, one that relies on a logic of flows and a networking of technologies to generate its spaces, including computer-mediated technologies. Such spaces exploit overexposure in a post-spectacular sensory interactivity, while at the same time challenging the dichotomy of spectator/spectacle and subjecting the transparency and authority of the image to the blur and noise of an image now too close.

After-image

Nevertheless, from the nuclear exposure of Nagasaki and Hiroshima to the violent effects of the tabloid streams of television news, the vision industry's "post-spectacular" space can be as bleak as the visions of it in Ballard, Baudrillard, or Virilio's imaginary. From the death of Diana, Princess of Wales—index of the excessive penetration of everyday life by the media, and of her body by that older, vehicular, network in an epiphany of Ballard's crash culture—to the obsessive media fascination with the imagery of 9/11—the implosion of the buildings mirrored with an explosion of coverage—the effects of media excess are familiar to us. The American military has developed a dazzling array of new optoelectronic technologies: satellite guided missiles launched by B2 Stealth Bombers and linked into the Global Positioning System network, soldiers equipped with shoulder-mounted thermobaric bombs that suck air out of confined spaces like buildings to create powerful levels of heat and pressure, back-pack satellite-connected laptops that communicate with aircraft by data-link to locate moving targets on the ground, un-manned spy drones able to map infrastructures or moving targets and launch remotely-operated Hellfire missiles capable of taking out the smallest moving target with precision, and Directed Energy Weapons, microwave bombs capable of releasing crippling waves of high-frequency electromagnetic pulses, shorting out computer systems and power supplies to whole urban areas (including schools and hospitals). In both these mediatic assaults the spectacular world has mutated into something else, at once both destructive and delirious, a channeling of energies, digital codes and circuitries that is both pure medium and pure effect.

Left
Thermal Baths and Spa
Peter Zumthor, Vals, Switzerland.

Endnotes

1 See Marshall McLuhan, *Understanding Media: The Extensions of Man* (Cambridge, Mass.: MIT Press, 2001 (1964)), and with Quentin Fiore, *The Medium is the Massage* (New York: Bantham, 1967).

2 Jonathan Crary, "The Eclipse of the Spectacle," in *Art After Modernism: Rethinking Representation*, ed. Brian Wallis (New York: New Museum of Contemporary Art, 1984); pp. 291-2.

3 Guy Debord, *The Society of the Spectacle*, trans. Donald Nicholson-Smith (New York: Zone Books, 1994 (1967)); pp. 12-24.

4 Debord, *The Society of the Spectacle*, p. 112.

5 Debord, *The Society of the Spectacle*, p. 22.

6 Richard Sennett, *The Fall of Public Man*, p. 125. Jean Baudrillard, for whom the nineteenth century private sphere is spectacular, albeit a private spectacle tied to psychoanalysis and the dramas of family and subjectivity (the space of the "scene" and the "mirror," operating through "a phantasmatic logic") also sees the nineteenth-century public sphere as the space of the "spectacle." See Jean Baudrillard, "The Ecstasy of Communication," in *The Anti-Aesthetic: Essays in popular Culture*, ed. Hal Foster (Port Townsend, Wash.: Bay Press, 1983); p. 126.

7 See William Wordsworth, "Residence in London," Book VII, *The Prelude* (Harmondsworth, Middlesex: Penguin Books, 1995); pp. 250-295.

8 Crary, *Techniques of the Observer*, p. 20.

9 Crary, *Suspensions of Perception*, p. 74-5, and *Techniques of the Observer*, p. 18-19. See also Richard Sennet, *The Fall of Public Man*, pp. 125-26, 195.

10 Debord, *The Society of the Spectacle*, p. 34.

11 Tony Bennett, "The Exhibitionary Complex," *New Formations* IV (Spring 1988); p. 76, emphasis added.

12 Bennett, "The Exhibitionary Complex," p. 76.

13 Guy Debord, *Comments on The Society of the Spectacle*, trans. Malcolm Imrie (London/New York: Verso, 1998 (1988)); p. 8.

14 Debord, *The Society of the Spectacle*, p. 42.

15 Debord, *Comments on The Society of the Spectacle*, p. 7.

16 Debord, *Comments on The Society of the Spectacle*, pp. 13-15.

17 Crary, "The Eclipse of the Spectacle," p. 284.

18 Debord, *Comments on The Society of the Spectacle*, p. 60.

19 Crary, "The Eclipse of the Spectacle," p. 291.

20 Beatriz Colomina, *Privacy and Publicity: Modern Architecture as Mass Media* (Cambridge, Mass: MIT Press, 1994); p. 15.

21 Manuel Castells, "An Introduction to the Information Age," in *The Media Reader: Continuity and Transformation*, eds. Hugh Mackay and Tim O'Sullivan (London: Sage, 1999); pp. 406-7.

22 Paul Virilio, "The Perspective of Real Time," in *Open Sky*, trans. Julie Rose (London/New York: Verso, 1997/2000); p. 26. "From now on, urban architecture must deal with the advent of a 'technological space time.' The access protocol of telematics replaces that of the doorway. The revolving door is succeeded by 'data banks,' by new rites of passage of a technical culture masked by the immateriality of its components: its networks, highway systems and diverse reticulations whose threads are no longer woven into the space of a constructed fabric, but into the sequences of an imperceptible planning of time in which the interface man/machine replaces the facades of buildings and the surfaces of ground on which they stand." Paul Virilio, "The Overexposed City," *Zone 1/2*; p. 18.

23 Paul Virilio, "The Vision Machine," *The Vision Machine* (London: BFI, 1994); p. 64.

24 Paul Virilio, "The Third Interval," in *Open Sky* (London: Verso, 1997); p. 11.

25 "A planetary data-communications network [is] physically implanted into the decaying digressive terrain of the automobile-based city." Crary, "The Eclipse of the Spectacle," p. 290.

26 Alex Wall, "Programming the Urban Surface," in *Recovering Landscape: Essays in Contemporary Landscape Architecture* (New York: Princeton Architectural Press, 1999); p. 233.

27 K. Michael Hays, "Prolegomenon for a Study Linking the Advanced Architecture of the Present to that of the 1970s through Ideologies of Media, the Experience of Cities in Transition, and the Ongoing Effects of Reification," *Perspecta* 32 (2001): 105-106.

28 See Paul Virilio, "The Law of Proximity," in *Open Sky*, p. 55.

29 Baudrillard, "The Ecstasy of Communication," p. 127.

30 Jean Baurdrillard, "The Precession of Simulacra," in *Simulations* (New York: Semiotext(e): 1983); p. 54.

31 Baudrillard, "The Ecstasy of Communication," p. 130.

32 Baudrillard, "The Ecstasy of Communication," pp. 130-131.

33 Crary, "The Eclipse of the Spectacle," p. 287. See also Samuel Weber, "Mass Mediauras, Or: Art and Media in the Work of Walter Benjamin," in *Mass Mediauras: Form, Technics, Media*, ed. Alan Cholodenko (Cambridge, Mass: MIT Press, 1994); p. 125.

34 Castells, "An Introduction to the Information Age," p. 403.

35 Michel Serres, *Hermès I* (Paris: Minuit, 1969); p. 66; published in English as *Hermes: Literature Science, Philosophy*, eds. Josue V. Harari and David F. Bell (Baltimore: John Hopkins University Press, 1982). See also Michel Serres, *The Parasite*, trans. Lawrence R. Schehr (Baltimore: John Hopkins University Press, 1982); originally published as *Le Parasite* (Paris: Grasset, 1980).

36 Michel Serres, "In the City: Agitated Multiplicity," republished in *Architecture Theory: A Reader in Philosophy and Culture*, edited by Andrew Ballantyne (London: Continuum, 2005); p. 190.

37 Michael Hardt and Antonio Negri, *Empire* (Cambridge, Mass.: Harvard University Press, 2000); p. 397.

38 Stan Allen, *Points and Lines* (New York: Princeton Architectural Press, 1999); p. 92.

39 Michel de Certeau, *The Practice of Everyday Life*, trans. Steven Rendall (Berkeley: Unviersity of California press, 1984); p. xix.

40 The Eameses were interested in communications theory and produced numerous films, diagrams, and multimedia presentations that both demonstrated and materialized new communications modes based on the increasing diffusion of information and the technologies that enabled this (esp. the computer). The most significant include "A Communications Primer" (1953), "Mathematica" (1961), "The House of Science" (1962), "IBM at the Fair" (1965), and "A Computer Persective" (1971). Importantly, they were to fuse these presentations with architecture, creating an immersive and distractive architectonics of information and mood: "Glimpses of America" (1959), IBM Corp. Pavilion for the 1964 New York World's Fair.

41 Barry Katz, "The Arts of War: 'Visual Presentation' and National Intelligence," *Design Issues* 12, no. 2 (1996); p. 12.

42 Marshall McLuhan, *Understanding Media: The Extensions of Man* (Cambridge, Mass.: MIT Press, 2001 (1964)); pp. 9, 13. McLuhan's methodology is most clearly formulated in the two publications he produced with Quentin Fiore in the late 1960s, *The Medium is the Massage*, and *War and Peace in the Global Village*.

43 "Francis Bacon never tired of contrasting hot and cool prose. Writing in 'methods' or complete packages, he contrasted with writing in aphorisms, or single observations… The passive consumer wants packages, but those, he suggested, who are concerned in pursuing knowledge and in seeking causes will resort to aphorisms, just because they are incomplete and require participation in depth." McLuhan, *Understanding Media*; p. 31.

44 See Edward Tufte, *Envisioning Information and The Visual Display of Quantitative Information*, (New Haven: Graphics Press, 1990).

45 "In contrast, the distracted mass absorbs the work of art. This is most obvious with regard to buildings. Architecture has always represented the prototype of a work of art the reception of which is consummated by a collectivity in a state of distraction." Walter Benjamin, "The Work of Art in the Age of its Mechanical Reproduction," in *Illuminations*, trans. Harry Zohn (New York: Schocken, 1968); p. 239.

46 Linked to habit rather than attention, perception of the built environment is only incidentally or peripherally optical, or "absent-minded."

47 See Samuel Weber, "Mass Mediauras, Or: Art and Media in the Work of Walter Benjamin," in *Mass Mediauras*, pp. 76-107. (Note: Benjamin noted auratic effects in photography's precursor, the daguerreotype. See "On Some Motifs in Baudelaire," in *Illuminations*, trans. Harry Zohn (New York: Schocken, 1968); pp. 187-188).

48 Samuel Weber, "Mass Mediauras, Or: Art and Media in the Work of Walter Benjamin," in *Mass Mediauras: Form, Technics, Media*, ed. Alan Cholodenko (Cambridge, Mass: MIT Press, 1994); p. 107.

49 Ben van Berkel and Carolyn Bos, "Effects: Radiant Synthetic," *Move*, Vol. 3 (UN Studio/Goose, 1992); p. 27.

50 See translator's introduction, Gilles Deleuze, *Francis Bacon: The Logic of Sensation*, trans. Daniel Smith (Minneapolis: University of Minnesota Press, YR); p. xxvi; quotation from Henri, Maldiney, *Regard Parole Espace* (1973).

51 On the question of delirious effects, see Rem Koolhaas, *Delirious New York: A Retroactive Manifesto for New York* (New York: Monacelli Press, 1994 (1978)).

52 McLuhan, *Understanding Media*, p. 26.

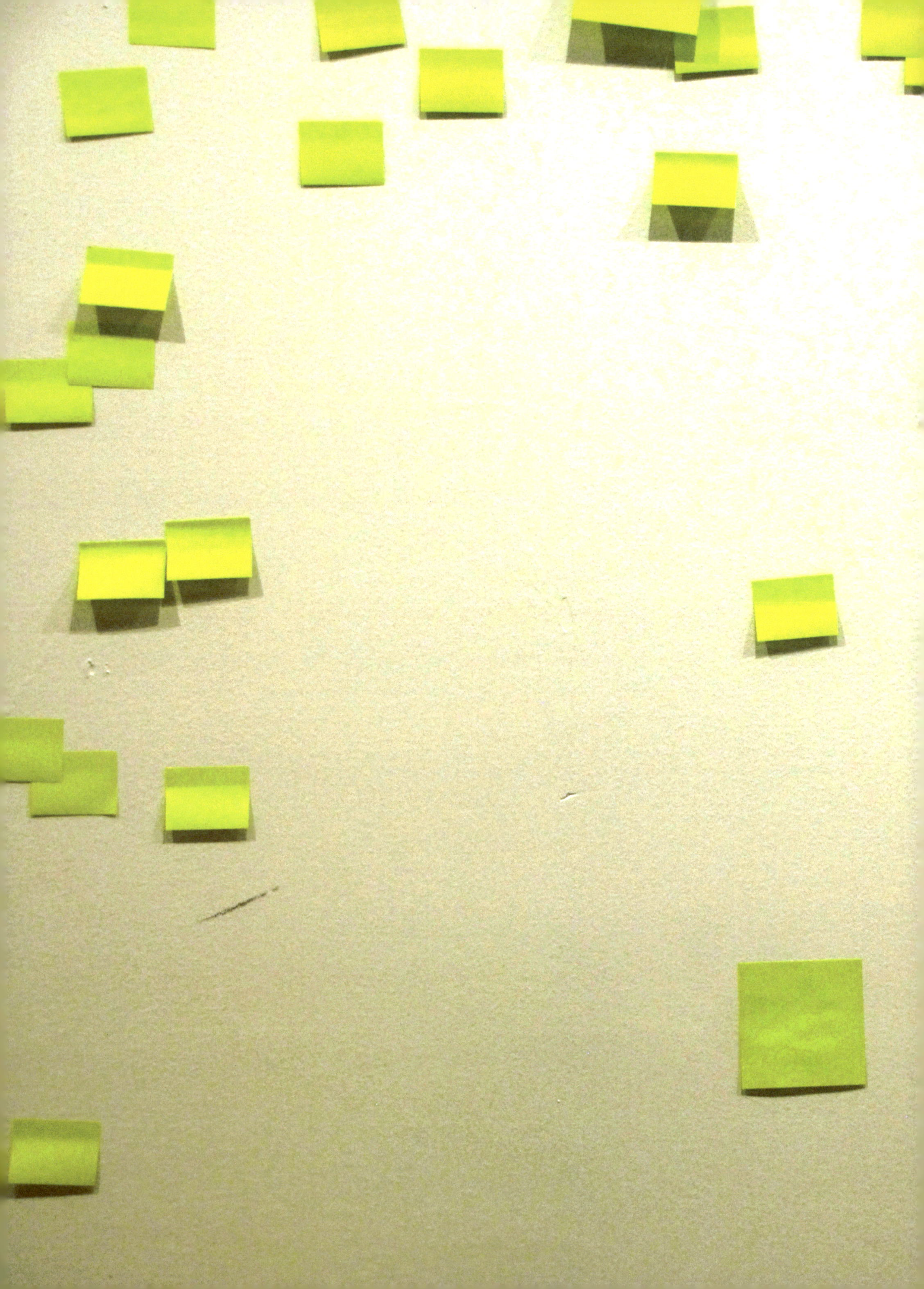

Process Work

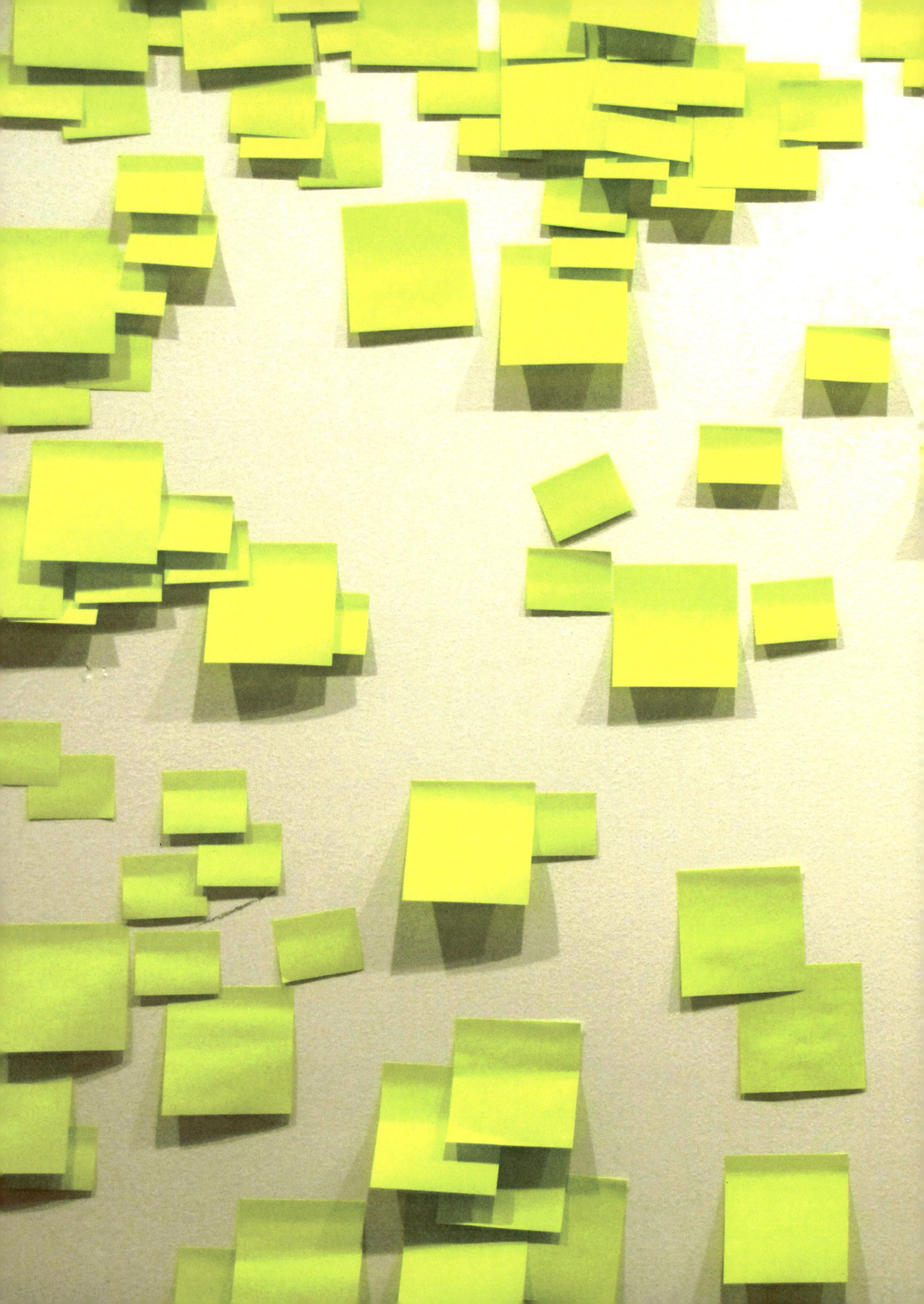

Dynamic Constellation of Post-It Notes

Accumulation 2

Previous Spread
Accumulation 1

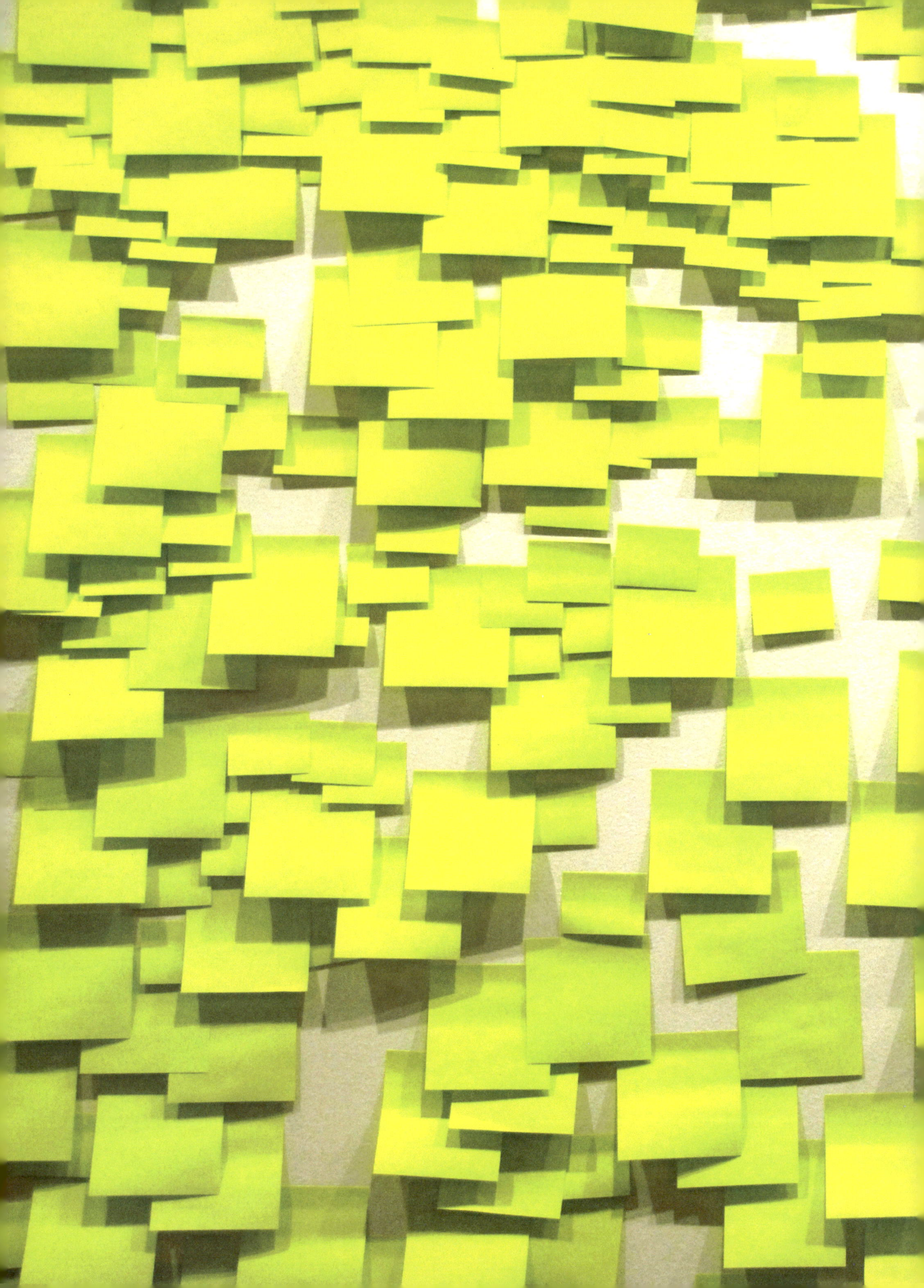

Accumulation 3

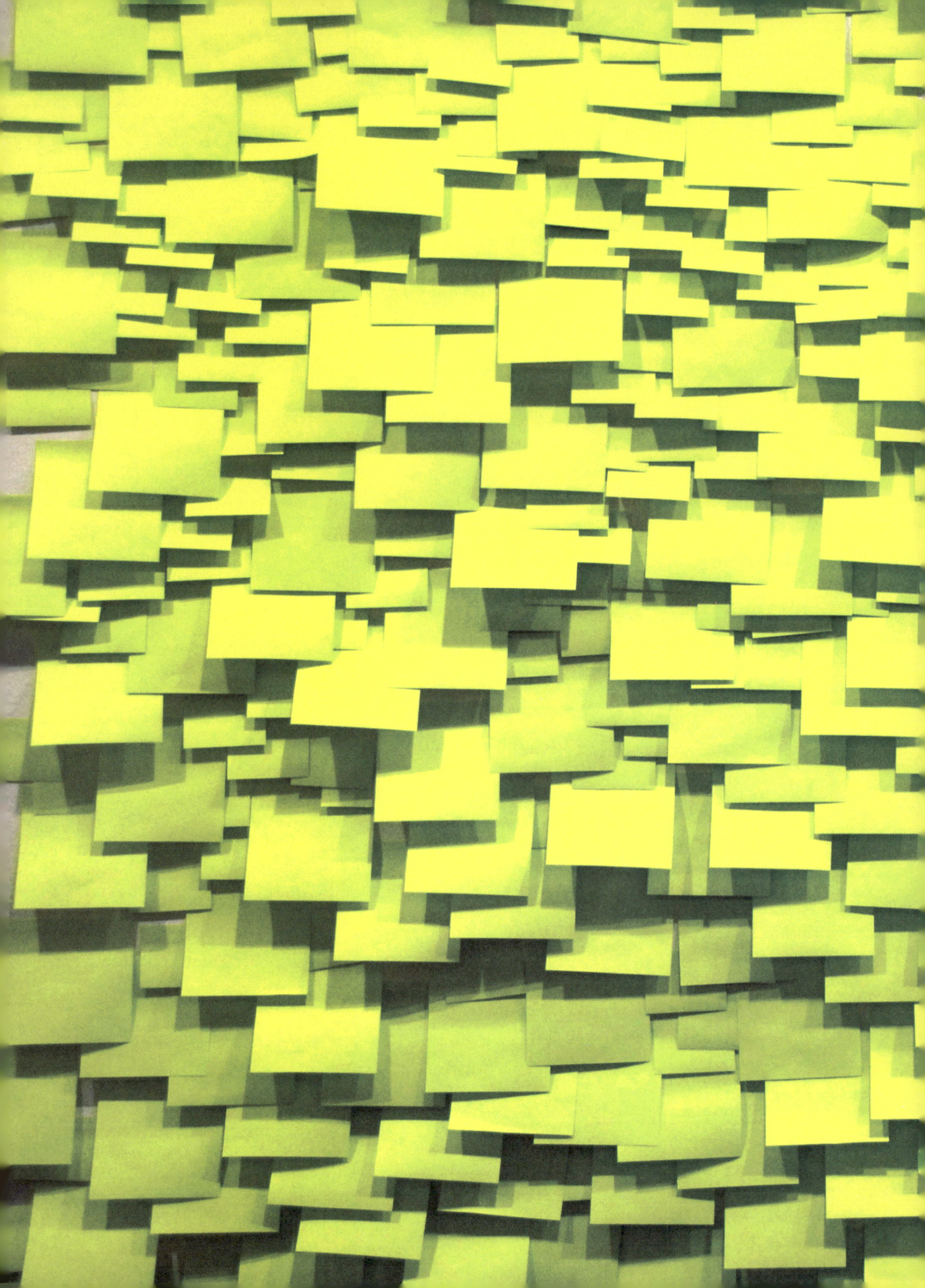

Accumulation 4

Orbigraphia

Rhett Russo

Bacon:
"Very often the involuntary marks are much more deeply suggestive than others, and those are the moments when you feel that anything can happen."

Sylvester:
"You feel it while you're making those marks?"

Bacon:
"No the marks are made, and you survey the thing like you would a sort of graph [diagramme]. And you see within this graph the possibilities of all types of fact being planted. This is a difficult thing; I am expressing it badly. But you see, for instance, if you think of a portrait, you maybe have to put the mouth somewhere, but you suddenly see through this graph that the mouth could go right across the face…"

David Sylvester and Francis Bacon,
The Brutality of Fact: Interviews with Francis Bacon (1987)

Unlike painting, architectural drawing must cater to the necessity of repeatability and to the frailty of our perceptions. This makes it a difficult topic to characterize. It is a temporal process that requires specialized drawing techniques at different stages, ranging from the painterly to the technical. It is often difficult to understand or explain where dimension emerges in this process, but in the best of circumstances—as I experienced with the *Orbigraphia*—the range of sensations elicited in the drawings are a constituent part of their technical development. Every architect is trained to draw and see differently; occasionally, architects invent new drawing formats to address the complexities of space, form and matter that occupy our imaginations.

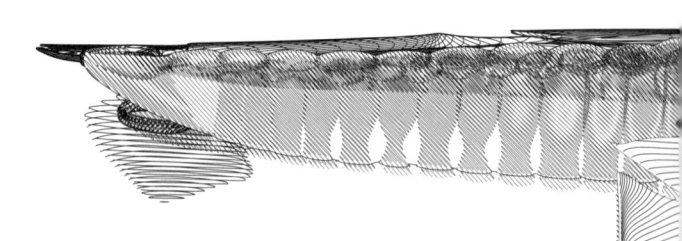

Drawing in Space

Distinctions have emerged in the last fifteen years between the practices of drawing manually, and drawing in the presence of three-dimensional modeling software.

First, it is no longer necessary to construct three-dimensional objects through a system of projections. With our current software, it is possible to achieve an infinite number of auxiliary views from virtual three-dimensional objects. It could be argued that two-dimensional drawing no longer exists in a three-dimensional environment, but what I sought to demonstrate with the *Orbigraphia* is that drawing persists, albeit under a slightly different scenario, whereby the degree of dimensional precision—0.001 mm—and computational speed are combined in ways that give rise to new effects.

Second, architectural drawing no longer requires the use of a single, fixed, picture plane.[1] Measure is no longer a singularity to be designated within the drawing; it exists at every point. It is a simple process to describe a line with equal precision on a curved surface anywhere in a coordinate space. The nature of our design space has shifted from a laminar or planar environment to a space that is more spherical or topological in character. In orthographic drawing, the effect of thickness is perceptual—it belongs to the phenomenal space

Figure 1

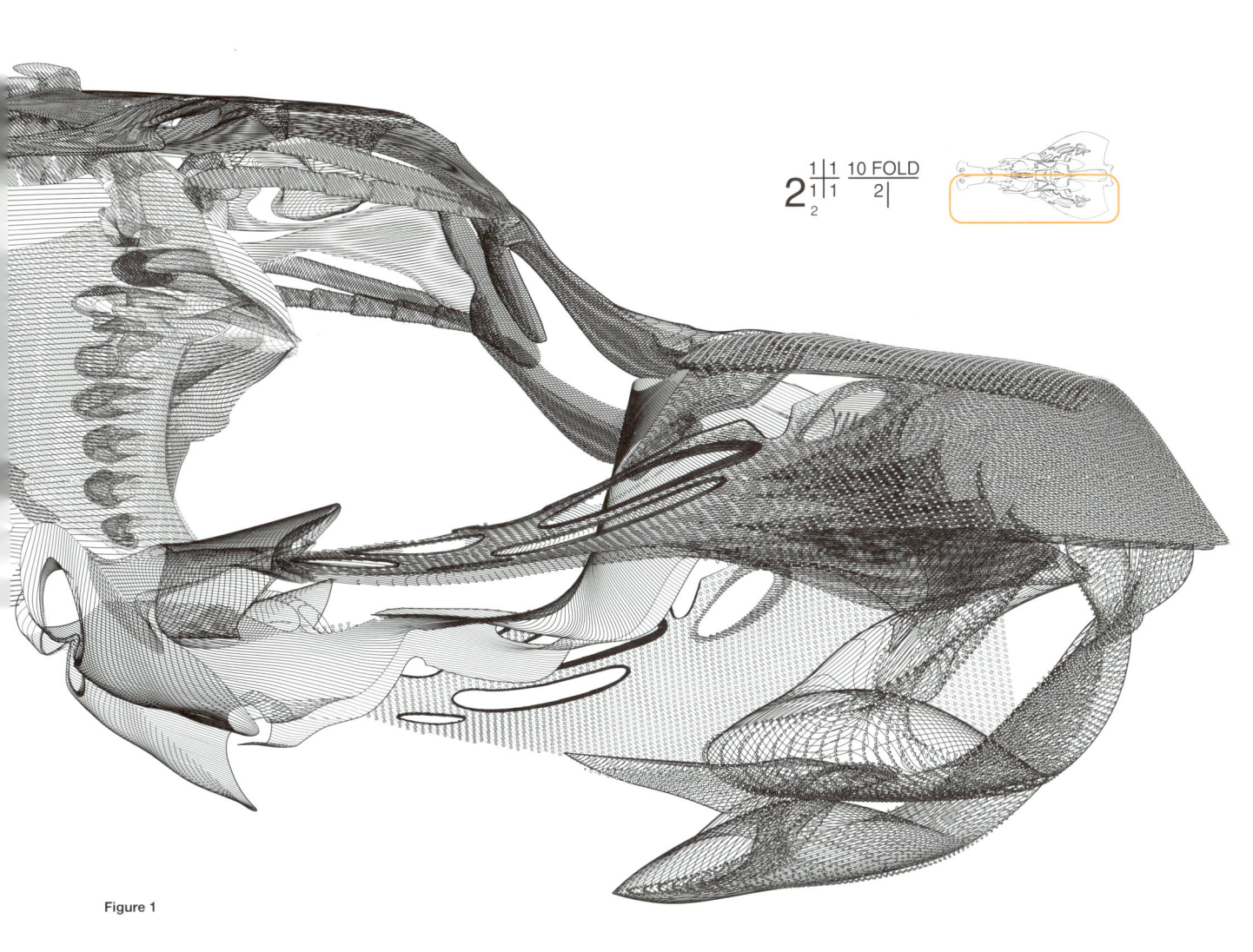

of painting, unmeasured, flat, and reserved for the imagination. In model space, on the other hand, thickness is not only measurable but it can be easily cut through to reveal two-dimensional geometry. It can also be used to obtain the section through a surface, or to reveal the interior of a volume.

Third, orthographic drawing is no longer the de facto instrument of measure that architects use to design buildings. The speed of computation has accelerated the act of drawing to the point that the calculation of form virtually disappears. Measure and transformation are no longer the challenge to drawing that they once were. The rules once anchoring measure to position have been replaced by virtual objects that always retain their representative length, surface area, and volume.

The *Orbigraphia* were generated topologically through distortion and deformation; that is to say, through movement and action, rather than by projection. In

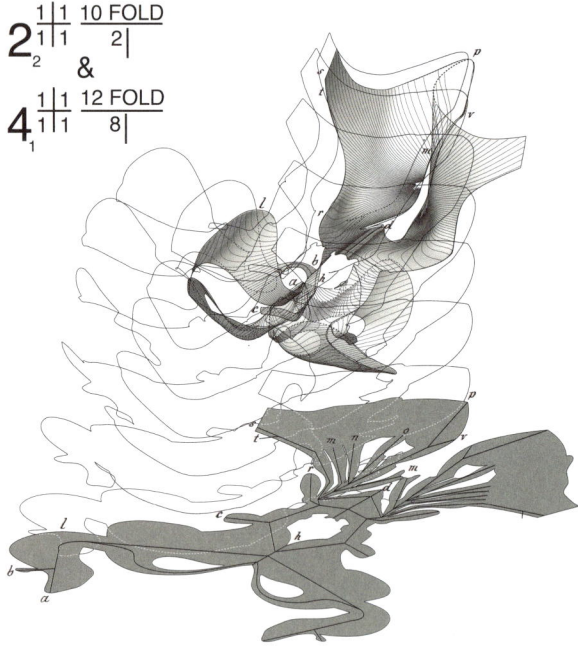

Figure 2
The development of the *bauplan* (bodyplan) as a two degree surface using a one degree plane.

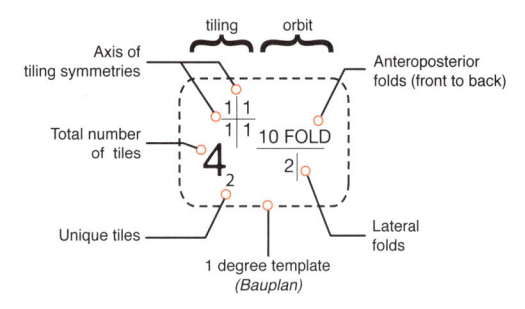

Figure 3
Nomenclature
Each model is annotated according to the number of tiles and the number of orbit folds used to develop its surface.

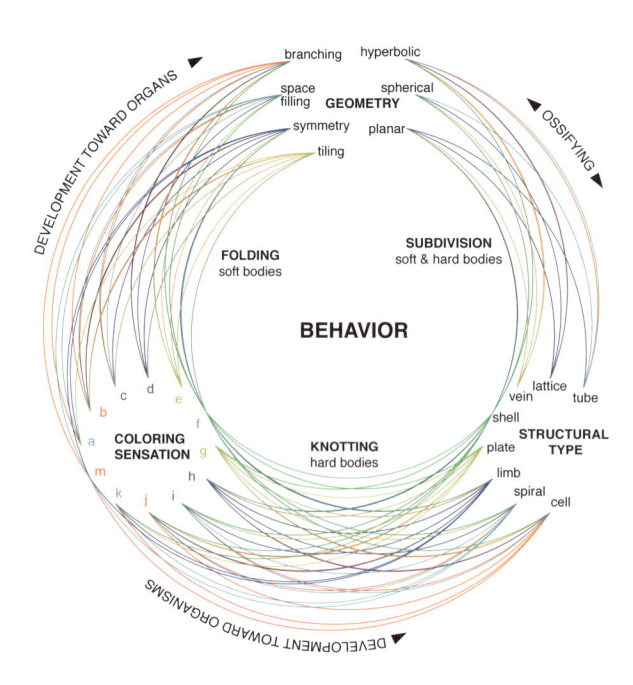

Species (Matter)
a. Tympanuchus cupido attwateri
b. Eumeces egregius lividus
c. Hypomesus transpacificus
d. Potomilus capax
e. Triodopsis platysayoides
f. Sternotherus depressus
g. Felis pandalis
h. Gopherus polyphemus
i. Oncorhynchus clarki stomias
k. Bufo houstonensis
m. Felis yagouaroundi

Figure 4
Genealogy
The genealogy of the models on a torus. Three sets of facts, sensations, geometry, and types are represented as spherical nodes. The actions, folding, subdivision, and knotting are located on the surface of the torus. The organism emerges from the combination of facts and actions. The *bauplan* is painted with information from a variety of species and the colors and intensities are developed into a set of organs.

drawing the *Orbigraphia*, the perception of thickness was supplemented by the design of volumetric parts. (Fig. 13) The phenomenal aspects associated with that thickness appear hollow in some instances, while in others the curves collapse to produce a flat pattern or moiré effect. (Fig. 2) In either case, these effects would be hard to achieve without the three-dimensional surfaces that are native to digital modeling.

The heterogeneous process of making things through discrete drawings is slowly disappearing from our discipline. Digital modeling has introduced a level of simultaneity and dynamism that was not previously accessible, and the effects of this present a new sensibility for design. We now have the power to incorporate and reproduce nonlinear deformations with remarkable clarity, and the precision to calculate the resemblance of the things we could only remotely imagine.

Drawing Models

When I set out to do this work I had little sense of what would transpire. What I wanted it to be was purely part of bringing together a set of facts or logics that were unrelated: topologies, bodies, and colors. I wanted a way of working that provided opportunities for all three facts to coexist in the design process. In this respect, it was a *dirty* process; clouded by the presence of interests in other disciplines that I had no formal training in—mathematics, biology, optics—and a desire to intermingle their traits. I had also become tired of the limitations of drawing, and was searching for a way to assemble things in the absence of rigid geometries, through the use of deformable, two-dimensional maps.

The *Orbigraphia* consists of two separate models (Figs. 5 & 8) that were never intended to represent buildings. Instead, they were constructed to explore a set of procedures that lie in-between drawing and building. Their development helped me to identify a new architectural format for handling topologic form. I was interested in how the architectural categories of structure, surface, and ornament could be linked together in a novel way, in the presence of both analog drawing techniques and digital tools.

The drawings were developed from a curiosity in the unstratified manner in which form, structure, and color are so closely intertwined in nature, and the rich topologic features that are common to both the physiology of animals and architecture. A genealogy was developed that identified specific species from the natural world according to three distinct categories: color, geometry, and structure. (Fig. 4) Each model was an attempt to understand how these disparate characteristics could be reconstituted to produce topological assemblies.

The flatness of the initial template drawings, and the fact that they would be folded, made it necessary to conceptualize the models as topological bodies—more specifically, as single surfaces with two distinct, orientable sides, which corresponded to a topological space. By definition, any "topology" has to maintain the limit form of a closed, three-dimensional surface, but it can be welded and knotted together in infinite ways as long as it retains its continuity—as long as it is "homeomorphic." This continuity was a key feature that made the structural behavior of the templates indeterminate. It led to buckling and twisting that aided the design and legibility of each model. By classifying the model as a body, it was also possible to establish a more robust set of parts—such as organs, and limbs—that could help identify whether their orbits—the transformation or "quotient" spaces of given points—belonged to the internal or external development of the model. In short, the body metaphor became an essential spatial reference or diagram that made it possible to trace where the various parts had been displaced, revolved through space, or turned inside-out.

A new drawing format was implemented to bridge between the two-dimensional drawings and the spherical space of the models. Its syntax includes two major parameters: the number of tiles and the number of orbits, with other parameters assigned to the lateral folds, anteroposterior (front to back) folds, unique tiles, and their orientation along lines of symmetry. (Fig. 3) Multiple pieces from this genealogy were loosely tiled together according to their color and the tangency of their outlines, and then manually arranged in clusters along the axis of a fold. Often the tiles—like the ones that appear in Fig. 7, for instance—were repeated and reoriented so that their orbit folds could occur simultaneously around multiple axes. The resulting templates were adopted as *bauplans* (blue-prints, "body-plans," or the design system), which in a literal sense served as two dimensional maps, but more importantly provided a latent taxonomy that would later give rise to an unpredictable arrangement of features.[2] (Figs. 6 & 7) The *bauplans*, were then folded—or orbited—and eventually welded together to produce topological surfaces. (Fig. 11)

I was interested in reformulating the role of the *bauplan* to refer to an indeterminate apparatus rather than an archetypal form, through its relationship to material. The overall form of the models was generated largely from the topology of the folded paper rather than a plan as such. This intention parallels the shift in biology away from a geometric means of classification in favor of a more non-linear and behavioral understanding of how forms develop in the natural world based upon their material. What transpired through the folding was the most important factor in the design of the models. It became clear that symmetry helped stabilize the paper, while the parts—especially the placement of the narrow pieces—made the overall topology very unpredictable, and on certain occasions the entire form would buckle to reveal a concave or convex configuration. It would have been impossible to predict or draw this behavior without the models.

As more tiles were added, they formed a network of complex symmetries that are similar in their disposition

Figure 5
The 3-Degree Body

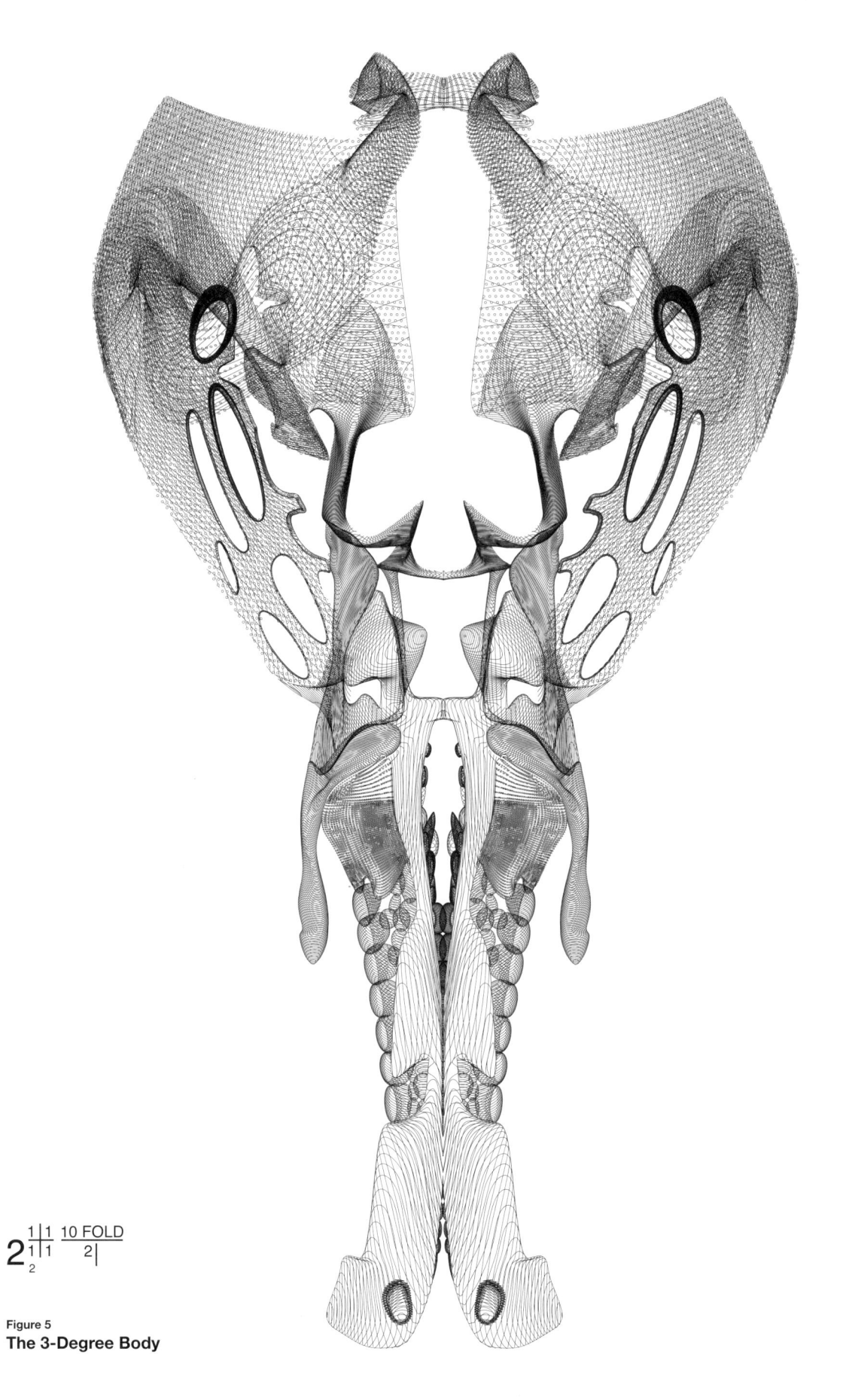

118 **Orbigraphia** Rhett Russo

ORBITS

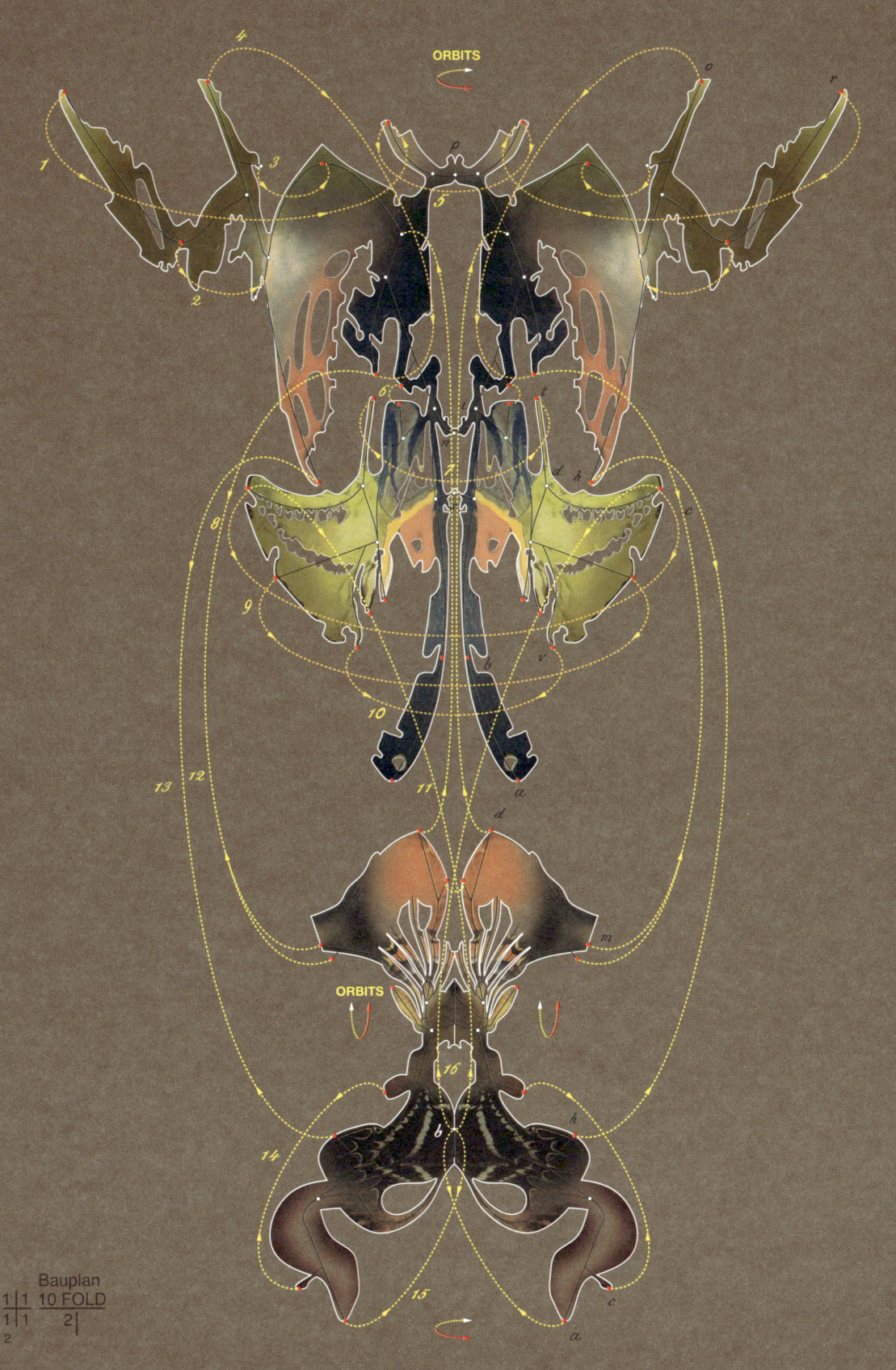

ORBITS

Bauplan
$2\,{{1|1}\atop{1|1}\atop{2}}\;{{10\;\text{FOLD}}\over{2|}}$

Figure 6
The 1-Degree Body

Process Work 119

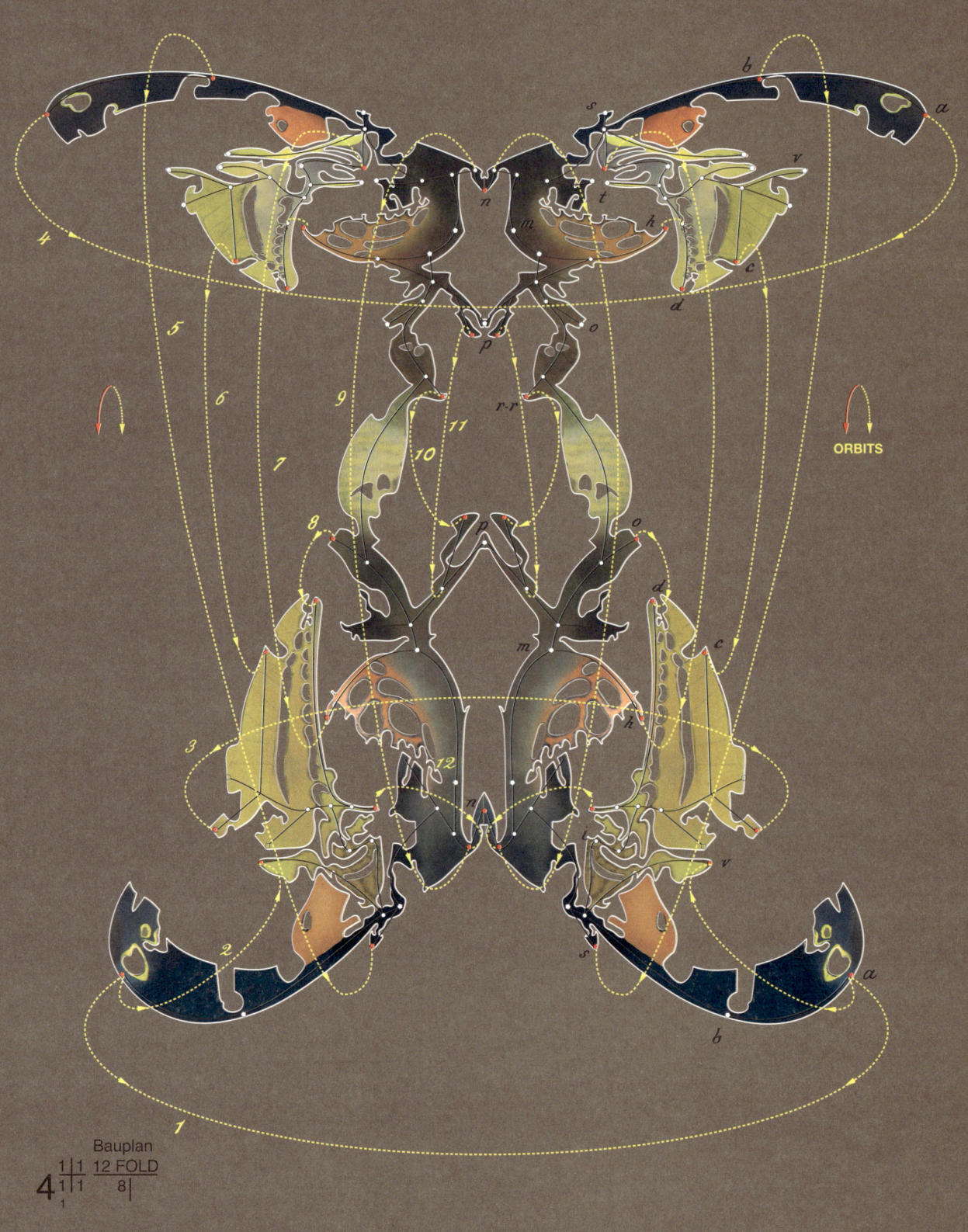

Figure 7
The 1-Degree Body

120 **Orbigraphia** Rhett Russo

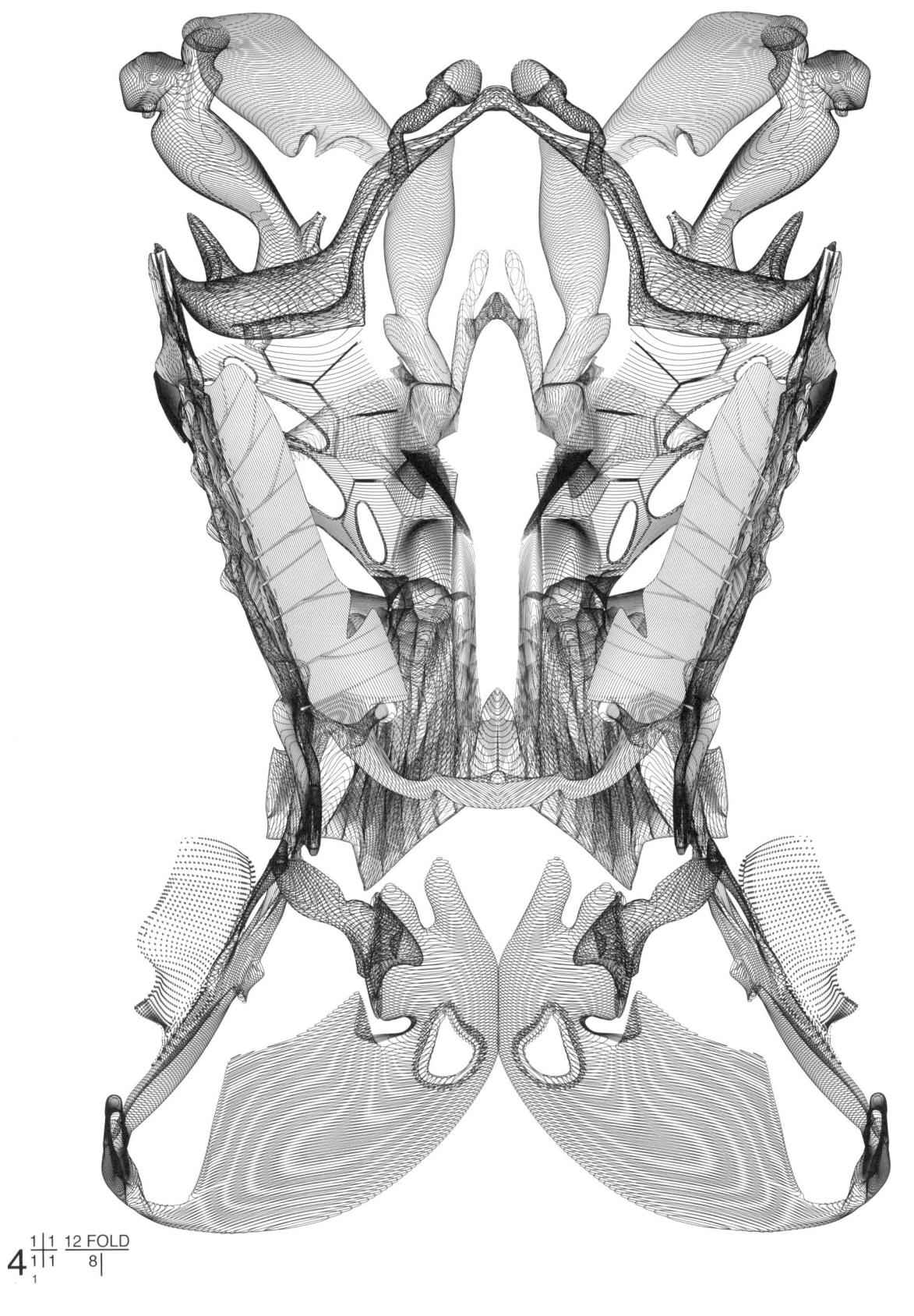

Figure 8
The 3-Degree Body

Process Work   121

Figure 9
The major structural organs from both models, exhibiting the variety of structural morphologies.

122 **Orbigraphia** Rhett Russo

Figure 10
A symmetrical tiling in a Euclidian space that results in an orbit of the tile's symmetry in a topological space. The vectors are flipped at six o'clock.

Figure 11
The folded topology as a development of Figure 6.

to the vertices of multi-faceted polyhedra or crystals, and this increased the number of times that the folding developed internally as pockets.[3] This type of symmetry is distinct from classical symmetry: it is less compositional and more topological. It emerged from a set of three-dimensional vectors and tiles that behave like the folding that occurs in soft tissue or plants. In nature, soft tissue possesses remarkable variability, and it can contract and expand at different rates as it grows.[4] While this change in surface area could not be accommodated by the nature of the paper, it became possible to achieve once the models were constructed digitally.

The coloring of the drawings served a variety of purposes. It helped segment the template into smaller regions. and it gave a more legible character to the opposing sides of the paper. In contrast to having abrupt transitions—outlines—between the parts, the paint was used to produce eddies or striations that were later reintroduced into the design of the joints. Each stage of the analog modeling was constructed so that at least one characteristic of the material—the paper or the ink—would produce uncertainty. Next to the malleability of the paper, the dispersion of the ink became the chief means of propagating intricacy to the next scale of development. (Fig. 11)

Topological Facts: Manifolds

At first glance, mathematical models seem a less likely place to search for facts that concern matter. However, there are at least two things that make them distinctly productive. First, mathematical facts are rarely constrained by the presence of material, and this means that surfaces can move freely through each other in mathematical space. Second, alternative possibilities of fact occur in the presence of a multi-dimensional space: for example, information that appears to be on the front of a surface may actually correspond to the opposite side. Such mathematical models are termed geometric manifolds—topological spaces that are locally Euclidean (intuitively, surfaces), and hence dimensional. William Thurston, professor of mathematics and computer science at Cornell, developed the "Orbifold" theorem in 1981, which identifies finite-volume three-dimensional manifolds, particularly hyperbolic knots. His theory led to significant advancements in knot theory, string theory, and crystallography.

Orbifold theory—"orbit manifold," literally combining orbits and folds—enables mathematicians to analyze complex manifolds and express them through the use of simpler Euclidian, spherical, or hyperbolic spaces.[5] Manifolds can be analyzed with homeomorphic curves located along lines of symmetry, allowing them to be transformed.[6] Thurston's theory contributed to two important possibilities in the models. The first development was the use of homeomorphisms—structure-preserving maps between two algebraic structures. This meant that outlines were transferable from one dimension of space to another. (Fig. 2) Thurston used simple sketches to illustrate this process in his lecture notes. This significant discovery created a new sensibility for working interchangeably with spatial maps. I came to understand how orbits, rotations, and reflections could all be used to flip a vector along a line of symmetry when they exist in a topological space, offering

Process Work 123

new possibilities for working with flat maps of a curved space. (Reflections in topological spaces can be hard to visualize: for instance, while the vectors positioned along the lines of symmetry of a 2d surface follow the same direction, the vectors become flipped when mapped onto a Möbius strip, as in Fig. 10.)

The process of inverting symmetries through their orbits was carried out through the tiling of the two-dimensional templates, and it was also extended to a spherical space once the templates were folded, but because of the limitations introduced by the paper—such as its inability to stretch, or be folded through itself—it became necessary to employ digital tools. While the models have an underlying mathematical structure, this operated in the presence of the paper rather than a formula, and thus made it possible to differentiate the typical forms from the novel ones *by choice* rather than by solution. The folding added a large degree of complexity. Each template had a limited number of possible folds and weld points (the weld points that were used are the red dots in Figs. 6 & 7), but a rather large matrix of possible outcomes, and the number increased dramatically if knotting—pulling one limb of the template through a hole in another limb—was permitted.[7]

Sensation and Action: Behavior

The term "organic" has many definitions, and the course of architectural history is marked by a variety of interpretations of the idea. But in contrast to morphological arguments concerning form, I am struck most by the assessments of nature that explore behavior as a type of formal transmission or feedback. Kantian biologist Jakob von Uexküll's 1920 treatise, *Theoretical Biology,* represents an important change in the philosophy of organisms. Uexküll pioneered the field of biosemiotics and is a forerunner of biocybernetics.[8] He based his theories on a distinction between "*Umwelt*," the subjective environment (an "environment-world" or the spatio-temporal context of an organism), and "*Umgebang*," objective reality.[9]

Uexküll's theories laid the groundwork for the study of animal behavior patterns—the field of ethology. He attempted to develop biology independently from physics and chemistry, through a closer examination of animal behavior and perception, studying how animals perceive their environment and how, in turn, perception determines their behavior. By introducing the concept of the "subjective environment," he identifies sensation as a form of knowledge that is unique for every organism. Insofar as each organism senses its environment differently, there is no universal perception. By grounding biology on perception, he departs from debates focusing on form and function. He acknowledges the role of morphology, but identifies it as a science of analogy, and proposes an alternative framework for addressing questions of causality. Under his theory, all physiologies are understood as implements that participate in a *function-circle* (*Funktionskreis)* an environment split into two parts, the *world-as-sensed* and the *world-of-action*.

For Uexküll, organisms are complex physiologies consisting of receptors and effectors. Behavior is an expression of how the organism sets its body-plan (*Bauplan*) into motion—how well its legs enable it to run over rocky terrain, or how effectively its spines penetrate flesh. Uexküll's assessment of the organism is important: he associates their degree of complexity with their bodily capacities. Regarding complexity he says, "In the highest animals, however, the creature's own *action-rule* penetrates further and further into the *world-as-sensed*, and there assumes direction and control."[10] In making the *Orbigraphia,* the action-rule emerged through the templates, with each part bringing a uniquely indeterminate capacity to the definition of the whole.

The influence of Uexküll's ideas played into the design process in a rather straightforward way. In making the *Orbigraphia*, I became very interested in the *function-circle* and the possibility that the degrees of transmission could produce variation. His theory offered two alternatives to form that I wanted to explore. Foremost, as Gilles Deleuze has pointed out, Uexküll's perspective is unique: he avoided distinguishing bodies by species or genus, and instead "sought to count their affects."[11]

This idea of capacity was something that I wanted to implement in the design process, as a means to sublimate the question of ornament by embedding every element with a transmissive capacity. In short, the form and

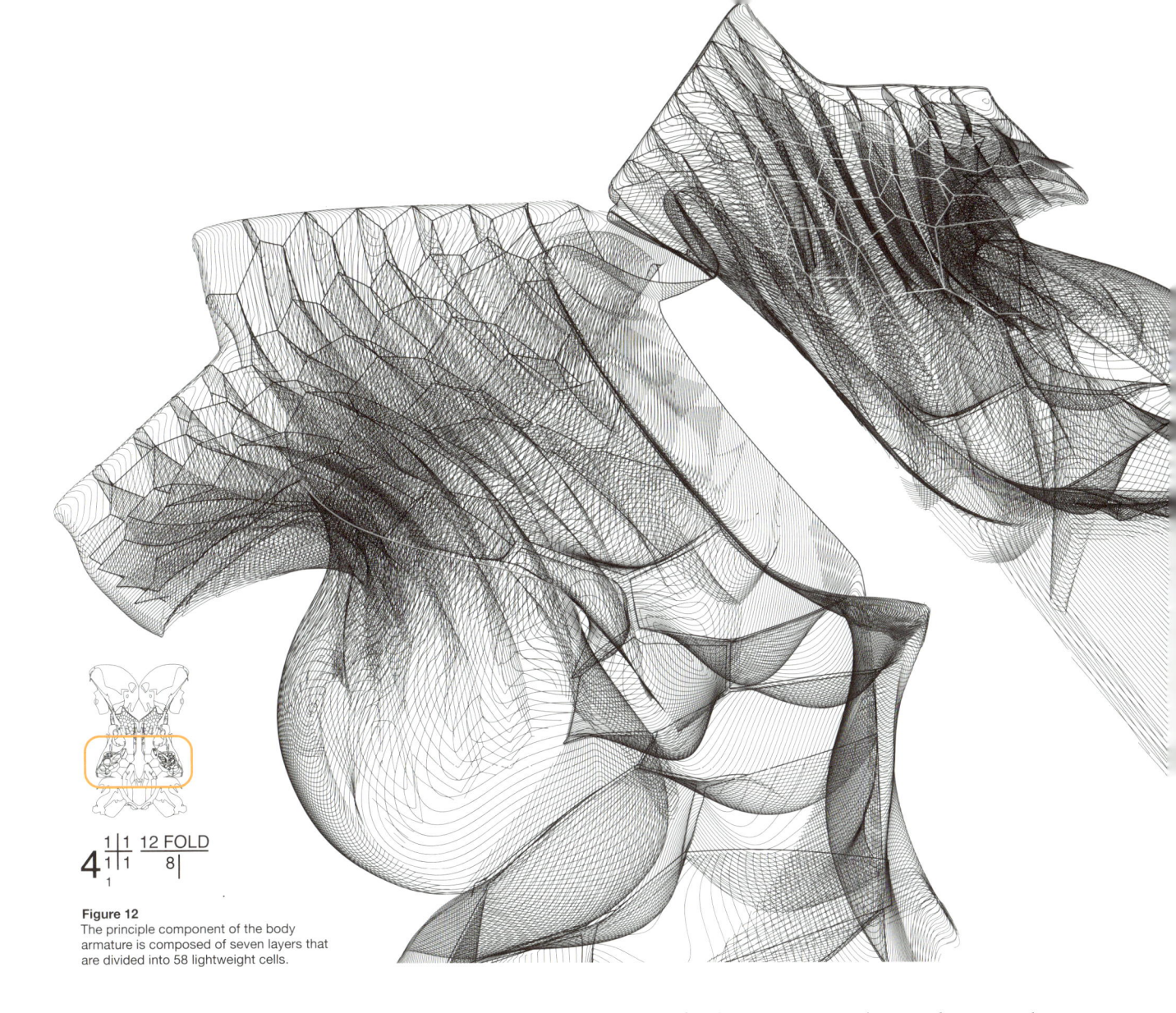

Figure 12
The principle component of the body armature is composed of seven layers that are divided into 58 lightweight cells.

surface area of every part and its outline responded differently to the pressure of the folding.

I wanted to draw up a way for the whole body to emerge through the communication of the disparate drawing methodologies and their material interactions without fully describing the form in advance. It is important to note that while the logic of capacity can be very precise, its transmission varies by degree.[12] This leads to an important distinction between biology and our current architectural discourse that associates variation with type, and variability with dynamical systems or changes in degree. With the *Orbigraphia* I sought to engage both logics, but it also became apparent that the design benefited the most from the variability of the material. The responsiveness between the parts and the paper folding gave way to character, and it also revealed that the capacities of each part were enough to produce a simple circuit, something that the drawings alone did not have the inertia to achieve.

I sought to formulate a similar attitude toward developing complexity: not through the morphology of the forms themselves, but through their unpredictable interactions. The tangency of the unrelated parts, the bleeding of ink washes, and the manicured discontinuity of the pre-existing patterns, established a working circuit. As new information was drawn in, its capacity to interact with other features was tested. These material interactions became the accepted behavior of designing any part and turning it into an organ, and by this I mean designing something that is inside of something else, as opposed to a feature or blemish that is developed superficially, on top of a surface. (Fig. 9) The interspersing of the ink, like the

Process Work

Dorsal   **Interior**   **Ventral**

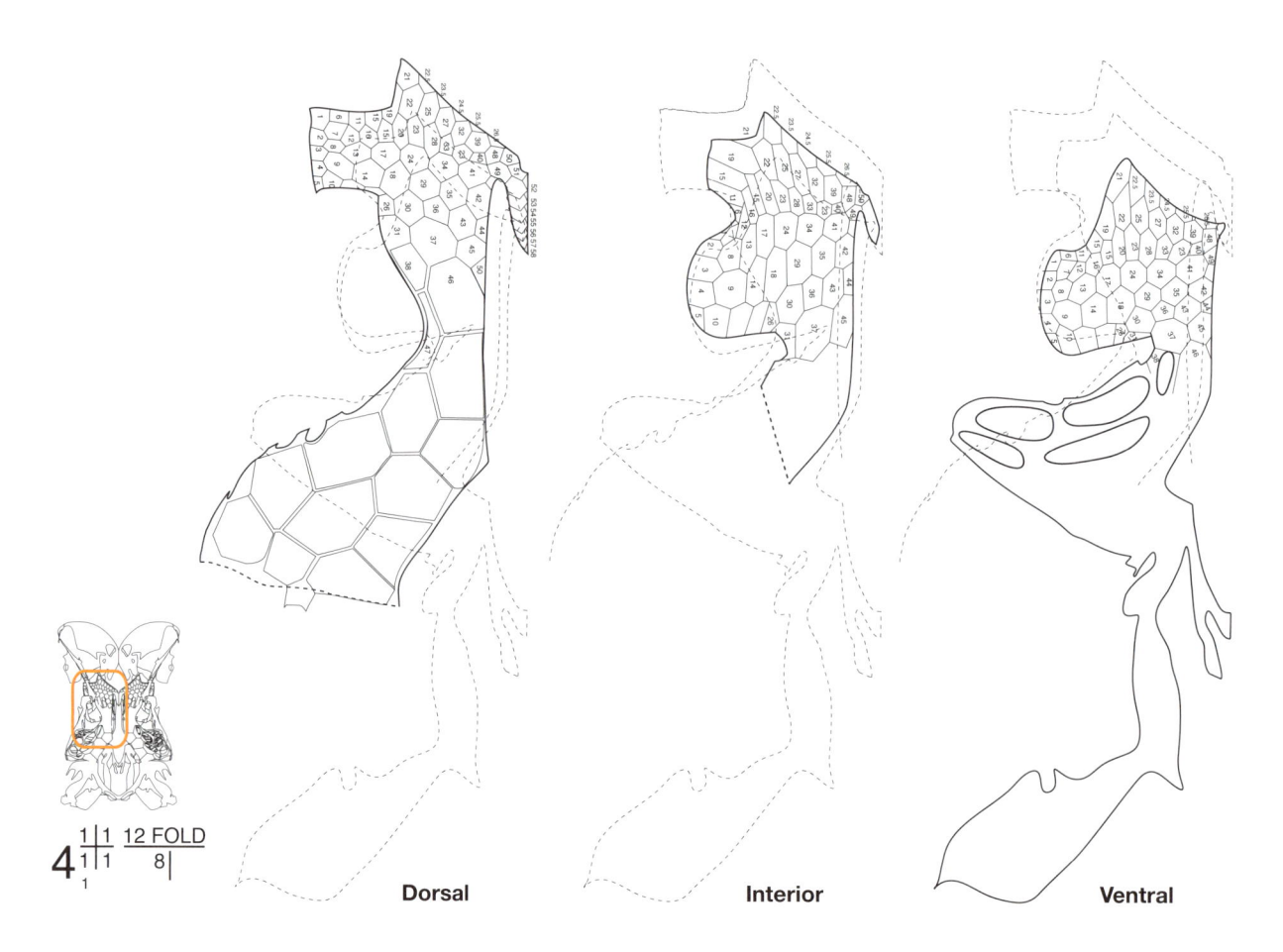

Figure 13
Three slices through the celluloid geometry. Top left is the dorsal layer. Pattern information from the surface is subdivided manually into cells and pulled through the section of the torso as a series of parallel membranes. These cells comprise the lower portion of the organism and stiffen its midsection.

folding, helped spur a sharper imagination for the depth of things. This is the part of making the drawings that I ascribe to developing a design behavior that initiates the form of things: it is a process that moved rather directly from the sensations of the drawings, to the formulation of heterogeneously interconnected parts.

Optical Facts: Microscopic

The microscopic observations of English eighteenth-century natural philosopher Robert Hooke provide another source of inspiration. A polymath, Hooke was an architect, urban planner, geometer, physicist (who aided Robert Boyle in his gas theory experiments), astronomer (he also designed and built telescopes), and biologist—an early proponent of evolution, the father of microscopy, and coiner of the term "cell" as the basic unit of life. Hooke was one of the most renowned inventors of his time, and his desire to invent things fueled his curiosity for nature.

In the *Micrographia*, a compendium of his microscopic observations, Hooke sets out to produce a catalog of exemplary illustrations of the natural world. To accomplish this, he uses the microscope to reveal what he identifies as the *subsensible* organizations of nature in great detail:

> The next care to be taken, in respect of the Senses, is a supplying of their infirmities with Instruments, and as it were the adding of artificial Organs to the natural; this one of them has been of late years accomplished with the prodigious benefit to all sorts of useful knowledge, by the invention of Optical Glasses.[13]

In the preface to the *Micrographia*, Hooke insists that his research will provide scientific certainty into the workings of nature, but he eventually conceded that there were territories that remained imperceptible to his microscope.[14] The subsensible is an important concept for several reasons: first, because it establishes the need for an alternate pictorial representation that renders things sharper than they appear; second, it reconfigures the relative scale between things; and third, it often requires its own instruments.

Hooke's microscope employed lenses he ground himself. His observations of the natural world were recorded as engravings and were widely distributed in England. The etchings are remarkable in their detail. He also complained that there were minute organizations that remained imperceptible through the magnifications provided by his microscope. Not only does he encounter the limits of his lenses, their optical distortions, air bubbles, and the like, but he also accepts that the optics were incompatible with achieving certainty—a fully objective, total, or exemplary view.[15] What makes his drawings even more remarkable is his ability to precisely communicate the physiologies without removing the aura of the microscope. His engravings portray the sensations of what it was like to see through the microscope and this was equally significant to the content of his observations. The intricacy of the surfaces and the character of the light presented the public with an often blurry, but entirely new sensibility.[16] His observations introduced a format for drawing that is unfettered by the distinctions between the essential and the supplemental, or the structural and the ornamental. The fidelity of his engravings leads us to forget that the act of drawing a subsensible world is a speculative process.

I wanted to extend Hooke's remarkable modulation of light and use of contours into the third dimension. I also wanted the thickness of each element in the *Orbigraphia* to reflect the intensity of the color that had been painted onto the templates. This was accomplished by tying the frequency of the colors to the frequency of a curve. (Fig. 15) Since color depends on frequency and wavelength, with reds having the lowest frequency wavelengths and violet the highest, it was possible to correlate the apparent vibrancy of the animal coloration—or its coloring sensation—to particular curvatures.[17] To study this, colors from the swallowtail patterning were used to construct a series of thickened NURBS surfaces with varying wavelengths and amplitudes. (Fig. 17) The resultant topology is similar to pushing inward on the surface of a cylinder from two sides until the surfaces intersect one another, producing a torus. This process was repeated multiple times, using two parallel surfaces with different amplitudes to attain the pattern. In this way, the false luminosity of the coloring sensation was used to generate the cross section of a new surface. Unexpectedly, the intersections of these amplitudes produced a new pattern with its own frequency of holes. (Fig. 16) The modeling gradually progressed from surfaces to solids, while the contouring involved slicing each of the sixty parts, separately, and at small increments, to reveal the cross section. The pitch—or angle—of the cutting plane was used to modulate the contouring effects. This was handled on a case-by-case basis to determine the proper density and cutting orientation for each part, including the appropriate level of overlap between the contours. (Fig. 9)

Conclusion

The *Orbigraphia* is a reflection on architectural drawing as a framework for thinking and sensing. These drawings emerge in opposition to the role of drawing as a mechanism of productivity while looking for innovative ways to redirect the speed and complexity of our tools. Much of what I have discussed here pertains to the act of designing, the limitations of our tools on our imaginations, and the molding of facts into a diagram. I have attempted to clarify how drawing is an extension of our human ability to sense, and that facts emerge in this process through reason, accident, and intuition. The act of drawing architecture is obligated with representing something physical, and lines serve this purpose well, but in painting, by contrast, marks are tied to sensation and can operate free of measure. This distinction separates our disciplines; I want to encourage its re-embrace. So many of an architect's lines are in the service of description rather than sensation; to the untrained eye it is difficult to distinguish them apart, and even more so once they are built. All of the theories that I have discussed here could be put to work as scientific economies of architectural production, or saddled with qualitative assessments of performance. Instead, I hope that the *Orbigraphia* offer enough evidence that these facts should persist as vital dimensions of our design culture and our discipline.

Figure 14
Detail of the 3 Degree Body

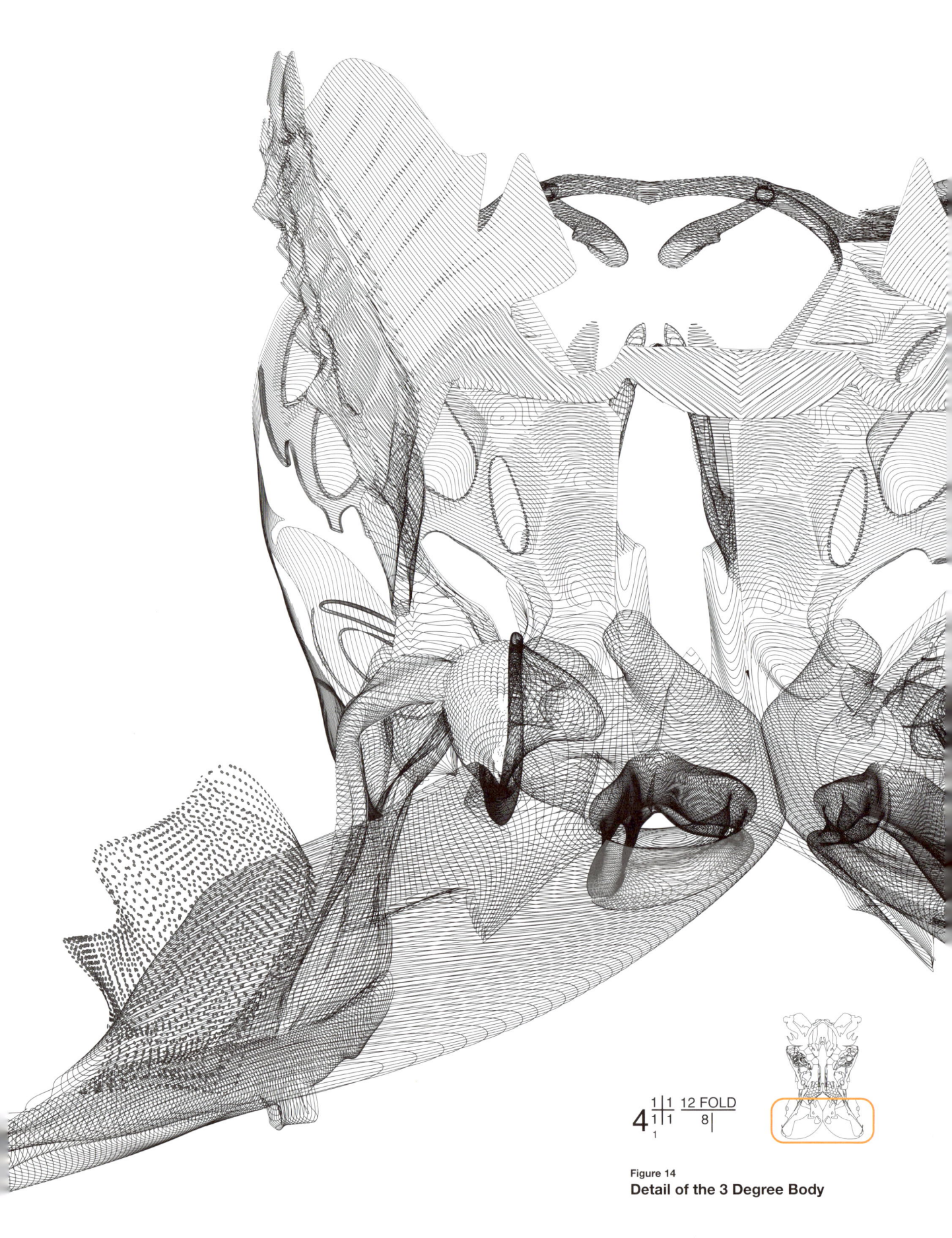

128   **Orbigraphia** Rhett Russo

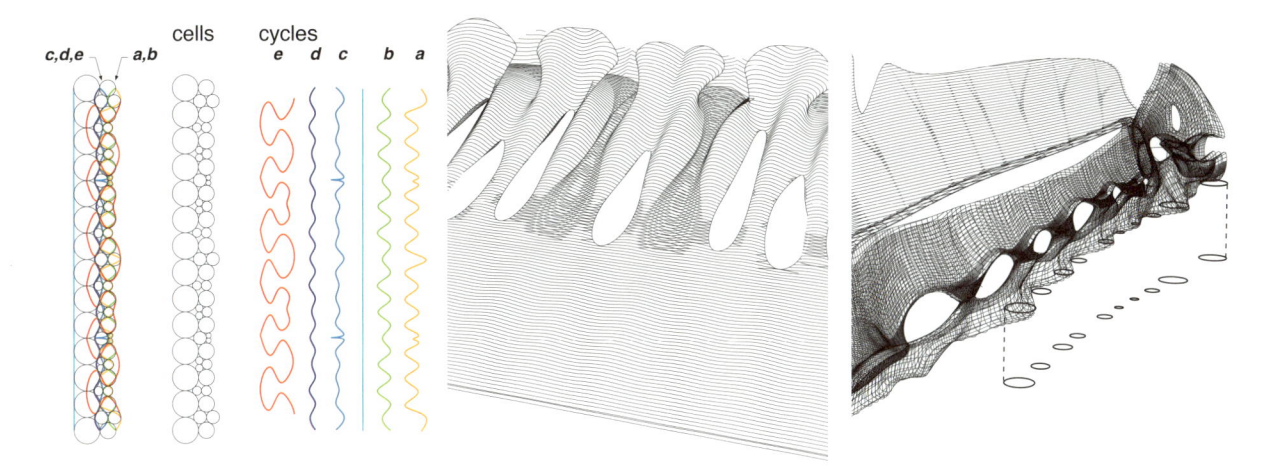

Figure 15
The coloring sensation expressed as amplitudes and lines. The frequencies were developed from the swallowtail butterfly wing. Each color is registered as a cyclic wave.

Figure 16
The waves are compiled into a pair of intersecting surfaces that cancel each other out, producing alternating holes and hollows.

Figure 17
As the cycles increase in length, the surface area of the wing ripples along its edge.

Endnotes

1 The invention of a UCS (User Coordinate System) in CAD software made it possible to reposition individual drawings anywhere in space so that each contains its own set of world coordinates. This is similar to the repositioning of the picture plane in descriptive geometry and stone masonry as a means to acquire the true length of any line segment, regardless of its position or orientation in space.

2 See Michael Allaby, *A Dictionary of Zoology* (New York: Oxford University Press, 1999). *Bauplan* is a zoological term that refers to "the generalized body plan of an archetypal member of a major taxonomy." See also Jakob Von Uexküll, *Theoretical Biology* (London: K. Paul, Trench, Trubner & Co, 1926); pp. 110-111. As a means of classification, morphology, or comparative anatomy, *bauplan* did not explain the relationship between form and function—according to von Uexküll, it was unsatisfactory because it overlooked the role of material.

3 See Steven Wolfram, *A New Kind of Science* (Champaign, IL: Wolfram Media, 2002); p. 1007. Biological systems often show definite discrete symmetry. In monocotyledon plants there is usually 3-fold symmetry; in dicotyledons 4- or 5-fold; animals like starfish often have 5-fold symmetry; higher animals usually only 2-fold symmetry. There are fossils with 7- and 9-fold symmetry. At microscopic levels there are sometimes other symmetries: cilia of eukaryotic cells can for example show 9- and 13-fold symmetry.

4 For more commentary on the folding of flat sheets of tissue in organisms see Wolfram, *A New Kind of Science*, p. 417.

5 See William P. Thurston, "The Geometry and Topology of Three–Manifolds," lectures given at Princeton University, 1980 (web edition at http://www.msri.org/publications/books/gt3m/); Ch. 2, p. 9. These classifications sometimes appear under other names. The Euclidian, spherical and hyperbolic dimensions are more fully described in his lecture notes.

6 See Thurston, "The Geometry and Topology of Three–Manifolds," p. 300. Thurston's sketch of the Borromean rings as a transformation of a cube accompanies his lecture notes on Orbifolds and helps to visually describe the transformation of the homological structure.

7 It is worth noting that many of the orbits failed to produce stiffness, and the redundancy of the stiffest solutions were often the least elegant.

8 Uexküll knew Walter Benjamin and influenced the development of phenomenology and hermeneutics, and philosophists such as Martin Heidegger, Maurice Merleau-Ponty, Gilles Deleuze, Félix Guattari and Giorgio Agamben.

9 This distinction likely influenced those made by Walter Benjamin and Martin Heidegger: "experience"—*Efrarung*—versus "existence"—*Erlebnis*—for Benjamin, or "being-in-the-world" versus measurable space for Heidegger.

10 Uexküll, *Theoretical Biology*, pp. 156-7.

11 Gilles Deleuze and Félix Guattari, *A Thousand Plateaus: Capitalism & Schizophrenia* (London: University of Minnesota Press, 1987); p. 257. Uexküll "looks for the active and passive affects of which the animal is capable in the individuated assemblage of which it is part."

12 Deleuze and Guattari acknowledge Uexküll's use of degree to describe how receptors respond to subtle changes in their environment—such as changes in temperature or smell—that in turn effect how animals behave. For more on this see Uexküll *Theoretical Biology*, pp. 76-7. He places the ability to sense thresholds, or *mark signs*, as a determining factor in identifying how complex an organism is.

13 Robert Hooke, *Micrographia, or, Some Physiological Descriptions of Minute Bodies Made by Magnifying Glasses: With Observations and Inquiries Thereupon* (1665); p. 8.

14 See Hooke, *Micrographia*, p. 8.

15 See Hooke, *Micrographia*, p. 15.

16 See Barbara Maria Stafford, *Body Criticism: Imaging the Unseen in Enlightenment Art & Medicine* (Cambridge, Mass.: MIT Press, 1991), p. 353. Barbara Maria Stafford has identified a fundamental paradox revealed by Hooke's work, particularly the observations he made of a sewing needle. Stafford sees the work of the biologist here as political—aiming to undermine the world of art and artifice by showing its "rudeness" compared to the sophistication of even the most "paltry fragments" of the natural world. The microscopic image of the needle destroyed its semblance of smoothness, and revealed its numerous imperfections: pock marks, divots and blotches that, along side, the organisms he studied, made it inferior. The research that began as an endeavor to encapsulate the complexity of nature, ended with the revelation that not only was the natural world superior in its refinement; but that the threshold for order was infinite.

17 See Gilles Deleuze, *Francis Bacon: The Logic of Sensation* (Minneapolis: University of Minnesota Press, 2005); p. 92. Deleuze describes the coloring sensation in the paintings of Cezanne: "It is thus a temporal diagram, with two moments. But the diagram connects these two moments indissolubly: the geometry is its "frame" and the color is the sensation, the *coloring sensation*." This relationship also holds true in animal patterning, except that the sensation that arises between the pattern and form is often exaggerated by the surface geometry to such a degree that it is misconstrued for another form. The relationship between color and curvature was explored as an alternative method for generating surfaces.

Branching Morphogenesis
A Tale of Imagination, Translation and Visualization

Sabin+Jones LabStudio
Essay by Annette Fierro

Branching Morphogenesis, originally installed at the 2008 SIGGRAPH Design and Computation Galleries in Los Angeles, and since exhibited in 2010 at Ars Electronica in Linz, Austria, is the tangible outcome of a collaboration of architects and biologists within the methodological precinct of both the laboratory and the design studio environment. Jenny E. Sabin of PennDesign and Peter Lloyd Jones of the Institute for Medicine and Engineering at the University of Pennsylvania, joined recently by Andrew Lucia, established the interdisciplinary LabStudio in 2007. This essay focuses on a particular aspect of this exploration: the errant, wild, and transformative leaps of imagination that result when material intuition encounters practices of visualization between two fields. When these conflate a fertile ground is generated where ideas hatch and are nursed and transfigured according to linear as well as elusive logics. What follows is a tale of a design process, with all its slippery rigor and a short scoop on translations between mediums and collaborators.

Branching Morphogenesis began in formal scientific observation, a real-time documentation in the Jones lab of branched vascular structures that form between lung endothelial cells and a three-dimensional biological matrix. Tracing the influence of the cells on this matrix and vice versa, the original microscopic movie evinces a silent communication between living tissues. Manifested as forces and movements through a viscous medium, a dance emerges between cells as they pull and stretch toward each other and upon their matrix to form an ensemble. Through a series of shifting phase states, random connections between them evolve from disorder to order. Like many—if not all—biological models, the images and videos of the cells are significant imaginative devices, immediately triggering associations far beyond their physical properties. The dance of these cells is one loaded with desire and rejection. Their tendrils become limbs flailing for contact. This communication is animalistic—meanings are suggested and intuited, but their ultimate draw is in an indecipherability that begs codes and translations in order to be understood.

A datascape was created to meet the hermeneutic need of this Dr. Seuss-like microworld. The original cell network modeling was posed as a set of sequenced rules, modeling the cell interactions against matrix points contrived as a system of attractors, and against continually redistributed forces that permeate the surrounding matrix.[1] The digital tools developed for the model expressed the intangible forces exerted by the matrix on the cells, emphasizing the influence of environment rather than the actions or compositions of the cells themselves. Through the next iterations, the datascape was still tied definitively to the

Facing Page
Branching Morphogenesis (Interior View)
The installation is a scaled datascape that captured a creative process encompassing design and science. Made from >75,000 interconnected cable zip-ties, with each one representing a datapoint, it simulated the computationally predicted forces generated by human pulmonary artery endothelial cells as they interact with one another and with their surrounding extracellular matrix environment in three-dimensional space over time during capillary formation. At all stages of the filtering and scaling process, the network was adjusted by new constraints. The final artifact was a synthesis, a *biosynthesis*, for people to inhabit.

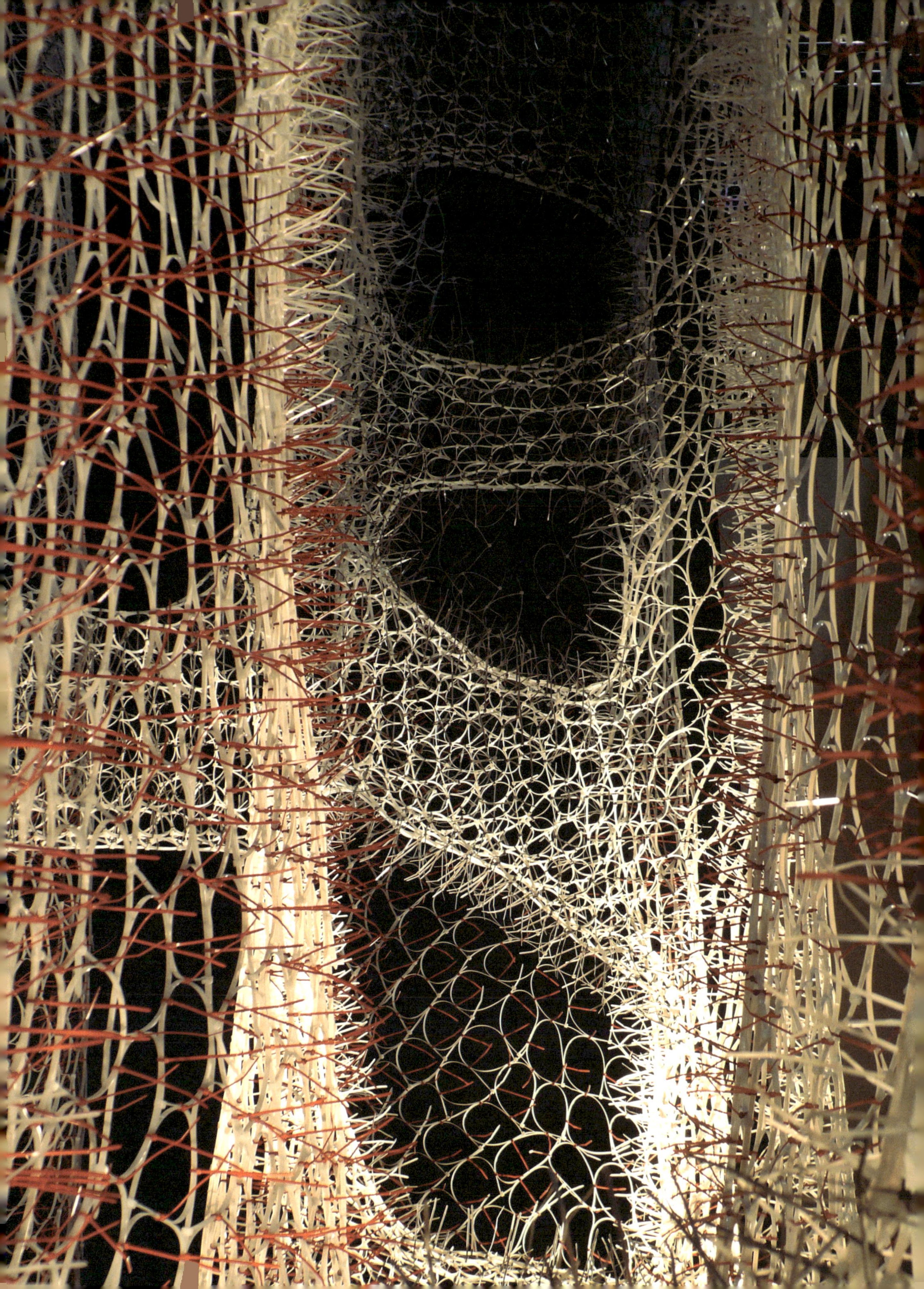

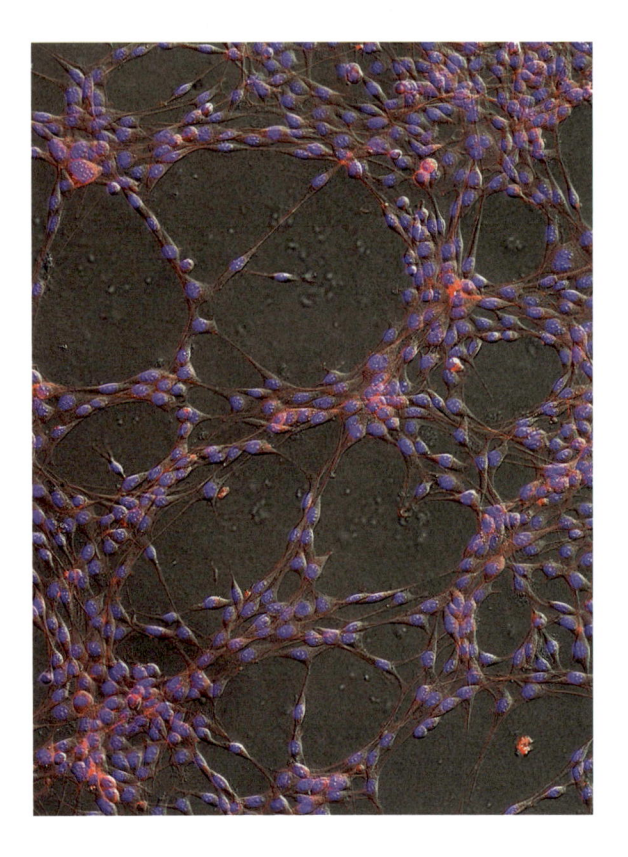

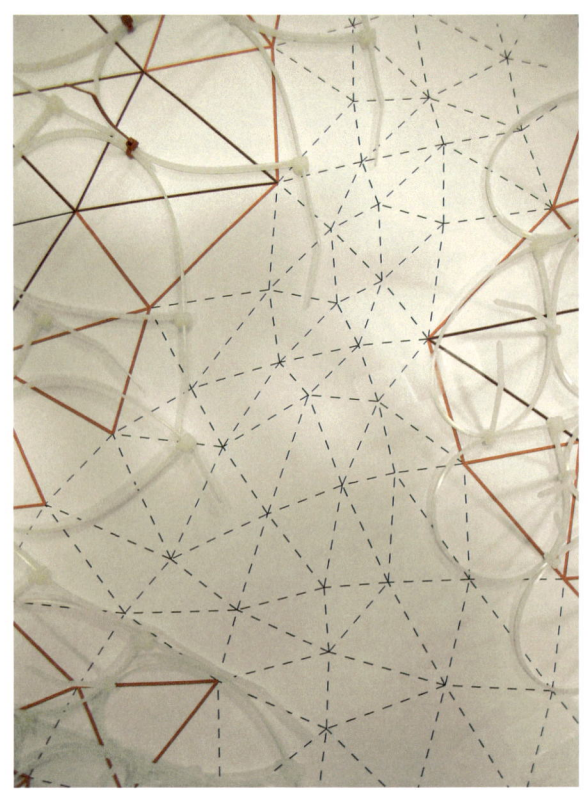

observed phenomena, ostensibly able to be measured and put to use by scientists as diagnostic or other immediately purposeful uses.

Not so at the next state, where this mapping device was materialized, and in this critical translation scientific description turned into architectural invention through a forced confrontation of pure data and physical material, in media whose properties were entirely other to the original phenomena. The material—or perhaps *input*—chosen by Sabin was the "zip-tie," the little plastic cord that magically bundles together a mess of electrical cables. This unit of material enabled large-scale installation at minimal cost, but was more importantly understood as a cognitive device, ordinary material recognizable upon quick scrutiny, a "ready-made." The final conception of the installation came from a happenstance attendance at a dance performance, where the stage consisted of a vast layering of hanging wires, a filmy stratification with bodies moving in and out of fore and background spaces.

How, then, to take an informational field—an objectively construed device—and call forth associational intentions while remaining devoted to the factuality of the data

within? How to manipulate an empirical reading into a visual quest, generated analogically, with a particular scale and material reality? How to transform the informational field into one that was episodically blurred, illegible at some moments and popping into clear focus at others? Five meshes taken from different time frames of the biological simulations were overlapped together; producing a kind of indeterminacy and blur resistant to immediate comprehension. At moments of difference between the overlaps, the eye strains to focus the lines back into rectitude. That the datascape was itself insistently elusive in its potential to be read easily, its resistance to immediate comprehension, is consistent: within the disjunction between knowing all but refusing to know-it-all, the imaginative operation works to keep the transformational capacity of the piece alive. We are meant to be frustrated in grasping the final image as composed and finite, and must pursue yet another hermeneutical jaunt, another imaginative ruse. What does it mean? And at this point, might that question matter less than what does it *looks like*?

The final transformation of the piece into full-scale construction began first by assigning each intersection of

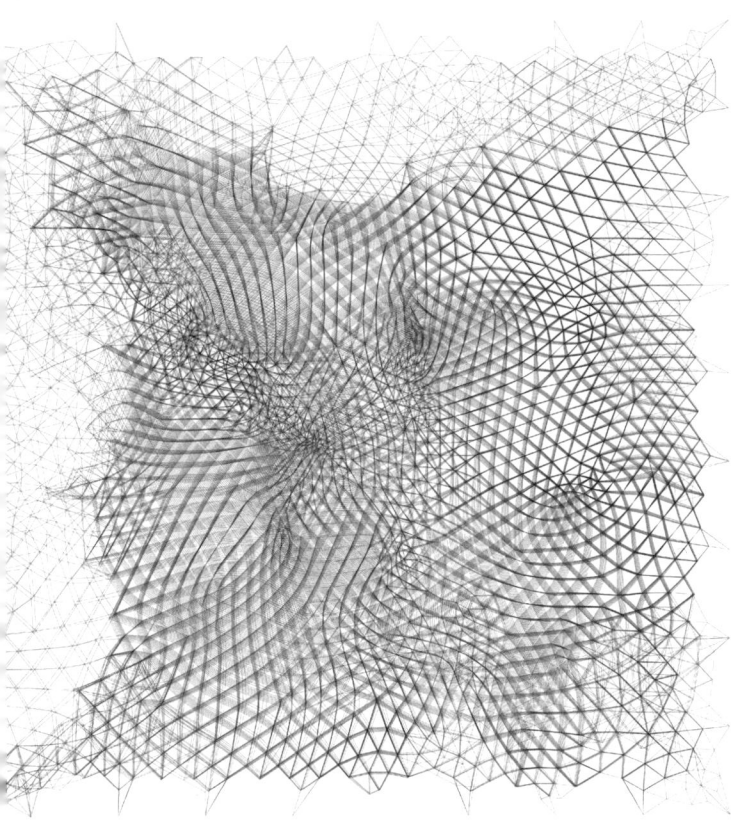

From Left

Endothelial Cell Matrix

The primary function of the lung is to allow for efficient gas exchange between the airways and blood vessels in post-natal life onwards. However, determining how networks of blood vessels are generated and maintained during development represents a major challenge in contemporary lung biology. The aim of this project was to sequentially model the networking process in tissue culture and *in silico*, and then to abstract this process into experimental architecture. To approach this, we studied the parameters that govern blood vessel development at the scale of capillaries in response to the surrounding extracellular matrix (ECM) microenvironment, and how modifying cell and ECM density affects the networking process. Along these lines, we investigated, via simulations, potential parameters that alter networking behavior, including intercellular communication, environmental instigators, and cellular geometry.

Assembly and Diagram

To generate *Branching Morphogenesis*, time-lapse microscopic images of networking endothelial cells cultured in the presence of a 3-D matrix were analyzed to generate computational tools that simulate this process. Next, large-scale 1:1 templates from simulations were overlaid with >75,000 inter-connected zip-ties.

Network Simulations

During the first phase of the design and production of *Branching Morphogenesis*, time-lapse images of cultured endothelial cells forming networks in response to an ECM were captured via videomicroscopy. These images were then used to generate custom-written algorithms in simulation software to abstract and visualize endothelial cell networking behavior. Importantly, at the cell biological level, this computational tool, devised by a close collaboration between architectural designers and scientists, allowed for pre-testing of experimental hypotheses *in silico*.

---

each mesh to one zip-tie, now looped. Repeated and lying together on a large two-dimensional field, the loops were tied tightly together by more zip-ties in the vertical plane, color-coded to reflect the force of the original matrix. At the most intense moments, the field projected vertically, funneling to the next layer, another slice in time.

Altogether there were 75,000 zip-ties. For months, up to twenty people could be seen tying the zip-ties together across full-scale templates laid out on a gallery floor. Through the tedium, music played, films were projected, gossip flowed freely; the production had spawned a social dimension, becoming a quilting bee of sorts and a material tracing of a summer's worth of associated experiences. Translated once again, material components, physically handled and manipulated over time, re-recorded the cell network and refigured it significantly by both the inexactitudes of the joinery and the indelibility of social narrative. In the gallery, *Branching Morphogenesis* took on a new life, a work founded on immutable scientific information open to viewers' personal associations, images and experiences. Each constituency had their own version: workmen on a job site hooted with glee as they recognized the component of the installation as dearly familiar; gallery-goers hesitated before entering, wondering if this was an artwork or fabric partition. An anatomical joke? A datascape.

The moment of straining for significant re-reading is a potent one, a space of heavy delay in which the silent meander of the imagination is engaged. In the end *Branching Morphogenesis* represents the polarities involved in regarding the generation of architectural form through computational iteration. Often represented as derived and driven by a set of automatic procedures, this misapprehension is confronted by the actualities of the configuration of this piece, as subjectively informed at every step as it was driven by the incorporation of the subject herself, in the micro and macro spaces of the body. It is also about the materialization of the body—no longer as medical specimen or data, but as art, material, aesthetics, and as expression, space, and aura. The piece operates within a tradition in which art recuperates the body, reciting its imminence, and thus both incorporating and transcending the political.

But what of the original obligation of *Branching Morphogenesis* to science—was this shelved in the

Final Installation
The final installation (12-feet high x15-feet wide x 8-feet deep), made up of five vertical sheets representing the forces that cells generate upon their adjacent ECM at specific phases in time during the formation of branched blood vessel networks. Gallery visitors are invited to walk around and in-between the layers, thereby immersing themselves within a newly created "Datascape", fusing dynamic cellular change with human occupation, all through the constraints of a ready-made.

quest for architecture? There is nothing measurable about the finally materialized and installed version of *Branching Morphogenesis*, but that is not its ultimate instrumental value. Bruno Latour has argued that it is within the innovations of the graphic representation of scientific information—where new types of images were contrived to "transport the objects of the world,"—that paradigmatic shifts in scientific thinking have emerged.[2] Noting that every new scientific discipline has been dependent on a new visual and written language, he marks the significance of these new languages not for practical implementation, but more fundamentally in their potential for cognitive ideation. His point is simple yet profound: different modes of intuition conflate through visualization. He gives a lovely example in the measuring of liquid in two types of containers, one a tall thin beaker, one a short flat one. While the measure of equal liquids is obviously the same in each container, the "notion of volume" is prompted by the different shapes, and this idea itself is more fundamentally provocative to the scientific imagination than are the actual measurements. The point: the image contributes the essence of the scientific idea far more effectively than the numerical reading.

By inscribing data in different media and materials through a rigorous process, *Branching Morphogenesis*

Detail View

spawns an imagistic device intrinsic to its instrumentality, perhaps more so than the datafield itself, simultaneously suggesting that modes of imagination in the two disciplines were never so far away as we had all presumed.

Endnotes
1   The models by Andrew Lucia and Christopher Lee were developed in Sabin and Jones' graduate seminar, *Nonlinear Systems Biology and Design,* at PennDesign.
2   Bruno Latour, "Visualization and Cognition: Thinking with Eyes and Hands," in Knowledge and Society: Studies in the Sociology of Culture Past and Present, vol. 6 (Greenwich: JAI Press, 1986); pp. 1-40. My thanks to John Tresch for this reference.

Secret Pact of Parts
Of Plants and Parametrics
Ferda Kolatan

Again ye come, ye hovering forms. I find ye, as early to my clouded sight ye shone! Shall I attempt, this once, to seize and bind ye?
> Johann Wolfang von Goethe, *Faust* (1806)

Anyone who has paid even a little attention to plant growth will readily see that certain external parts of the plant undergo frequent change and take on the shape of the adjacent parts – sometimes fully, sometimes more and sometimes less.
> Johann Wolfang von Goethe, *Metamorphosis of Plants* (1790)

In 1786 the poet, historian, and naturalist Johann Wolfgang von Goethe left his native Germany to embark on a momentous journey to Italy. During this visit, which lasted for months and took him as far as Sicily, he became so intrigued by the rich and diverse occurrences of plant life in the Mediterranean climate that he began a series of scientific observations that would eventually culminate in his famous work, *Metamorphosis of Plants,* in 1790.[1]

In eighteen short chapters, *Metamorphosis* describes in minute detail the formative processes of plant development. Chapter titles such as "Of the Seed Leaves," "Transition to the Flower," and "Formation of the Stamens" along with a concise narrative seemingly demonstrate the author's desire to front an empiricist view and position this treatise in the realm of pure science. The linear, step-by-step progression of his descriptive prose further enforces a strict causal logic, inevitable and incorruptible. And yet, reading through the first few chapters, the text quickly transcends the systemic, methodological language and begins to formulate a much deeper concept.

Goethe was already enthralled for some time by what his friend and congenial classicist poet, Friedrich Schiller, would later call a *philosophical idea*.[2] This idea revolved around the notion of the "Urpflanze" (archetypal plant), a singular leaf or cell from which all variety sprouts both within a particular species as well as in all flora.[3] For Goethe, this idea was far more essential than just an isolated exercise in morphology, since he believed that all material manifestations were manifold expressions of a single, all-encompassing principle developed over time.[3] In this context, his descriptions of the formative processes of plants become both proto-evolutionary, as well as an exposition on totality.

This alone was a remarkable scientific insight, given that Goethe's observations preceded both Darwin's theory of evolution and Mendel's genetic experiments.[4] This is particularly so if one considers that Goethe was passionately derided by many of his peers as a hobby scientist and an amateur naturalist altogether better suited for poetry than research. However, it was precisely this Universalist attitude that enabled Goethe to engage his topic in an interpretative and intuitive fashion. Objectivity was confined to the description of the transformative nature of plant morphology and then eloquently guided to support and verify his *philosophical idea*. Only in this intricate combination of knowledge and idea did Goethe see a meaningful approach toward an understanding of the principles of nature.

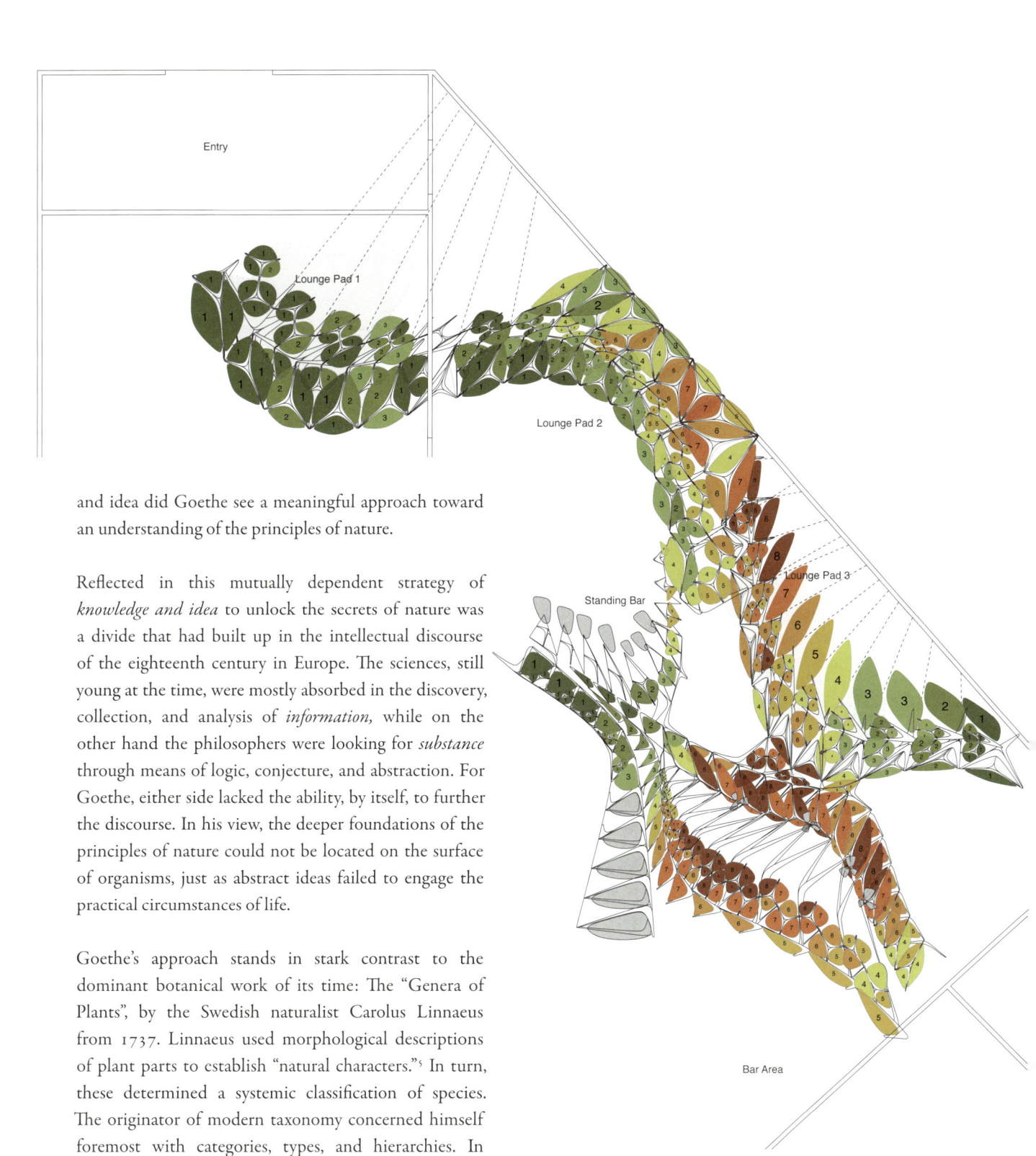

Reflected in this mutually dependent strategy of *knowledge and idea* to unlock the secrets of nature was a divide that had built up in the intellectual discourse of the eighteenth century in Europe. The sciences, still young at the time, were mostly absorbed in the discovery, collection, and analysis of *information,* while on the other hand the philosophers were looking for *substance* through means of logic, conjecture, and abstraction. For Goethe, either side lacked the ability, by itself, to further the discourse. In his view, the deeper foundations of the principles of nature could not be located on the surface of organisms, just as abstract ideas failed to engage the practical circumstances of life.

Goethe's approach stands in stark contrast to the dominant botanical work of its time: The "Genera of Plants", by the Swedish naturalist Carolus Linnaeus from 1737. Linnaeus used morphological descriptions of plant parts to establish "natural characters."[5] In turn, these determined a systemic classification of species. The originator of modern taxonomy concerned himself foremost with categories, types, and hierarchies. In Linnaeus' understanding, character is based on the anatomic feature-set of a part that identifies an origin. In other words, it is a measure of differentiation. For Goethe, on the other hand, character is expressed by the interaction of parts, continuity, and transmutation.

CHROMAZON

Process Work 137

Figure 1
CHROMAZON
Stem, Leaf, and Petal Configurations.

Figure 2
CHROMAZON
Perspective View

While the former is mainly concerned with a definition of *what is*, the latter concentrates on an approach to *what becomes*.

This shift from a static notion of character to a dynamic one is critical because it necessarily reaches into the realm of environments, forces, and fields. Sanford Kwinter writes about Goethe's concept of type "as an abstract formative principle to be acted upon by other primary transformative processes."[6] These processes, whether internal or external, are fundamental as they create a multi-directional, material information exchange within which, over time, form is manifested. The organism's origin is not revealed in any one particular shape, but by continual formal expressions of its generative forces. In an interesting twist, Detlef Mertins refers to the shift from static to mobile form as a "transformation that leads *to and from the product* and eventually to a generative field of movement."[7] The product in this case is not just the result of forces, but rather an enabler of growth through which any change needs to be calibrated—at once a point of departure *and* arrival.

To study Goethe's and his contemporaries' positions on form, laws, and nature is illuminating as they echo in many ways aspects of the discourse surrounding parametric design today. The interpretation of the role of parts in relationship to the organism (whole) and the varying definitions of *character* in reference to shape, identity, and concept are useful devices to set up criteria for evaluating parametric work, but also to help speculate about larger cultural ramifications that lead to interesting questions: How are part-to-whole affiliations advanced by parametric processes? What governs the relationship between the systemic and the intuitive? Is there a novel character emerging in designs that are produced with this tool? These questions belong together and proved instrumental in designing a number of projects in our practice, su11 architecture+design. I would like to introduce two of them in more detail below.

CHROMAZON

CHROMAZON was one of the finalist projects for the 2008 MoMA/PS1 Young Architects Program (YAP). The brief called for a leisure installation in the PS1 courtyard that incorporated sun shading, reclining areas, and a stimulating backdrop for the weekly rave parties held there during the summer. The project title sums up our main ideas for the installation: to create an atmosphere of tropical exuberance through a simple, yet highly *manipulable,* systemic device. We also wanted to generate a *synthetic organism* with characteristics that would oscillate between familiar references to nature as well as unknown and strange ones. The "strange" quality was to be addressed by synthesizing the floral connotations of the forms through digital and parametric processes.

Secret Pact of Parts Ferda Kolatan

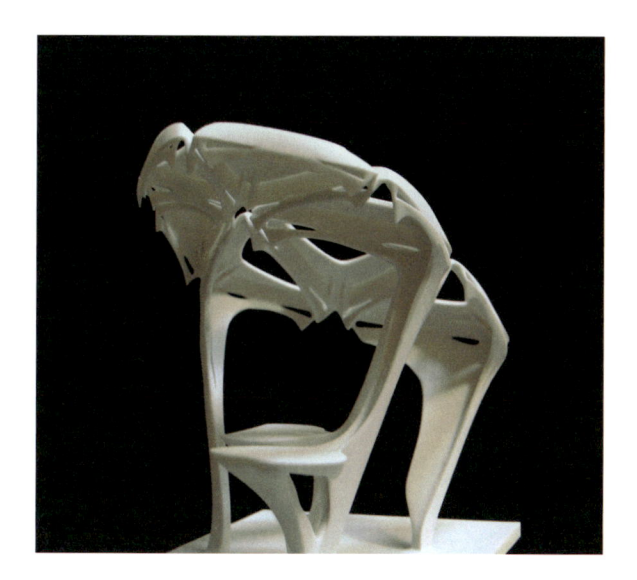

Figure 3
PS_Canopy
Model showing morphological transformation.

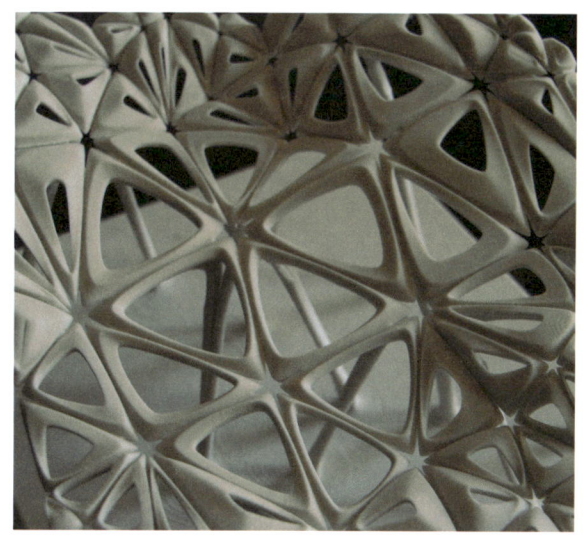

Figure 4
PS_Canopy
Model top view with varying petal formations.

The first problem we approached was the initial part-to-whole setup. While we did have an image or *idea* in mind before we began, we did not immediately translate it into a fixed organization of components. Instead we established a parametric system with networked relationships that could produce a range of behavioral effects, controlled by global variables. The morphology of the whole was driving the process as we sought to create expressions of movement, rhythm, and pulse. To support this strategy, the parts themselves needed to become incremental, serial, and *differentiated*. Thus, each component is defined by a number of features and classified as a single character, forming stem (structure), leaf (table), or petal (shade) (Fig. 1). The scale and geometry of the parts vary without transmuting from one to the other or transgressing their own boundaries.

While the subordinate character of the parts was necessary to achieve some of the desired effects of CHROMAZON, we also wanted to introduce a component that would willfully undermine a singular and categorical reading of the parts. This component was color. We created a palette of eight swatches with a color range typically found in tropical forests and distributed them over the whole project. We followed two main criteria in doing so: first, to further amplify effects of rhythmic pulsation and to create different atmospheric intensities, shades of red, orange, and green that generate vastly different moods were utilized to change the spatial feel along the underbelly of the canopy; and second, to blur the distinction between the individual parts and to bleed them into a single totality.

In CHROMAZON parametric systems were applied in almost a *musical* way. The original setup displayed a constant beat with no variations at all. Changing the variables allowed us to introduce different tempi without having to break the coherence of the overall organization. The interconnected nature of the model assured that any rhythmic change would have repercussions that would flow through the rest of the structure, sometimes accelerating the effects, sometimes slowing them down. The color component acts as an additional layer, dependent on the parts yet autonomous enough to blend them further together. The character of this piece is determined by the contiguous relationship of parts as they transform gradually within a totality that localizes physical and visual intensities and by the atmospheric effects they produce.

PS_Canopy

PS stands for Pluripotent Structure. Pluripotency is a term used in cellular biology to describe cells with more than one potential outcome.[8] Stem cells are pluripotent as they can develop into specialized types with different capacities. Invited to participate in SIGGRAPH's Generative Fabrication exhibition in 2009, we developed PS_Canopy as a prototype with the aim to

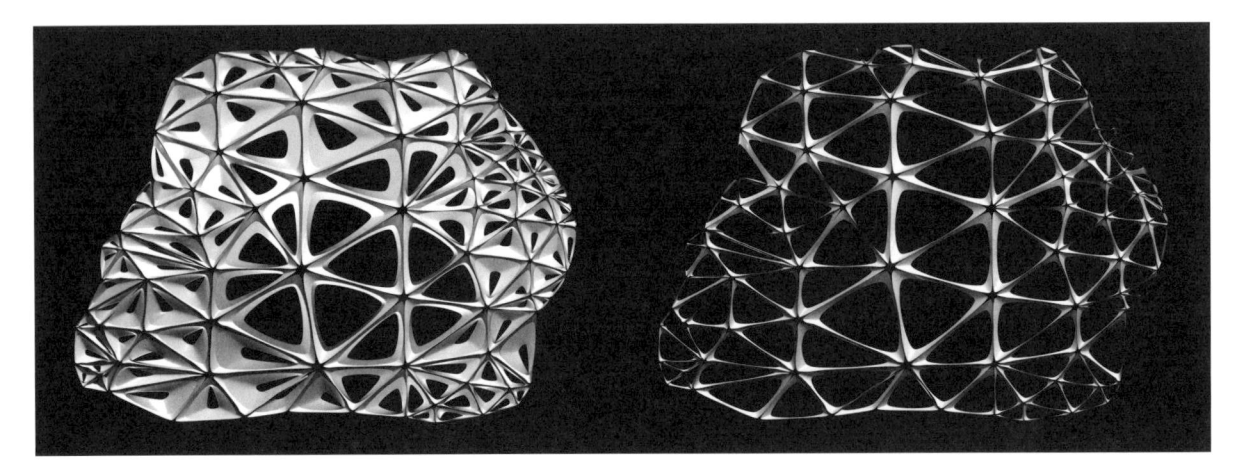

Figure 5
PS-Canopy
Parametric Variations of Shade Aperture Sizes.

explore ideas of pluripotency in regards to architectural applications. We also viewed this as an opportunity to expand on some of the strategies that we had originally developed with CHROMAZON. In this sense both of these projects share common traits, but they also have significant differences.

Unlike in CHROMAZON, our initial approach here was not at all concerned with the whole. There was no particular site, scale, or context to which we needed to relate. We also did not have a clear concept as to what emotional response we wanted to elicit from the observer. What we did have was a precise definition—pluripotency—and we decided to focus our efforts towards a component logic that had the ability to express difference from within rather than in its differentiation to neighboring parts. In other words, we wanted to explore the notion of character as it is evoked by a part's ability to display fundamentally different capacities.

The parametric setup for PS_Canopy thus needed to concentrate on the transformative qualities of a single component rather than the interplay of a series of parts. The question of the whole was to be addressed during a later phase when issues of size and distribution of parts would become the focus. Three main structural/programmatic capacities were quickly identified: shades, posts and counters. The post or main structure could be parametrically "triggered" to *grow* into two appendixes along its z-axis, one at the bottom portion that turned into the counter, and the other one at the top, which became the shading device (Fig. 3). If left un-triggered, the post remained as a simple structure with dormant but unformed shading/counter capacities. This option was important since the larger conglomeration of these components did not require all functions simultaneously.

The model's appendixes were then arranged to take on more specific performance tasks, such as a flexible aperture size for the shades (Fig. 5), or height-to-width ratios for the counter pieces. These performance criteria were controlled with a secondary parametric system, which was imbedded into the original one. Finally, the main components were linked together via a tertiary set of variables to form larger field conditions. A minimum of three individual post components is required to make the canopy stand on its own, while the connection of the triangulated shade parts gives the canopy lateral stiffness. The larger the assembly of components gets, the fewer structural posts are needed unless more counters are desired. To take advantage of this we switched the reciprocal dependency between post and shade, so that the posts could be left un-triggered as well if not needed. This last feature demonstrates an important quality of parametric work flow, as it allows for hierarchical changes within the system, based on analysis and feedback.

Secret Bonds (Conclusion)

In the fourth paragraph of *Metamorphosis*, Goethe uses the words "geheime Verwandtschaft" (secret kinship) to characterize the bond through which the individual parts of a plant are tied together. The German word "geheim" translates literally to *belonging-to-home*, thus evoking a sense of intimate secrecy, undertakings behind closed curtains—invisible yet effective.[9] It seems through his choice of words that Goethe protects and pulls out of reach the very principles he seeks to uncover. In the bright climate of enlightenment, suddenly the alchemist in him abounds and his "philosophical idea" reveals yet another facet: a desire to uphold arcane laws, moreover to establish their indispensible role in our perception of nature. While this smartly shields his vision of *idea and knowledge* from pragmatist attacks, it also provides an atmospheric, even aesthetic claim to his argument: that all phenomena share ultimately an elusive quality. It is in this spirit, I believe, that Faust wonders if he should "seize and bind ye hovering forms," fully aware of the risk that the attempt alone could mean losing them forever.

The *secret bond* eludes the emphasis on process without denying its existence. It favors aspects of discovery over analysis. It displays a pattern of behavior without uniformity. Most importantly, it conceals the effects it has on the totality it governs over. As the parts merge into the whole, they remain the agents through which the object moves, grows, and organizes itself. The philosopher and architect Rudolf Steiner writes about *Metamorphosis*:

> One observes also that an organism thus comes to life within one, even down to its most minute parts: that one conceives it, not as a lifeless, self-enclosed object, but as something evolving, becoming, as the continuously unresting within itself.[10]

The quality of "unrest" is crucial as it not only forbids standstill, but also insinuates an internal struggle, an unease with the current situation, and the desire to immediately reconstitute into new formations.

There could hardly be a more sensible assessment of part-to-whole relationships than the one Steiner offers in regards to *Metamorphosis*. Parametric modeling provides a unique opportunity to re-formulate part-to-whole affiliations in a deeper and more integral fashion. While the rigor of parametric modeling allows for unprecedented control over countless individual bits and pieces, it does not *per se* introduce novelty into design. Equally, the ability to customize from the bottom up and avoid strict standardization does not lead to real difference. In fact, it often overwrites it by placing the emphasis on the mechanistic organization of efficient parts and downplaying the importance of *idea*. For Goethe, knowledge alone cannot provide a meaningful understanding of nature, at least not in a cultural sense. This can only be achieved through an interpretative investigation by the author, one in which the systems of design he deploys allow for intuitive explorations and leave space for discoveries.

Endnotes

1 Johann Wolfgang von Goethe, *Versuch die Metamorphose der Pflanzen zu erklären* (*The Metamorphosis of Plants* (1790). English translation from the British "Journal of Botany" (1863).

2 Franco Volpi, *Grosses Werklexikon der Philosophie* (Stuttgart: Kröner, 2004); p. 579.

3 Goethe's use of the term Urpflanze refers to a larger concept of Urforms (Archetypal Forms), which constitute phenomena at the "border of idea and perception" of which all living matter is made of." Volpi, *Grosses Werklexikon der Philosophie*, p. 579. For Goethe, this concept extends beyond botany.

4 Darwin published his *On the Origins of Species* in 1859. Gregor Mendel conducted his genetic pea experiments in the 1850s.

5 "Carolus Linnaeus," *Encyclopædia Britannica Online*, accessed 30 Mar. 2010 at <http://www.britannica.com/EBchecked/topic/342526/Carolus-Linnaeus>. "*Genera Plantarum* was considered by Linnaeus to be his crowning taxonomic achievement. In contrast to earlier attempts by other botanists at generic definition, which proceeded by a set of arbitrary divisions, *Genera Plantarum* presented a system based on what Linnaeus called the "natural characters" of genera—morphological descriptions of all the parts of flower and fruit."

6 Sanford Kwinter, "Who's Afraid of Formalism," *ANY* 7/8 (1994): p. 65.

7 Detlef Mertins, "Variability, Variety and Evolution in Early 20th-Century Bioconstructivisms," in *Research & Design: The Architecture of Variation*, ed. Lars Spuybroek (London: Thames & Hudson, 2009), pp. 48-59.

8 The Encyclopedia Britannica describes cells as pluripotent if they are "able to give rise to any cell type of the adult organism" and Wikipedia defines pluripotent as "having more than one potential outcome." "Pluripotent Cell," *Encyclopædia Britannica Online*, accessed 30 Mar. 2010 at < http://www.britannica.com/EBchecked/topic/1072302/pluripotent-cell> and "Cell Potency," Wikipedia, accessed 30 Mar. 2010 at <http://en.wikipedia.org/w/index.php?title=Cell_potency&oldid=371670674>.

9 "Geheim, zum Haus gehörig," *Deutsches Etymologisches Wörterbuch*, ed. Gerhard Köbler (1995); p. 147, accessed 30 Mar. 2010 at <http://www.koeblergerhard.de/der/DERG.pdf>., p. 147.

10 Rudolf Steiner, "Origin of the Theory of Metamorphosis," in *The Metamorphosis of Plants*, Johann Wolfgang von Goethe (Junction City, OR: Bio-Dynamic Farming and Gardening Association, 1993); p. 5.

Live Models

Jason Kelly Johnson and Nataly Gattegno, Future Cities Lab

Live models are dynamic formations that register and continuously adapt to shifting atmospheric and microclimatic conditions. These models can be used as analytical engines to understand the patterns around us, and in some cases, as conceptual frameworks for architecture. The most compelling of these models do not merely depict the appearance of things, but seek to reveal the irreducible nature and behavior of processes in transition. Not only are they capable of calculating the underlying logic of these processes, they also reveal emerging organizations of energy, form, and flow in visually discernible patterns.

Our design practice routinely employs what we call live models and a promiscuous mixture of design tactics from the fields of interactive design, robotics, biology, material sciences, and advanced fabrication. Closer to a research laboratory, our practice operates as a loose collaborative bringing experts and practitioners into the studio environment mixing disciplines and tactics. Alternative modes of exploration, representation, and design emerge from this crosspollination, yielding a conflation of dynamic representation, modeling, and simulation that has deeply affected our approach to design. How does the cross-knitting of modes of representation and simulation—including physical modeling and dynamic cartography—suggest a productive framework for design practice? What is at stake when a model attempts to exceed the world of pure simulation, and demands some form of analogical reasoning and perceptual analysis? What is at stake when a map or a model not only demands interaction, but also relies on the participation of viewers or its environment for the activation of meaning? At which point does the model exceed its representation?

Models are intriguing in their ability to analogically represent the nature of things and to simultaneously reveal conditions previously invisible. This perceptual oscillation between the analogical and ontological reading of models is of particular interest to us as it allows for the indexing and transformation of actual energies at play. Historian of science D. Graham Burnett suggests that "what makes models so powerful is precisely the slipperiness of this distinction. The move from 'as' to 'is' can happen fast, can happen for only a moment, can subsequently be denied—it is in this instability, this indeterminacy, that models ultimately do their real work."[1] Live models thrive in this instability; they rely on their grounding in existing forces and live energies, while flourishing in their unpredictable and blurred interpretations.

Interestingly, the word 'model' is an auto-antonym, containing two antithetical definitions. It simultaneously defines a fake and an ideal; it describes the representation of a given condition and an exemplar, prototypical order. This representational fluctuation is core to live models in the way they operate, to simultaneously represent existing and ideal conditions. Live models are triggered by

Facing Page
The Aurora Project
Future Cities Lab, installation at Van Alen Institute, New York, 2009. Detail view of Aurora installation surface.

Aurora
Plaster cast buoys, stainless steel structure, PETG surface, LED, and CRT Aurora field.

existing forces and energies. They represent those energies and strive to articulate their unpredictable and surprising consequences.

Historically, orreries and astronomical clocks are clear examples of this perceptual fluctuation of models. They consist of gears and rotating orbs that not only mechanically simulate the interaction of planets in the solar system, but also model spatial relationships including the relative position, volume, scale, and trajectory of planets and satellites. They operate as dynamic models and allow users to see, experience, and juxtapose information from differing perspectives. Astronomical clocks powered by gravity allow the slippage between the represented (the simulated) and the ideal to go even further. The forces applied to the model are real, live forces and energies surrounding both the simulated and the idealized representations. In other words, the model is dynamic, kinetic, and live; its sole limitation lies in the mechanics of its gears.

Contemporary examples such as Sachiko Kodama and Minako Takeno's *Protrude, Flow* use a material's properties as a mechanism to slip between analogical and ontological representations.[2] Ferro-fluid is a liquid that becomes strongly magnetized and transformed in the presence of a magnetic field. *Protrude, Flow* indexes the sonic energy surrounding the installation through a series of magnets that control the magnetic fluid and reconfigure it relative to the sound levels present. The ferro-fluid does away with mechanics and relies on a phenomenon—magnetism—to propel the representation of energy exchange. *Protrude, Flow* behaves as a model, a live model—or system—that slips between the representational interpretation of a phenomenon and the exposure of latent potentials within the system.

As a result of the blurred and highly interconnected environment generated by live models, new dynamic cartographies emerge that are latent with real-time, open-source, user-generated data.[3] With the advent

Aurora
Layering of buoys, stainless steel structure,
surface and light field.

of immersive technologies, these models are rapidly becoming experiential worlds unto themselves, dynamic cartographic manifestations of energies and flows, parameters in flux and in constant transformation relative to their microclimates. These representations blur distinctions between models as mere depictions and models as vital sensorial spaces that are live and impregnated with mutable data. Live models absorb information from their surrounding environment—temperature, weather, pollution, circulation—and through a reformulation of live inputs yield formal logics and live outputs that are simultaneously representational frameworks and spatial armatures for design. As a design practice, we are interested in this latency and believe there is a fundamental shift taking place in how we expect models to perform as analytical machines and how in turn those machines become dynamic, and perhaps intelligent, frameworks for architecture and design. These frameworks set the boundaries and outer limits of performance and ultimately describe the inextricable relationship and design interdependence between energy and form.

The *Aurora Project* was instigated as a way to explore these questions, and to experiment with the perceptual oscillation of live models.[4] By enabling us to work with a constantly fluctuating set of inputs, the Arctic became a site for experimentation with a transient and dynamic dataset. The fluctuation in the dataset did not only exist in the pure phase change of water to ice, but also in the dramatic effects of climate change on the Arctic region and the simple fact that new ground is constructed—or more aptly emerges—seasonally and annually. The *Aurora Project* was initiated as a series of three distinct design explorations that emerged out of an extensive study of how the Arctic region has been represented, and in many cases, misrepresented throughout time. The intention was to use these representations as points of departure for engaging contemporary political, social, and ecological issues. The *Aurora Project* was comprised

Process Work

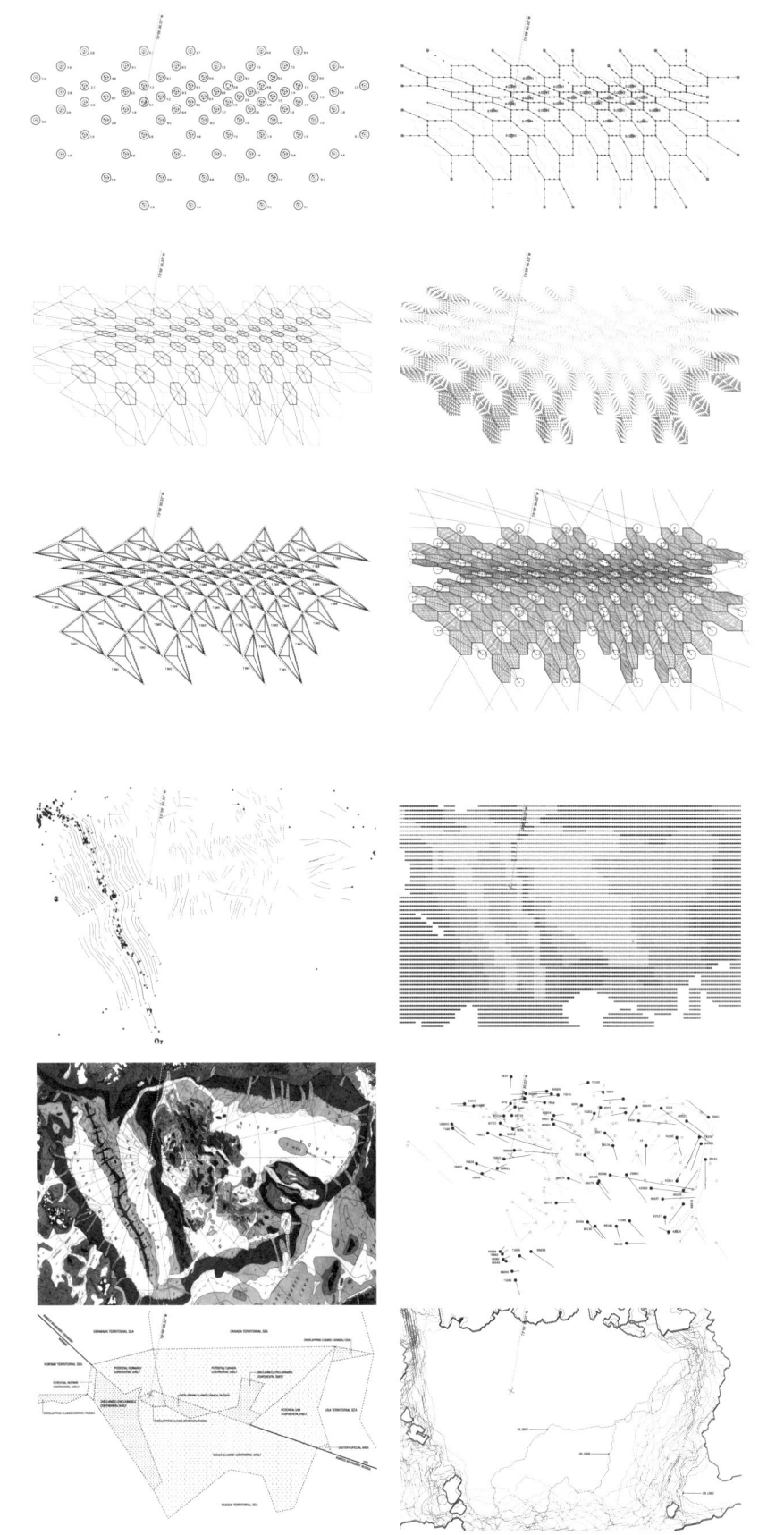

Maps of Aurora

Left Column from Top
Inaugurate, Intermesh, Array

Right Column from Top
Actuate, Perforate, Synthesize

Maps of the Arctic

Left Column from Top
Shift, Deposit, Dominate

Right Column from Top
Cache, Drift, Erode

146 **Live Models** Jason Kelly Johnson and Nataly Gattegno

of three components: *Terra Incognita*, the *Aurora Model*, and the *Glaciarium*.

Terra Incognita consisted of maps and diagrams that provided a view into how the Arctic region has been represented, claimed, and mythologized in the past and present. This graphic experiment concerned itself primarily with the dilemmas of representing—ice—that is in constant fluctuation. Through the study of historical maps and abundant contemporary real-time data from the Arctic, *Terra Incognita* experimented with ways to synthesize, remap, and remodel these representations that consciously oscillated between modes of dynamic modeling, cartography and creative fiction.

The main interactive piece—the *Aurora Model*—superimposed the ephemeral qualities of these representations with the dynamic behavior of multiple users, translating the shifting dimensions of the ice into a responsive light field. The model was constructed using a series of horizontal layers that indexed both static and dynamic relationships occurring in the Arctic: bathymetry, temperature, salinity, and ice thickness defined the organization of the surface. The responsive qualities of the *Aurora Model* described the way natural and artificial systems interact and adapt to one another. Left unattended, the surface of the *Aurora Model* would be brightly lit through a series of LEDs populating the interior of the surface. Approaching the model as a spectator would trigger a reverse reaction: the LEDs dimmed away from the viewer and a series of 'auroras'—blue cold cathode tubes—lit the middle of the surface.

The *Glaciarium* was an interactive instrument that engaged a smaller group of users' senses through the sight and sound of a melting ice core. The influence of the individual viewer was linked directly to the materiality and sensation of the project. Increased observation amplified the internal lighting effects and, depending on the duration of interaction, dramatically accelerated the melting of the ice core rendering the environmental degradation visceral and real.

The *Aurora Project* experiments with the perceptual fluctuation between vast scales of both geography and time, and reveals the potential for models—and perhaps by extension, architecture—to simultaneously index, synthesize, and engage climatic, cultural, social, and politically charged fields. Live models describe a promiscuous, polluted, and dirty design process with unexpected design outcomes. The oscillation, in what we call live models, between metaphorical and ontological data is integral in their ability to become design tools—tools that represent existing, but also refer to latent potentials. Olafur Eliasson claims that what we "are witnessing is a shift in the traditional relationship between reality and representation. We no longer progress from models to reality, but from model to model while acknowledging both models are, in fact, real... Models have become co-producers of reality."[5]

Models are beyond real—they are active, evolving and live.

Endnotes

[1] D. Graham Burnett, "Masters of the Universe," in *Models: 306090 Books, Volume 11*, eds. Emily Abruzzo, Eric Ellingsen and Jonathan D. Solomon (New York: 306090, Inc., 2007); p. 44.
[2] Conny Freyer, Sebastien Noel, and Eva Rucki, *Digital by Design: Crafting Technology for Products and Environments* (London: Thames & Hudson, 2008); p. 122.
[3] Some examples include real time climate data from Pachube (see www.pachube.com); texture-mapped, multi-layered three-dimensional models from Google Earth (see www.earth.google.com); real-time data flow between the digital and physical worlds from Firefly (see www.fireflyexperiments.com).
[4] For full credits of the Aurora Project, please visit www.future-cities-lab.net; photography: Zechariah Vincent.
[5] Olafur Eliasson, "Models are Real," in *Models: 306090 Books, Volume 11*, eds. Emily Abruzzo, Eric Ellingsen and Jonathan D. Solomon (New York: 306090, Inc., 2007); p. 19.

Tickle the Shitstem

Phoebe Washburn in conversation

It all started with some old t-shirts and the letters ORT. New York based artist Phoebe Washburn found this odd syllable, possibly a misspelling of "art", or a nickname from childhood, layered haphazardly over little league baseball logos and slogans for used car parts. The word became a catalyst in an elaborate and convoluted system that provides t-shirts, industrial trash, and words, new significance. In August of 2008, during the art gallery world's sleepy summer hiatus, Washburn exhibited Tickle the Shitstem at Zach Feuer Gallery in New York.

The installation, an intricate system of production and consumption, sold the ORT t-shirts for $25. The t-shirts were just the tip of the iceberg. As thrift store finds these shirts needed to be washed. This washing produced a volume of residual graywater, which was initially problematic; What to do with this excess of waste? For Washburn, problems are good things: they spur invention and creativity. Washburn creates problems for herself, so that she has the opportunity to devise solutions. Nuit Banai describes Tickle the Shitstem as, "a never-ending battle to keep the system functioning as production and consumption, usable material and waste become outlandishly interchangeable. With supply exceeding demand, defeat seems inevitable".

Tickle the Shitstem would not run properly without its daily production of dirty water, in fact it would not exist without it. The water motivates and structures this mini-reality that stretches through several gallery rooms with a soda and trinket shop, graywater treatment basins, pumps, hoses, tubs, stacked display tanks, and an artificial pond. Yet the system is imperfect; an artificial pond sits at the end of the line to accept the overflow of the net-waste system.

Waste, consumption, and productivity are continuing threads through Washburn's work. Her earlier installations include large architectural topographies made of scrap wood and cardboard found on daily scavenger hunts through skips and demolition sites. These aggregate pieces, exhibited at Zach Feuer/LFL, the Whitney Museum in New York, and the ICA in Philadelphia are exquisite. Their beauty challenges the viewer's expectations of the limits and burdens of waste.

From these early works Washburn's practice has become more systematic as she has become intimately involved with the cycle of production and consumption. Rather than using other people's waste to produce work, she creates her own cycles. Beginning with *Regulated Fool's Milk Meadow*, a solo exhibit at the Deutsche Guggenheim in Berlin, Washburn engaged processes of production and consumption. In this work, she constructed a micro-factory of plywood and conveyor belts which produced sod that was then planted on the museum's roof. *Tickle the Shitstem* builds upon these works, adding the notion of consumerism into the already dense layering of ideas and agendas.

Facing Page
Tickle the Shitstem (installation view)
Zach Feuer Gallery, 2008.

Process Work

Tickle the Shitstem (interior view)

The *Dirt* editors, along with Debs Hoy, sat down with Washburn in the summer of 2008 to discuss her work. The interview took place in two sessions, one in the early stages of *Tickle the Shitstem*, and the other a week prior to its installation.

Dirt

Tickle the Shitstem. We love this title. Where did it come from? What does it reference?

Phoebe Washburn

The *Shitstem* is the system; it is a messed up, shitty, failing system. The tickle is the invite for people to come and participate.

Dirty System as Creative Generator

Dirt

Dirt is the stuff that makes the system jump, forcing a new kind of internal logic. In terms of your piece, one of your starting points seems to be the dirty water. How has dirt helped you to create this system for the soda shop?

Phoebe Washburn

One of the interesting and productive aspects about my working method is that I focus on one problem and then realize somewhere in the process that that is not actually the real problem. The problem is somewhere else. It tends to creep up on me a little bit and becomes the thing that is really interesting about the project. The dirty water was a huge part of this project. It became a problem when I had to start dealing with the reality of what to do with the water generated by the washing machine. The washing machine and the resulting twenty gallons or so of water is the heartbeat of the piece. It was the main problem and the main burden. It was my exploration of the ways around that problem, or the ways of trying to work, overcome, play, and aestheticize that problem that became the piece.

Dirt

So, in a sense, in each project, there are initial problems and unexpected problems. Was the dirty water from the washing machine an initial problem or an unexpected one?

Phoebe Washburn

It wasn't completely unexpected, but it became a bigger issue than I thought it was going to be. When I was designing it on paper it made enough sense, but once I was on site there was a reality to it that required me to go deeper with the elements. Ultimately it became the focal point of the piece.

Dirt

It must be exciting to be constantly surprised by problems and issues as they arise in your working process. Your installations are often dynamic and *Tickle the Shitstem* is no exception: this work involves caretakers as well as a participatory audience. It is always in motion.

Phoebe Washburn

There is no guarantee that the installation will look the same upon a repeat visit. Things shift and change during the course of a single visit. This aspect of the work is very important to me. My early pieces have hinted at this dynamism, and I've been able to creep closer in this installation. In a way, it is how things exist in the world naturally. Any environment or landscape that you look at is never a fixed thing. If you look under the surface there is some sort of war happening everywhere. It is exciting to me if the piece can somehow reflect that.

Ways of Making Accumulation and Process
Dirt

Can you talk to us about your working process? Where does an idea come from? Do you sketch? How do you move from ideas to installation?

Phoebe Washburn

It happens in a lot of different ways. I get from project to project by revisiting and taking down the exhibitions, or maintaining the installation once it is up. Certainly taking it down helps me think about the next project or think about what I truly never want to do again. Seeing the pieces in transport helps too. I'm really hands on in that I help dismantle and move the work. It is always a monstrous amount of material and an ongoing burden. But I see things happening and get an idea for the next thing that looks cool, or stupid, or dangerous.

Dirt

There is an interesting shift in your work from your earlier pieces, like *Vacational Trappings and Wildlife Worries* at the ICA in Philadelphia (2007), where you had a distinct process in making and accumulating the material, to your more recent pieces, such as *Regulated Fool's Milk Meadow* at the Deutsche Guggenheim and *While Enhancing a Diminishing Deep Down Thirst, the Juice Broke Loose (the Birth of a Soda Shop)* at the 2008 Whitney Biennial, in which your working process has become a more critical element of the piece. Do you see that as an evolution in your work?

Phoebe Washburn

Yes, I definitely see that in the development of my work. It is interesting how some of the earlier pieces were built in a way that revealed their own construction. You could see the structure and with close observation you could figure out how it was put together. These pieces told their own stories. My newer pieces compress and distill this notion; they *show* their creation and process rather than simply *tell* it. They are created, built, and evolve on-site.

The first piece that alerted me to this shift in process was a piece called *Poor Man's Lobster*. I made this piece for a group show titled *Make it Now* at the Sculpture Center in 2005. I wanted to do everything on site: generate the material; build the structure; et cetera. I was sick of the idea of collecting all of the stuff and bringing it back to the studio to process it. I wanted to eliminate the step in the studio, so I tried to do everything on site. I liked that feeling, but there was a disconnect in the piece since it was all new to me. I enjoyed the notion of compressing the steps of the process and having it happen more on site. I went to the space early and spent two weeks ahead of time producing the material on site.

Glitches and Leaps
Dirt

We started off talking about the problem of the gray water and how to fit all of the excess water into the gallery installation. At the gallery, we were very surprised to walk through the space to discover the empty pond and the undulating hillside at the end. It was a very different aesthetic from the rest of the work. How did you arrive at that?

Phoebe Washburn

I knew that I wanted to have an anchor somewhere in the gallery that acted as the dumpsite of the piece. I thought that back room was appropriate since it was removed. I loved the idea that the hose would go all the way to the back of the gallery and allow you to follow the path to where it would end up at this puddle in the back. At the last minute I decided not to put plants into the pond because it felt like an artificial, gross space deep in the gallery. There was no light and it didn't seem right for plants to be in that pond. It turned out to be just a place to dump the extra water. The towels evolved late in the game too. I knew that I wanted to have towels in the piece because I had been using towels so much in the studio to mop up spills. The towels seemed to nicely reference maintenance in a basic way.

There was one pretty significant disappointing moment during the installation. Originally, all of the t-shirts were going to be stacked up in the structure, but that became hugely problematic in a number of ways. Visually, it was too dense and busy looking to have all of the different t-shirts stacked up, so I decided not to display them. Ultimately I removed them from the towers and replaced them with the stack of towels. This may be silly to talk about since it is so intuitive at the time, but this is a way to work through things, to solve problems. It is hard to chart it after the fact, although it is important so that I know for the next project where the weak points are and what I want to push further.

Dirt

It is interesting to hear you say that those little glitches are on your mind and could lead to new pieces.

Phoebe Washburn

I definitely think that things that are troubling and don't make perfect sense are the things that are going to be the next step.

Facing Page
Tickle the Shitstem (water cleaning tanks and aquariums)

Above
Tickle the Shitstem (detail view of aquarium)

Process Work 153

Between Line and Shadow

Marion Weiss in conversation

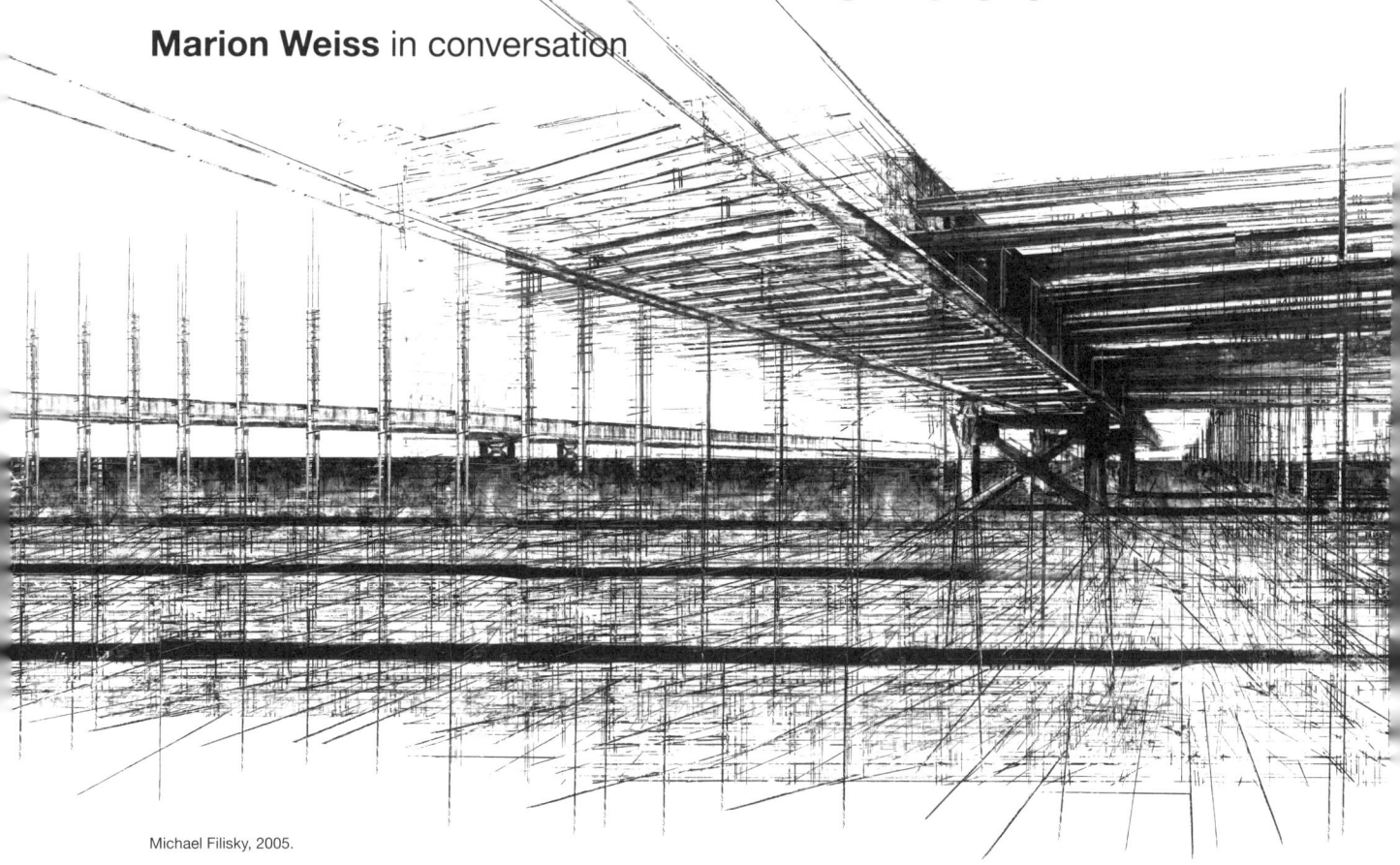

Michael Filisky, 2005.

Over the past ten years, Marion Weiss has taught an advanced drawing course titled *Advanced Drawing Procedures: Between Line and Shadow*. The course begins with a single photograph, taken in the railyards of Philadelphia's 30th Street Station. The image, cut down to no larger than three by four inches, is the seed of invention for a much larger and more complex reality. A world is created through constructed perspective; lines extend, objects scale and repeat to fill eighteen by twenty-four inches of Strathmore. More lines, drawn in a specific forty or forty-five degree zigzag depict light, shade, and shadow, giving body to the skeletal framework of construction lines. The drawing is then repeated, in the less controlled medium of ink on plastic film. Texture and depth are discovered through the messy and indeterminate nature of the fluid technique. The drawing is once again repeated. This time the pencil and ink iterations are conflated digitally, layering constructions and qualities of both into one image. The fourth iteration takes life through digital manipulations of stretching, shrinking, growing, repeating. Final iterations of the drawings range in scale from six to twelve feet long and four to six feet high. The drawings, which share the same humble and tightly prescribed beginning, depict highly specific and unique environments—immersive, textural, and spatially rich worlds. Techniques of drawing and the process of making multiple iterations of the same image are highly stressed in the course. Invention slowly emerges from a process of precision and repetition. *Dirt* Editors Megan Born and Lily Jencks sat down with Marion Weiss to discuss *Line and Shadow*, the process of making drawings, and how this relates to the process of making spaces and buildings.

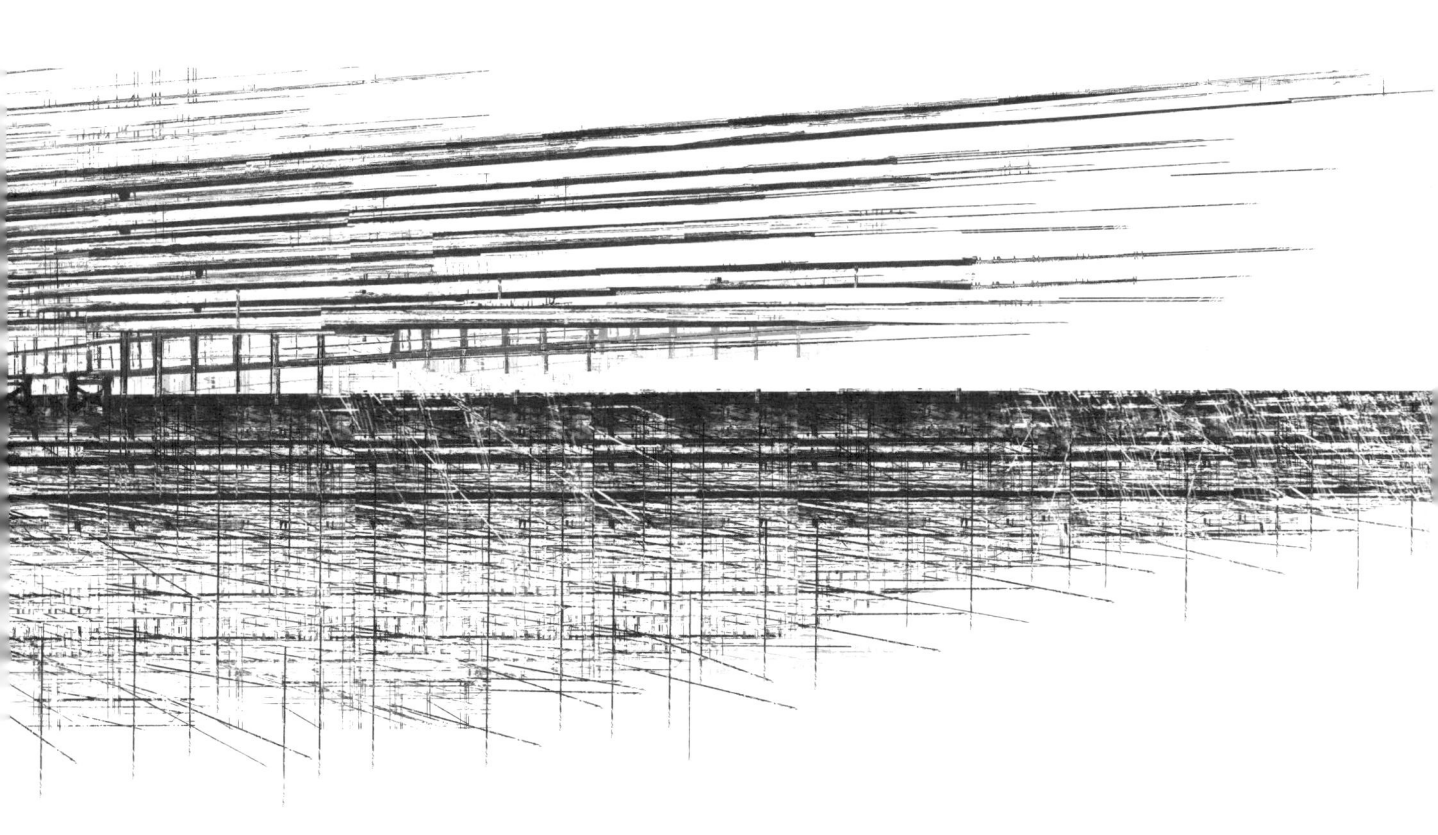

Representation

Dirt

The drawings produced in your *Line and Shadow* course, and their complements in your own work, are for us "dirty": heavily layered, intricate accumulations of marks on a surface. These drawings are also "dirty"

Gavin Riggall, 2005.

ideologically—they are not the "au currant" means of representation (the glossy digital rendering), but rather insist on the amalgamation of analog and digital. What is of interest and at stake in this technique? And more broadly, how do they relate to a broader question of representation and its disciplinary role today?

Marion Weiss
I am preoccupied with a drawing's capacity to sustain ambiguity and provide multiple readings. How do you look at lines? They are fully abstract elements that don't exist in real life, but they are nonetheless meters and boundaries. We build by them, and we understand the measure of things by them. But, lines remain an abstraction that is set in two dimensions on a flat piece of paper. Shadow describes the result of light hitting an object and giving it dimension, but it too is a fiction. We (architects) are always working on the flat. As a result, our ability to do certain things is established first and foremost by the framework of this flat: how big it is, how small it is, what texture it is, what medium it is (paper, screen, etc.), whether we are working by hand or remotely. These are all factors that contribute to thinking about what a line is; a description of boundaries, of limitations, of this side and that side, and the implication of a form it describes or does not fully capture. These elements (being described by a line) can remain ambiguous in a drawing in ways that they cannot in a physical model.

We work across various mediums, doing the same thing in different ways, with each tool and accompanying technique offering particular resistances and freedoms. Within the translation across media—when the resistance of one and the freedom of another come together—something new is found. The drawing course is aimed to think about the loops of media, using a precise cycle of iterations and translations to generate end results one would never imagine from the starting point. It's about reiteration and build-up, about getting lost in the debris of these layers, in doing things again and again. This leads to a new set of discoveries. In practice, these iterations lead to a set of mistakes that engender new spatial potentials—repetition, expansion, extension, or the ability to go from the finite to a point of infinite possibility.

Dirt

How do you view the issue of representation, and what is its place in contemporary architectural discourse? Or, alternatively, how does the analog, and especially the loose sketch, relate to the highly processed and controlled digital rendering?

Marion Weiss

Through iteration we gain a mastery of technique so that we can work without thinking too hard. The medium (in this case the sketch) acts to translate our intuitions.

Megan Born, 2007.

It has to do with skill, agility, and practice. Ideally, you want to have a foundation of all of the representational media available to architects, and that's the point of this course. It's about immersing yourself in a range of media and their transitions: from the photograph to the constructed drawing, to the wet medium on plastic, to the digital environment. In going through each one of these environments, the limitations, predispositions, and strengths of each become finite and real.

The digital environment has a certain set of predispositions amplified by each specific software. The drafted line has a predisposition as well—it doesn't lend itself very easily to curves but can easily produce lines. Ink on plastic, too, has its own predispositions: Higgins ink mixed with water produces sediment tracking so if you've got a tilt on your board, that sediment describes the force of gravity on the medium, producing a series of drip marks that suggest age. The coincidence of the material and the medium is truly interesting to me, as is the process of layering. The superimposition of graphite, line, ink sediment, and charcoal intensifies the potential to produce something utterly different from what would have emerged working exclusively with one material.

Pushing the same subject matter through all of these media, you see it differently each time, you feel it differently, you discover things in a different way. This is an investment in the artifact of the drawing, as a single product, the whole way through. *Line and Shadow* is effectively one drawing that's done over the course of the semester, with many different results.

Dirt
Do you find that moving between the analog and the digital environments is very difficult for the students?

Marion Weiss
Actually I've found that it's liberating. The shift from analog to digital is where the process becomes exciting. It allows people to scale up very quickly, to draw complex forms and spaces and to test effects at high speed. But

it's also tricky: we discovered the importance of needing to scale up texture without it becoming cartooned, for instance, which is a nuanced skill. I'm often amazed, though, at what a student can bring to the table once they enter the digital environment. And in the end, the course's product is digital: *as if* the drawing has been constructed by hand, but about seventy percent has been so modified through the digital translations that it has become something else altogether.

The risk of using only the digital environment is homogeneity: everything looks alike. When the layers of the analog drawings are brought into the digital environment, they're already so powerful on their own that they bring a voice and a set of demands to the digital environment. So the analog drawing brings in a very tactile and personal bias before it goes into the digital, a medium that tends to the generic if you're not fully in control of the software. The rich analog input thus has the capacity to compensate for—or resist—the generic. The digital environment tends to stay very "clean." It has a phenomenal capacity to do certain things so well that it becomes powerfully seductive, so much so that it's hard to actually resist those capacities. The *Line and Shadow* drawings, on the other hand, are all about resistance.

Technique and Process
Dirt
The process of creating drawings in the *Line and Shadow* course begins with very strict, prescribed techniques and media. There is a right way to construct a composition, draw a line, and render light and shadow; the drawings all utilize a combination of projective and free-hand techniques. At a certain point during the seminar, you have the students move from a very steadfast rule system to intuition and invention. How does technique inform process, and vice versa?

Marion Weiss
I studied as a classical pianist, a similarly gradual process of learning the rules. I was kept away from jazz by my piano teacher, who didn't want me to be distracted by

Jackie Wong, 2007.

jazz until I was sixteen. A classical musician operates under the belief that a rigorous foundation is essential so that when you depart from that foundation, a full array of tools are at your disposal. Mastery of technique is essential to maximize intuitive capacity. Similarly, the class begins with strict constructed drawings and moves to the sketch. It begins with the benefits of order—of constraints that are established as a place to depart from. Over the course of the seminar, we literally draw over drawings, sketch over them, tear, rip, pull, repeat, remove, and create yet a new layer. The sketch is the mode of translation.

The sketch is the most intuitive mode of drawing and is quite different from drafting or other techniques of representation. The sketch recognizes the radial positions of your wrist and your elbow, and the intuitive movement of a small radius of your fingers. It's physically dependent on that field of connection, of bodily and sensory integration—of moving, seeing, recording.

For those of us who draw, seeing and making are always connected. This is a generational difference: unlike learning to draw on the computer, drawing by hand has a physical dimension.

For a pianist, practice aims to develop and sustain the physical memory of technique—by doing the exercise often enough that it becomes automatic and you don't have to think about it. It's the same thing with sketching.

Hand media encourages you not to think but to do, to act, to throw things down, to test, to remove; effectively, to sculpt on a two dimensional surface. So, the aim is to introduce "unthinking" after the abstract, rigorous construction methods of the earlier drawings.

Practice/Pedagogy
Dirt
Iteration is at play in your work, and in your teaching: internal to the process, as we've discussed, but also in the reuse of processes. How have both the method and the results evolved over the seven to eight years you have offered the *Line and Shadow* course? How has this evolution in turn informed your work and your teaching? Have there been mistakes?

Marion Weiss

The first time I taught *Line and Shadow*, it was a bust of a course. After a few iterations, it acquired momentum. In the initial classes, for instance, we had trouble figuring out how to deal with texture. There were some pretty crude experiments. There were just lines that became more and more lines. There were cool lines on some dark backgrounds, and some of them were actually great, but, nonetheless, spatial richness and dirtiness were missing. It took a while to become relaxed enough for the push toward failure, and for me to feel confident enough to make this push.

We could refer here to Jasper Johns; the palimpsest of his preoccupations is evident in the self-conscious

Peter Rae, 2007.

repetition seen in the body of his work. He has said, "If I like something, I do it. If I still like it, I do it again." If you look at his *Savarin* series (1977-81), for instance, of a Savarin coffee can stuffed with paintbrushes in his studio, he's produced paintings of it, he's produced sketches of it, he's produced drawings of it, he's drafted it, he's silk-screened it, he's cast it in bronze, he's produced it as a kind of libretto. There are other series like this in Johns' work, such as letters, in works like *Grey Alphabets* (1956). He keeps on messing with them. He develops an addiction for the subject matter and a set of techniques, and then develops a kind of meditation, which leads him to represent the same subject in different ways again, and again, and again.

Dirt

You mentioned not having a goal-orientated view with this class. It seems as if technique and process are more important than the final product. How does that relate to the working methods utilized in your practice?

Marion Weiss

It's important to discover that mistakes are often far more compelling than the thing you set out to do. You need to defer to the discoveries that happen along the way. Often there's an idea that's robust enough to make it through to the end, but sometimes a radical mistake takes ownership of the direction you're moving in. Every project has a DNA and if it's strong it can succeed in different ways. You can pass that DNA to seventeen different designers and it will thrive in those seventeen different hands. This realization can provide a certain fearlessness to be able to allow yourself to risk failure.

One of our current projects, for instance, started with the roughest charcoal sketches, the roughest pen drawings, the roughest clay models, the roughest scraps. But it became clear that through the repetition, and more and more exacting approximations, we could tease out sectional agendas that could carve through the project and create a whole new set of topographies, ones that were totally against the initial, obvious moves. We discovered these through approximations and mistakes.

Drawing and/as Architecture
Dirt
The *Line and Shadow* drawings are very spatial in nature, yet none are specifically architectural proposals. How does the nature of the drawing shift in the context of your practice? Do you find drawing helps to understand details? The sketches for Smith College, for instance, look at the window mullions and how they articulate space: they seem to be exploring an understanding of structure.

Marion Weiss
We are interested in meter and measure, and effect and environment—we start to intuit these things as we work initially through the sketch, and these sketches make their way into the architecture. Even if it's just the debris of a charcoal line, which may compel us to bring texture to the surface of an all glass building. We might want something else to be immaterial and reflective, and not about texture, again in part because of the discoveries produced through the drawing. So often the first sketch remains powerful. Sometimes, things keep reasserting themselves even when we try to abandon them. You abandon it only to come back to it later in the process a lot more informed.

Dirt
For an architect so invested in the question of representation, you have a huge portfolio of built work. People who are very interested in representation tend to

Ashley Wendela, 2007.

remain "paper architects" but you are committed to the built. One could argue, nonetheless, that architects don't produce buildings as such, they produce drawings. What is your view of this argument?

Marion Weiss
We set up the framework; we set up the script. We are setting up everything for the actors so to speak; in this case, the contractors who build, who take a project into a reality that we cannot execute ourselves. There are architects that specialize in crafting projects as design/build but that work tends to remain at a small scale, the scale of the house, for instance. It can be quite beautiful. But it's difficult to work at the scale of a large landscape or a city with just a few skilled colleagues. Representation is very compelling to me, but so too is the urge to sculpt at a full scale, to realize built work.

Dirt
Is there an impetus to push both the drawings and their processes further in your practice, allowing architecture to evolve out of representation?

Marion Weiss

When we think about what we do as architects, we're always hopeful the architecture we create will transcend the object that is created, that it will engage things that are far more expansive, beyond the confines of architecture and perspective. In *Line and Shadow*, all of the drawings, particularly the strongest ones, end up suggesting something way outside the periphery and the vision of the frame. For us, creative drawing is part of a hook, impossible to resist, that pulls you to a place you don't know but you want to explore. It's like music or dance, it only becomes possible after you've gone too far, stayed up too late, felt exasperated with everything about it and yourself and everything you're doing, and then only, when you've gone over the edge, does something come out that you feel reinvested in again.

Dirt

We're hooked.

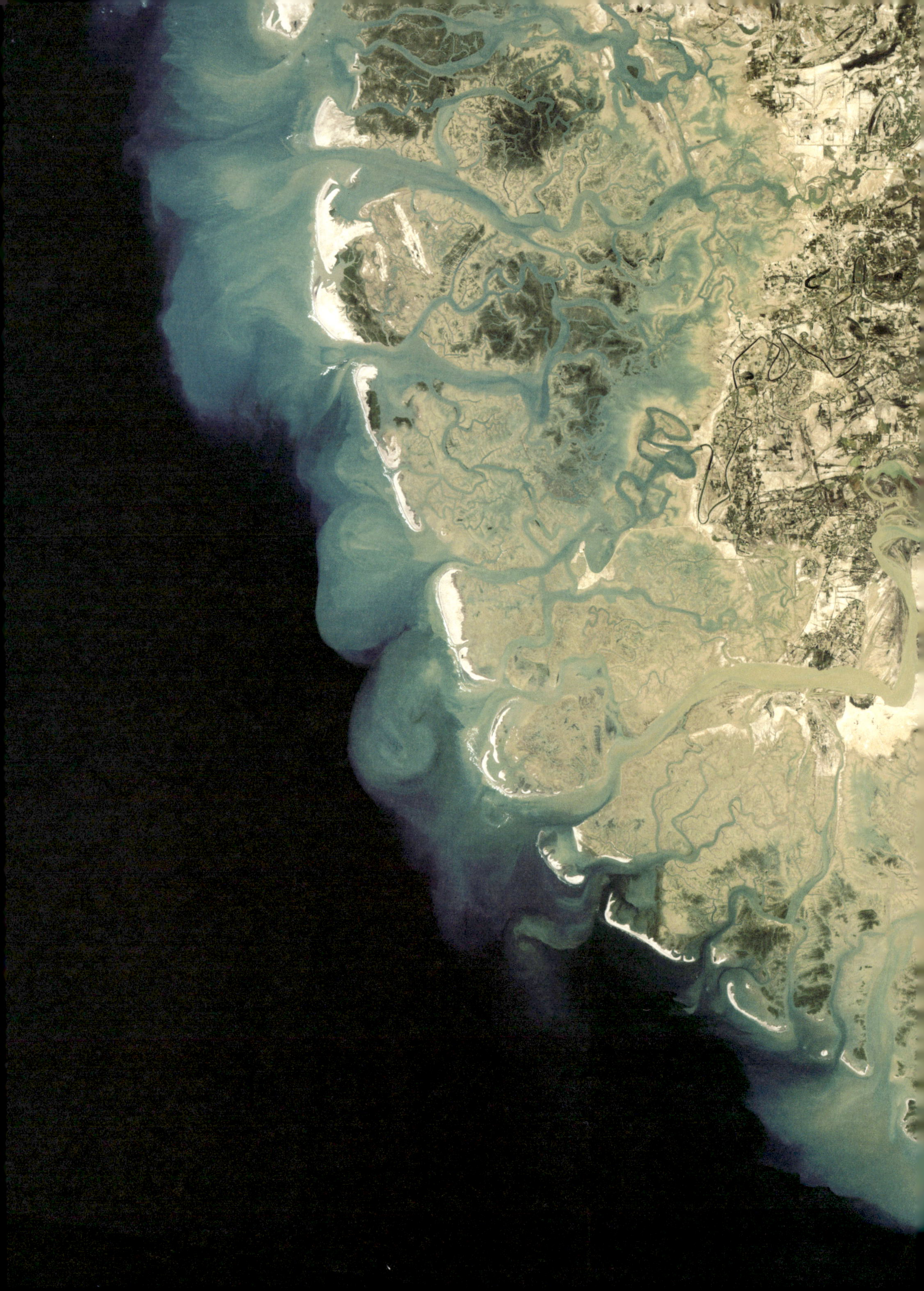

Active
Agents

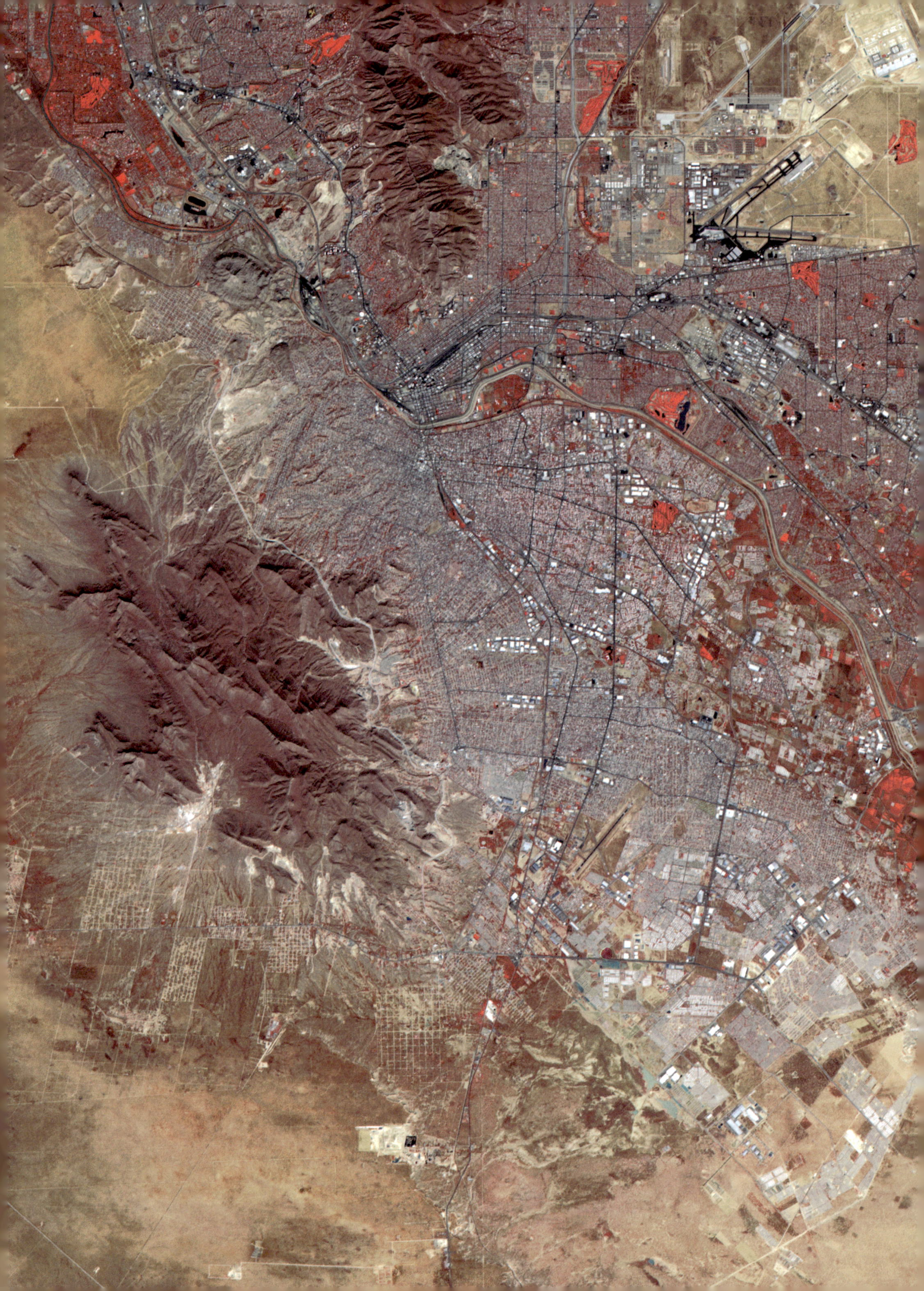

El Paso, Texas and Juarez, Mexico

Although governed by different nations the cities of El Paso and Juarez appear to belong to the same metropolis. The false-color imaging—acquired by the Advanced Spaceborne Thermal Emission and Reflection Radiometer (ASTER) on NASA's Terra satellite on October 15, 2008—depicts vegetation as red and hardscape as gray. The built environment and agricultural fields of these two cities negotiate the physical landform and the flow of the Rio Grande River.

Previous Spread
Indus River, Pakistan

The Indus River begins in Tibet and flows though the Himalayan Mountains. Before it empties into the Arabia Sea southeast of Karachi it meanders over a coastal plain. The course of the river shifts frequently in this area creating the land effects captured here by the NASA/USGS Landsat 5 satellite.

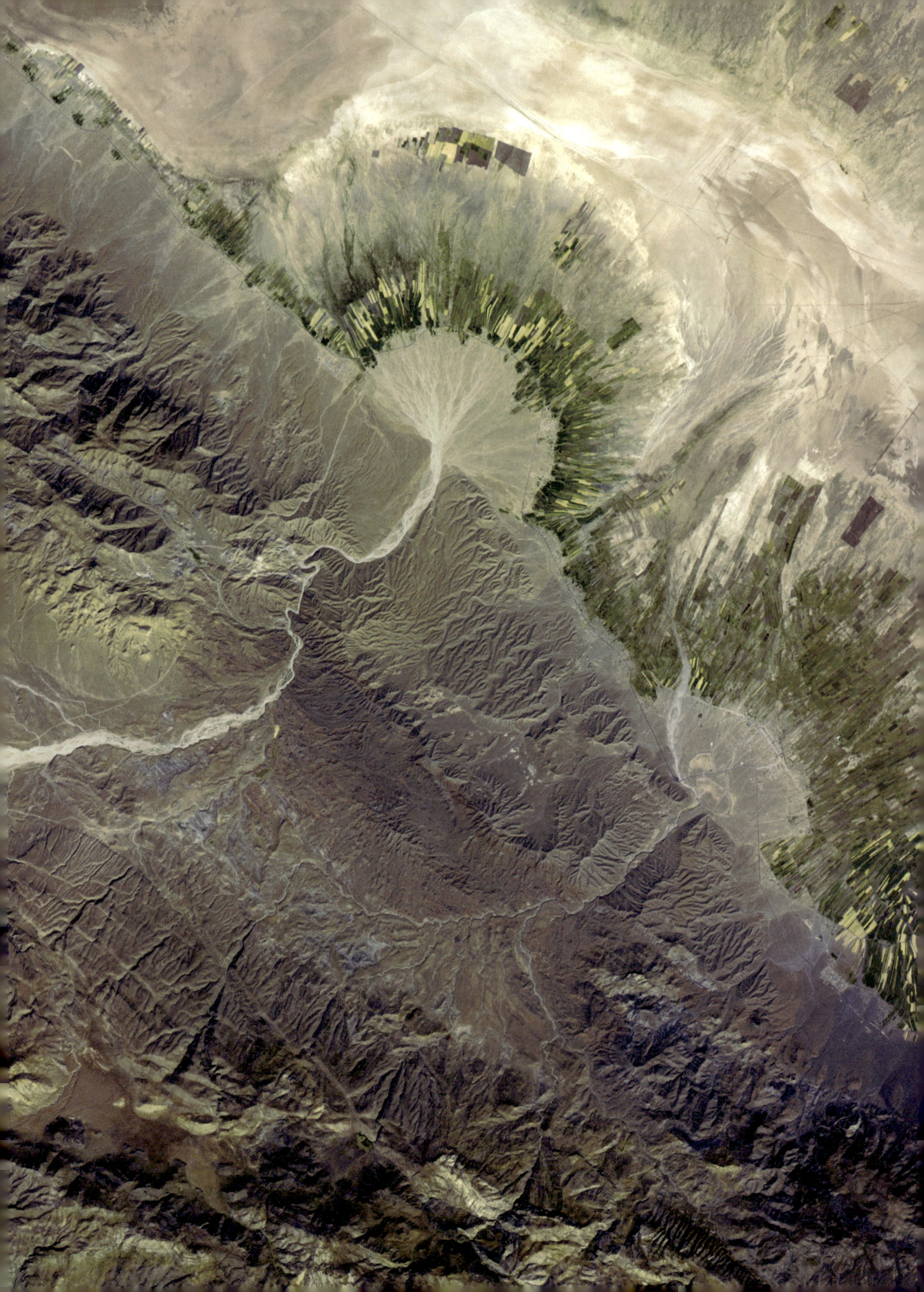

Alluvial Fan in Southern Iran

This image, taken by the Advanced Spaceborne Thermal Emission and Reflection Radiometer (ASTER) on NASA's Terra satellite on October 12, 2004, captures a dry river channel and adjacent agricultural land in the Fars Province in southern Iran. The river is dry throughout most of the year but subterranean water flows along the same pathways, creating opportunity for access through wells. The fields mark the hidden presence of water in this region.

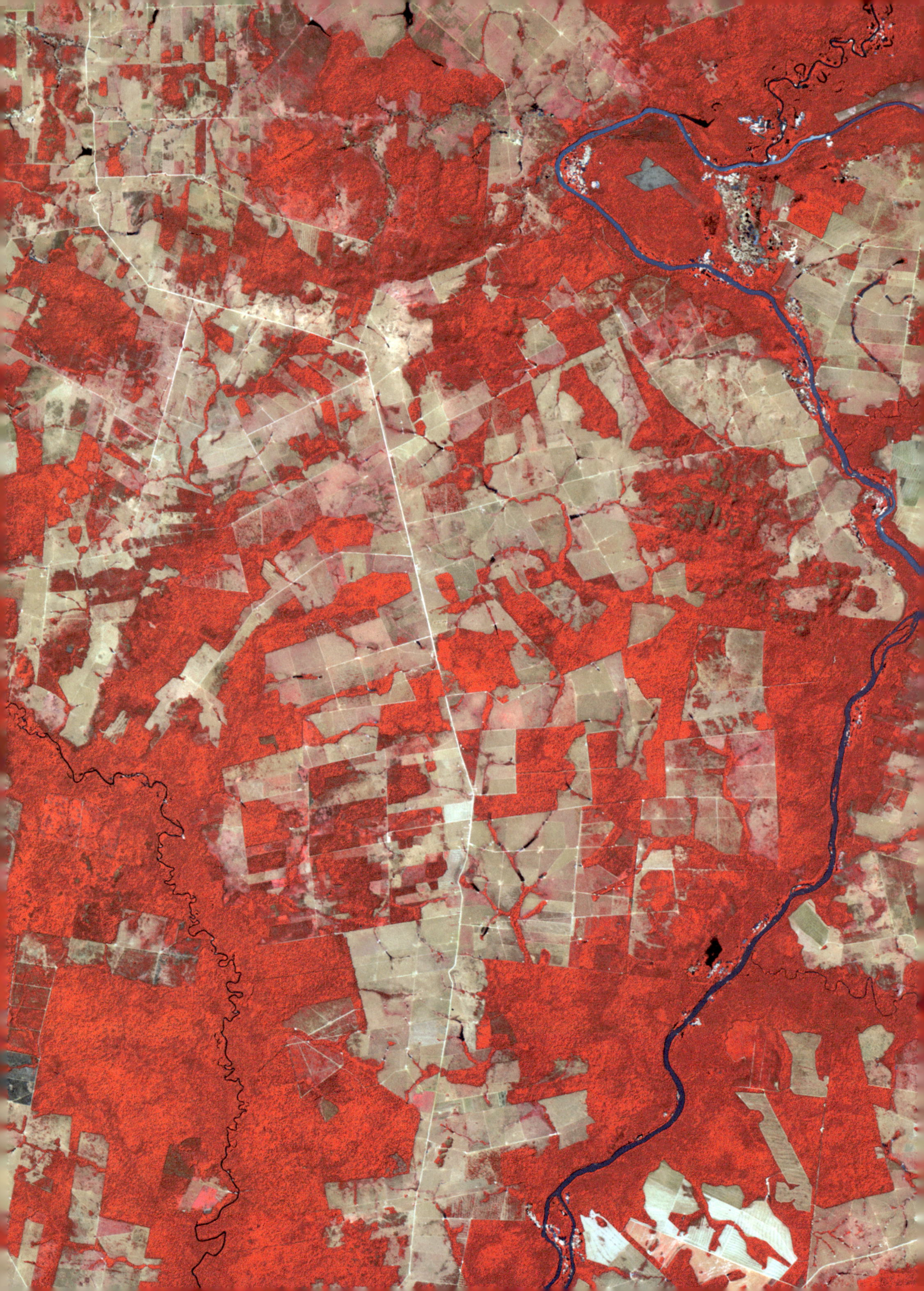

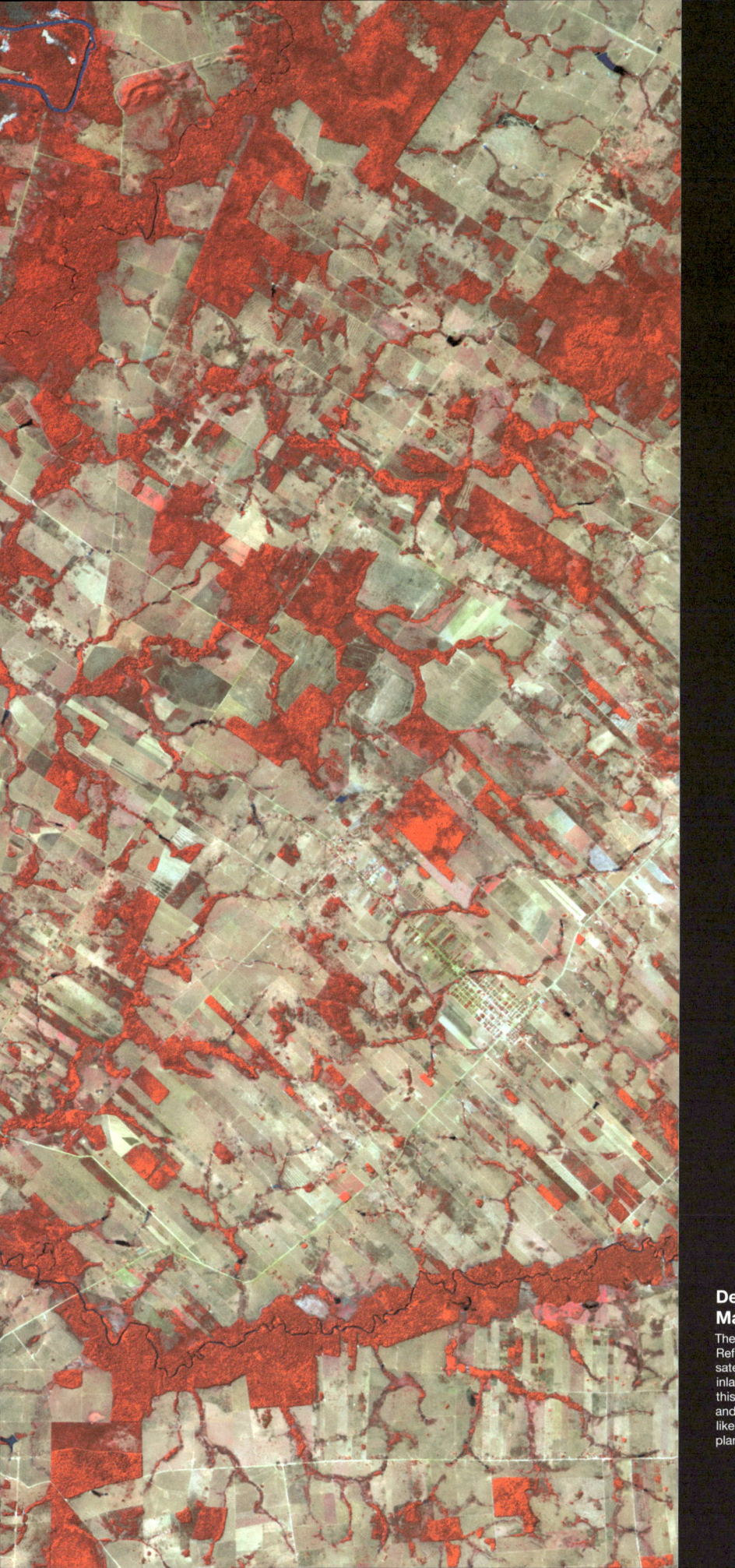

Deforestation in Mato Grosso, Brazil

The Advanced Spaceborne Thermal Emission and Reflection Radiometer (ASTER) on NASA's Terra satellite captured this image of Mato Grosso, an inland state in Central Brazil, on July 28, 2006. In this false-color image, red indicates vegetation, and the beige-grey marks areas of deforestation, likely cause by clearing for pasture and agricultural plantations.

Rising Currents
Contemporary Design Discourse
Barry Bergdoll

Since 2007, when I ventured out of the academy to take the reins of the Department of Architecture and Design at the Museum of Modern Art, we have traversed an unexpected set of challenges, ones in which the centrality of the design professions have become again manifestly clear, even if larger forces—in which architects are all too often complicit—are enormous in acting to marginalize the disciplines of architecture, landscape architecture, urban planning, design, and the fine arts. Having worked side-by-side with a diversity of disciplines, I am even more convinced of my strong belief that a cooperative, interdisciplinary approach is fundamental to the future vitality of the design professions. At MoMA we have been trying to discover meaningful positions and prospects even as the design professions have been jolted as almost never before into discussion of just where the moral compass should be set.

The horizon of expectations—the matrix in which decisions were made and values assessed—just a few short years ago seems now quite distant—distant from the uncertainties that accompany passage into the second decade of this now not-so-new century. Even what seemed like the emerging new paradigms of a few years ago—the rapid maturation of digital fabrication, an explosion of new materials, a widespread acceptance of the priority of sustainability, a slowly reawakening ethos of social responsibility—are, and need to be, continually submitted to intensive questioning and new exploration from perspectives that are gaining daily in urgency.

The End of the Starchitect

In 2007, the overlapping worlds of architecture and design, much like the worlds of politics and finance, and thus of building and spatial development more generally, were very much persuaded that old laws of cycles and periods had definitively yielded to new models of uninterrupted growth, limitless possibilities, and perhaps even the transcendence of the disruptive paradigm of the cyclical, and sometimes, violent, swings of economic growth and building demand. That mood seems hard to recapture. The neologism "starchitect" has lost much of its luster, a term which did little service even to the handful of design talents whose works were regarded from a very superficial set of criteria of relevance largely to the affluent citizens of the G20 countries. It is no longer a viable role model for future designers, the collapse of Lehman Brothers, the sub-prime mortgage crisis, and now the sovereign debt crisis emerging in Europe accompanied by an equally impressive crash of new commissions for expensive private houses and showy museum additions, the prime building types that sustained that "starchitect" attention.

A few short years ago, it seemed that the reduction of the range of tasks for architecture was in direct relationship to the small percentage of the profession who could hope to excel within the paradigms of early twenty-first century media culture. Of course there were other outlets, and some of the most innovative design work even entered

Facing Page
Rising Currents Exhibition
Organized by The Museum of Modern Art in cooperation with P.S.1, 2010.

in a rarified way into public discourse through limited-edition objects, on sale in the overheated art market. Research seemed limited to the academy, ensuring the traditional rift between academy and the profession had widened. But this is not a sustainable model for the interface between design and the world, if it ever was.

I am not among those who believe that we are currently experiencing a temporary downturn; nor that we need simply to wait it out. I am no economist, political scientist, or financial analyst. But it is now abundantly clear—to any of us following the historical information revealed by each new excavation of our assumptions brought on by the crisis—that there were ample signs that that euphoria was untethered long before the band ceased to play, that many of the causes are structural rather than ephemeral. We are living through a paradigm shift as fundamental as that launched when the Reagan and Thatcher revolutions in the English-speaking world set in motion the dual doctrines of unregulated markets and the winnowing of government's role in large-scale planning and intervention for the public good (even as the public sector has continued to grow). These doctrines have become an international paradigm with the accelerated march of globalization that followed in the wake of the sudden thawing of the Cold War. What is certain is that we need to be thinking of new ways of intervening in the world rather than wait for things to return to a "normalcy" that is now a historical artifact—and this is nowhere truer than in architecture and design.

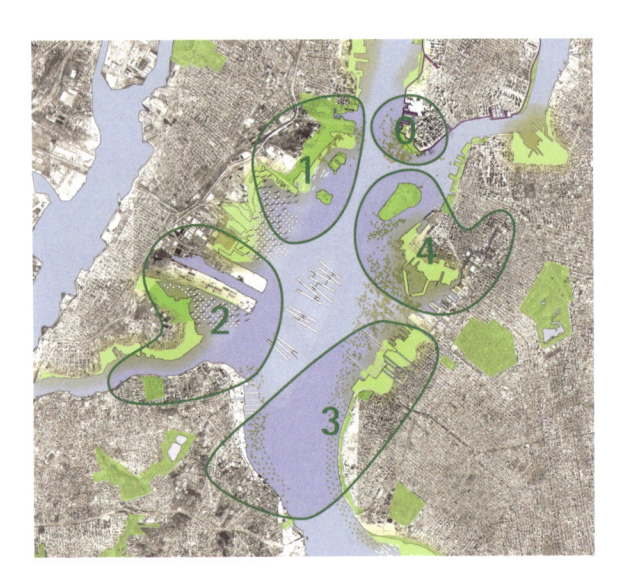

Rising Currents
Projects for New York's Waterfront Architect Teams and Zone Locations.

Zone 0
A New Urban Ground
ARO and dlandstudio, New Urban Ground transforms Lower Manhattan with an infrastructural ecology.

Innovation and Collaboration

Educational institutions are particularly well placed to accelerate the practice of design in emerging new paradigms, not waiting for them to come into focus clearly enough to see where the opportunities lie but building those very opportunities, and engendering the continuation of the exploration of these challenges out into the demanding but very needy environment that exists today for designers. For instance, PennDesign at the University of Pennsylvania, has distinguished itself over and over again as a leader in innovation from the days of Louis Kahn, Robert Venturi, Romaldo Giurgola, and Ian McHarg. The current generation of teachers exploring diverse new paradigms for the delivery of design in the digital age at many leading institutions, along with interdisciplinary connections between landscape and architecture, between regional planning and economic analysis, between design and the current demographic crisis make universities the most interesting laboratories of design potential in the world. If one thing is clear it is that the various professions taught in design schools will only prosper, and will only have the transformative power that is their potential when practiced in taught dialogue and collaboration, in feedback with one another.

This role parallels the challenges I have posed for myself, and it is one that I have tried to facilitate in my own redefinition of curatorial practice. I was hired to guide the architecture and design program of a museum still in the throes of one of the great expansions of the last generation, with ambitious plans on the book for a second expansion in less than a decade. A year later, I found myself negotiating with my colleagues a museum with reduced budgets, eroded endowments, and a smaller staff. Happily—with the Mies van der Rohe archive as one of our greatest assets—we were well placed to face a new age of "Less is More;" and to do so not with the idea that the challenges represented so many problems to solve, but that they must be embraced as new opportunities and new challenges to think unconventionally.

From the first, I gave myself the mandate of making the museum a platform for the stakes of architecture as it is practiced now, a platform where public and professionals alike could confront the process of "design thinking," rather than merely a place to observe the end results. Beautiful buildings on display divorced of the contextual framework of their genesis is an old art museum paradigm that runs ever the risk of reducing architecture to so many consumer or media objects, no matter what the intent of their makers or clients.

This was the goal of the 2008 MoMA exhibition, "Home Delivery," with its complex presentation of the stakes of digital fabrication read against the larger history of the multiple replications of architectural solutions, in the

Zone 1
Water Proving Ground
LTL Architects, Aquatel Pier.

Zone 1
Water Proving Ground
LTL Architects, Concert Pier.

dream of pre-fabrication that has existed since the dawn of the Industrial Revolution. This was also the profile of my colleague Andres Lepik's 2010 exhibition, "Small Scale, Big Change: New Architecture's of Social Engagement," which presented the work of architects around the world who define and invent ways of "getting it done" for the betterment of local populations, rather than waiting for a competition or a commission to come along that might serve as the occasion for such innovation. The coupling of superb, innovative architecture with wholly new ways of transforming an urban or social situation was a revelation for many.

In such exhibitions visitors are shown a profile of the architect as an interdisciplinary artistic and intellectual entrepreneur, rather than simply as the artist who can give brilliantly memorable form to briefs written by others. In avoiding frequent monographic displays, we are determined to promote not individual architects, but rather architecture, landscape, and design as such. We also aim to forefront the full gravitas of their centrality in our public realm, a task all the more important in a period in which the public posting of private wish lists on social media sites often passes as a form of public discourse.

Design Is Central

The challenges of poverty, disaster, or climate change, for instance, require "design thinking." We need emerging design talents to respond to the long-term challenges posed by climate change, especially the accompanying sea level rise, where anywhere from two to six feet more water is expected on a daily basis in our continent's largest metropolis, New York. This is an urgency in which design has not often been seen as central, but our self-given mandate at MoMA was to reveal exactly the contrary: that design is central.

The approach is glocal, an attitude towards acting locally on issues shared planet-wide that has been gaining increasing traction in the face of the uncritical acceptance of globalizing normalization. In 2010, for the first time, more than half the world's population lives in large cities. And of the twenty largest metropolises on the planet, fifteen of them lie substantially in floodable zones that will be remodeled by climate change even without design intervention. *SOAK: Mumbai in an Estuary*, by Anuradha Mathur and Dilip Da Cunha, was one of our inspirations for "Rising Currents."[1]

Even as the "Rising Currents" workshops were underway at MoMA's transformed schoolhouse P.S.1, the estimates of sea level rise were adjusted radically upward, with evidence of more rapid polar ice cap melt. The specific challenge posed to the five interdisciplinary teams of architects, landscape designers, ecologists, engineers, and artists who accepted our invitation to a residency

Active Agents

Zone 2
Working Waterline
Matthew Baird Architects, Bayonne piers and glass reefs.

at P.S.1 was to respond to the AIA College of Fellows Latrobe Research Prize team, a group emblematic of this new interdisciplinarity, led by engineer Guy Nordenson, landscape designer Catherine Seavitt, and architect Adam Yarinsky, which called for a radical expansion of the palette of techniques for intervention. Implicit was a critique of the ruling doctrine of both the U.S. Army Corps of Engineers and the developers who have made a bee-line for New York City's waterfront: to include not only traditional hard infrastructure approaches, but also a whole range of "soft" infrastructure techniques and design interventions which are multi-functional and protective as well as energy producing.

At a time when the national debate on infrastructure and new energy sources was focused on "shovel-ready" projects that would stimulate the economy, it seemed to me vital to demonstrate—even on the modest scale of a small set of case studies, or "soundings"—that we have an important opportunity to foster new research and fresh thinking about the use of urban coastlines, about the collaborative designs of architects and landscape designers, and the fact that design is a forum for imagining wholly new solutions rather than a way of decorating solutions found by others. Rather than running from the rising sea levels and leaving the problem solving to engineers who will build the defenses, we sought to harness the new interdisciplinary experiments that have been emerging in the design world and in academia to embrace the coastline, to mediate the environmental challenges, and to provide both solutions and images. The production of images that can actually motivate public discourse is as important as the solutions themselves for thinking of mid-twenty-first century urban life differently.

The audiences were multi-fold, as they must be for an architectural gallery inside one of the world's most visited and popular museums of art: the general public, government policy makers who de facto form the physical fabric of the region, and the design professions themselves in a period when the economic recession provides challenges not experienced for two generations. Attendance at MoMA was been beyond our wildest hopes, even if the level of exchange on the accompanying web site revealed that we all still have a long way to go to bridge the gap between speaking to one another as designers, and to the vital task ahead of us: claiming a central place at the national public debate about infrastructure, climate structure, the post sub-prime crisis development, the aging of the population, and myriad other urgent issues where design should be at the table from the earliest planning stages.

Some are bewildered by this new use of the museum not as a sanctuary for continually re-launching a battle in a war I believe won long ago—namely the status of architecture as art—but rather my posturing of the museum as a form of advocacy. MoMA was founded

Zone 3
New Aqueous City
nARCHITECTS, Viewed from Sunset Park, showing residential buildings hung from shared bridge structures, floating treatment wetlands, and wave attenuating public piers.

Zone 4
Oyster-Tecture
SCAPE, An approximation of the "fuzzy rope" oyster nets proposed for the shallow waters just south of Red Hook, Brooklyn.

within days of the stock market crash of 1929 and came of age in the Depression. From the first its agenda was multi-fold. Even if most architectural histories have preferred to retain the aesthetic manifesto of Philip Johnson and Henry-Russell Hitchcock's seminal "International Style" exhibition of 1932, in fact the most sustained activity of the department's first decade was in exhibitions and programs advocating for better public housing. These had direct impacts on the creation of the New York City Housing Authority in 1934, and on the passage of the Federal Housing Act of 1937, much of this due to the activism of the young Catherine Bauer, in her 20s at the time, and the advocacy of Lewis Mumford.

It is the renewal of this advocacy role that has seemed to me increasingly urgent in defining the role of a Department of Architecture and Design, not only as a mirror of the range of invention, innovation, and artistry to be found today in the design professions, but also as an instrument, even an agent, for the engagement of the design professions with the most pressing issues of the day. I hope that we might agree that this form of engagement is the most viable posture for a design professional as the twenty-first century enters its second decade—with a sense of anxiety more justly felt than that which accompanied the ephemeral Y2K threat, a momentary blip in an unthinking faith in technology. Since then, the digital forces of the globe have revealed themselves capable of causing radical destruction and shifts of wealth in automatically programmed sales and purchases of stocks by mega-computers malfunctioning for a nanosecond, even as computer-driven armaments often fail to reach their real targets.

While there is indeed real cause for anxiety, and new crises continue to emerge, the most pertinent stance young designers can take is to translate the wealth of research in which they have engaged in design school into further activist engagement. Their challenge is to convert the daily stakes they took on as students into new research opportunities and to advocate for the central role of design in the robustness of the societies within which they elect to practice as a central part of any national agenda. But this is something a designer can only do once he or she has calibrated their own ethical compass, set a standard for what it means to act as a designer, and engaged to work collaboratively with the other disciplines that have been trained side-by-side, and with the issues that the fast changing global situation is bringing us every day. The architecture of the future will not be a new set of formal experiments, but rather a new approach to working together to craft a meaningful public realm resilient to the challenges already evidently manifest before us.

Endnotes
1   Anuradha Mathur and Dilip da Cunha, *SOAK: Mumbai in an Estuary* (New Delhi: Rupa, 2009).

The Suburbs are Dead, Long Live the Suburbs!
John D. Landis

In the June 2010 issue of *The Atlantic Monthly,* urban planner and real estate developer Christopher Leinberger declared the era of the postwar suburb to be at long last over.[1] The demise of the suburb was brought on by long commutes, falling real estate prices, commodity-like subdivision designs, and a lack of walkability. Fueled by growing population and household diversity and rising popular concerns over sustainability, future suburbs, Leinberger argued, would consist of walkable, mixed-use, higher density urban-like centers closer to traditional downtown cores. Viewing this shift as desirable, Leinberger further suggested that local governments help it along by partnering with private developers to finance new or improved transit service and pedestrian-oriented infrastructure improvements, and by establishing special assessment districts to capture the property value increases associated with these investments. Most city planners and urban designers will surely welcome Leinberger's predictions as a long overdue change from the essential sameness of too many American suburbs.

Not everyone agrees with Leinberger. Geographer Joel Kotkin, author of the 2010 book, *The Next 100 Million: America in 2050,* sees the traditional postwar American suburb as much more durable *and* more desirable.[2] Kotkin argues that while many American suburbs will gain city-like amenities, particularly walkable downtowns and a greater sense of place, the characteristics of American suburbs that have made them so attractive in the past—the ability to own one's own home, the flexibility of the detached single-family home to accommodate many different demographic and social preferences, and the opportunity to live among people who, while not always similar, share aspirational values—will ensure that suburbs remain America's dominant land use form. Moreover, whereas Leinberger points to declining housing prices among fringe suburbs as foresaging their end, if anything, the fall in condominium values in urban cores has been much greater. In both cases the cause of the decline was overbuilding and over-leveraged borrowers, not a fundamental shift in household preferences.

Kotkin and Leinberger aren't completely in different worlds. Whereas Kotkin agrees that *some* suburbs may become more urban, Leinberger acknowledges *some* need for suburban expansion to accommodate future population growth, especially in the South and West. These two points of overlap aside, Kotkin sees the future of American metro areas as occurring through a more benign form of sprawl, whereas Leinberger sees it largely as one of infill and urban redevelopment.

Sprawl by the Numbers
What does the data show? A recent study of residential building permits in the fifty largest metropolitan areas by John Thomas of the Environmental Protection Agency seems to support Leinberger's view.[3] Thomas identified twenty-one metro areas in which central cities more than doubled their share of residential building permits between 2003 and 2008 compared to the early 1990s.

(Fig. 1) Counting older suburban communities, there were eight metropolitan areas in which 2003-2008 residential building permits in the downtown and core suburban areas accounted for a third or more of total metropolitan permits: San Jose, New York, Los Angeles-Anaheim, San Diego, Virginia Beach-Norfolk, Miami-Ft. Lauderdale, San Francisco-Oakland, and Chicago. As Figure 2 indicates, the factors most strongly associated with core area construction activity were population growth, metropolitan area size (core areas grew more in larger metropolitan areas), and a coastal location.

Even as many older, dense suburbs regain their former attractiveness, newer suburbs are also densifying. Between 1990 and 2000, the average population density of *all* large U.S. metropolitan areas rose from 460 to 520 persons per square mile, an increase of 16%.[4] (Fig. 3) Compared by region, average densities increased most among Western metros (rising from 490 persons per square mile in 1990 to 580 persons per square mile in 2000) and least among Midwestern metros (rising from 410 persons per square mile in 1990 to 450 in 2000). Compared by size category, average densities rose the most among very large metros (from 1,220 persons per square mile in 1990 to 1,370 in 2000) and least among very small metros. Two factors are behind these increases and differences: geography and sewers. For the most part, metropolitan regions in the Mountain region and West have less easy-to-build land available for new development. Developers and planners seeking to accommodate new population and business growth must therefore do so at higher densities. Most

Figure 1
Central City Share of Metropolitan Residential Building Permits
Sorted by growth in Central City share.
Source: U.S. EPA, 2010.

	1990 - 1995	2003 - 2008	2003 - 2008 Share / 1990 - 1995 Share
Miami	2%	17%	8.5
Washington DC	1%	6%	6.0
Boston	2%	10%	5.0
St. Louis	1%	5%	5.0
Baltimore	2%	9%	4.5
Philadelphia	3%	13%	4.3
Denver	5%	21%	4.2
St. Paul	1%	4%	4.0
Chicago	7%	27%	3.9
Atlanta	4%	14%	3.5
Minneapolis	2%	7%	3.5
Richmond	2%	7%	3.5
New York City	15%	48%	3.2
Ft. Worth	5%	16%	3.2
Milwaukee	6%	18%	3.0
Portland	9%	26%	2.9
Sacramento	9%	23%	2.6
Detroit	2%	5%	2.5
Birmingham	5%	11%	2.2
San Francisco	5%	11%	2.2
Oakland	3%	6%	2.0
Seattle	11%	21%	1.9
Kansas City, MO	12%	21%	1.8
Los Angeles**	11%	17%	1.5
Cleveland	4%	6%	1.5
Cincinnati	4%	5%	1.3
Hartford	4%	5%	1.3
Salt Lake City	6%	7%	1.2
San Jose	11%	12%	1.1
Dallas	13%	12%	0.9
San Diego	42%	37%	0.9

Active Agents

Figure 2
Central City and Core Suburban Residential Building Permits
As Share of Metro Permits by Metro Size, Population Growth, and Location, 2003-2008
Source: Author's tabulations, based on U.S. EPA, 2010.

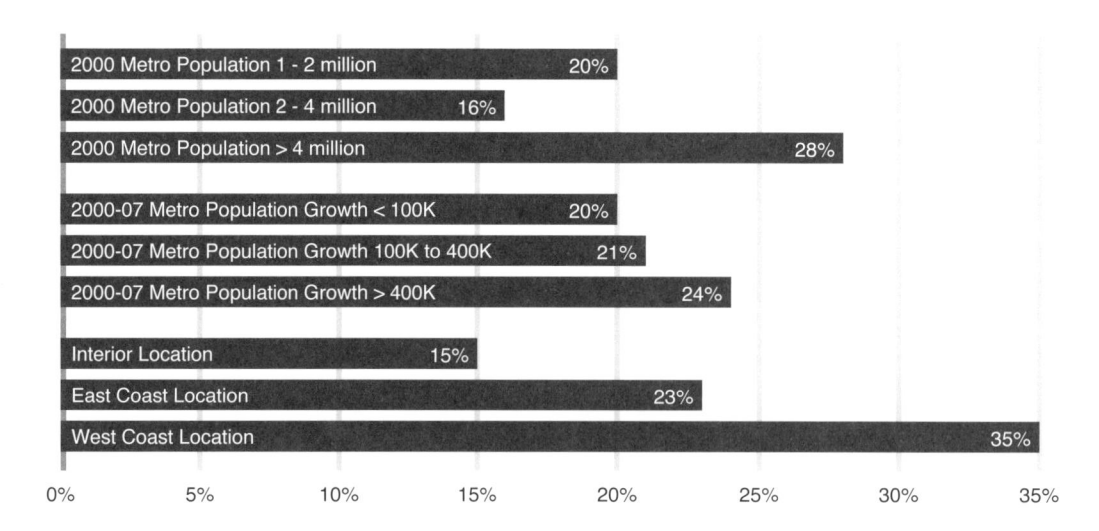

Category	Percentage
2000 Metro Population 1 - 2 million	20%
2000 Metro Population 2 - 4 million	16%
2000 Metro Population > 4 million	28%
2000-07 Metro Population Growth < 100K	20%
2000-07 Metro Population Growth 100K to 400K	21%
2000-07 Metro Population Growth > 400K	24%
Interior Location	15%
East Coast Location	23%
West Coast Location	35%

suburban subdivision codes require new homes to be attached to public sewer lines, and as Fulton, Pendall, et. al. discovered in their analysis of changes in metropolitan densities between 1982 and 1997, sewer requirements are strongly correlated with higher densities.[5]

Architects and designers look at sprawl from the perspective of density and design homogeneity. Urban and environmental planners also look at it in terms of resource land consumption. Between 1990 and 2000, new development within U.S. metropolitan areas consumed an average of 0.36 acres of total land and 0.30 acres of resource land (including farms, forests, and pastures) per additional resident. (Fig. 4) Compared by metro area size, rates of land conversion were lowest in large metropolitan areas and highest in smaller ones.[6] Among large metros, each new resident accounted for 0.29 acres of newly urbanized land, whereas in small metros, the rate was 0.62 acres. Among regions, land conversion totals were highest among Midwestern metros and lowest among metropolitan areas in the West. Indeed, at 0.7 acres per new resident, urban growth among Midwestern metros consumed more than three times the amount of undeveloped land per person as urban growth in Western metros. What accounts for these differences? Land prices are higher in large metropolitan areas, encouraging developers to use available sites more intensely. This results in lower conversion rates. In the West and Mountain regions, the combination of strong population growth, limited land supplies, and more extensive land use and environmental regulations encourages developers to build at higher densities. In the Midwest, population growth has been much more meager, and easy-to-develop farmland is abundant. This keeps land prices and densities low, and conversion rates high.

Higher densities come with smaller lots and sometimes, smaller homes. After rising continuously for four decades, there is some evidence that new home sizes are finally leveling off, or even declining slightly. (Fig. 5) It used to be that bigger houses (those with additional bedrooms and bigger garages) appreciated more rapidly, but no more. Today, appreciation rates are more a matter of location (neighborhood and metro area) than size or features. Rising energy prices, shrinking lot sizes, and a more restrained ending environment are also putting a break on home sizes. This does not mean that Americans are falling out of love with single-family homes. There is something about the single-family home, with its separate entrance, lack of common walls, private front and back yard (however small), and ease of upgrading and modification that, according to homebuilder surveys, continues to make it the housing style of choice for every household type.

Figure 3
Average Metropolitan Densities
By MSA Size and Region, 1990 and 2000
Source: The author, compiled from U.S. Census Tiger data.

	Average Population Density, 1990 Persons per sq. mile	Average Population Density, 2000 Persons per sq. mile	Density Change, 1990 - 2000 Persons per sq. mile	Percent Density Change, 1990 - 2000
All Metropolitan Areas	450	520	70	16%
Northeast MSAs	825	890	65	8%
Midwest MSAs	410	450	40	10%
Southern MSAs	310	370	60	19%
Western MSAs	490	580	90	18%
Very Large MSAs > 4M Population	1,220	1,370	150	12%
Large MSAs 1M - 4M Population	610	710	100	16%
Medium-Sized MSAs 500K - 1M Population	350	400	50	14%
Small MSAs 250K - 500K Population	270	310	40	15%
Very Small MSAs 100K - 250 Population	160	180	20	13%

Re-inventing Suburban Town Planning

With many American suburbs now approaching middle age, the central task facing today's city planners and urban designers is how to remake them *in place* into something still recognizable but better—that is, into something in which single-family homes are still the dominant development form, but in a manner in which they are better connected to neighborhood and regional commercial centers (and to public facilities such as parks and schools) via multiple modes, especially walking. What makes this task difficult is that we lack good baseline studies of how different suburban formats perform in the real world. Transportation planners, for example, use empirical trip generation rates based separately on land uses, densities, and household characteristics; and not on how these factors combine to create 'travel opportunity spaces.' Nor do we have a particularly good understanding of neighborhood change trajectories—how the forms and function of particular suburban morphologies change over time and why.

For those who care about the future of American suburbs, the first task must therefore be to benchmark the social, economic, and environmental performance of different suburban types and forms in different metropolitan contexts. Do New Urbanist suburbs really have a smaller carbon footprint than more traditional suburbs? Is building a higher-density, master planned community at the urban fringe really all that different from building conventional residential subdivisions of quarter-acre lots? In areas of poor or mediocre transit service, will higher densities or more walkable urban designs really move the mode choice needle? For example, a recent National Research Council study of the effects of alternative development patterns on car versus transit use found that the degree of incremental densification required to get people out of their cars and into buses or onto light-rail would be so extreme as to be unpalatable.[7] Before we embrace alternative suburban forms and designs as more desirable, we first need to do our homework. Out of such research should come a new set of empirically based principles for modern suburban town planning. These principles may ultimately come to resemble those articulated by New Urbanists, or for those with longer memories, by Clarence Perry in the 1920s regarding the proper design of the 'neighborhood unit.'

Some challenges are obvious. In older neighborhoods, architects and designers must develop locally-appropriate templates for upgrading and up-sizing older homes, many of which are too small for today's households and have obsolete floor plans. Urban designers and transportation planners will have to re-conceptualize existing street systems, alleyways, pocket parks, older public buildings,

Housing Development, Markham, Ontario

and the occasional vacant lot as a *network of neighborhood infrastructure*. Urban planners will have to recast local zoning laws to neutralize the purely anti-change sentiments of local NIMBYism, attract pedestrian-oriented and neighborhood-based retail uses, and following Leinberger's suggestion, adopt new financial mechanisms to pay for these improvements.[8]

Many newer subdivisions will also require modification if they are to retain their long-term value and attractiveness. Backyards will have to be opened up to connecting pedestrian ways, front yards and street frontages will have to be redesigned and landscaped in ways that stitch subdivisions together while disguising the cookie-cutter designs and close-packed nature of recent suburban homes. Neighborhood commercial centers will have to be turned inside-out as buildings move to the front of the lot and parking moves to the back. Larger power centers should be redeveloped as smaller town and recreation centers. In some places, fragmented and dysfunctional open spaces and empty lots should give way to small-scale neighborhood retail projects. Voluntary *suburban investment districts*, modeled after center city business improvement districts, will have to be established to pay for these improvements.

Longer-term, and beyond the redesign of residential subdivisions, urban planners must face the fact that employment will likely continue decentralizing, and provided that new employment locations are within walkable distances of residential areas, this trend could actually contribute to metropolitan environmental and

Figure 5
Average Square Footage of New Single-Family Homes
1990-2009
Source: U.S. Census Bureau.

	Acres of All Land Types Converted to Urban Uses, 1992 - 2001	Acres of Farm, Forest, and Pasture Land Converted to Urban Uses, 1992 - 2001	Population Change, 1990 - 2000	Per capita Land Conversion 1992 - 2001 Acres converted per additional resident	Per capita *Resource* Land Conversion 1992 - 2001 Acres converted per additional resident
All Metropolitan Areas	151,943	126,008	26,053,651	0.36	0.30
Northeast MSAs	25,707	24,539	4,355,210	0.36	0.35
Midwest MSAs	40,795	39,111	3,603,705	0.70	0.67
Southern MSAs	58,871	50,400	9,972,125	0.36	0.31
Western MSAs	26,570	11,958	8,122,611	0.20	0.09
Very Large MSAs > 4M Population	31,572	24,689	6,321,864	0.31	0.24
Large MSAs 1M - 4M Population	47,538	39,361	10,130,641	0.29	0.24
Medium-Sized MSAs 500K - 1M Population	23,744	19,866	3,880,348	0.38	0.32
Small MSAs 250K - 500K Population	25,796	21,839	3,411,304	0.47	0.40
Very Small MSAs 100K - 250 Population	23,293	20,253	2,309,494	0.62	0.54

Figure 4
Total and Resource Land Converted to Urban Uses
By MSA Size and Region, 1992-2001
Source: The author, compiled from U.S. Geological Survey Land Cover Data.

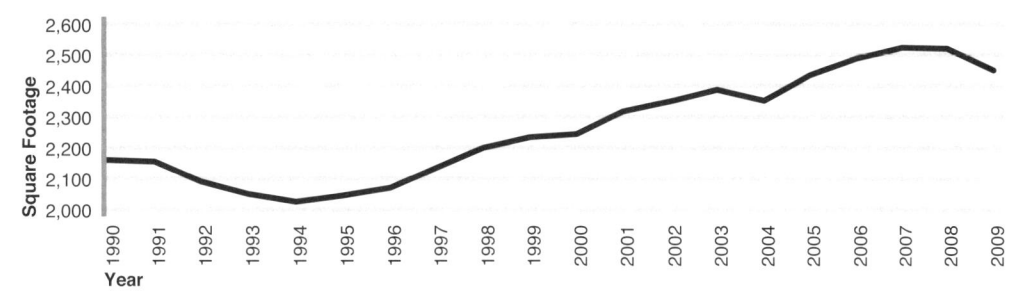

financial sustainability. This will require retrofitting existing office parks and retail power centers (most likely with residential uses) and joining them together into new town centers. This is already happening. In Belmar, Colorado for example, an obsolete regional shopping mall has been redeveloped as a new town center incorporating regional employers, residential condominiums, live-work space, and national and local retail tenants.[9]

Endnotes

1 Christopher Leinberger, "Here Comes the Neighborhood," *The Atlantic Monthly* (June 2010).
2 Joel Kotkin, *The Next Hundred Million: America in 2050* (New York: Penguin Press, 2010).
3 John V. Thomas, *Residential Construction Trends in America's Metropolitan Regions* (Washington, DC: U.S. Environmental Protection Agency, 2010).
4 These estimates were obtained by dividing the total MSA population by total land area net of federal and state lands; they include non-residential land uses and rural residential sites as well as residential land uses.
5 William Fulton, Rolf Pendall, Mai Nguyen, and Alicia Harrison, *Who Sprawls Most? How Growth Patterns Differ Across the U.S.* (Washington, DC: The Brookings Institute, 2001).
6 Low per capita land conversion rates indicate that land is being used efficiently; high rates indicate that land is being used inefficiently. Low rates are associated with a smaller urban footprint and less sprawl. Higher rates are associated with a larger footprint and more sprawl.
7 National Research Council, *Driving and the Built Environment: The Effects of Compact Development on Motorized Travel, Energy Use, and CO2 Emissions* (Washington, DC: Transportation Research Board, 2009).
8 Christopher Leinberger, *The Option of Urbanism* (Washington, DC: Island Press, 2010).
9 Ellen Dunham-Jones, *Retrofitting Suburbia: Urban Design Solutions for Redesigning Suburbs* (New York: Wiley & Sons, 2008).

Pathos and Irony
Industrial Still-Life in Japan
Tetsugo Hyakutake

Active Agents

Top
Pathos and Irony: Industrial Still-Life 1, 2006

Bottom
Pathos and Irony: Industrial Still-Life 2, 2006

Previous Spread, Left
Nihonbashi, 2007

Previous Spread, Right
Pathos and Irony: Industrial Still-Life 21, 2007

The inherent duality of industrialization in Japan: the strength of progress and the fragility of the human lives that make it happen, are visible in these photographs. They show industrial landscapes imbued with a sense of pathos, as well as an ironic beauty, that reveal the emotional complexities of advancing modern society. While there is no visual evidence of human lives in these industrial structures, they cannot be stripped of the humanity that created them.

Post-war Japanese identity has been largely shaped by recovery from defeat and the physical destruction of cities for super-speed economic development imported from the West. The economic disaster of the "Lost Decade" in the 1990s, a result of this high-speed development, left little room for the Japanese people to reflect upon, understand and create a uniquely japanese identity. The work is partly a tribute to those who toiled to build Japan into a superpower, providing a space to contemplate both sides of the development story.

Active Agents

Top
Pathos and Irony: Industrial Still-Life 16, 2007

Bottom
Pathos and Irony: Industrial Still-Life 17, 2007

Active Agents

Shibuya Station, 2007

Pathos and Irony Tetsugo Hyakutake

Active Agents

Dirty Cities, Dirtier Policies
The Philadelphia Office of Sustainability
Mark Alan Hughes and William W. Braham in conversation

Dirt Editors Helene Furján, Lily Jencks and Gabriela Sarhos brought together Mark Alan Hughes and William Braham for a discussion of the links between policy and design.

Dirt

We are interested in roles and goals: when you were a blogger and columnist for the Philadelphia Daily News, you were dirty—operating as critic, trying to change the system from the outside-in; now that you are the establishment, you're messy—working from within but, as you will explain, horizontally, in order to change the system from the inside-out. We are interested in how a sustainability director might operate, how you have set up your department, and what your combined background in policy and architecture might uniquely provide. How are you able to operate in this position in a way that we would call productively 'dirty'?

Mark Alan Hughes

One of the really unexpected and tricky parts of this process has been that it takes time to build an apparatus for accepting help. Interestingly, I have been 'loaned' executives: from the Clinton Foundation, the federal government, and especially Laurie Actman, the chief policy adviser from the Chamber of Commerce, who has functioned as a fulltime deputy in the creation and operation of the Office of Sustainability. Less formally, I've gotten literally hundreds of people and institutions expressing their desire to help. Their momentum, their appetite, and just being able to acknowledge all of them, for the obvious political reasons, is very important—but, being able to sort it in a way that I can really make use of it is a full-time job.

William W. Braham

Mark you're on an interesting trajectory, having dipped into architectural education—yet gotten so incredibly much out of it—and then set up an entirely new Department of Sustainability for the City of Philadelphia. Your link to architecture, coming to the field out of policy as you did, is an interesting proposition for me as an environmentalist-architect. I've been trying to make the case to architects for a long time that ecology matters, a topic which so often seems to fall outside the normal realm of what architects do and think about.

Mark Alan Hughes

Architects are well situated not only for the public discourse but also the professional activity of making energy conservation happen. And the extent to which I was prepared at all [laughs] for what I'm doing now is what I learned here at PennDesign, both in specific courses and in the general culture that the School provides.

This is precisely what tempted me away from policy to architecture: I couldn't think of any place on earth where I would learn more every day than architecture school. So what then drew me away from architecture school and back to policy is not loyalty to the mayor, and it's certainly not any appetite for governing; it was the chance to put into practice what I'd been learning about sustainability while I was in the school, which in itself will continue to require an even greater learning.

Dirty Systems
William W. Braham

In the spirit of the name of the issue, which is both provocative and brings various topics together, I want to think seriously about the connection between dirt and the "ecological question". On the one hand, there is what I jokingly call compost theology. It is perhaps more common in California, though it's certainly become more prevalent here on the East Coast. And it's usually characterized as the narrow subset of people you think of as traditionally caring about these kinds of environmental subjects: for the people who have compost piles, they are in a way the source of a whole body of belief. But when the same idea is put in economic terms, the debate shifts. In essence, I take stuff from here that's nasty and dirty and I put it there, and within a matter of weeks or months it becomes valuable, fertile. Trash becomes value, becomes a new kind of "dirt". It's the business of closing loops. Mark, I think all the time about the diagram you made last year: a spatialized flow-diagram of a typical row house in Philadelphia that examined the scales at which processes occur.

Dirt

The notion of "home economics" that Bill's talking about, and that you diagrammed, imply that you can't think about the house or the building without thinking of the whole infrastructure, which is a systems approach,

Solar Powered Bin
One of hundreds of solar-powered trash compactors being deployed in Philadelphia.

Philadelphia's Recycle Truck

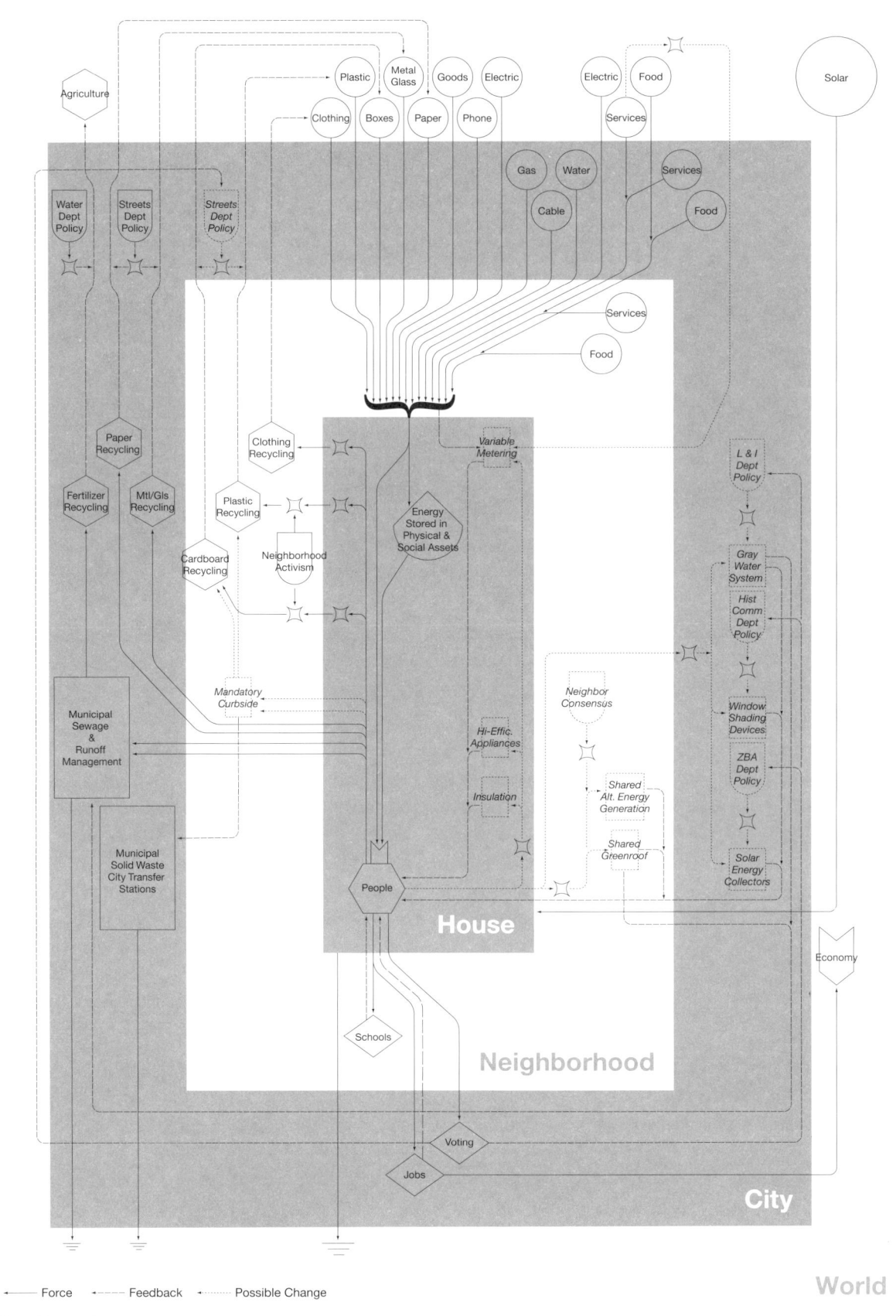

Dirty Cities, Dirtier Policies Mark Alan Hughes and William W. Braham

or ecological thinking. Otherwise you can't really understand the energy systems and flows that this one little node is a part of. That has a direct implication back to a school of design: architecture, landscape, urban design, economics, and socio-political factors have to be thought of together to understand the problem, which forces architecture in particular to rethink scale.

Mark Alan Hughes

One good example comes from the retrofitting of buildings, especially their envelopes and mechanical systems. Both clients and the public now understand that recapturing energy alone—the thirty or forty percent of energy reduction available to us through conservation in buildings—would mean that we never have to build another fossil fuel-powered plant again. That kind of understanding and the ability to articulate it simply, decouples all kinds of processes: for instance, the utility companies are now getting out of the commodities business where the only way they can get paid is to sell you a fuel. Now they get paid to help you conserve. Philadelphia Gas Works is trying to get into the Public Utilities Commission (PUC) that regulates utilities in Pennsylvania before the 2010 electricity caps go off to say to the PUC "give us a rate hike of twenty-five million dollars at the meter, and we will promise and verify to spend that twenty-five million on energy conservation." In other words, they have a scheme by which they will be paid indirectly through the rates for conservation, of ultimately reducing the total amount of gas they actually sell. So they are decoupling their business. But you can't get there, and you certainly can't build the politics that support such a move, without an understanding of the bigger picture, and what that means in costs and benefits.

Gabriela Sarhos

Jose Castillo writes about informal communities in Mexico City that happen because there isn't a governmental infrastructure to create them. The political cycle is very short, a mere two years, so a project must be done within those two years to get done at all. As a result, people are building outside the system of government, and feed back into it only when the city comes in to formalize the services that in reality simply support what is already there. Philadelphia, meanwhile, is teetering towards becoming the next Portland, which perhaps could not happen to a more calcified city like New York or Boston.

Mark Alan Hughes

This is a great question. To push us over that edge, Philadelphia will have to give up the central control that governments, even local governments, have traditionally held over the behaviors needed to affect change at the urban scale. I think technology is central to a more dirt-centric approach to policy, although what we are talking about here are systems, if "dirty" systems. Barack Obama, as one example, has been incredibly savvy at a systemically "dirty" mode of thinking: encouraging people at rallies to text a number that, on election morning, sent a text back from the campaign not only worked to retain energy and excitement, but also allowed his team to capture all those cell phone numbers! It's an amazing organizing device.

Bloomberg's million trees, as another example, it is of course absolutely impossible in the traditional sense—a city government can't plant a million trees—but what you can do is build a web page, accessible to both computers and mobile phones for maximum reach, where people who want to help can go and say, "I have a tree bed where a tree died five years ago, it's ready for a tree, please send one when you can," or "I planted a tree in a tree bed, please credit the city for that tree that I planted," or "I am willing to plant four trees in my side yard, please send two as I have two myself." You create an opportunity that technology can inventory, but also promote, galvanize, and reward, while letting citizenry or external-to-government actors actually implement the government's agenda, and in a way that probably survives government transition.

Part of our traditional response to this in the United States has been to celebrate our NGO infrastructure, which has been terrific in many ways, but can get ossified and often has to be rethought and revolutionized every generation or so. Technology, on the other hand, is so decentralized that it can get you very far very quickly, but you lose all kinds of control as a result. Cities are exploring ways in which technology can be deployed to engage public momentum because under-resourced governments simply can't tackle problems alone.

William W. Braham

You made me wonder, to what degree is the whole spectrum of things that falls under your new sustainability oversight similar to or different from traditional local government concerns? Things like trash, the snow, and so on.

Mark Alan Hughes

We could have designed a Department of the Environment—instead of an Office of Sustainability—as has been done to some degree in New York, and more fully in Chicago and Los Angeles. You could build such a department, as you probably would have to do, by consolidating things that now exist in other departments. But in practice that means you end up with the issues and problems that nobody really cares about, and you never get to touch the core missions of those big, powerful departments that really matter. Partly by necessity—because it's just me and nobody's going to ask me to come in and do a bunch of bureaucratic heavy-lifting—and partly because I'm an idea advocate, this is a large experiment in matrix management. Because I'm largely on my own but in the cabinet among peers who each control thousands of employees, I have to rely on other people's reporting lines and budgets. But the advantage is that sustainability is understood as pervasive throughout government. Rather than locate it to a singular place in government, it's inherently thematic across government: a horizontal model in which the Office of Sustainability is distributed across every other department, across the entire city government. Every department uses energy, every department generates waste, every department has a stake in how we do capital and operating budgets, and therefore every department is implicated in and by sustainability.

Dirt

Mark, my interest in systems theory is identical to yours, which is to say that it isn't systems theory as systems theorists think of it, it's actually thinking of systems from the point of view of infiltration. Your method is a method of infiltration. It's kind of a stealth move.

Mark Alan Hughes

We just instituted a performance management system in city government for the first time in Philadelphia, under the Managing Director's Office. It's modeled on "CityStat", already implemented in cities like New York and Baltimore, which we're calling "PhillyStat". All city government departments are given a set of goals and a set of metrics that measure their progress towards those goals. Every quarter, they have to publicly report on their progress toward those goals to the entire executive team and to the managing director, and account for the ways they have or have not met their goals. The system thus operates on a feedback mechanism, with well-specified goals complemented by incentives, and public derision or congratulations, all of which relies on performance measured by reporting.

At the moment, all departments draw their budgets from what's called the General Fund, except for the two Enterprise Funds—the Airport and the Water Department—which have their own huge amounts of money. What that means is that the Police Department, Licences and Inspections, Planning Department, Health Department, and so on, never directly pay their energy bills. Departments simply aren't aware of the costs of running their buildings: whatever the electricity, gas, and water bills turn out to be that month get paid centrally, and they don't even see the bills. It's the worst possible scenario. The Municipal Energy Office, which has been absorbed by the Office of Sustainability and is our one line management function, gets boxes of PECO Energy Company bills that look exactly like the PECO bills you get at home. They are for individual buildings, such as Rec Center 27 or Rec Center 35, but if you look at the top-line account for the whole Recreation Department, for instance, it's $700,000 for electricity for the month of March. Since January 2008, the Energy Office reports on energy use by the city, and we have now centralized data management to give the numbers to the commissioner or director of each department, who then reports on what her energy use is and accounts for its trajectory. We're also working with the budget director to realign this budget process so that departments pay for their own energy bills directly.

Dirt

Do they get incentives if they use less?

Mark Alan Hughes

Exactly.

Dirt

And hopefully the sticker shock will promote change when each department finds out just how large the bills are.

Mark Alan Hughes

Yes, again. We plan to institute a sustainability fund that will be a shared savings fund. We will keep year-to-year energy records listing what each department has saved, but each department must come up with their own plans, using innovation, new management practices, new budgeting methods, building monitoring systems (especially for dispersed facilities), and so on. We help by investing in their proposals to make them feasible and help implement them. But they are also tasked with working out how to get their own employees to change their behavior to reduce energy consumption in their facilities. Then we split those savings with them. Energy is eminently measurable, and hence easy to hold departments accountable for, but to really change usage, you need this simple proposition of aligning incentives with behaviors, so that people get rewarded. Through this method, we predict we can get five million dollars worth of savings in the first year.

P(h)lans

Mark Alan Hughes

The hidden agenda is to publish Philadelphia's own PlanNYC. I have my own copy of PlanNYC. I walk around with it. It's the best such document I have ever seen because it's not a plan, it's a campaign. So, we're going to have a P[h]lan that will be an organizing device for programmatic initiatives and we'll have seven years of implementation by bringing it out at the beginning of the Nutter administration. By designing the process that allows Philadelphia city government and its external constituencies and partners to produce our version of that report, we'll create a venue that allows for the highest level policy alignment and priority setting. Right now we don't have a way, and there's just too much going on in any one day to do any strategic thinking. We need to think about how we align, about opportunities for synergies. For me it's all about speaking to people by speaking for them, raising the level of discourse both in government and among citizens. You have people now talking about open space, how to generate support for green infrastructure.

Greensgrow Farm
Philadelphia, Pennsylvania

Active Agents

William W. Braham

So what is the link between dirt and sustainability?

Mark Alan Hughes

You can talk about dirt at the scale of the city of Philadelphia. We are a grey city. We are dirt. In the world of the United States as a metropolitan settlement system, we are as thrown away, as dirty as you could possibly get in that settlement system, except maybe Youngstown. But at our scale, we account for more dirt than any other settlement in the urban system. So we need to recycle the city, reengineering it in a way that helps it find its new place. There is no waste; waste is food. The greenest building is the one you've already built. The cheapest unit of energy is the one you conserve rather than generate. All these aphorisms favor cities, and figuring out how those aphorisms get oriented to a specific city, a dirty city like Philadelphia is a big piece of what this agenda is about.

The hidden agenda is about this green infrastructure: how do you get people excited about this, how do you see that dirt as fertile rather than abject?

William W. Braham

On the one hand you are successfully launching off from the old sense of ecology: household management. Any farmer does what cities would like to do as a matter of course: recycling dirt. "Of course I'm not going to throw that away because I might be able to use it or sell it." On the other hand, there is the urge towards health. It's easy to imagine the most dramatic contrast between dirt and the kind of health offered in a hospital, the cleanest possible place, at least in theory. I'm wondering about the convergence of "dirt" and health.

Mark Alan Hughes

Let me give you some examples of how this is playing

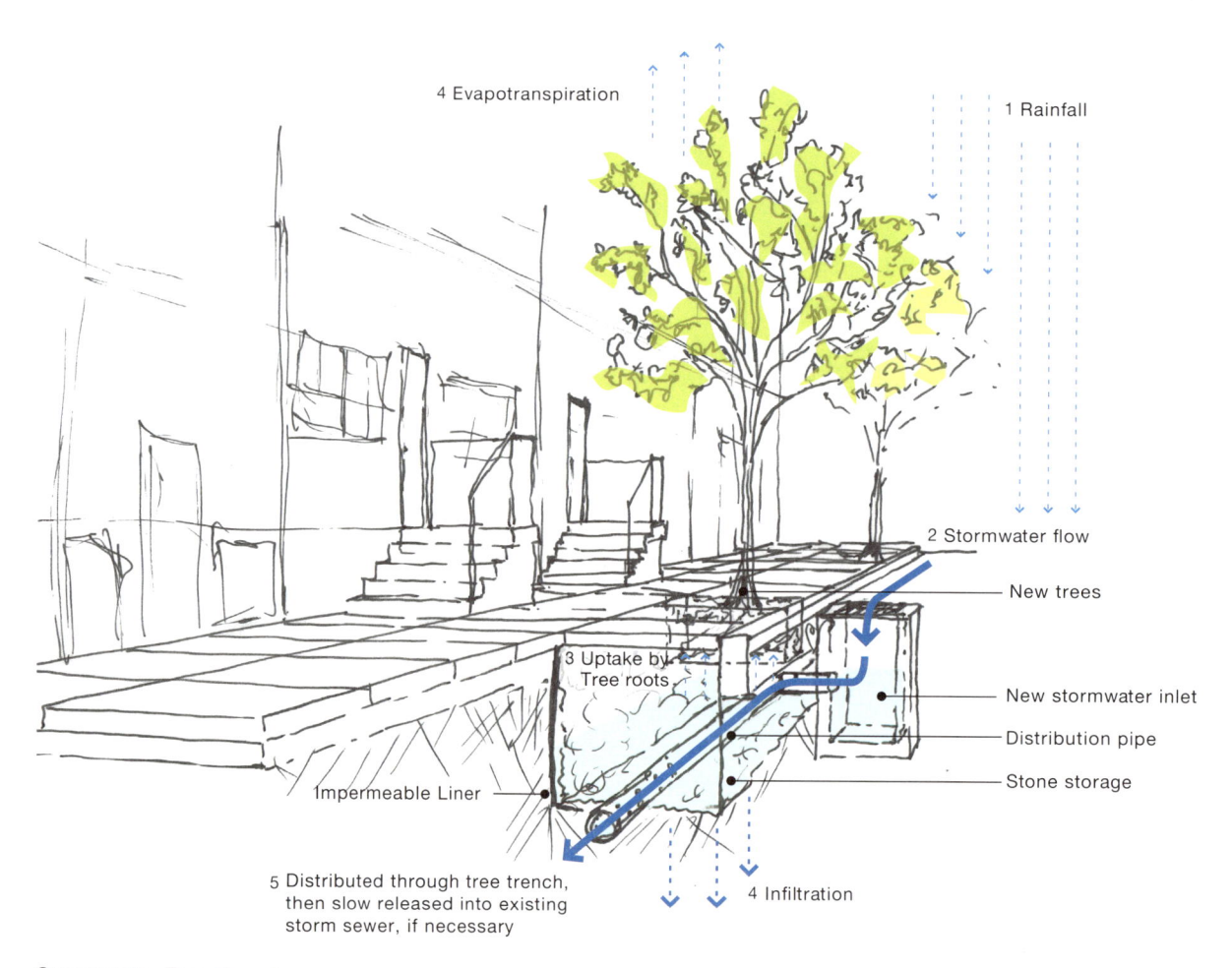

Stormwater Tree Trench
Sub-Surface View

out. We have a big effort right now regarding regional food policy: the Mayor has issued an executive order announcing the Food Charter and establishing a new Food Policy Council. Many big cities around the world now are talking about food security. As the distance between the dots grows larger (source to sales point, for instance), national chain stores like Whole Foods reprint their bags with "locally grown food," and the IVCC (The Innovative Vector Control Consortium, combating insect-borne diseases) talks about global food security, people understand the issues, and we see initiatives developing here in Philadelphia: Penn's Urban Nutrition Initiative (a K-16+ education program), the Food Trust (nutritional, education access, and public policy promotion, including school food programs and farmers markets), Weavers Way (natural food coop and community-funding body), Philadelphia Green (PHS, Philadelphia Horticultural Society's urban greening program), community gardens, and gardeners in schools tapping into research, finding that teenagers respond to the healthy eating habits of their peers to a far greater degree than they do to smoking or sexual activity.

We have gardeners in about three dozen schools, perhaps the most amazing of which, because it's a school not without troubles, is Martin Luther King High School. The students have about two acres cultivated, and as they are harvesting the farming students have a fresh fruit and vegetable stand outside the school doors so that other students can buy fresh fruit and vegetables. They are selling to corner stores and therefore getting involved in the supply chain of food distribution into the neighborhood. As a result, the small local stores don't have to go to the food distribution center or buy from the grocery store where they buy high and then mark it up. By the time it gets to the customer it's both more expensive and older, which is why small stores rarely stock fresh produce. The net effect is to make an impact on local nutrition and community health. The school students are saying, "We'll give you fresh produce that's been grown right here, and if you start selling it into this community, we'll give you a discount until it takes off, so we can then start improving local eating habits."

City Harvest is a partnership between thirty-two of the city's larger and better established community gardens and food pantries throughout the city. There are two destinations for City Harvest's fresh produce: the first is food pantries that are usually stocked with donated canned goods, which are supplemented with lessons and help about how to prepare and store that food.

The second destination is local prisons: community gardens are raising seedlings and transferring them to prisoners, and the prisoners harvest the produce and send it back to the food pantries of the neighborhoods where the prisoners were first arrested. Healthy eating meets restorative justice.

On a slightly different scale, I'm tempted to talk about our biosolids proposal. This is an emerging policy that goes back to nineteenth century ideas of urban health and comes out of the Water Department in Fairmount Park. We are the only city on the east coast that's operating without a consent decree from the EPA for our combined sewer overflows. Every time it rains hard in the city, sewage flows into the rivers because we have a combined system, in violation of the Clean Water Act, and requiring cleaning at great expense to the city. This is a huge problem. Over the last decade and a half or so, other cities have signed consent decrees. They got in early, but they also got in very unimaginatively: solving this problem by building bigger pipes with bigger tanks so sewage doesn't overflow, spending billions and billions of dollars. We're proposing to spend about twenty billion dollars to build sufficient gray infrastructure to remediate to federal standards our Combined Sewer Overflows (CSOs)—less than replacing the system entirely as other cities have done. Our pipes are already amazing: we invented large-scale urban sewerpipe networks when we closed all of our creeks and streams. London turned the Fleet River into a pipe under Fleet Street, but we did it at a citywide scale. But this incredible system is old and still too small. By treating CSOs rather than up-scaling the pipe system, we can add back value. As a pilot, we're converting an outdoor sewer processing facility, which currently produces a Class B biosolid product for the market, into a facility that can produce a palletized Class A product. All we can do with the Class B product is use it for acid mine remediation and in reality we're sending some of it into a landfill. But the Class A product is good quality fertilizer.

William W. Braham

Before Paris installed its sewer system, the walled city was a net exporter of green goods to surrounding communities and farmland. It was a business. Human waste (sewage) was gathered up and then sold or taken to garden plots throughout the city, which were hugely productive because they were so intensely fertilized. But the minute that waste was channeled out of the city in sewer water, the productivity of the city dropped. I was wondering if the Class A fertilizer that's now produced could come back into the city to augment the green infrastructure you are talking about.

Mark Alan Hughes

Absolutely. There are forty thousand vacant parcels in the city, which the city owns most of. The one thing that Philadelphia has a lot of is dirt. We are the only county in the region that has been adding to our open space inventory, famously for all kinds of bad reasons—because we are constantly demolishing. And so we have a lot of dirt. And that dirt can be deployed in ways that have not been traditional to the city in a long time. In fact, those open plots can now be seen as an asset: urban farming, storm water remediation, water retention and detention, bio-remediation, and so on.

There are already farms in the city: Mill Creek, Greensgrow, Martin Luther King High, the new Weavers Way Farm that's at Aubrey Arboretum, for instance. Greensgrow, one of the very first, and established on the brownfield site of a former galvanizing plant in Kensington (which requires raised beds), is extremely entrepreneurial. Mary Seton Corboy, co-founder and Chief Farm Hand, is constantly experimenting. For one thousand dollars and the assistance of an enthusiast, she collects biowaste from Standard Tap and three or four other restaurants in the neighborhood to make biodiesel with modified water heaters. She has not bought diesel for the farm's trucks in a year, and has surplus—she's got four hundred gallons of diesel stored because she can't use it fast enough. One of the by-products of this process is glycerine that contains a methanol gas, illegal to pour down the drain. Mary centralizes glycerine processing for a community of five or six other small biodiesel manufacturers into legal effluent, and she ships the toxic residue offsite.

Mill Creek Farm, meanwhile, makes use of a bioswale that replaced a traffic island. The Streets Department, in collaboration with the Water Department, came in and engineered the bioswale, providing an inlet coming in right off the curb that the farm uses for irrigation. The intersection doesn't flood anymore, and the storm water doesn't run into the sewers anymore. Three wins from a very simple, ancient device. And everybody loves it.

Incentivize to Innovate

Dirt

For you, Mark, sustainability in cities critically has to take on economic sustainability, along side and perhaps even before other forms of sustainability. The environmental debate is not always configured in these terms. The other side of this debate is the improvisational and entrepreneurial solutions that can be found across the socio-economic spectrum of society—the 'messy' and informal grass-roots ideas you focus on and support, which provides a way to avoid the typical fetishization of poverty as a source of inspiration to designers, but rather looks at the ways in which everyone, whether poor or otherwise, might have design solutions to offer that need to be located, and, if viable, enabled.

Mark Alan Hughes

For the first time in fifty years, the assets that the city controls or contains are going up in value rather than going down for reasons beyond our control. We've tried to manipulate the asset value through policy for generations, but it rarely works very well. But at the moment, things like density, transit-oriented development, energy conservation that is inherent to building stock, are going up in value—a kind of gentrification writ large, in a way. We need to identify small-scale innovations, perhaps protect them from some of these other forces, and perhaps augment them. Do you scale-up these projects? Do you formalize them or not?

Dirt

You're looking at existing grass roots networks in the city to recognize their value, making these bottom-up processes more apparent. You don't want to formalize them or even implement them because they won't work as an implementation strategy.

Mark Alan Hughes

One of the things I've noted by observing these many different informal networks and their products is that they often undergo continuous improvement. The people who started Greensgrow worked out how to use raised beds; then how to contain some of their water costs; then how to make their own biodiesel; then how to organize CSAs, community organized agriculture systems where people buy shares and the farm distributes two or three shares of their produce to investors rather than customers. They are constantly innovating. So, we either protect them as integrated communities or take to scale ideas that they've already made successful and free them to focus on the innovation frontier. It appears to me that in fact what many of them do best is to get an idea working, to figure out what the next barrier is.

This is how the idea of the Common Market came up. The city has a lot of food production going on, and increasing demand for local food in all communities and neighborhoods across the city. But the question has been how to connect those two? Food distribution happens to be our competitive advantage in Philadelphia, because thirty or forty years ago we passed on the offer from the guys who invented shipping containers to become the world's first cargo container port and instead it went to Newark. Newark and Baltimore are the east coast container ports while Philadelphia stayed with labor-intensive bulk freight.

That's why we handle, say, Chilean grapes; we have fruit and vegetables because we didn't build a cargo container port. You can buy it pretty cheaply on a per transaction basis at the food distribution center if you've got a big supermarket chain. But if you're Weaver's Way what you want to do is buy from the MLK High School farm—you can't go down to the food distribution center and do that deal. You've got to do it on the phone, and it gets very expensive when you have one person who has to do two hundred food purchases each week. So the Common Market was launched to try to build an infrastructure to support these small-scale dealmakers.

William W. Braham

This is a B2B for food?

Mark Alan Hughes

It's a B2B network with a delivery-truck component. The truck coming through the neighborhood with fresh produce used to be common in Philadelphia, of course.

William W. Braham

Examples still exist. There's a truck that stops in West Philly, though the produce probably comes from the food distribution center. The "fruit guy" used to park at 37th and Locust Walk and just open up the back of his truck.

Mark Alan Hughes

The aim here is to restore these smaller connections which at first blush look like they have to be more expensive because they're smaller, but with a little bit of infrastructure investment like the Common Market become viable.

Dirt

You're just trying to keep the dirt fertile. It sounds like what you're doing in policy terms is trying to set up policy that sets incentives for both innovation and conservation. That's really how it works, which means that you still have some top-down control, but it's a top-down method that's fostering bottom-up. You're operating in both directions.

Mark Alan Hughes

Yes. I've got some specific examples of incentive structures that would be designed from the top but will be intended to change behaviors from the bottom. For example; the most literal one is we could probably reduce the city's total energy bill by ten or fifteen percent without spending a single dime on an ESCO or retro-commissioning buildings' HVAC systems. It's just about getting people to turn off the lights, and turn down the thermostats. 'Building control systems' can be about simple behavior: the imperative is to get behavior to change. But rather than getting people to remember to do the right thing every time they have to act, you need to train that behavior to become automatic. Incentives can influence that behavior.

Postscript

Dirt

Much has happened since we sat down for this interview. The Obama Administration is investing billions of

Green Roof Bus Stop
Built to celebrate the unveiling of the Philadelphia Greenworks annual report.

Philadelphia Horiticultural Society's Pop Up Park
A temporary public garden in Center City Philadelphia acting as a plant nursery and vegetable farm for City Harvest, a non-profit feeding the homeless.

dollars in greening programs as part of its economic stimulus, you were named the Mayor's Chief Policy Adviser in addition to Sustainability Director, the City's Greenworks framework has been adopted and released to the public by the Mayor, and perhaps most surprisingly you have announced your departure from government. Can you provide us with a postscript to our forward-looking interview?

Mark Alan Hughes

Yes, lots of water over the dam. The least surprising item on that list is that I've handed over my position. It's not so much that I resigned as much as I simply finished. The Greenworks policy frame was really my task at hand. Let me say a few words about that.

Greenworks is the policy framework to guide the City and its partners through 2015. It consists of five goals: energy, environment, equity, economy, and engagement. These goals organize fifteen specific targets and 169 mutually-reinforcing initiatives to achieve them. These targets are extraordinarily ambitious. You can read the full report or a summary at http://www.phila.gov/green/greenworks, but let me provide three overarching points about Greenworks.

First, it's a framework not a plan. What's the difference? A plan is a pre-conceived set of steps designed to achieve a well-defined objective. A framework is a tool built to simplify something otherwise too complex to understand or act on. What does it mean to become the "greenest city in America"? That is a paralyzingly complex planning objective. Greenworks provides a tool to guide the dozens of decisions that a city government makes every day, week, month, and year. Its goals, targets, and initiatives give dimension to sustainability in Philadelphia.

Second, there is no Grand Canyon between creating Greenworks and implementing it. The people who built the framework who will implement the framework, both inside and outside of government. Every target, every initiative is tempered by the realities of implementation by virtue of this fact. The last year was both top-down in the sense of the Mayor's commitment *and* bottom-up in the sense of how grounded in implementation every aspect of Greenworks is. The best evidence is how much implementation is already underway.

Third and finally, Greenworks has been embraced by this government. Not just across all the many departments and agencies represented in the making of Greenworks, but also at the very highest levels of the administration. And for that, I can provide some evidence, too. One of my key findings after one year in government is: always make a movie. Just watch the movie at http://www.phila.gov/green/greenworks to see what I mean about buy-in at the highest levels.

So, they've done their part and I now want to turn the tables and talk about us, the so-called private sector in this most private of cities. This government has given us an anvil on which to hammer and hammer. Now private interests must pick up the hammer and start to forge change. Greenworks is a tool for evaluating every decision this government makes. As I used to say about former Mayor John Street, in a very different context: it's not about the Mayor, it's about us. I came back outside of government because this is where the action is—where it must be, and where it should be. This sustainability constituency, which I have gotten to know quite well over the last year, needs to play much bigger. Local green advocates either fail to recognize or fear to exercise their potential power. They need to speak on every issue confronting this City, especially the budget and our relationship with Harrisburg and Washington, D.C.

I am not an environmentalist, that's not what brings me to this table. The future of cities is my real endgame. Sustainability is a means to that end, and that's why I need the green movement to bring its best game. Sustainability is the most pro-urban organizing device for policy we've had in a long time. Because it's only a national interest that ever trumps the old local divisions of city-suburb-rural that keep us barefoot and ignorant. Remember it was Manifest Destiny that built the transcontinental railroad and the Cold War that built the interstate highway system.

So the question is: In the twenty-first century, is there a national-interest politics that can harness American capitalism to invest and build a whole new infrastructure of place? Yes, and it's the politics of sustainability. The challenges of climate change and energy independence can harness American capitalism to redevelop metropolitan areas through green building practices, sustainable food production, transit and pedestrian-oriented development, and distributed and renewable energy generation and consumption.

That's why Philadelphia must lead American cities in unleashing a sustainability movement as strong as possible: to compel a set of national actions equivalent to the fifty-year closing of the frontier and the fifty-year construction of the interstate highway system. So, it is huge. But Greenworks is also doable. Regional collaboration based on self and shared interests and Washington's new appetite for change fueled by enormous new federal resources *all* conspire in our favor.

In closing, let me say that this experience has kindled my curiosity about the nexus of design and policy. My interest in the studio as a teaching device is one of the things that led me to enroll in architecture school. But now I have a whole set of questions about the substantive crossover between design and policy. Sustainability is a great organizing device for studying this nexus. We know the issue connects a variety of programmatic areas, but it also implicates an interaction between design and policy that we're only just beginning to understand. Students who develop a facility with that interaction will be the young professionals most in demand in coming decades.

FLUXscape
Remapping Philadelphia's Post-Industrial Terrain
Andrea Hansen

In the case of the ruin, the fact that life with its wealth and its changes once dwelled here constitutes an immediately perceived presence. The ruin creates the present form of a past life, not according to the contents or remnants of that life, but according to its past as such.

Georg Simmel, *The Ruin* (1911)

Like many rust-belt cities, Philadelphia is experiencing an ever-increasing presence of urban "ruins," as rapidly-evolving technology makes industrial fabric obsolete and city-dwellers flee to the suburbs. Allowing these leftover structures to remain unmonitored in their current state is potentially dangerous due to crime, vagrancy, and physical safety hazards. However, demolishing the structures destroys a part of Philadelphia's architectural and cultural history. Moreover, demolition is often economically prohibitive due to extensive mitigation processes.

Thus, the city is in need of a comprehensive solution that reimagines the vestiges of post-industrial vacancy not as liabilities, but as assets. *FLUXscape* provides the solution to Philadelphia's problem of post-industrial vacancy by networking ruined sites along infrastructural corridors into catalytic, productive ribbons of flexible, hybrid program that will course life through Philadelphia's long-dormant veins. In this network, the ruin is given new life within a contemporary context through the insertion of hybrid program, which can dynamically respond to the needs of a city in flux.

Romancing the Ruin

Humans have a longstanding fascination with ruins: While the ruin reveals its age, it does not always its history. Thus, we can imagine any number of romantic scenarios—often causing the ruined structure to be imbued with a reverence that it was not granted in its original state. Ken Worpole explains:

> Ruins, like skeletons, are...emblematic of a lost whole, whether it is a building, a body or an organic society. They represent the passage of time, decay and absence as much as physical presence: roofless and windowless creaking structures are about worlds and lives through which the winds now blow.[1]

While ancient ruins are often picturesque and architecturally interesting, they are few and far between in most parts of the world. Moreover, they present few problems in the milieu of contemporary architectural and urban theory. On the other hand, ruins of a more modern nature are a dime a dozen, especially in the northeastern United States, as technological improvements and globalization increasingly reduce the need for heavy industry and related transportation infrastructure in urban cores around the globe.

Rem Koolhaas names vestiges of industrial globalization "junkspace"—the residue mankind leaves on the planet—while not of the quality of our predecessors ("We do not leave Pyramids"), not totally devoid of value, either.[1] Dealing with these obsolete urban sites has become

Active Agents

Citywide Maps of Ruin Intensities
Philadelphia

Site Prioritization (Blight-based Incentivization)

Cultural Obsolescence (Crime and Poverty)

Decay

Previous Page
View of Port Richmond Rail Yards

more pressing in recent years because they are taking up valuable, developable space in city centers yet often possess enough historical and aesthetic significance to make demolition an undesirable option. Undesirable, that is, from a preservationist standpoint, but also environmentally and economically. Thus, efforts must be made to adaptively—and creatively—reuse modern ruins: to reclaim space in urban centers, reconnect areas divided by the barrier of vacancy, introduce sorely-needed resources into gaps in the urban fabric, and reframe the post-industrial ruin's historical and aesthetic value so that it can be appreciated rather than neglected.

FLUXscape follows two conceptual approaches to keeping ruin as ruin—in spirit if not in form or function—both of which require cognizance of time periods outside of the building's immediate frame of reference:

1. Look to the past by incorporating ruins into a new environment that expresses memory and history—whether canonical or vernacular.
2. Look to the future by anticipating the process of ruination to trace the physical transformations that will occur over a building's life.

Both approaches have in common the pervasiveness of change, the continuity of time, and the submission to ruination which, rather than being taken as strictly detrimental, can be construed as potentially advantageous.

The advantage of intentionally incorporating decomposition and weathering into design is that the building or landscape has an integrated flexibility to change over time. As such, by embracing ruination, whether subtly or overtly, *FLUXscape* attempts to provide a solution to the contemporary dilemma of making a building dynamic without actually making it move. In contrast to physical dynamism expressed through complicated mechanization, *FLUXscape* expresses temporal dynamism, both cyclical and accumulated. Not only is this form of transition easier to construct and maintain, but, due to its variety and unpredictability, it is far more interesting.

Context: Transcending Boundaries

Without a doubt, one cannot reinterpret and readapt Philadelphia's modern ruins—defined here as spaces designed in the recent past that can no longer be used as they were originally intended—without first gaining

Structural
Instability

Climatic
Unsuitability

Environmental
Contamination

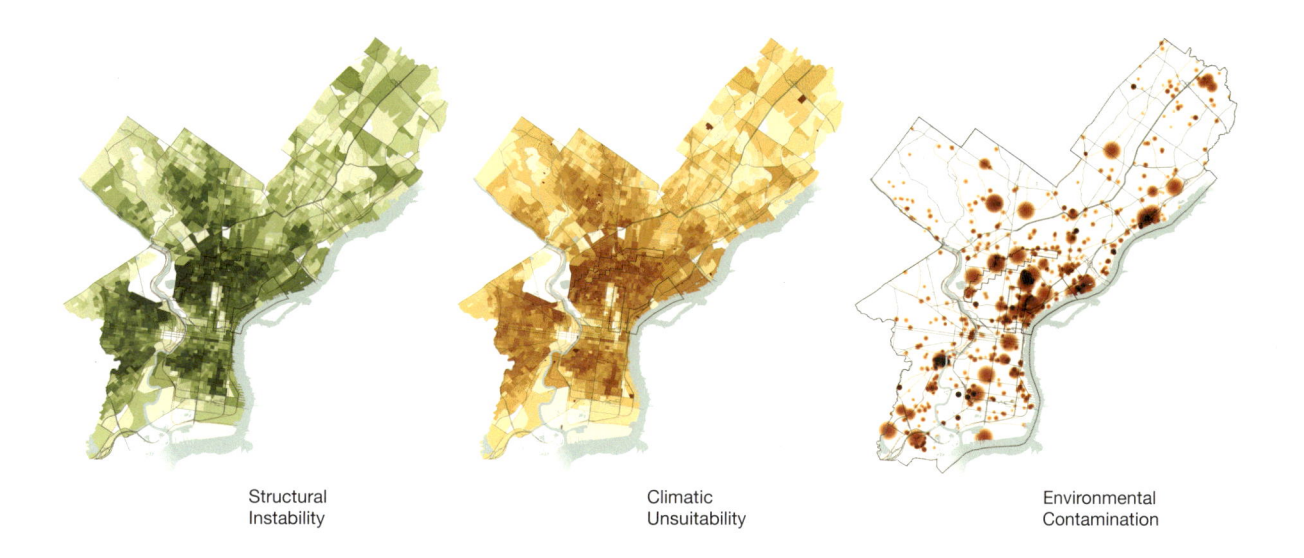

a thorough understanding of their history—both as individual structures and as part of the Philadelphia story. Moreover, the ruin's history is not limited to its original state, but rather is marked by a series of past, present, and future events. Likewise, a ruin's history includes both a written (or anecdotal) record of attitudes and perceptions and a physical record of the changing contours of the building, landscape, and surrounding urban fabric. This archive of history, space, and culture of the site and its surrounds is the ruin's contextual framework.

FLUXscape approaches contexts as generative continua that reflect the changing nature of a ruin over time—the temporal spectrum of the ruin's history, the fluctuating space of the site and its surrounding infrastructure, or the changing dynamics of the city's demographics and social values, for instance. By seeing context as the framework for a design strategy, the project is able to fluidly respond to the dynamic needs of a contemporary city in flux. Furthermore, the system ensures responsiveness by avoiding the tendency to fetishize a frozen moment in the site's past, present, or future—instead reflecting a spectrum of temporal states. By focusing on making both functional and formal transitions that transcend linear time, the system becomes richer, as it weaves together a tapestry of diurnal, seasonal, and historic gradients.

To navigate the city's social context, *FLUXscape* seeks to engage disparate parties within Philadelphia's municipal government agencies in a much-needed dialogue on how to best approach the city's numerous industrial ruins and associated vacant properties and infrastructure. As a rust-belt city, the city has struggled to define itself in the post-industrial era like many of its counterparts in the northeast.

With much of the fabric outside Center City and University City consisting of 19th and early-20th century industrial sites and related industry-oriented infrastructure, much of which is in various states of ruin due to technology-induced obsolescence, Philadelphia is a prime location for a city-wide investigation into repurposing structures that fall into a challenging gray area of development. Sites such as the Port Richmond Rail Yards and the Willow Street Steam Plant have outlived the relevance of their original industrial intent

The *FLUXscape* Network
The citywide strategy for the *FLUXscape* network transforms industrial corridors into remediative landscape infrastructure, reintegrating sites into the city's open space network and restitching communities divided by rail and highway barriers.

and have been abandoned. As such, they have reached too advanced a state of decay to be used intact, but as monuments of a representative era in Philadelphia's history, they are also too historically significant to be razed. It is clear that a compromise must be reached.

Proposal:
From Industrial Corridor to Green Network

FLUXscape proposes a network of "thick landscape infrastructure" concentrated along Philadelphia's deteriorating industrial corridors, to be developed through public-private partnerships. Inhospitable program and decrepitude currently inhibit network proliferation along these corridors, but by remediating ruin and reprogramming the corridors for production, transit, and recreation, the city can incubate smart growth in its neglected districts.

Espousing a systematic approach to post-industrial ruin, *FLUXscape* operates simultaneously on a citywide and local scale. The process inputs weighted mappings of ruin conditions into decision-making matrices to produce a schematic design framework that guides and catalyzes flexible, dynamic, and responsive site design. The system was applied to three demonstrative sites—the Amtrak Northeast Corridor, the Reading Viaduct in Philadelphia's Callowhill neighborhood, and the I-95 Corridor at Port Richmond—to test the process as well as to show a range of design possibilities. The designs present three ways in which neighborhood transformation is catalyzed by landscape infrastructure, with an emphasis on bioremediation of contaminated sites, urban agriculture, and partnerships between the City of Philadelphia, developers, and community stakeholders.

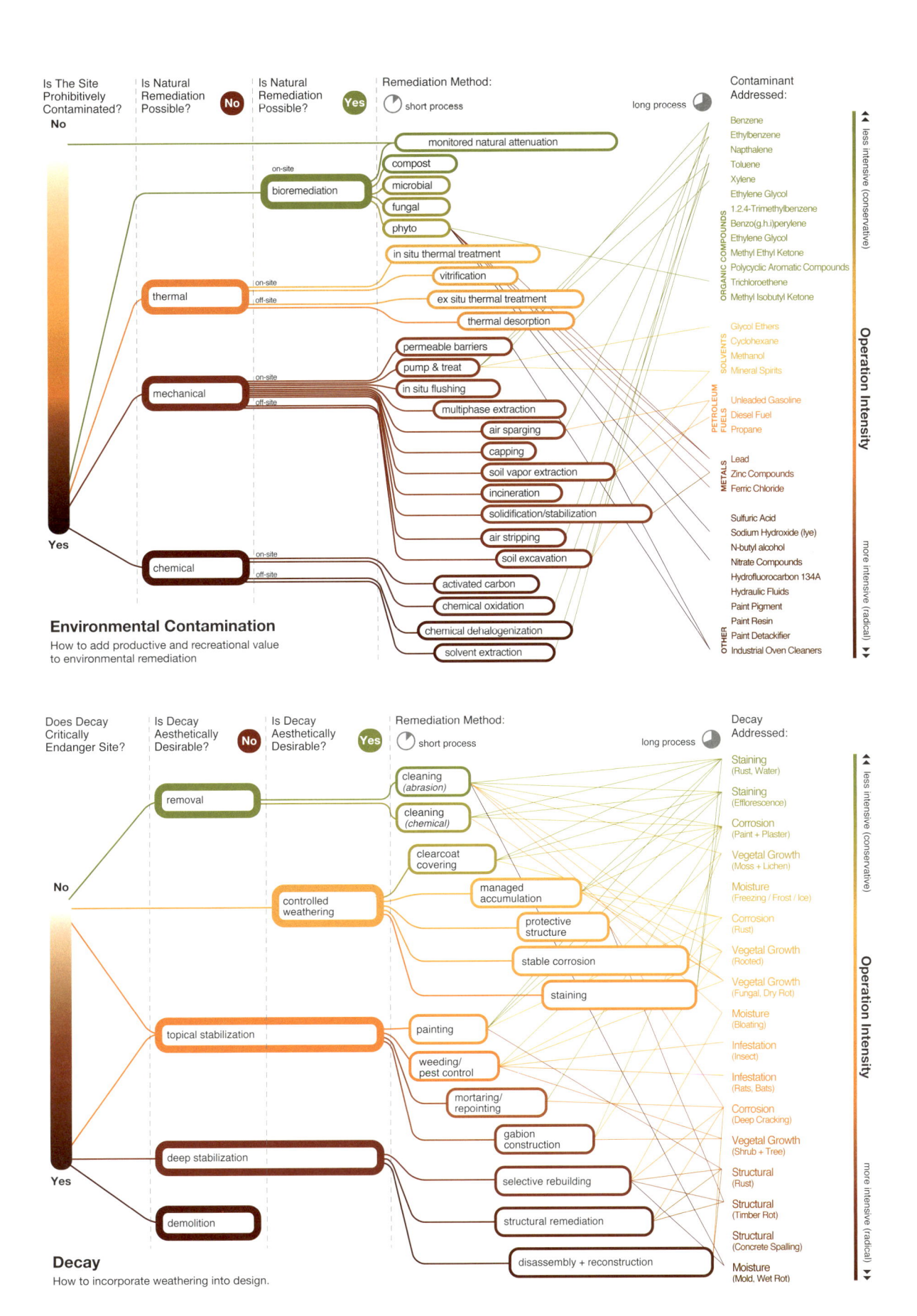

Environmental Contamination
How to add productive and recreational value to environmental remediation

Is The Site Prohibitively Contaminated?
- No
- Yes

Is Natural Remediation Possible? No / Yes

Remediation Method: short process / long process

Contaminant Addressed:

Branches (No — Natural Remediation Possible: Yes):
- monitored natural attenuation
- bioremediation (on-site): compost, microbial, fungal, phyto

Branches (Natural Remediation Possible: No):
- thermal (on-site / off-site): in situ thermal treatment, vitrification, ex situ thermal treatment, thermal desorption
- mechanical (on-site / off-site): permeable barriers, pump & treat, in situ flushing, multiphase extraction, air sparging, capping, soil vapor extraction, incineration, solidification/stabilization, air stripping, soil excavation
- chemical (on-site / off-site): activated carbon, chemical oxidation, chemical dehalogenization, solvent extraction

Contaminants:

ORGANIC COMPOUNDS:
- Benzene
- Ethylbenzene
- Napthalene
- Toluene
- Xylene
- Ethylene Glycol
- 1,2,4-Trimethylbenzene
- Benzo(g,h,i)perylene
- Ethylene Glycol
- Methyl Ethyl Ketone
- Polycyclic Aromatic Compounds
- Trichloroethene
- Methyl Isobutyl Ketone

SOLVENTS:
- Glycol Ethers
- Cyclohexane
- Methanol
- Mineral Spirits

PETROLEUM FUELS:
- Unleaded Gasoline
- Diesel Fuel
- Propane

METALS:
- Lead
- Zinc Compounds
- Ferric Chloride

OTHER:
- Sulfuric Acid
- Sodium Hydroxide (lye)
- N-butyl alcohol
- Nitrate Compounds
- Hydrofluorocarbon 134A
- Hydraulic Fluids
- Paint Pigment
- Paint Resin
- Paint Detackifier
- Industrial Oven Cleaners

Operation Intensity: less intensive (conservative) ↔ more intensive (radical)

Decay
How to incorporate weathering into design.

Does Decay Critically Endanger Site?
- No
- Yes

Is Decay Aesthetically Desirable? No / Yes

Remediation Method: short process / long process

Decay Addressed:

Branches:
- removal: cleaning (abrasion), cleaning (chemical)
- controlled weathering: clearcoat covering, managed accumulation, protective structure, stable corrosion, staining
- topical stabilization: painting, weeding/pest control, mortaring/repointing
- deep stabilization: gabion construction, selective rebuilding, structural remediation, disassembly + reconstruction
- demolition

Decay types:
- Staining (Rust, Water)
- Staining (Efflorescence)
- Corrosion (Paint + Plaster)
- Vegetal Growth (Moss + Lichen)
- Moisture (Freezing / Frost / Ice)
- Corrosion (Rust)
- Vegetal Growth (Rooted)
- Vegetal Growth (Fungal, Dry Rot)
- Moisture (Bloating)
- Infestation (Insect)
- Infestation (Rats, Bats)
- Corrosion (Deep Cracking)
- Vegetal Growth (Shrub + Tree)
- Structural (Rust)
- Structural (Timber Rot)
- Structural (Concrete Spalling)
- Moisture (Mold, Wet Rot)

Operation Intensity: less intensive (conservative) ↔ more intensive (radical)

Active Agents

Territory 1: Amtrak Northeast Corridor

The Amtrak Northeast Corridor Master Plan uses a significant initial public investment on a productive infrastructural park to incubate private development, especially in rehabilitating the architecturally significant warehouses and brownfield lots in the district. The plan includes affordable housing, office space for locally-owned businesses, and urban agriculture fields. Its main feature is an elevated cap park that spans over the active Amtrak rail line to restitch the North Philadelphia and Fairhill neighborhoods. In partnership with the federal Rails-to-Trails program, the cap park and adjacent vacant parcels provide recreational space that will eventually become part of a regional trail system following the proposed Northeast Corridor High-Speed Rail project. In additional, the adjacent lots will be incentivized for dedicated energy and food production, in keeping with the EPA's recommendations. Finally, two superfund sites that border the cap park are phytoremediated with a poplar-birch forest and contaminant-specific forbs that can be used for educational and recreational purposes by the area's many nearby schools.

Linear Cap Park: A dendritic cap park restitches the residential areas separated by the rail corridor and adjacent industrial parcels. It connects at-grade energy-production, urban agricultural, and recreational zones by spanning the rail, whether below ground or at-grade, providing a twenty-two feet clearance to anticipate the requirements of the future high-speed rail.

High-Speed Rail: In the spirit of an energy-producing corridor, the high-speed rail can be designed to actually create energy, resulting in a negative carbon footprint. The magnetosphere of the maglev rail, along with the latent kinetic energy of the deflection of the ground beneath the rail, can be harvested to create enough electricity to power the lighting and services required by the park and rail infrastructure.

Flexible Productive Zones: By facilitating public acquisition of dilapidated and vacant parcels adjacent to the rail corridor, the corridor can be transformed from an inaccessible barrier to a connective vein. The parcels become an informal park and trail system while the cap park is being constructed, and later become fertile ground for public and private investment in energy farms and urban agriculture.

Poplar-Birch Forest: Two superfund sites along the R5-R6 Regional Rail line are remediated with a Poplar-Birch forest, which can extend the linear park system along the Amtrak Corridor and can also be used as an educational resource for nearby schools. Poplars, which are extremely fast-growing, excel at degrading and removing chlorinating solvents and aromatic hydrocarbons.

Amtrak Northeast Corridor
North Philadelphia Station (Amtrak/SEPTA Regional Rail), 1992.

Amtrak Northeast Corridor
Graffiti along Amtrak railroad, 2009.

Poplar-Birch Forest
Linear Cap Park

Flexible Productive Zones

High-Speed Rail

Amtrak Northeast Corridor
Above **Below**
Site Plan Bird's-eye view

Active Agents 213

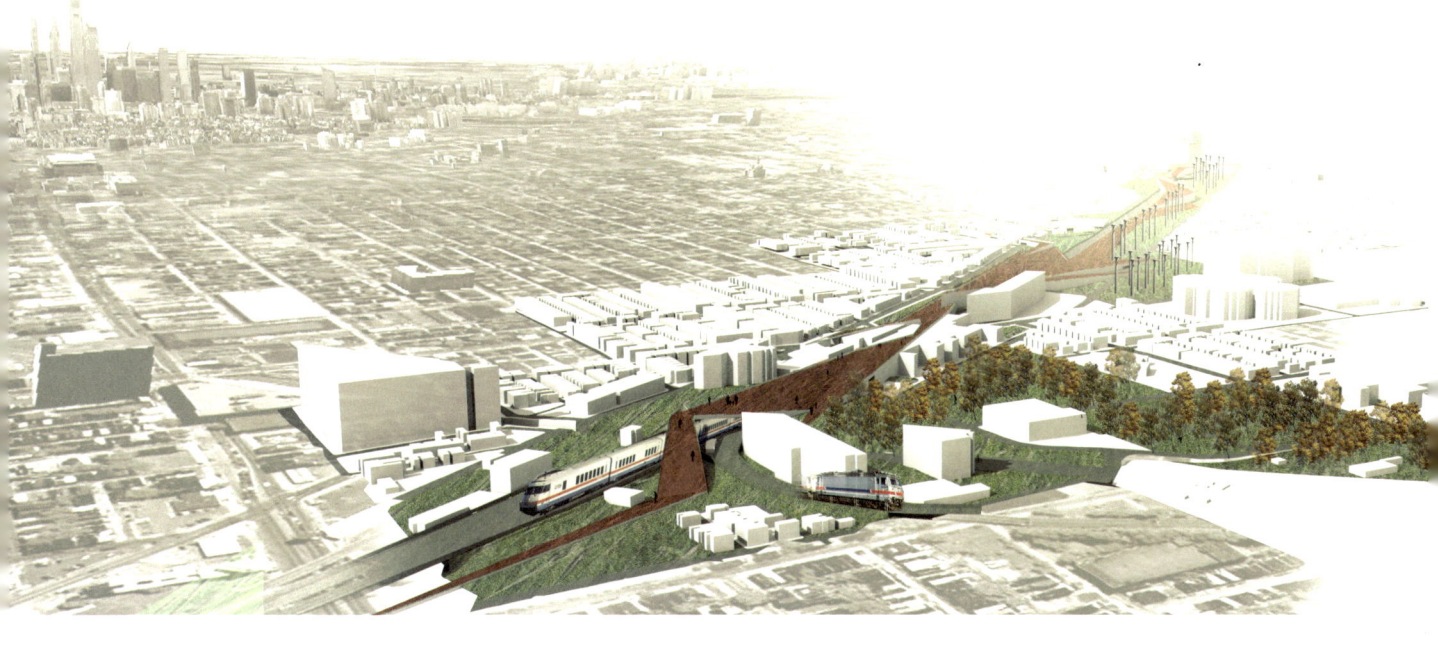

Territory 2: Reading Viaduct Corridor

The Reading Viaduct Corridor Master Plan involves moderate public investment to revitalize Philadelphia's abandoned Reading Railroad viaduct and transform it into a linear park. This viaduct park is capped on either end with expansive new tracts of open space: at the southern end, a green roof park is constructed on top of the convention center on Eleventh Street, while at the northern end, a series of sloped green roofs is built as part of a new transit hub and mixed-use development along the viaduct at Fairmount Avenue. This new park system, coupled with the prevalence of attractive historic warehouses in the district, will draw extensive private investment and development of high-density, innovative architecture—both rehab and infill construction—with mixed-income loft, hotel, and creative office space. The calling card of this architectural playground will be the hybrid symbiosis of old and new, where new construction respects the colors and textures of the industrial patinas—with materials such as Corten steel, copper mesh, and vegetated walls—and rehabilitation emphasizes managed decay and creative structural reinforcement.

Viaduct Park: The Reading Viaduct is largely supported—with the exception of roadway crossings—by earth berms and retaining walls. As such, it is possible to turn the viaduct into a park with minimal structural intervention, necessary only where the ground-plane is unsupported by earth. The extant structure also means the viaduct is able to support trees: a planting gradient of larger trees and smaller shrubs expresses the underlying structure of the park.

Convention Center Green Roof: One of the largest open spaces in Center City is the roof of the Philadelphia Convention Center. Located directly across the Vine Street Expressway from the current termination of the Reading Viaduct, converting the roof to a habitable green roof provides the perfect opportunity to bridge the crevasse created by the expressway, reconnect the two neighborhoods, and provide a centralized access point to the viaduct. Moreover, the roof can become a significant storm-water collector, much needed in a heavily impervious area. Lastly, greening the roof has significant energy implications, from both a conservation and production standpoint.

Transit Hub and Terminus Park: The Viaduct Park culminates at its far end with a multi-use transit hub and park that includes affordable and market-rate housing, art space, community gardens, and retail and dining. Moreover, the sloped green roofs of the complex provide public access to the elevated park as well as a grand open space that awaits visitors at the end of the narrow viaduct.

Loft District: The area around the viaduct is characterized by large, historic lofts, many of which have been lying dormant for years. The completion of the elevated park will attract new development to the area on top of the steady growth the district is now experiencing due to low rent and proximity to downtown. Like the Lower East Side in New York, forecasted growth makes the neighborhood a prime target for high-density residential and mixed-use development that is structurally symbiotic with the existing industrial fabric.

Reading Viaduct, c. 1980
The active Reading Viaduct before closure in the mid-1980s.

Reading Viaduct Today
View from Callowhill section of the viaduct towards Center City.

Transit Hub and
Terminus Park

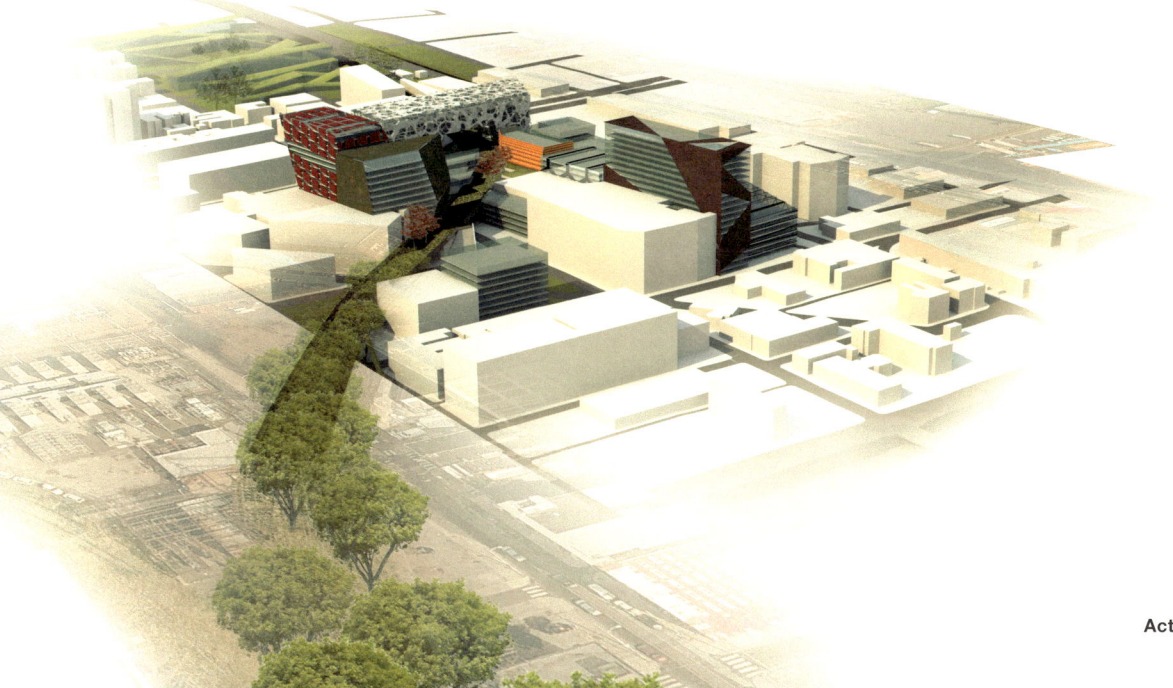

Viaduct Park

Loft District

Convention Center
Green Roof

Reading Viaduct Corridor
Above — Site Plan
Below — Bird's-eye view

Active Agents   215

Territory 3: The Port Richmond/I-95 Corridor

The Port Richmond/I-95 Corridor Master Plan would be developed through a partnership between the City and Greensgrow Farms to create an agricultural park and subinfrastructural farmers' market under I-95 where goods and produce can be sold. After sufficient funds are raised, a dedicated year-round farmers' market will be built as part of the new Richmond Waterfront District, which will be populated with day and night entertainment, recreation, and food venues serving local produce. In addition to creating a hub for Philadelphia's thriving urban agriculture industry, the greening and remediation efforts on the Port Richmond site serve to bridge the divide between the Richmond neighborhood and the Delaware riverfront: both by enlivening the ground underneath the interstate and by leveling a large wall along Richmond Street. Additionally, the elevated band along which the Reading Railway tracks used to converge into Port Richmond would be converted into a forested trail for biking, jogging, and hiking down to the river.

Greensgrow Farm Expansion: Much of the drive behind the concept for this site is a partnership between the city, developers, and local stakeholders. Greensgrow Farm is a key community partner with vested interests in innovative green redevelopment and bringing urban agriculture to Philadelphia, so this site is partially dedicated to the expansion of Greensgrow's agricultural efforts. Following moderate phytoremediation to mitigate the site's industrial past, large tracts of farmland are coupled with space for community gardens in order to engender further partnership between community organizations and neighborhood residents.

Port Richmond Farmers' Market and Freeway Park: Phase 1 of the farmers' market sees the area under I-95 being transformed into a park and open-air market. By turning a barrier into an active attractor, a connection between urban fabric and riverfront is forged. This connection is amplified by Phase 2 of the farmers' market, in which the seasonal outdoor market is supplemented with a daily all-seasons market selling food, goods, and crafts—the northern analog to the Reading Terminal Market.

Richmond Waterfront District: To accompany the daytime use of the farmers' market and the trails system, and make the park active both day and night, the waterfront piers will be thickened with space for restaurants, bars, clubs, and retail. The infrastructure is woven into the landscape and the farmers' market, tracing the paths of the historic rail lines and integrating planting, views, storm-water swales, and active and passive districts.

Rail-to-River Trail: The unused portion of the Reading Railway flows through a residential neighborhood. By converting it into a wildlife trail, it becomes a valuable resource for the community and is seamlessly integrated into the *FLUXscape* network of thick green infrastructure.

Port Richmond c.1928
Aerial view of the Reading Railroad Terminus at Port Richmond.

Port Richmond Today
Port Richmond Coal Elevator, now abandoned.

- Rail-to-River Trail
- Greensgrow Farm Expansion
- Port Richmond Farmers Market and Freeway Park
- Richmond Waterfront District

Port Richmond Corridor

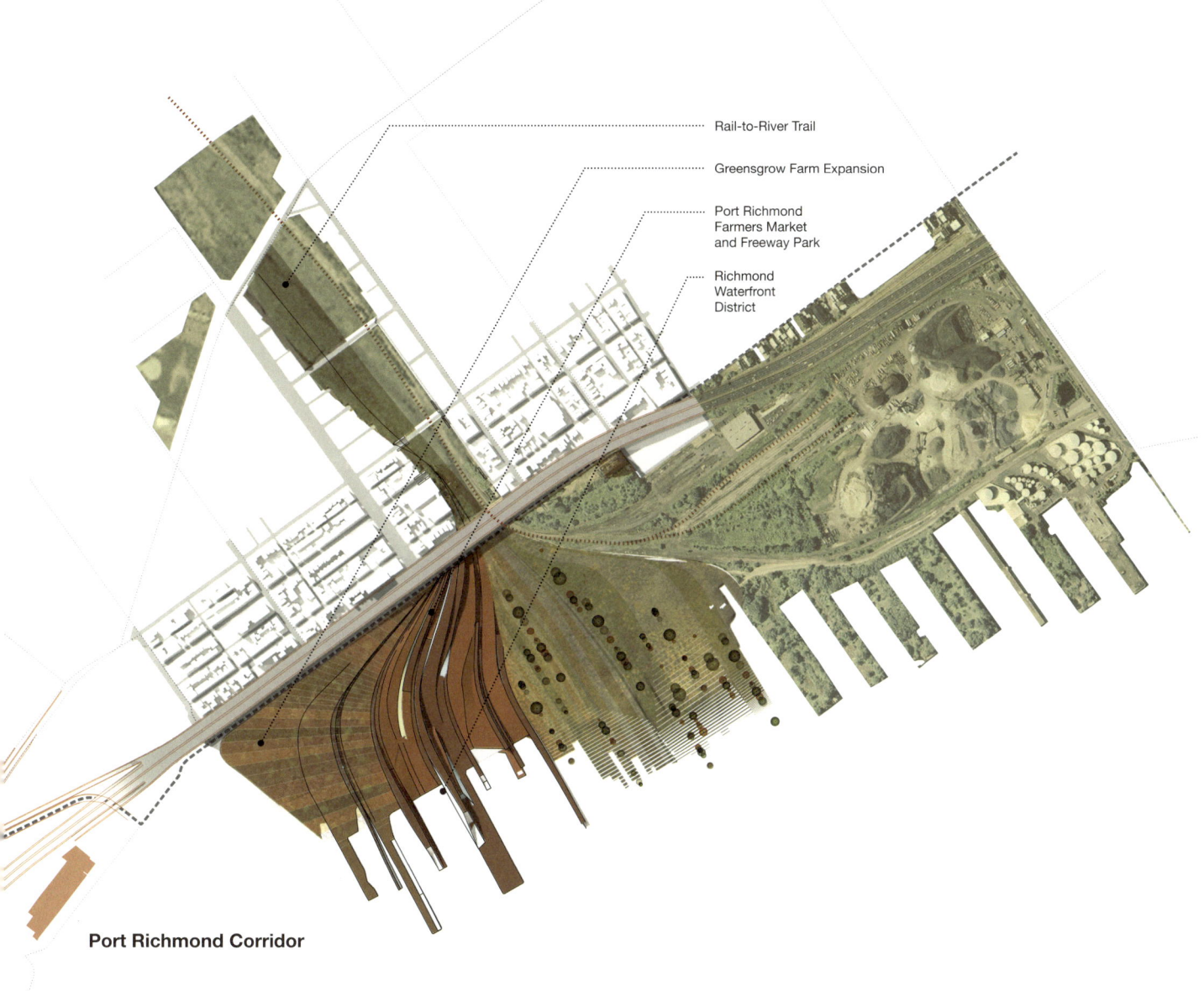

As shown by the citywide strategy and interventions for the three demonstrative sites, *FLUXscape* emphasizes design in conjunction with policy in an effort to rethink traditional planning models that have failed time and again for relying too much on policy-heavy master plans and zoning codes or on grassroots activism. The flexible strategic frameworks laid out by *FLUXscape* are visually accessible, with the intent of encouraging partnerships between municipal government, designers, independent organizations, and individuals. At the scale of urbanism a striking design is useless without implementation, thus it is informed partnerships that lie at the core of the *FLUXscape* strategy. The project provides a means for thorough site evaluation with an open range of intervention options to suit the needs and changing agency of a city in flux: options for green infrastructure, urban agriculture, stormwater management, transit, and other productive uses are explored exhaustively and linked to potential conditions so that the strategy is ensured longevity and maximum applicability no matter the site, scale, or players involved.

Endnotes

1. Ken Worpole, *Last Landscapes: The Architecture of the Cemetery in the West* (London: Reaktion, 2003), p. 128.
2. See Rem Koolhaas, "Junkspace" in *Content: Triumph of Realization,* eds. Rem Koolhaas, Brendan McGetrick (Köln: Taschen, 2004), pp. 162-171.

Active Agents

Holey Urbanisms
Phillip M. Crosby

Since the late 1990s the discourse of landscape urbanism has emerged as one of the most promising approaches toward the design of the contemporary city. Charles Waldheim coined the term in 1996, defining it as "a disciplinary realignment... in which landscape replaces architecture as the basic building block of contemporary urbanism."[1] Waldheim further underscored the central role of landscape in urban design in his 2001 essay "Decamping Detroit," stating that landscape is "the only medium capable of dealing with [the] simultaneously decreasing densities and indeterminate futures" of postindustrial American cities.[2] It is thus significant that Waldheim, an architect, was named Chair of the Department of Landscape Architecture at the Harvard University Graduate School of Design in July 2009. This transdisciplinary appointment marks Waldheim's own "decamping" to a discipline positioned by him as better placed to tackle the questions of the contemporary city, and suggests an important blurring of the boundaries between the design disciplines.

But questions remain. If, as Waldheim suggests, landscape can act as a model for urbanism, then the continued focus of the discourse on the design and construction of actual landscapes, largely in the form of large parks, begs the question: Where is the urbanism of landscape urbanism?

A Landscape Urbanism Primer
The traditional history of the landscape urbanist discourse traces its origins to the early 1980s with the 1982 competition schemes of Bernard Tschumi and Rem Koolhaas for Paris's *Parc de la Villette* looming particularly large as the ostensible point of origin for Waldheim's "disciplinary realignment." Waldheim says of this competition that it "began a trajectory of postmodern urban park making in which landscape itself was conceived as a complex medium capable of articulating relations among urban infrastructure, public events, and indeterminate urban futures for large, post-industrial sites."[3]

Earlier antecedents, where they are mentioned at all, are in each case cited only to be rejected, acting to announce a definitive break from the tradition they represent. For example, Frederick Law Olmsted's *Emerald Necklace* and *Back Bay Fens* in Boston are cited for their conflation of landscape with infrastructure. However, according to Waldheim:

> [C]ontemporary practices of landscape urbanism reject the camouflaging of ecological systems with pastoral images of nature that intend to provide stylistic and spatial exceptions to the gridded urban fabric. Rather, contemporary landscape urbanism recommends the use of infrastructural systems and the public landscapes they engender as the very ordering mechanisms of the urban field itself, capable of shaping and shifting the organization of urban settlement rather than offering predictable images of pastoral perfection.[4]

The importance of the work of Ian McHarg is also recognized. However, once again this work is dismissed by Waldheim: "Landscape urbanism benefits from the long-standing lineage of regional environmental planning—from Patrick Geddes through Lewis Mumford to Ian McHarg—*yet remains distinct from that tradition.*"[5] McHarg's work—as illustrated in his seminal book *Design with Nature*—is seen as "a rear guard defense of a supposedly autonomous 'nature' conceived to exist a priori, outside of human agency or cultural construction."[6] But this reading of McHarg is flawed. As Lewis Mumford has pointed out, "McHarg's emphasis is not on either design or nature by itself, but upon the preposition with, which implies human cooperation and biological partnership."[7] Furthermore, McHarg himself goes so far as to suggest:

> The Judeo-Christian creation story must be seen as an allegory; dominion and subjugation must be expunged as the biblical injunction of man's relation to nature. In values it is a great advance from "I-it" to "I-Thou," but "we" seems a more appropriate description for ecological relationships.[8]

In contrast to McHarg's mandate, many large-scale landscape-urbanist parks, such as *Fresh Kills,* tend to stress the importance of the ecology of plants and animals over that of a social ecology. In other words, these projects tend to operate in the mode of landscape as landscape rather than landscape as urbanism.

Having dismissed the canonical landscape architecture precedents of Olmsted and McHarg, much of the literature on landscape urbanism focuses on the newness of the discourse. For instance, James Corner posits landscape urbanism as "a *new* hybrid discipline" in which "the merging of landscape with urbanism suggests an exciting *new* field of possibilities."[9] But this location of the emergence of landscape urbanism in a particular condition of the late twentieth century turns a blind eye to the rich body of thought that emerged out of similar problems in the years following World War II.

Corner has also praised landscape urbanism for its "productive attitude towards indeterminacy, open-endedness, intermixing and cross-disciplinarity."[10] This is clearly an attack on the perceived failures of the top-down, technocratic techniques associated with Modern, CIAM-style urbanism. But this argument echoes that put forward by key participants in postwar avant-gardes, in particular, the group of architects known as Team 10. This loosely affiliated group—which included among others Alison and Peter Smithson, Aldo van Eyck, Jaap Bakema, Georges Candilis, and Shadrach Woods—is best known for their role in dissolving the influential Congrès Internationaux d'Architecture Moderne (CIAM) in 1959. The architects of Team 10 were adept at dealing with the holey nature of the postwar urban fabric that resulted from extensive wartime bombing.

The physical condition of many postwar cities like Berlin and Rotterdam that confronted the architects of Team 10 is not all that different from the postindustrial urban conditions that landscape urbanism focuses on: in both cases large swaths of formerly booming cities lay fallow. However, whereas landscape urbanism—at least as formulated by Waldheim—is framed to accept and address "the increasingly common urban conditions of de-densification and sprawl," many of the urban projects of Team 10—particularly those of Alison and Peter Smithson—conceive of small scale landscape and landscape-like interventions as precursors to future (re-)urbanization.[11] The architects of Team 10 were as interested in the space between buildings as they were with the buildings themselves.

Sixty Years of Indeterminacy

Reyner Banham credits the entry of the terms "indeterminacy" and "open-endedness" into architectural discourse to the London architect Richard Llewelyn-Davies in a paper presented at the Architectural Association in 1951 entitled "Endless Architecture."[12] Primary among the paper's arguments was an analysis of Ludwig Mies van der Rohe's *Alumni Memorial Hall* at the Illinois Institute of Technology:

> No single element is treated as self-contained, nor is it isolated from the rest by special treatment. The part is subservient to the whole. The whole, again, is left unbounded. There are no stop-ends, nor any dominating feature limiting the extension of any particular plane, or concentrating interest at any point in the plane. I think that a wall is conceived by van der Rohe as a portion cut from a plane, extending infinitely into space, and that this quality, which could be called endlessness, is at the bottom of this approach to design.[13]

This conception of an endlessly extendible and indeterminate architecture was developed by Llewelyn-Davies' partner, John Weeks, in a series of lectures and papers throughout the 1950s and would finally be crystallized into built form with their design for *Northwick Park Hospital* in northwest London. The programmatic requirements for *Northwick Park* included over 800 beds, laboratories, and research facilities, as well as the need to "cope with the increasingly rapid growth, change and obsolescence of hospital departments."[14] In response, Weeks offered strategies for both inter- and intra-generational change. At the short-term, intra-generational scale of change, Weeks provided a kit-of-parts system of movable walls, partitions, mullions, and other structural units that allowed individual hospital departments to modify their spaces as necessary without much interruption to hospital services. This kit-of-parts constructional system also aided longer-term, inter-generational processes of growth for the hospital as a whole.

To meet the various requirements of the future growth of individual hospital departments, Weeks arranged the departments in independently flexible buildings along an extendible corridor. This strategy allowed each department to grow (or shrink) independently without adversely affecting the comprehensibility of the overall arrangement. This was made possible both by the structural kit-of-parts, and by a system of "extendible ends," consisting of removable corrugated steel panels and temporary fire stairs that allowed for easy extension of the linear buildings. These end walls could simply be unplugged to allow for departmental expansion. This so-called "plug-in architecture" would be influential for a number of London-based architects, including Alison and Peter Smithson, who were central to Team 10.

Connective Holes

The Smithsons adopted indeterminacy and open-endedness in one of their earliest and most well known projects; their 1957 entry for the *Berlin Hauptstadt* competition. (Fig. 1) This iconic project featured a "platform net" that hovered ten meters above the existing street level of central Berlin and stretched in a dendritic pattern across the existing war-ravaged city fabric. Like the many large scale reclamation projects of the landscape urbanist canon, the Smithsons understood that the reconstruction of Berlin would be a long term project that could not be overseen by a single architect: "The greatest difficulty in working towards urban forms that can accept growth and change is that of communicating the general intention to those who follow."[15] They thus developed "a plan that could present a non-rigid idea, a way of indicating by means of drawings, a direction that an urban form could take."[16] As Alison Smithson noted, these new urban forms were "intended to be anticipatory, open-ended, and adaptable."[17] A sketch of the Hauptstadt project's antler-like administration buildings illustrates two possible future conditions: a series of sprawling mid-rise extensions or an interconnected series of towers.

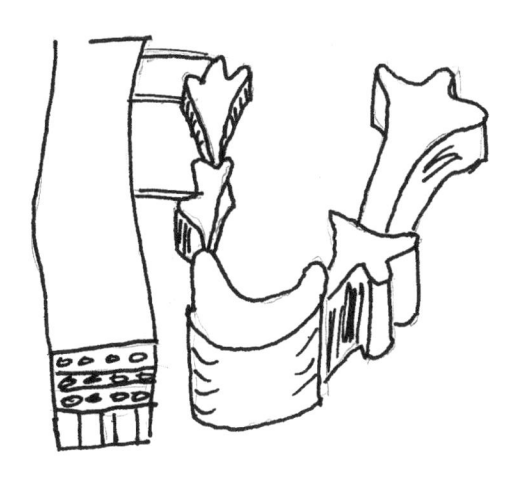

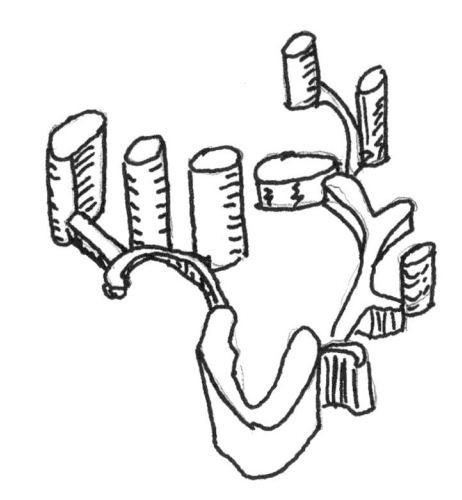

Figure 1
Berlin Hauptstadt Competition
Sketch by author after Alison Smithson.

Left
Ministry Building with Midrise Extensions.

Right
Ministry Building with Interconnected Towers.

The concepts at work in the Smithsons' *Berlin Hauptstadt* project also form the basis of two further explorations within Berlin: the 1975 project for the *West Berlin Railway Yards*, and the 1988 project *Wild Ways Berlin*. Each of these projects explored reuse tactics for the abandoned railway yards surrounding the center of Berlin that echo those used by James Corner Field Operations at the *High Line* in New York. The Smithsons described this "disused network of places" as "remarkably spacious areas of inner city, often touching the city centre, yet also often secret from the rest of the city by their being a level above or below their surroundings."[18] The intervention in the abandoned railways was not only intended as new way to move through the existing city fabric—much like the *High Line* allows one to move uninterruptedly through western Manhattan—but also as an "armature to a new urban structure, on which would cluster those functions Berlin wishes to attract, or needs to generate."[19] These "connective holes" were understood as a tactic for reinvigorating the central city that had the ability to "refocus attention inwards."[20]

Quality Effective Sites

Alison Smithson's 1977 essay "The City Centre Full of Holes" includes a sketch that illustrates her idea for the selection of "quality-effective sites in cities." (Fig. 2) In this sketch Smithson compares the "old style" approach to rebuilding that focuses on the "comprehensive development" of large sites to that of a "place response" approach in which a dispersed network of smaller sites are chosen for their "power of renewal."[21] This dispersed approach to healing holes within the city can be seen in the work of another Team 10 participant, Aldo van Eyck.

Between 1947 and 1978 Aldo van Eyck designed more than seven hundred public playgrounds in the city of Amsterdam. For van Eyck, these playgrounds were designed to reanimate a "series of forgotten spots, left over because a road takes a particular route, triangular squares lying there lifelessly."[22] As these "forgotten spots" were infilled with van Eyck's playgrounds, they gradually came to form a "finely-meshed network" of public spaces that enhanced the experience of the city by closing up holes in the urban fabric. In contrast to top-down rational planning espoused by the modern architects of CIAM, this approach represented a "strategy of the interstitial and the polycentric."[23] Furthermore, the siting of these playgrounds were not part of a comprehensive masterplan, but were instead requested by the public: "groups of citizens in Amsterdam would see a playground, or hear of one, and write the public works department in order to request one for themselves."[24] For example, a letter dated 11 May 1954 reads:

> As a resident of the Waalstraat I would like to ask you whether the unproductive plot of land at the end of the street between Moerdijkstraat and Waalstraat cannot be turned into a playground with a sandpit as in other districts of Amsterdam.[25]

Active Agents

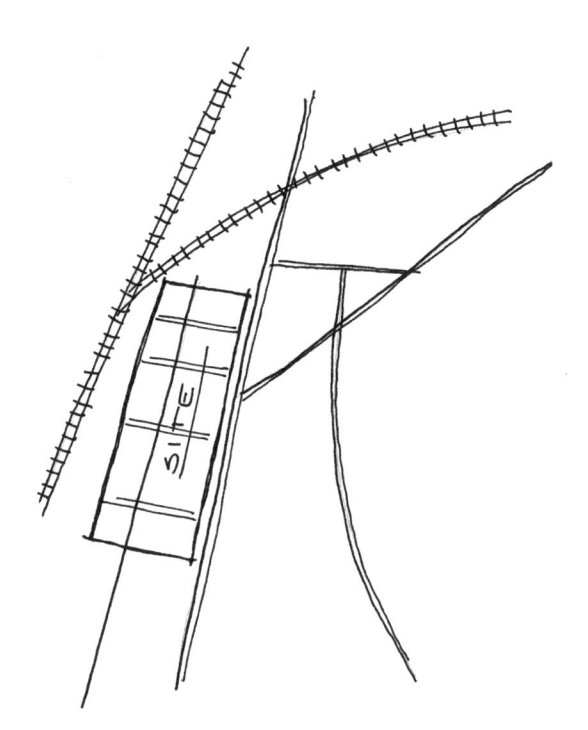

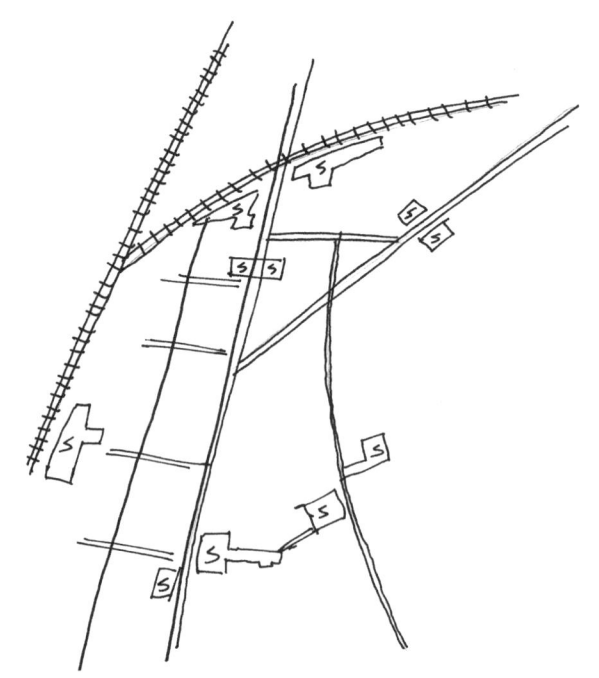

Figure 2
Choice of Quality-Effective Sites in Cities
Sketch by author after Alison Smithson.

Left
Old Style Approach. Comprehensive development but neither place-maker nor place restorer.

Right
Place Response Approach. Sites chosen for power of renewal.

The success of van Eyck's Amsterdam playgrounds is indicative of the power of the bottom-up, polycentric, place-based approach described in Alison Smithson's "quality effective sites" sketch. (Fig. 2) Fellow Team 10 participant, John Voelcker, described these interstitial playgrounds as "active agents of urban reintegration."[26] Even more important than their success as playgrounds is the role that these "active agents" played in reinvigorating a city that had been damaged by war.

Conclusions

In "The City Centre Full of Holes," Alison Smithson suggests that the tactical conception of open space utilized in the projects discussed here can operate as an agent in healing the city:

> The city centre is not dead, only resting [and] that it is becoming available, a place for the nature of change to make itself manifest, a place for change for the better in a climate of hope.[27]

In other words, these projects are not considered to be an end product. Instead, they are instigative tactics for rejuvenating the city.

This conception of the interstitial and unbuilt as a tool for engendering future re-urbanization—whether in the form of landscapes or hardscapes—is missing in many of the iconic landscape urbanist projects. Despite creating functioning ecosystems while reclaiming and cleaning large postindustrial sites, projects like *Fresh Kills* and *Downsview* remain parks, their plant and animal succession diagrams about creating landscapes, not cities as such. As Smithson recognized, "cities where depopulation has taken place are likely to have holes in them for some years to come."[28] She goes on to suggest that the "greening of the depleted city centre may even be the most obvious characteristic of the future city centre."[29] In these ideas we can see a clear antecedent to Waldheim's conception of landscape as the medium for addressing de-densification and sprawl. However, in contrast to Waldheim's acceptance of the shrunken city, Smithson conceives of these pockets of landscape as "a holding operation until more prosperous and confident times."[30] In other words, landscape is not a goal in and of itself, but rather a temporary remedy intended to engender dense urbanity.

The discourse of landscape urbanism was founded upon the realities of dealing with shrinking postindustrial cities. If it is to remain efficacious in a world where the percentage of people living in urban areas around the world continues to grow, it must now turn its attention to creating dense, sustainable urban forms. The understanding of ecological processes that has been embedded in the first generation of landscape urbanist projects will be essential to that goal. However, we must supplement this knowledge of ecology with the deployment of strategies that result in the construction not of parks, but of cities in all of their complexity. The projects of the Smithsons and Aldo van Eyck offer one possible approach to this problem. These projects can be described as a type of "dirty realism" that emerges from the complex everyday situation of existing urban fabrics. Rather than consigning ourselves to a future of dispersed suburban-style cities, these projects suggest an alternative future in which postindustrial urban cores and new-growth cities alike undergo a process of densification instigated by landscape urbanist tactics. In the end, in order to create an urbanism of landscape urbanism, we must not give priority to either architecture or landscape architecture, but rather to a rich and inseparable mixture of them both.

Endnotes

1 *The Landscape Urbanism Reader*, ed. Charles Waldheim (New York: Princeton Architectural Press, 2006); p. 11.
2 Charles Waldheim and Marili Santos-Munné, "Decamping Detroit," in *Stalking Detroit*, ed. Georgia Daskalakis, Charles Waldheim, and Jason Young (Barcelona: Actar, 2001); p. 110.
3 Charles Waldheim, "Landscape Urbanism: A Genealogy," *Praxis* 4 (2002); p. 13.
4 Waldheim, "Landscape Urbanism," p. 13.
5 Waldheim, "Landscape Urbanism," p. 13. Emphasis added.
6 Waldheim, "Landscape Urbanism," p. 13.
7 Lewis Mumford, introduction to *Design with Nature*, by Ian McHarg (Garden City, NY: The Natural History Press, 1969); p. viii. Emphasis in original.
8 Ian McHarg, *Design with Nature* (Garden City, NY: The Natural History Press, 1969); p. 197.
9 James Corner, "Landscape Urbanism," in *Landscape Urbanism: A Manual for the Machinic Landscape*, ed. Mohsen Mostafavi and Ciro Najle (London: AA Publications, 2003); p. 58. Emphasis added.
10 Corner, "Landscape Urbanism," p. 59.
11 Waldheim, "Landscape Urbanism," p. 12.
12 Reyner Banham, "A Clip-On Architecture," *Design Quarterly* 63 (1966); pp. 2-30.
13 Banham, "A Clip-On Architecture," p. 6.
14 Jonathan Hughes, "The Indeterminate Building," in *Non-Plan*, ed. Simon Sadler and Jonathan Hughes (Oxford: Architectural Press, 2000); p. 96.
15 Alison and Peter Smithson, *The Charged Void: Urbanism* (New York: The Monacelli Press, 2005); p. 56.
16 Smithson, *The Charged Void*, p. 56.
17 Smithson, *The Charged Void*, p. 56.
18 Smithson, *The Charged Void*, p. 194.
19 Alison Smithson, "Berlin's Railway Yards: Connective Layering," manuscript dated February 1978 found in the Smithsons/Team 10 Archive at the Netherlands Architecture Institute, Rotterdam (TTEN-52).
20 Smithson, *The Charged Void*, p. 194.
21 Alison Smithson, "The City Centre Full of Holes," *Architectural Association Quarterly* 9/2, 3, (1977); p. 8.
22 Aldo van Eyck, "On the design of play equipment and the arrangement of playgrounds," in *Aldo van Eyck: Writings*, ed. Vincent Ligtelijn and Francis Strauven (Amsterdam: SUN Publishers, 2008); p. 112.
23 Liane Lefaivre, "Space, place and play," in *Aldo van Eyck: The Playgrounds and the City*, ed. Liane Lefaivre and Ingeborg de Roode (Amsterdam: Stedelijk Museum, 2002); p. 27.
24 Liane Lefaivre and Alexander Tzonis, *Aldo van Eyck: Humanist Rebel* (Rotterdam: 010 Publishers, 1999); p. 17.
25 Quoted in Erik Schmitz, "Let our children have a playground. They need it very badly!" in *Aldo van Eyck: The Playgrounds and the City*, ed. Liane Lefaivre and Ingeborg de Roode (Amsterdam: Stedelijk Museum, 2002); p. 62.
26 John Voelcker, "Polder and Playground," *Architect's Year Book* 6 (1955); pp. 89-94.
27 Smithson, "The City Centre Full of Holes," p. 13.
28 Smithson, "The City Centre Full of Holes," p. 11.
29 Smithson, "The City Centre Full of Holes," p. 11.
30 Smithson, "The City Centre Full of Holes," p. 11.

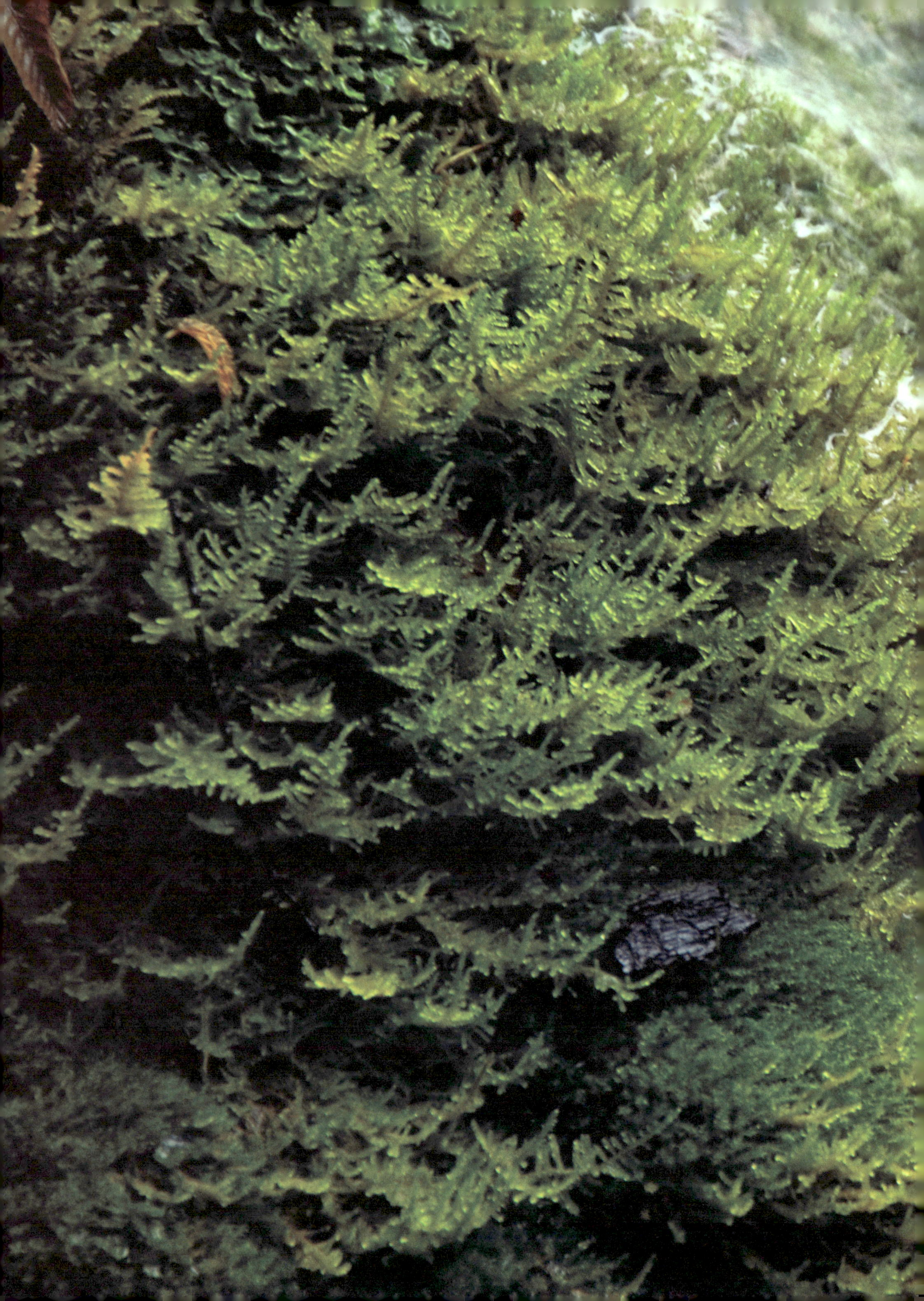

Rich Ground

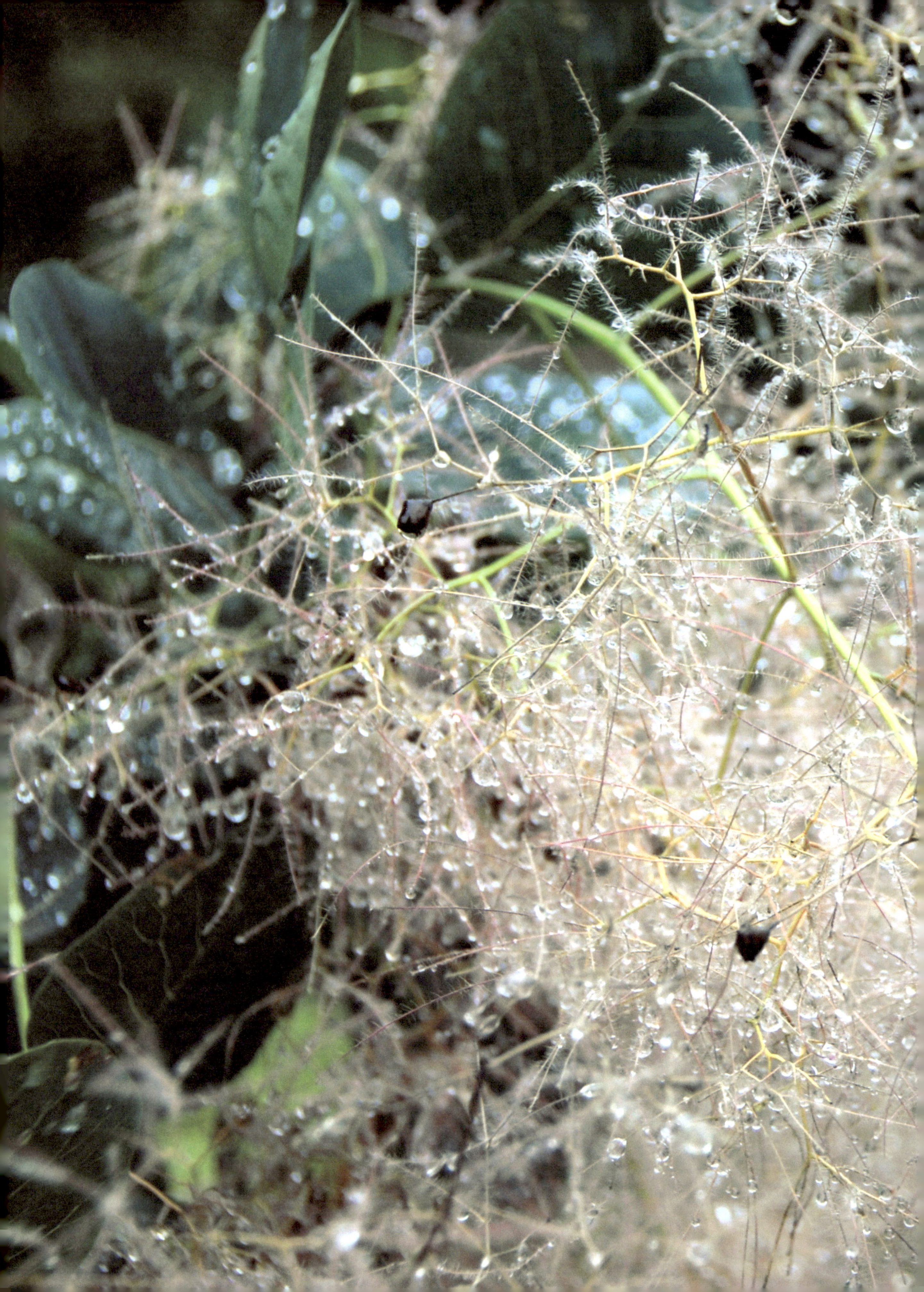

Dew formation on Eurasian smoketree
Plitvice Lakes National Park, Croatia

Previous Spread
Moss Splashed by Cascades
Plitvice Lakes National Park, Croatia

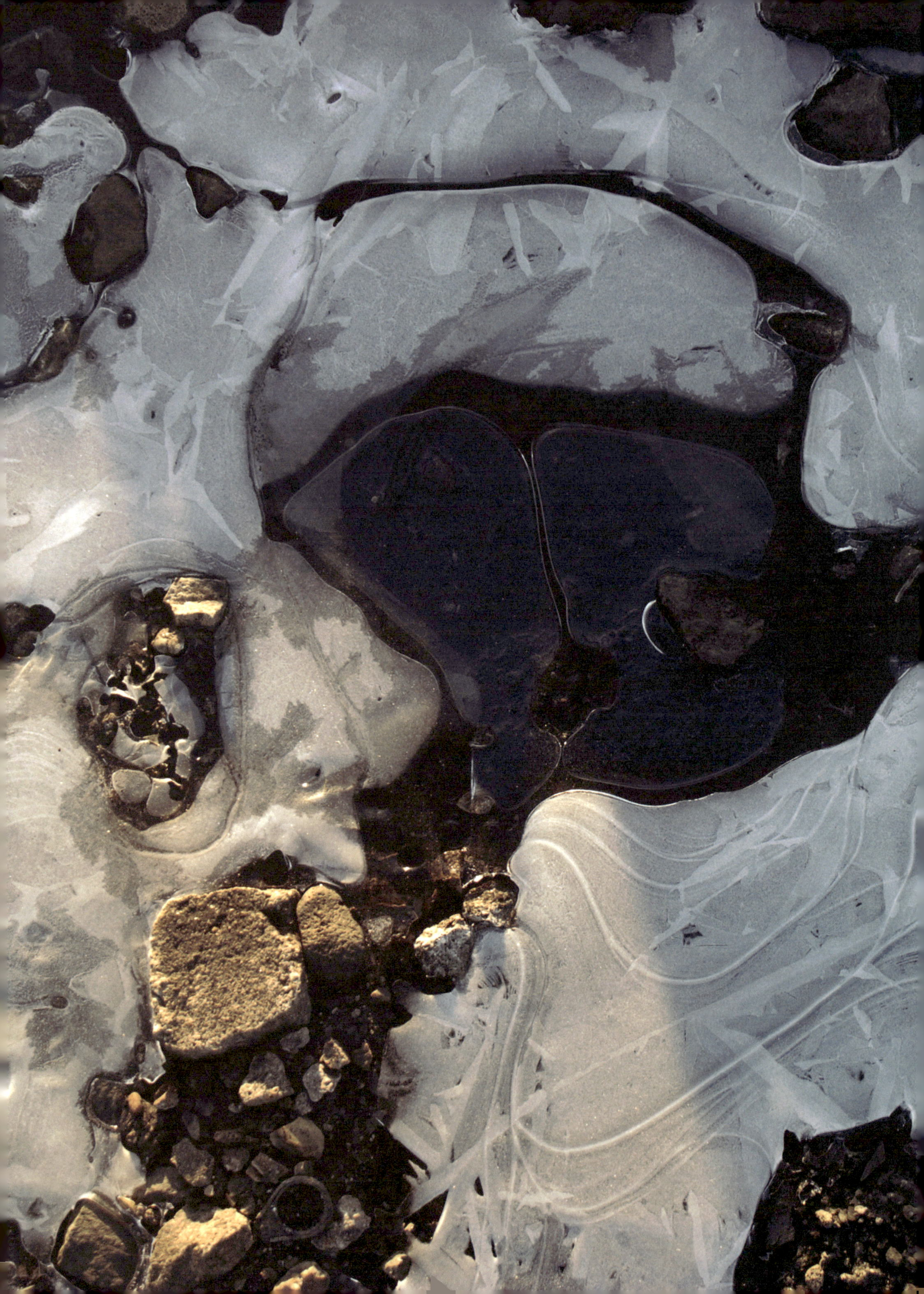

Frozen track ballast and debris
Near 30th Street Station, Philadelphia, PA

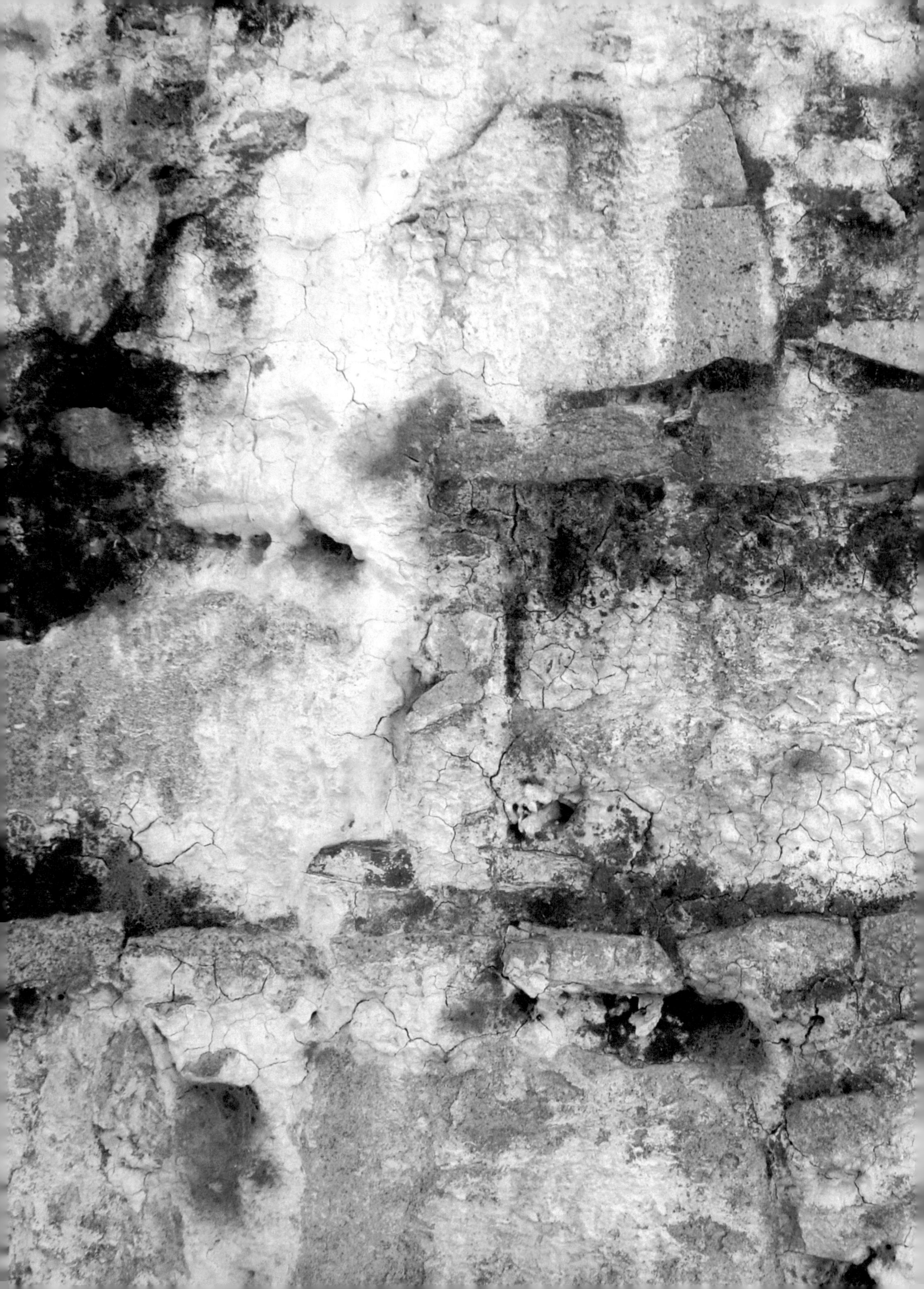

Exposed masonry work
Drepung Monastery in Lhasa, Tibet

Root Words
Introduction to *Ecology, for the Evolution of Planning and Design*
Megan Born

Search the term "ecology" in the Avery Index of Architectural Periodicals (the trusted database of design academia) and you will find 1,178 entries. Ian McHarg is the author of three of the first five articles, including "Ecology, for the Evolution of Planning and Design," reprinted in this volume[IV] Published in 1968, the article is a seminal work linking the natural sciences—specifically ecology—to the design fields of landscape architecture, architecture, urban design, and city planning. This essay pioneers the practice of ecological design, a concept that is now totally engrained in contemporary design thinking and practice.

It is difficult to imagine a time when interdependent networks, complex relational hierarchies, and site specificity were not terms of creative engagement. On the one hand, the ubiquity of ecologically-minded design can be seen as great progress. Conversely, now that an ecological approach is requisite in progressive design schemes, there is potential for it to become flat, trite, and prescribed. Reading the following essay prompts us to re-engage ecology as a critical design tool, recall its fundamental meaning, and reinterpret its relationship to design in fresh and precise ways.

McHarg's Context
To appreciate and accurately read McHarg's words we must know a bit about the time and circumstances in which he was writing. During the late 1960s and early 1970s, McHarg investigated American cities overripe with industry and the changing pressures of an urban population and suburban development. In *Design with Nature*, he describes cities as "imprisoning gray areas that encircle the center...their symbol is the abandoned carcasses of automobile, broken glass, alleys of rubbish and garbage"[2] He focused on the physical and environmental detriments that cities such as New York, Philadelphia, and Baltimore sustained during the previous century and he criticized the exclusive focus on economics and the social sciences to drive their urban design.

> It is clear that the principles which contributed to historic successes in urban form have failed dismally since the industrial revolution. The success of the subsequent city as provider of employment and social services is its best feature, but as a physical environment it has continually retrogressed.[3]

In the following essay McHarg calls on designers and planners to employ the natural sciences, specifically ecology, in method and process to counteract the ubiquitous force of economics that shapes the industrialized city, allowing ecology to form the basis for intervening at the urban and regional scale.

Ecological Principles and Methods
To understand McHarg's use and interpretation of ecology, we must first define the term. Ecology is the branch of science that studies relationships and interactions between organisms and their surroundings. It assumes that all organisms are interconnected and the actions of one will undoubtedly affect those within

its relational web. These connections are complex and at times unseen, often linked together via webs, clouds, or other networks.

When McHarg wrote the following essay, connections between ecology and design were nascent and unfamiliar. What makes McHarg so effective in linking ecology with design is his ability to be both a rousing generalist and didactic instructor. He interprets ecology through two lenses that are useful for designers and planners, framing both a paradigm within which to operate as well as a definitive set of principles and guidelines to follow. McHarg's words first inspire designers to think ecologically and then teach them how to design using an ecological method.

McHarg's first ecology frames a broad worldview. In *Design with Nature* he summarizes his vision of nature: "Let us accept the proposition that nature is process, that it is interacting, that it responds to laws."[4] This leads to an "ecological view that requires that we look upon the world, listen and learn. The place, creatures and men were, have been are now and are becoming. We and they are here now, co-tenants of the phenomenal world, united in its origins and destiny."[5]

Moving from universal to specialized application, McHarg outlines his "ecological method" in ten succinct steps. First is the gathering of existing histories, ecologies, and physical conditions, followed by analysis through layering, weighting, and conflating of these conditions, and finally design and uses are applied based on the analytical findings. Not unlike the scientific method, McHarg's process is based on principles rather than intuitions, leaving little room for interpretation or improvisation by an individual designer. The specificity of McHarg's process balances the inspirational broadsides.

Interdisciplinary Connections and Disciplinary Relevance

Fundamental to the ecological principle are notions of connection and interdependency. In light of this, McHarg was a pioneer in interdisciplinary collaboration. Ecology thus forms a model for working between fields as well as within one's own practice. By connecting to the natural sciences, McHarg sparked an interest in cooperation and collaboration across disciplinary boundaries. He states, "The natural scientists have been pointing out the interdependence which characterizes all relationships, organic and inorganic, in nature. Ecologists stress that an ecological community survives as a result of the interdependent activity of all the species within it."[6]

McHarg believed that without the consistency and rigor of an ecological process, designers are left with only their intuition, which is inconsistent and lacks accountability. With ecological methods and principles, designers were able to quantify and rationalize new and innovative strategies and rethink the urban condition. Previously, the cities and spaces shaped by economics left little room for designers to do anything more than cosmetic and superficial improvements. After McHarg, designers

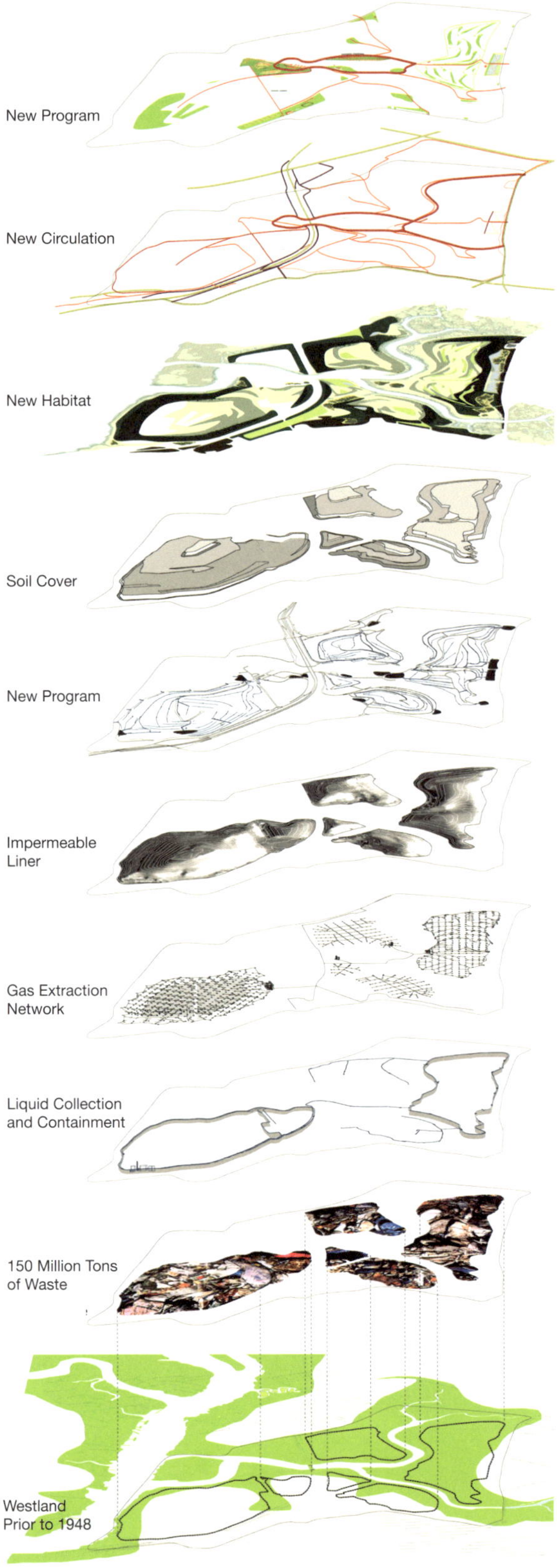

Figure 1
Fresh Kills Lifescape
The components of the park are layered to create a diverse mix of ecology, infrastructure, and recreation.

would become essential to the growth and development of cities, rather than peripheral players.

Consequently, McHarg's ecological method ushered in a new relevance for the discipline of landscape architecture. This in turn effected the scale and scope of work, which landscape architects engaged. Landscape architects became strategic visionaries and experts in ecology and environmental design—critical players in contemporary urban planning and discourse. Moreover, during the same period planners and architects became increasingly interested in landscape, realizing how—like iconic buildings and master plans—it could shape and organize cities.

Despite the enormous progress that McHarg sparked in landscape architecture, something was lost in the deployment of the ecological method. Place-making, formal investigations, and economic development were pitted against ecological planning and design. The quality of space, the social history of a place, the imaginative possibilities and future development potentials of a site's future were set aside by McHarg in favor of an ecological agenda, and a rigorous accountable scientific method. Ecology became narrowly defined and synonymous with environmentalism. In the time since McHarg wrote "Ecology, for the Evolution of Planning and Design," multiple generations of designers and thinkers have been grappling with how to fully realize McHarg's ecological method and how to re-incorporate neglected aspects of landscape architecture and urban design.

McHarg's Legacy

McHarg's legacy is enormously evident in the work of today's leading practitioners and theorists in the fields of landscape architecture and urban design. In the 1960s he reinvigorated and reshaped the Department of Landscape Architecture and Regional Planning at the University of Pennsylvania, which helped to elevate the critical discourse, research, and design methods in the study of landscape architecture and urban planning. Following McHarg's tenure, a group of designers have emerged who together shape the contemporary field of landscape architecture under the influence of his ideas, ideals, and pedagogy.

The projects, writings, and teaching of James Corner are heavily rooted in McHarg's definition of ecology. A student of McHarg's at Penn in the early 1980s, Corner's work expands McHarg's views by deepening the understanding and application of ecology in the fields of landscape, planning, and urbanism. "Since the publication in 1969 of Ian McHarg's *Design with Nature*, landscape architects have been particularly busy developing a range of ecological techniques for the planning and design of sites. But...ecology has been used only in the context of some thing called the 'environment,' which is generally thought to be of 'nature' and exclusive of the city...We have yet to understand cultural, social, political, and economic movements as embedded in and symmetrical with the 'natural world.'"[7] While remaining true to the core concept of ecology, Corner broadens its scope and approach by incorporating urban, social, and economic dynamics with natural processes to understand site conditions. Corner furthers McHarg's notion of interdependence by interpreting site as an open-ended horizontal working surface.[8] This "field of action" is McHarg's networked connections re-imagined for urban sites and situations.

Corner's design for the park at *Fresh Kills Landfill* in Staten Island, New York and his competition entry for *Downsview Park* in Toronto exemplify this expanded ecological approach. At both sites Corner designed physical frameworks that emerge from specific local conditions to amplify existing ecological networks and create new ecological corridors through earthworks and planting strategies. Along with the shaping of the physical site, Corner creates large, open program spaces for recreation and infrastructural activities. Program, infrastructure, and nature coalesce under the umbrella of ecology.

Along with McHarg's ideologies, Corner is inspired by McHarg's representational techniques. The layering and conflating of information, a technique pioneered by McHarg, is evident in Corner's work. Clearly seen in the diagrams and exploded axonometric drawings for both *Downsview Park* and *Fresh Kills*, Corner delaminates the components of the park, revealing the complexity and organization of the physical site along with the support infrastructure, and programmed or emergent activities. (Fig. 1)

Figure 2
The Lower Cuyahoga River Valley

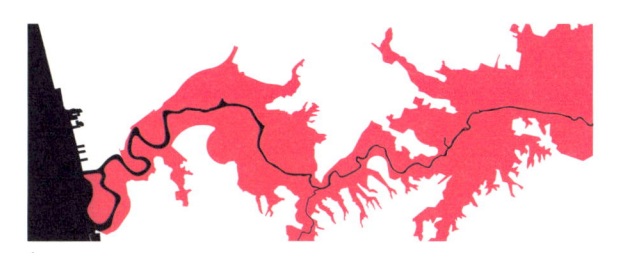

1
Topographic Valley Figure
12,480 acres, Nearly 20% of the total area of Cleveland

Our approach begins by first defining the entire valley as a recognizable urban figure within the city. By studying the topographic composition of Cleveland and Cuyahoga County, we are able to establish a clear boundary for this territory.

2
Reforestation Regime
5,420 acres, 22,000 metric tons of CO2 sequestered annually

The interior of this territory is organized by configuring ten broad land-use categories across the entire area. These categories include remediation, recreation, habitat, agriculture, industry, production, energy, water, preserve, and circulation.

3
Production Surfaces
3,520 acres, 89.4m lbs of potatoes or 148m lbs of strawberries

This figure is physically articulated by extending the native successional forest from the south, north to the shore of Lake Erie along the steep slopes, and escarpments of the territory's perimeter.

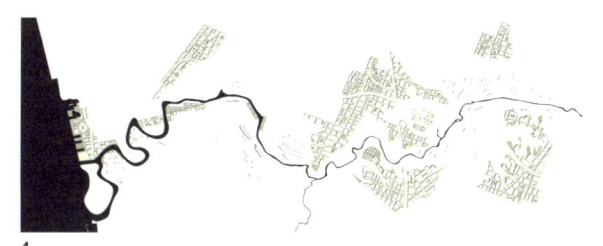

4
Economic Development Zones
2,250 acres, Clean/Green Industry clusters at perimeter

Though the lower Cuyahoga River Valley is the primary area of intervention, we have designated 5 development zones adjacent to the valley that are ideal areas for concentrated redevelopment catalyzed by the valley's transformation.

Rich Ground

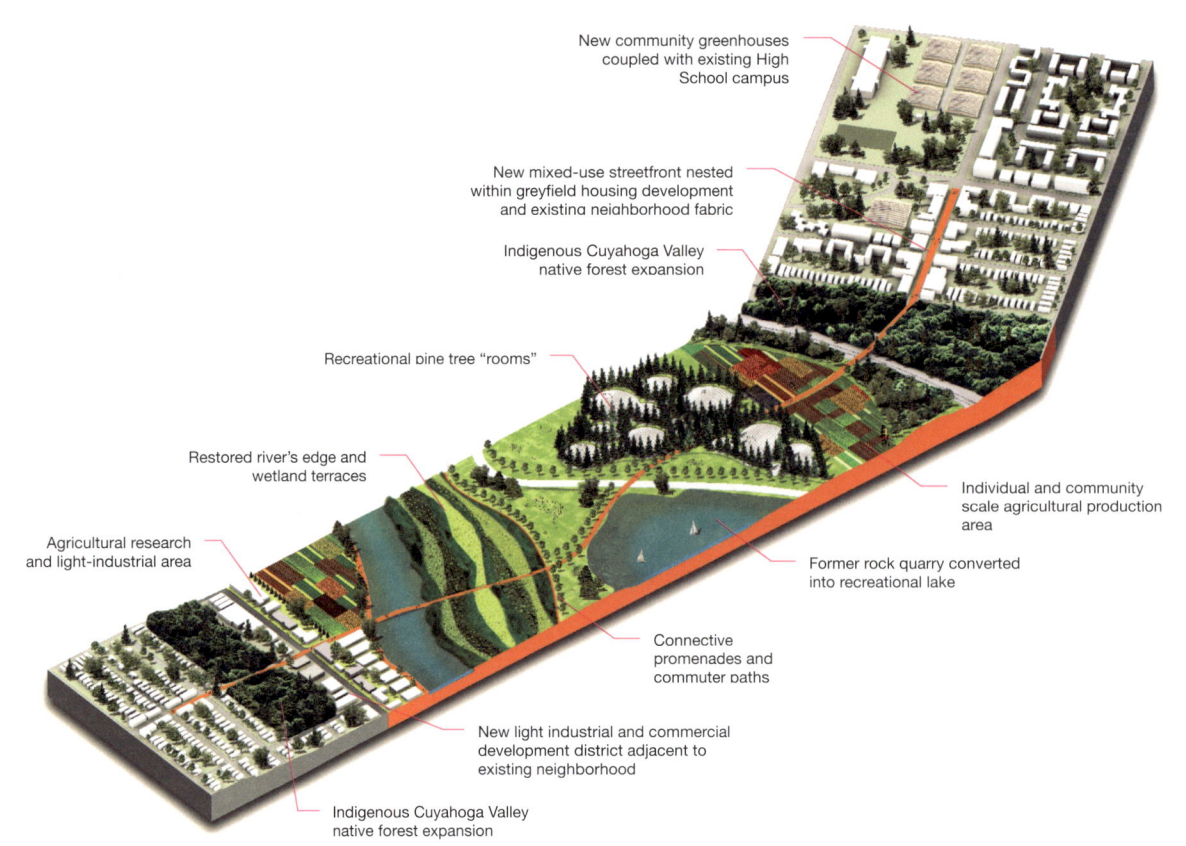

Figure 3
The Remediation Floor
The remade lower Cuyahoga River Valley comprises a variety of land uses and programs ranging from recreation to agriculture to clean industry. Initially, remediation is a major programmatic activity, but within the very near term, the valley once again becomes a place of significant agricultural production utilizing a 1:1 ratio of development to agricultural areas.

Following Corner, a group of contemporary designers and thinkers continue to expand the fields of landscape and planning in light of McHarg's work. Anuradha Mathur, along with her partner Dilip da Cunha, have produced design research studies of the Mississippi River, the Deccan Traverse in Bangalore, and the Mithi River in Mumbai that highlight the complexities and specificities of each site to include physical and ecological conditions with multiple histories, social and cultural traces through the territories. Mathur and da Cunha's work reveals how integral human intervention can be to the shaping of landscape. The representation of landscapes in their work also includes a complex layering of information, revealing a complex web of interconnected factors affecting a site. Unlike Corner's more analytic drawings however, Mathur and de Cunha expand a more painterly technique and use a large range of media including photography, digital and hand drawing, and screen-printing to access a qualified reading of the site.

McHarg's ecological approach is also evidenced by the work of PORT, a young urban design practice led by Christopher Marcinkoski and Andrew Moddrell. PORT's work focuses on post-industrial sites, similar to those described by McHarg, ranging from the scale of an urban district to a metropolitan region. And like McHarg PORT's work is grounded in careful analysis of a site's physical form and processes. PORT has traded McHarg's dogmatism for opportunistic pragmatism, strategically layering sites with relevant social programming, economic development, and emerging technology. For example, in their *Re-Cultivating the Forest City* project in the Cuyahoga River Valley, Marcinkoski and Moddrell begin by framing the post-industrial site geographically, as strategically located between the region's two major physical features, Lake Erie and the Cuyahoga River, and cutting through the center of Cleveland. (Fig. 2) They note that the environmental health of these two water bodies has improved as the economic and social wellness

Figure 4
View of the Remediation Floor

of the area has declined, which is the reverse effect of cities McHarg profiled in 1968. PORT proposes to pair ecological improvements with economic development through urban agriculture, sustainable energy production, and native forest expansion. (Fig. 3) PORT does not trade the influences of social science for ecology (as McHarg does) rather they layer the two for maximum effect. (Fig. 4)

Moving beyond McHarg

In the following essay, McHarg evaluates his theory of ecology as a tool for design as rudimentary, and his application of an ecological method to be primitive. The direct and simple nature of his words is a benefit to designers both then and now. It provided a rich ground from which the most compelling and influential contemporary work in landscape architecture and urban design has stemmed. It also provides today's students and practitioners of ecological design with a clear historical moment to study, critique, and interpret. The field of contemporary landscape architecture, with its subtle, complex, and richly layered mode of practice, is indebted to McHarg's straightforward ecological principles originally expressed in "Ecology, for the Evolution of Planning and Design."

Endnotes

1. Ian McHarg, "Ecology, for the Evolution of Planning and Design," *VIA 1* (1968): p. 44-66.
2. Ian Mcharg, *Design with Nature,* (Garden City, NY: The Natural History Press, 1969), p. 20.
3. Ian McHarg, "Ecology, for the Evolution of Planning and Design," *VIA 1* (1968): p. 44.
4. Ian McHarg, *Design with Nature,* p. 7.
5. McHarg, Design with Nature, p.29.
6. McHarg, "Ecology": p. 66.
7. Corner, "Terra Fluxus," in *The Landscape Urbanism Reader* (New York: Princeton Architectural Press, 2006); pp. 29-30.
8. Corner, "Terra Fluxus," p. 30.

Ecology, for the Evolution of Planning and Design

Ian McHarg

In the Western world during the past century, transformation of natural environments into human habitats has commonly proved to be retrogressive. In earlier times, because of the slowness of change, this was not so. Few among us regret the loss of ancient marshes for Venice and Amsterdam, or the loss of ancient hills for Athens and Rome. History testifies to human adaptations, accomplished with wisdom and art, which were and still are felicitous. Yet the principles which these successes were based upon are inadequate for the speed, scale, and nature of change today.

In the 17th century it required a third of the treasury of France, the mature life of Louis XIV, and the major effort of André Le Nôtre to realize Versailles. Three centuries later, Greater New York will urbanize at the rate of 50,000 acres and 600,000 people per year—without a plan. Paradoxically, in this period of change the city plan has remained like the Renaissance one which motivated Versailles, a poor symbol of man-nature in the 17th century, inexcusable as a prototype for the 20th century.

It is clear that the principles which contributed to historic successes in urban form have failed dismally since the industrial revolution. The success of the subsequent city as provider of employment and social services is its best feature, but as a physical environment it has continually retrogressed. New principles must be developed for human adaptations—for city, metropolitan region, and megalopolis.

Today, the prescriptions for urban location, form, and growth derive almost exclusively from the social sciences. Both analytic and predictive models are based upon economics. Yet the natural sciences have not become engaged, even though understanding of physical and biological processes is indispensable for good judgment in the problems of environment. Many central questions can be answered by natural scientists; for example, "What are the natural determinants for the location and form of development?" The answers are vital to administrators, regional and city planners, architects, and landscape architects. The landscape architects, in fact, work within a profession historically concerned with the relation of man to nature and of the natural sciences to the making of urban environments.

In the Western tradition, with the single exception of the English 18th century and its practitioners, landscape architecture has been identified with garden-making, be it Alhambra, San Gall, D'Este, or Versailles. In this tradition decorative and tractable plants are arranged in a simple geometry as a comprehensible metaphysical symbol of a benign and orderly world. Here the ornamental qualities of plants are paramount; no concepts of their communities or associations becloud the objective. Plants are domesticated like pets (lawn grasses, hedges, flowering shrubs and trees), tolerant to man and dependent upon him, man's cohorts.

This is the walled garden, selected out of nature—a symbol of beneficence, an island of delight, tranquility, and reflection. It is quite consistent that the climax of this garden is the flower. Not only is this a selected nature, but the order of its array is, unlike the complexity of nature, reduced to a simple and comprehensible design. Yet there is always the knowledge that nature reveals a different form and aspect beyond the wall. Loren Eiseley has said that "the unknown within the self is linked to the wild."

The role of garden-making remains important. Man tries to find a personal paradise on earth, at one with nature. In these, man may find peace, and in tranquillity discover, in Rexroth's words, "the place of values in a world of facts." He may respond to water, stone, herbs, trees, sunlight and shadow, rain, ice and snow, the changing seasons, birth, life and death. Such a garden is a special microhabitat, a healthy cell in the organism of the city, a most humane expression. Yet clearly its role, based on ornamental horticulture and simple geometry within the wall, is limited.

In 18th century England, landscape architects "leap'd the wall and discovered all nature to be a garden," but not until a new view of nature had dispelled the old, and a new aesthetic had been developed consonant with the enlarged arena.

Starting with a denuded landscape, a backward agriculture, and a pattern of attenuated land holdings, this new landscape tradition rehabilitated an entire countryside. It is testimony to the prescience of Kent, Brown, Repton, and their followers that, lacking a science of ecology, they used native plant materials in a way which reflected natural processes so well that their creations have endured and are self-perpetuating.

The objective was a productive, working landscape. Hilltops and hillsides were forested, while great meadows occupied the valley bottoms where streams meandered and lakes were constructed. The extensive meadows supported cattle, horses, and sheep. The forests provided valuable timber (the lack of which Evelyn had earlier deplored) and supported game, while free-standing copses in the meadows provided shade and shelter for animals. The planting reflected the needs of shipbuilding, but the preferred trees, oak and beech, were climax species and they were planted anew. On sites where these were inappropriate—northern slopes, thin soils, elevations—pine and birch were planted. Watercourses were graced with willows and alders. The meadows supported grasses and meadow flowers. As long as the meadows were used for grazing, a productive sere was maintained.

The objective however was more than production alone. Paintings of the 'campagna' by Poussin and Salvator Rosa, a eulogy of nature which obsessed poets and writers, had developed the concept of an ideal nature. Yet it clearly did not exist in the landscape of 18th century England. It had to be created. The ruling principle was that "nature is the gardener's best designer." Ornamental horticulture, which had prevailed within garden walls, became the object of disdain, and a nascent ecology replaced it. The meadow was the single artifice. The remaining components were natural expressions; their dramatic qualities were exploited, it is true, but derived in the first place from processes observed in nature. Nature itself provided the aesthetic; the simple geometry (not of simplicity but of simple-mindedness) of the Renaissance was swept away: "Nature abhors a straight line." The discovery of an established aesthetic in the Orient based on occult balance, asymmetry, confirmed this view. In the 18th century landscape, the revolution began which banished the giant classicism and the imposition of its geometry as a symbol of man-nature.

It founded applied ecology as the basis for function and aesthetics in the landscape, wherein form and process were seen to be facets of a single phenomenon. It is important because of the scale of operation. One recalls that Capability Brown, when asked to undertake a project in Ireland, retorted "I have not finished England yet." It is also important as a creation. Here the landscape architect, like the empiricist doctor, found the land in ill-health and, understanding nature's laws and forms, accelerated the process of regeneration so well that who today can discern the artifice from the untouched?

The successes of this tradition are manifest. No other movement has accomplished such a physical regeneration and amelioration. It is hard to find fault with this tradition, but one must observe that although the principles of ecology and its aesthetic are general, the realization of this movement was particular. It reflected an agricultural economy based principally upon cattle, horses, and sheep. It never confronted the city, which remained the Renaissance prototype. Only in the urban squares, parks, and circuses, in natural plantings, is the 18th century city distinguishable from its antecedents.

Particularly at the scale of the city, metropolitan region, and megalopolis, the creation of a 20th century tradition requires modern ecology as the basis for intervention. Today we need an understanding of natural process and its expression, and, even more, a realization of the true relationship between man and nature. Aldo Leopold writes of this need: "There is as yet no ethic dealing with man's relation to the environment and the animals and plants which grow upon it. The extension of ethics to include man's relation to environment is, if I read the evidence correctly, an evolutionary possibility and an ecological necessity. All ethics so far evolved rest upon a single premise, that the individual is a member of a community of interdependent parts. His instincts prompt him to compete for his place in the community, but his ethics prompt him to cooperate, perhaps in order that there may be a place to compete for."[1]

If nature is viewed from the vantage of the man who would intervene with intelligence and even aspire to art, then we can see that nature is process; it has values and opportunities for human use, but it also reveals constraints and even prohibitions. Furthermore, process can be measured in terms of creation or destruction. That process—be it cell, organ, organism, or community—which is creative will, by definition, be fit and will reveal its fitness in form. We can employ this concept for both diagnosis and prescription, in both planning and design. The application of ecology to human affairs is so recent, however, that there is not yet a formal method. I offer my own rudimentary conception of the ingredients of an ecological method.

1. Ecological inventory. An analysis of climate, historical geology, physiography, hydrology, soils, plant and animal associations, and existing land uses.
2. Description of natural processes. An analysis of the major physical and biological processes and their interactions, limiting factors, degrees of stability or instability, health or pathology.
3. Historical inventory. An analysis of the adaptations accomplished by man over time, considered in terms of their degree of success.
4. Expression of the 'given' form. An analysis of the ecological inventory to recognize the natural identity of the place and the components of its expression revealed in physiography and plant communities.
5. Expression of the 'made' form. An analysis of the historical inventory to recognize the man-made identity of the place, viewed as a formal vocabulary and a symbolic system of values.
6. Attribution of relative value. An analysis of each area in terms of its relative value for all prospective land uses, and the allocation of relative social values.

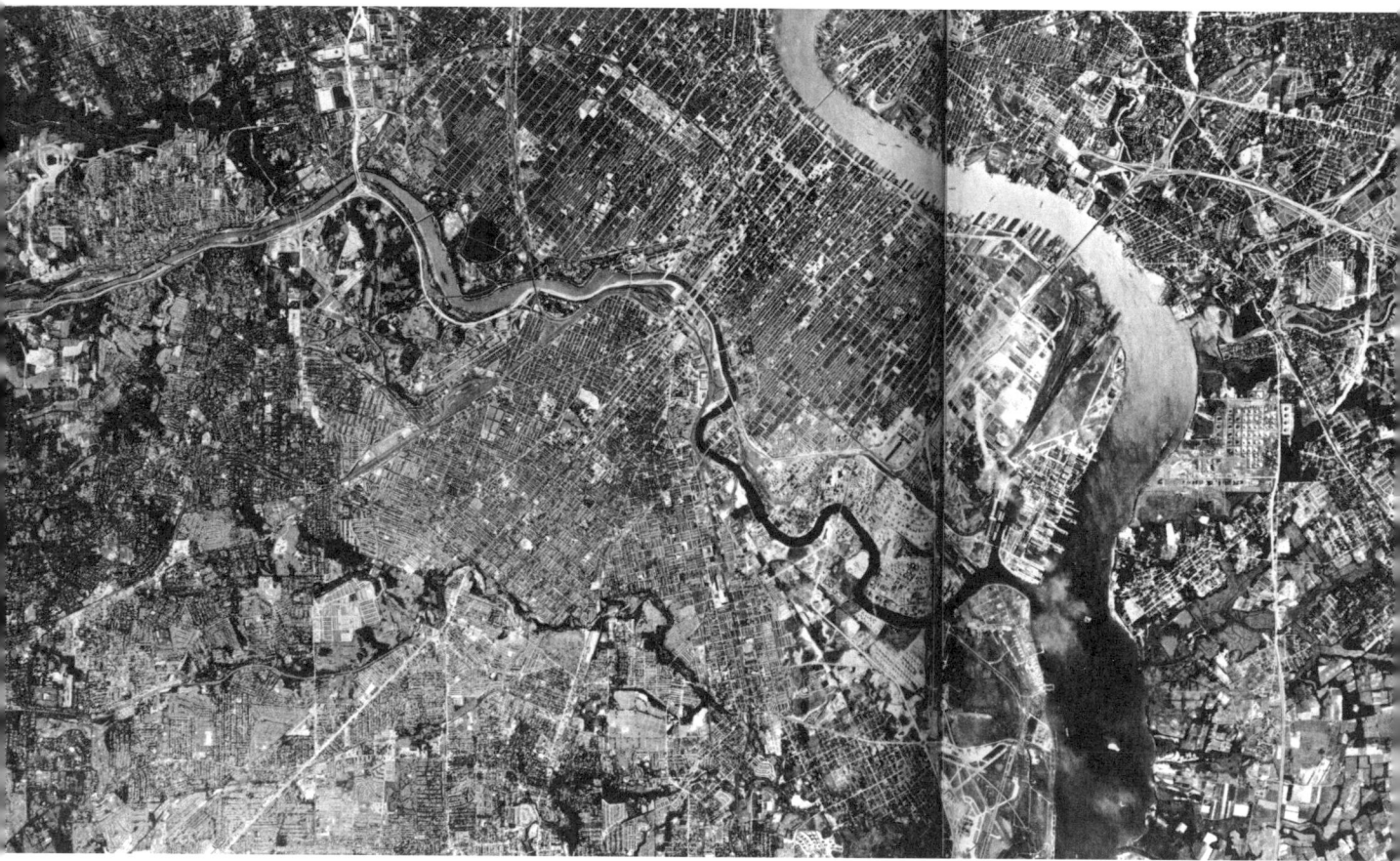

Figure 1
Aerial Photograph of Philadelphia, 1968

7. Interpretation of intrinsic land use. Selection from the foregoing of the most intrinsic land use for each area under study.
8. Conclusions as to compatible land uses. By the use of a matrix with all possible land uses on both axes, a selection is made of the maximum number of compatible, concurrent land uses.
9. Formulation of alternative land use plans. The selection of those prospective land uses which best satisfy multiple compatibility from the matrix, linked to the natural determinants of such uses and to the consequences of managing them.
10. Implications for the new 'made' form. Formulation of the determinants in natural and social processes which are revealed in existing form and hold implications for the form of new adaptations and their success.

In the past, unusually perceptive planners and designers have been able to create adaptations which are indeed fit and which demonstrate this in their form. Yet this has not developed from principle, and so the intuitive professionals are seldom able to transmit the bases for the rare successes to colleagues or students, who must then improvise to select a working method. The particular value of the ecological view is that it permits adaptations by man to be examined against the criteria which hold for all physical and biological processes. There is the promise, then, of an emergent body of principles for those concerned with molding the physical and social environment; with this the professional can rise to a new relevance. If the theory is rudimentary, it follows that the application will be somewhat primitive, and the case studies which are presented here, in part, for examination are pioneers in the enterprise of ecological planning.

Metropolitan Open Space from Natural Processes

The Urban Renewal Agency and the states of Pennsylvania and New Jersey supported a research project to develop criteria for the selection of metropolitan open space.

Figure 2
Urbanized Area
20% total

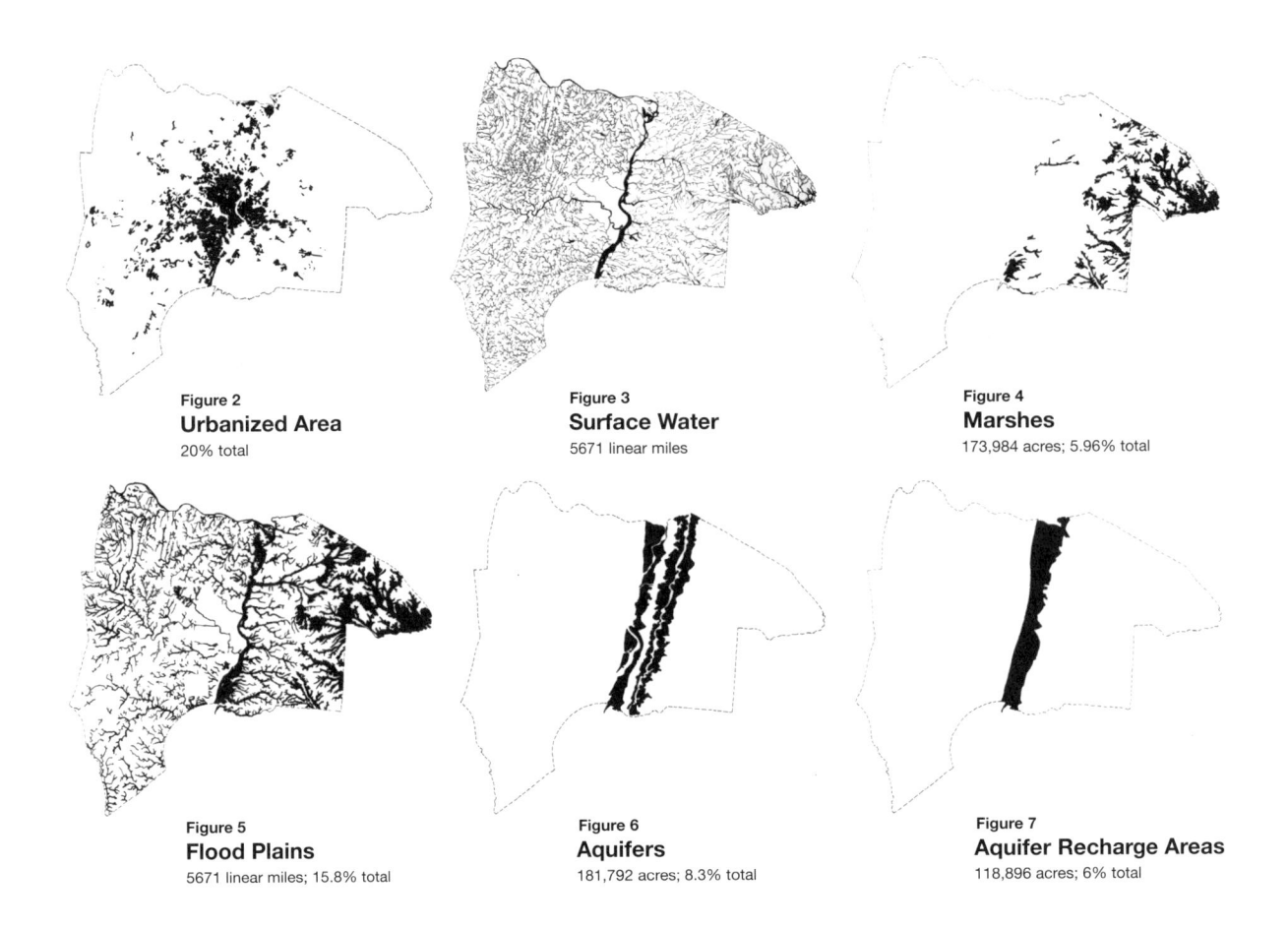

Figure 3
Surface Water
5671 linear miles

Figure 4
Marshes
173,984 acres; 5.96% total

Figure 5
Flood Plains
5671 linear miles; 15.8% total

Figure 6
Aquifers
181,792 acres; 8.3% total

Figure 7
Aquifer Recharge Areas
118,896 acres; 6% total

(Fig. 1) The hypothesis advanced was that such criteria can best be discerned by examining the operation of the major physical and biological processes in the region. When this is understood, and land use policies reflect this understanding, the values and structure of natural process would be ensured and would suggest form, both for metropolitan open space and for urbanization.

Before we employ this method, it is necessary to air two other views. The first is the economist's view of nature as a generally uniform commodity, which is appraised in terms of time-distance, cost of land and development, and allocated in terms of acres per unit population. Nature, of course, is not uniform, but varies as a function of climate, physiography, plants and animals, and thus varies in resources and appropriate land uses. The geometric planner, on the other hand, urges that the urban area be laid out with a green ring or some other form in which 'green' activities—agriculture, institutions, and the like—are preserved or introduced. Such designs, where enforced by law, do ensure the perpetuation of open space and, in the absence of an alternative, they are of some value. But the green is set aside arbitrarily and may not be distributed in the most suitable way.

In the 3,500 square miles of the Philadelphia Standard Metropolitan Statistical Area, only 20% is urbanized today (Fig. 2), 80% open (Fig. 11). Even should the population increase to 6,000,000, 70% of the area would still remain open.

The problem of metropolitan open space lies not in absolute area, but in distribution. The commodity concept of open space for amenity or recreation would suggest an interfusion of open space and population. But the low attributed value of open space ensures that it is transformed into urban use within the urban area and at the perimeter. Normal process of urbanization excludes interfusion and consumes peripheral open space. As a result, unlike other facilities, open space is most abundant

Figure 8
Steep Slopes

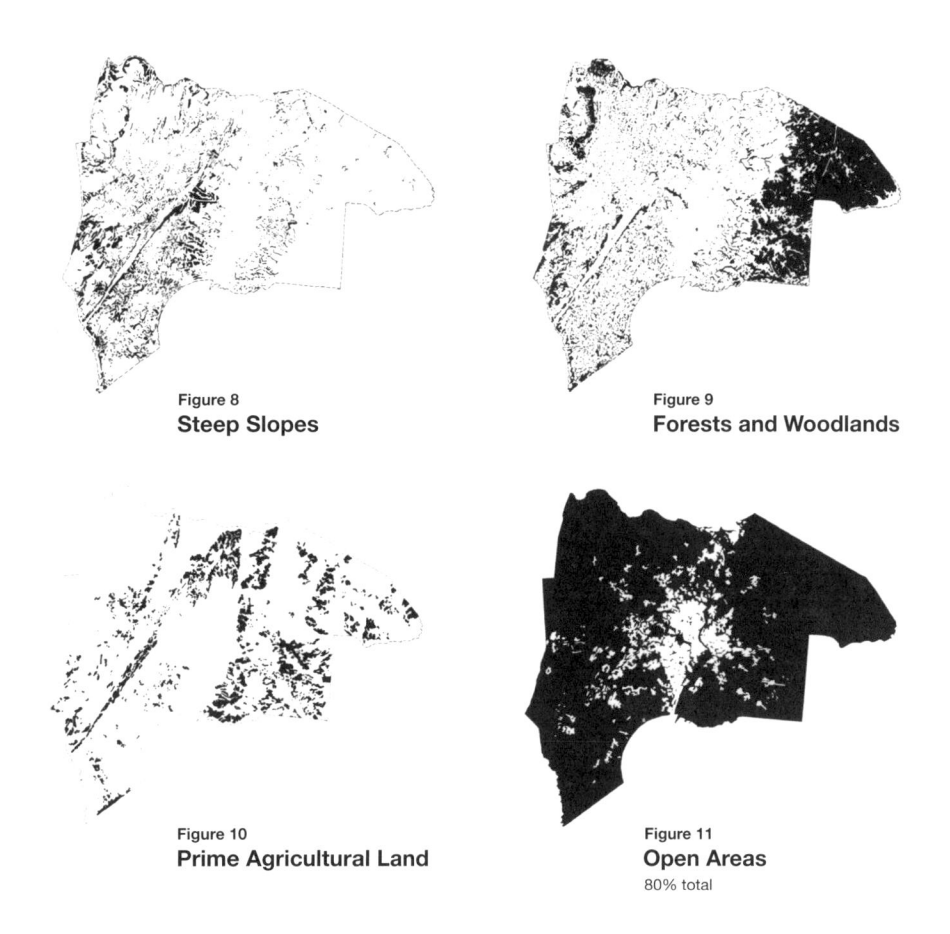

Figure 9
Forests and Woodlands

Figure 10
Prime Agricultural Land

Figure 11
Open Areas
80% total

where population is least concentrated. However, significant open space based on patterns of natural process can still exist within the urban area without greatly expanding the time-distance from the city center to points on the urban fringe.

Optimally, one would have two complementary systems within the metropolitan region: one, the pattern of natural process recognized in certain open space; and the other, the appropriate pattern of urban development. The ecological method would determine a better relationship between them and establish the place of nature in the city.

In this study we initially examined the characteristics of natural processes and attempted to identify intrinsic value, work performed, and protection offered. Large-scale functions were identified with the major physiographic divisions: uplands, coastal plain, and piedmont. Smaller-scale functions along air and water corridors were identified. And finally, eight discrete parameters generalized from basic phenomena were selected for examination. The prohibition and relative permissiveness of each one to certain land uses were then described.

Natural process, unitary in character, must be considered in the planning process. Changes to parts of the system affect the entire system. Natural processes do represent values, and these values should be incorporated into the accounting system of society, relating short-term private profits to long-term public costs sustained when natural processes are spoiled. It is unfortunate that there is inadequate information on cost-benefit ratios of specific interventions. It seems clear, nevertheless, that laws pertaining to development must be elaborated to reflect such a comprehensive accounting system, and to encourage the positive interfusion of natural processes and human developments.[2]

Surface water (Fig. 3) 5671 linear miles. In principle only those land uses inseparable from waterfront locations should occupy them, and only if they do not diminish the present and prospective value of surface water as resource or amenity. Industrial land uses consonant with general principle are harbor facilities, water and sewage treatment plants, and in certain cases, water-using industries. Even satisfying industry's demands, extravagantly predicted as 50 linear miles, 5000 miles remain and could be used for agriculture, forestry, recreation, and institutional and residential open space.

Marshes (Fig. 4) 173,984 acres; 5.96%. Land use policy for marshes should reflect their roles of flood and water storage, wildlife habitat, and fish spawning grounds. Compatible land uses include certain types of agriculture, notably cranberry bogs.

Flood plains (Fig. 5) 339,706 acres; 15.8%. All development should be excluded from the 50-year or 2% probability flood plain save those functions which are either benefited or unharmed by flooding, such as open space, recreation, and water-related uses.

Aquifers (Fig. 6) 181,792 acres; 8.3%. In the region under study, the great deposits of porous materials in the coastal plain are immediately distinguishable from all other aquifers because of their extent and capacity. The aquifer parallel to Philadelphia and New Jersey has an estimated yield of one billion gallons per day. Clearly this not only should be protected, but also could be managed and used as a valuable source of pure water for the city. Agriculture, forestry, recreation, and low-density housing pose no danger to the resource, while industry producing effluents generally does.

Aquifer recharge areas (Fig. 7) 118,896 acres; 6%. The aquifer recharge area consists of critical points of interchange between aquifers and surface waters, often areas of porous soils which replenish the aquifers through percolation. Development in these areas should be restricted so that large areas of impermeable cover and storm-water drainage systems do not interfere with natural interchange. Deep construction and projects of channel widening and dredging should be thoroughly checked, because they can create points of instantaneous recharge which contaminate the pure water resources of the aquifer, especially in the case of polluted rivers.

Steep slopes (Fig. 8) The problems of flood control, erosion, and rapid runoff restrict development on steep slopes. Compatible land uses are forestry, recreation, and low-density housing.

Forests and woodlands (Fig. 9) The natural vegetative cover for most of these areas is forest. Where present, it moderates the microclimate, helps to balance the water regimen, and diminishes erosion, sedimentation, flood, and drought. The forest is a low-maintenance, self-perpetuating landscape which can be employed for timber production, water management, wildlife habitats, airsheds, recreation, low-density housing, or for any combination of these uses.

Prime agricultural land (Fig. 10) 248,816 acres; 11.7%. These soils are uniquely suitable for intensive cultivation with no conservation hazards. Market values of farm lands do not reflect the long-term value or irreplaceable nature of these living soils. Such soils, if lost to non-agricultural uses, can be replaced only by bringing inferior soils into production, requiring capital investment. This would suggest, if agriculture is no longer appropriate, retirement of prime soils into woodlands, institutional open space, recreation, or housing at densities no higher than one unit per 25 acres so that the potential for agriculture is not diminished.

Landscape for Washington, D.C.

The ecological method has been used to counter both the unplanned development of rural areas and the arbitrary patterns of an ever-expanding city. (Fig. 12) But we can proceed with a method to examine the city in an ecological way, including natural evolution as well as cultural evolution. To do this we make a distinction between the 'given' and the 'made' forms. The former is the natural landscape identity; the latter is the present city. By using the ecological method we can discern the reason for the location of the city, comprehend its natural form, discern those elements of identity which are critical and expressive of both physiography and vegetation, and then develop a program for the development and enhancement of that identity. A similar method can be applied to the made form, perceiving the morphology of the city as a sequence of cultural adaptations reflected in the plan of the city, its constituent buildings, and particular

Figure 12
Aerial Photograph of Washington D.C., 1968

places—some of which are successful and endure, others of which do not. Those which have endured enter the inventory of values, and thus are, along with natural process, determinants of new forms of adaptations. This inquiry is an investigation into the given form (the natural landscape identity) and the made form (the created city).

In many cities the given form of the site, with all its ecological implications, has been lost irretrievably—buried by undiscerning building, its rivers confined, streams culverted, hills bulldozed, marshes filled, forests felled, escarpments graded into inconsequence—unknown and unexpressed. Not so in Washington, where the major elements of natural identity persist in various conditions.

Historic Washington is in essence a neoclassical composition set in a half-bowl defined by two confluent rivers and an escarpment with a backdrop of low hills. The entire city is an inclined fan with the symbolic city as a base and with the valleys—Potomac, Glover Archbold, Rock Creek, Goose Creek, and Anacostia—as ribs.

Both physiographic and plant expression are likely to endure and be evident in open space. When one examines the area of Washington in open space—public, institutional, and private—it is apparent that many critical elements of expression remain recognizable to an extent unusual for a major city. Along Rock Creek and the Potomac and Anacostia Rivers is a discontinuous system of open spaces. (Fig. 13) Here the constituent

Rich Ground

Figure 13
A Discontinuous Open Space System

ecological communities vary dramatically—magnolia bogs and wild rice marshes along the Anacostia, the mixed mesophytic association of Rock Creek and the major valleys, the short-leaf pine association on the eastern ridge, the great mixed oak association of the plateau with its variants emphasizing sassafras and tulip poplar. The identity of these areas is not impaired by the formal 18th century plan for the city. With the single exception of the extension of the Mall to the Potomac, there is no reason for these open spaces to derive their form from the formality of the Renaissance plan.

While urban building may obliterate plant expression, certain physiographic elements—hills, escarpments, ridges, palisades, and valleys among them—may still be expressive when built upon. In these areas building can either obliterate the given form or exploit and dramatize it to some degree, being dramatized in turn.

Although physiographic relief is not great in Washington, varying some 400 feet, the configurations are consequential. It reveals in its surface the great spectrum of geologic time from Pre-Cambrian to the present. It contains two major geological divisions, piedmont and coastal plain. It is dramatically transected by the fall line, visible in the falls of the Potomac. In addition to these epochal divisions, there are major physiographic variations—the Potomac, Anacostia, and Rock Creek with its dissected valleys and ridges, the two clearly defined terraces of the coastal plain with their bordering escarpments (the "Flats" of L'Enfant's Washington), the encompassing hills including Mount Hamilton, Hickey Hill, and Fort Totten. (Fig. 14)

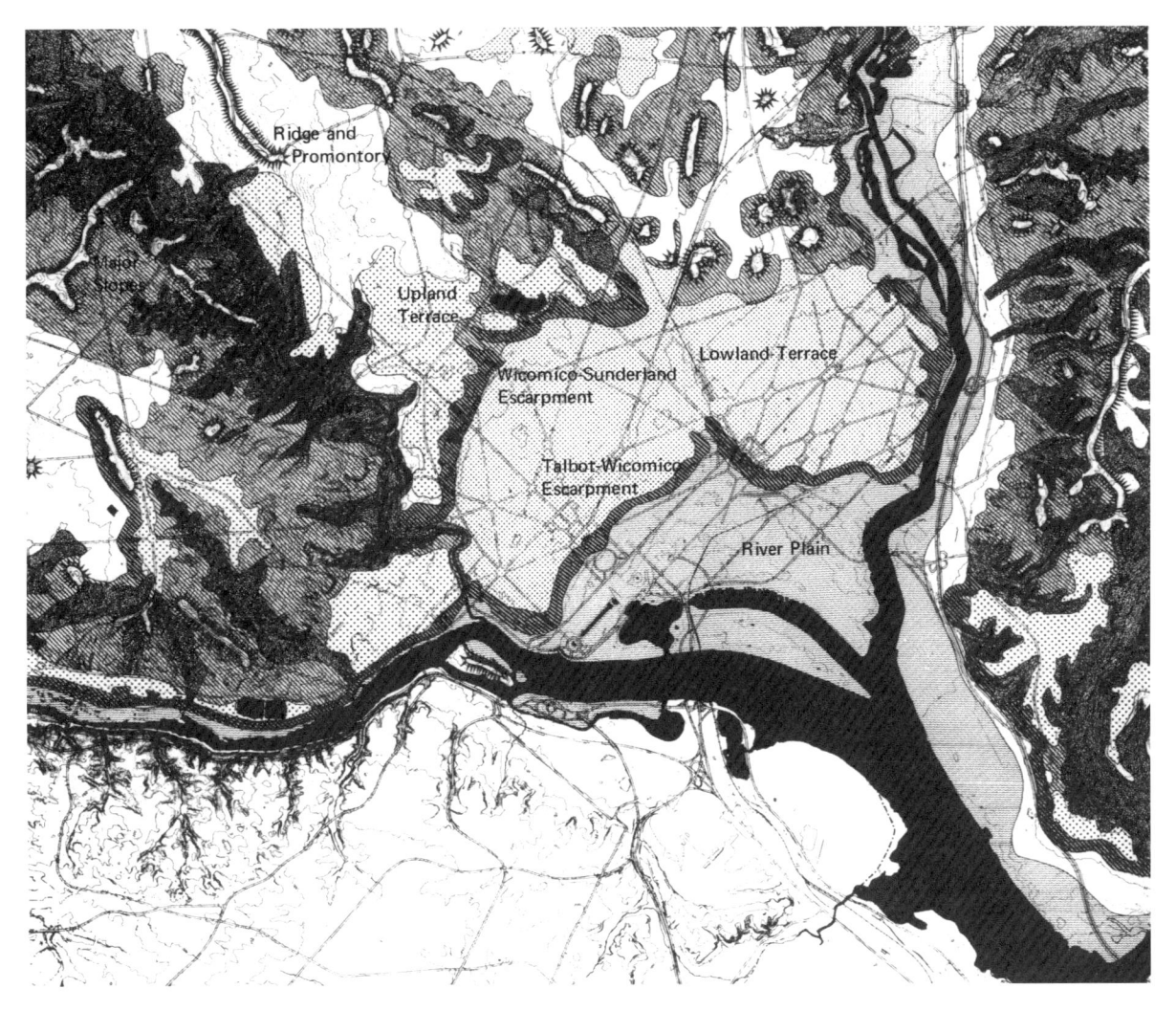

Figure 14
Physiographic Variation
Ridges and valleys, terraces and escarpments.

If a city had to be created on the Potomac in the 18th century, then Washington was the prime location, situated just below the fall line, at the end of the navigable part of the river. Given the location, the site of the city became the next consideration. Had L'Enfant been an Italian, he would have selected an 'ideal' site, on the hills above the Potomac, facing southeast. But he was a Frenchman, oriented to flat sites. Vaux le Vicomte and Versailles were his models and thus he chose the flat flood plains of the Potomac. Here, in an amphitheater, the city would extend its avenues to embrace the surrounding countryside, as was demonstrated at Versailles. The grand axis leading out from the Capitol becomes the basis of the entire composition. Thus, Washington's location, site, and made form are entirely comprehensible in terms of 17th century French Renaissance garden art and planning.

In 1791, George Washington sent L'Enfant and Ellicott to survey the area. Though L'Enfant had not yet been commissioned to design the city, he is presumed to have applied his talent in visualizing a plan which was later revealed when the survey and analysis of the site were presented. As reported by William Loughton Smith on April 22, 1791, "Major L'Enfant has noted all the eminences, plains, commanding spots, projects of canals by means of Rock Creek, Eastern Branch, and a fine creek called Goose Creek..." While presenting the site analysis, he had said that "Nature has done much for it, and with the aid of art it will become the wonder of the world." He described the most prominent position of the Talbot-Wicomico escarpment as a "pedestal waiting for a superstructure" and reserved this for the Capitol. The other prominent location on the same escarpment he

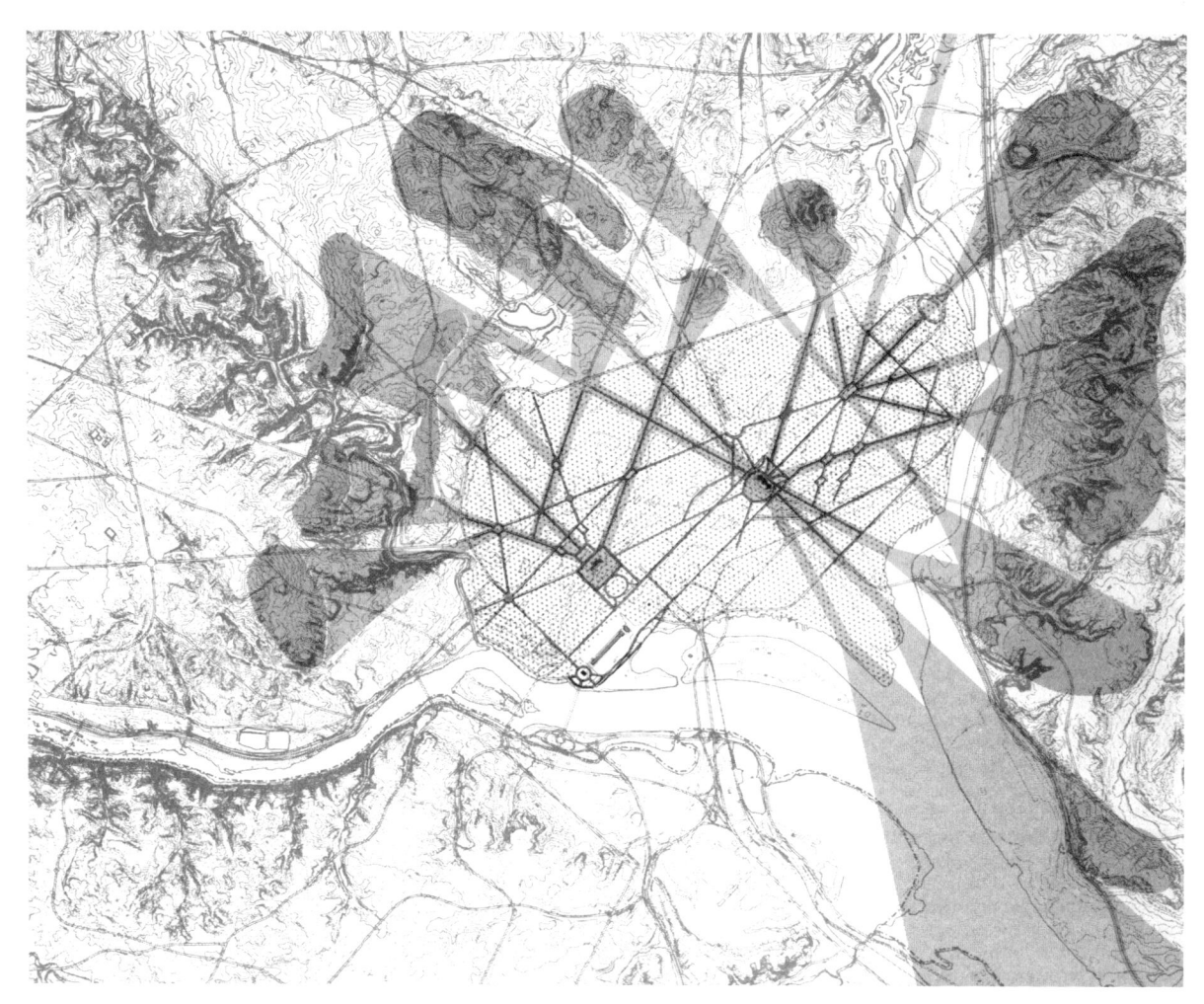

Figure 15
L'Enfant's Plan

chose for the White House. Trained in a formal tradition, he had an overriding concern for axial treatment of building masses and open spaces, and a delight in sweeping diagonal avenues. But this he coupled with his perceptiveness in reading the subtleties of land form. In his statement to the President, he recommended the avenues not only to contrast with general regularity and to make the real distance less from place to place by giving them reciprocity of sight, but also to "afford a greater variety of seats with pleasant prospects which will be obtained from the advantageous ground over which these avenues are chiefly directed." (Fig. 15)

The Flats are of particular importance as the site of the formal city. The Mall occupies the course of Tiber Creek, the Talbot Wicomico escarpments support both the Capitol and the White House, and Pennsylvania Avenue parallels it at a lower level. The limits of the formal plan coincide exactly with the Wicomico-Sunderland escarpment. Within this, L'Enfant united the Potomac with the Mall, and created a cross-axis connecting the latter with the White House; from these major features radiated diagonal avenues into the backdrop of hills.

At least in the L'Enfant City there is a basic consonance between the given form and the made form. The realization of the made form does not require the obliteration of the natural identity. Indeed, both may be complementary. A natural Potomac, Anacostia, Rock Creek, wooded hills, and ridges, encompassing the L'Enfant City, would provide the best and most dramatic contrast between calculated artifice and nature.

Washington is a neoclassical, Renaissance city form, heroic in scale, rhetorical in statement. Capitol, Mall, White House, Washington Monument, Jefferson Memorial,

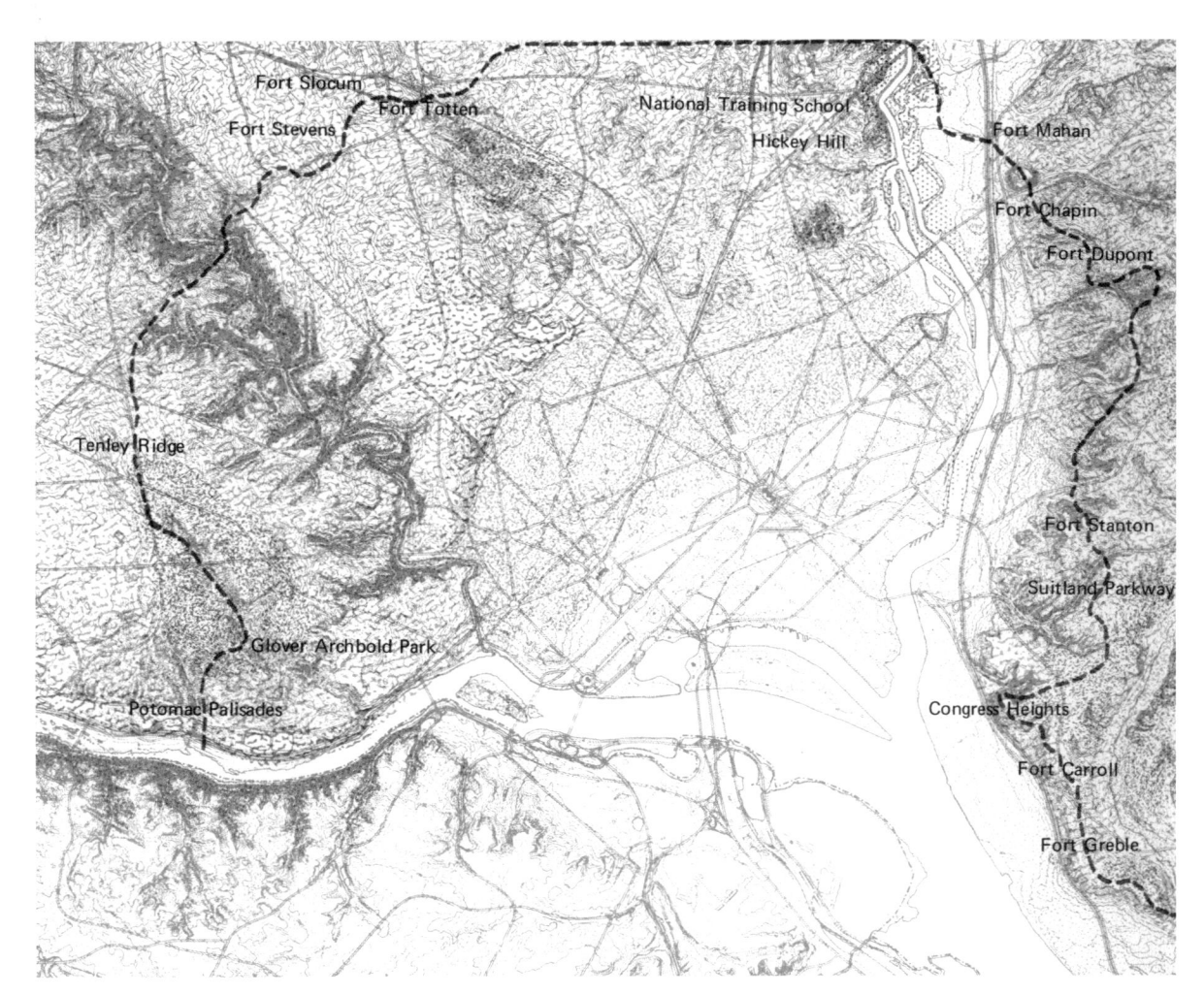

Figure 16
Proposed Parkway Route

great avenues, squares, parks, monuments, and above all tree-lined streets—these are the most conspicuous components of the made form of Washington, one of the most consistent and identifiable forms created since the 18th century. They, as well as the components of the given form, enter an inventory of values and must be considered determinants for future action, as opportunities and restraints. One might not have selected the image of Louis XIV and Le Nôtre as the most propitious expression for the capital of American democracy; but such was chosen, and remains to be managed.

The city of Washington, even outside the formal city, has now been extensively urbanized. Although, as a consequence, the pre-existing conditions have been radically altered, this cannot be cited as an argument for abandoning ecology as the indicator of fitness. On the contrary, perceiving transformations of the environment ecologically leads to appropriate adaptations in the present, artificial conditions.

While the Renaissance concept of man-nature insisted that the phenomenal world subscribe to an apparent and superficial order, the laws of physical and biological processes were not suspended in Versailles and Washington. Plants in these areas were and are responsive to conditions of sunlight, rain, ground water, soil, micro-organisms, and nutrients; they live, seed, and die. Consequently, ecological principles obtain in formal compositions as well as in the field. If plants are not accorded the appropriate conditions, or more importantly, if plants are not selected on a basis of existing conditions, they will die and fail. When a monoculture exists, be it a field of wheat or a boulevard of similar tree species, they are inordinately subject to epidemic disease. The conditions of soil aeration, compaction, temperature, and water which may be tolerable to a young tree may become increasingly intolerable to the aging specimen. In addition, species should not be associated in numbers radically different from their distribution in natural habitats. Plants live not as individuals, but as communities; even in formal compositions they should be associated as such.

Ecology would, then, provide the single indispensable basis for design in an area, formal or not. A method including the ecological inventory, if realized, would provide the basic palette. It reveals the natural landscape identity of the place, the given form, the components of this identity, and their dynamics. It would also suggest criteria with which to test existing conditions and the relative 'survival' of past made forms in the sequence of cultural adaptations that continues through the present.

Once the identity of any place has been perceived, the means by which it can be experienced and expressed become important. The freeway or parkway common in our culture is one device that could be used. Its alignment could be set to express features of the topography and the associated ecological communities. (Fig. 16) In certain areas the geology might be revealed in road cuts and other construction. An example taken to illustrate these opportunities is Fort Drive, connecting the series of historic fort sites surrounding the city. The drive commences at Fort Greble, which is situated at the southern end of the Anacostia ridge, and follows the top of the escarpment facing the Potomac River to Congress Heights. This affords a constant panorama of the city, the Potomac, the Flats, and the surrounding hills. At Fort Carroll, situated on this escarpment, one experiences the axial effect of the L'Enfant plan, with a clear view of the Capitol at the end of the vista, demonstrating how unique aspects of the formal city and certain natural features are integrally bound.

Where the drive follows the escarpment, a variety of oaks, mixed with tulip trees, form the vegetation experience. However, on leaving the escarpment, following the flat top of the ridge, one sees slight changes in the vegetation, revealing a predominance of pines with the presence of some scrub oak. As the drive crosses the Suitland Parkway, located in a stream valley, a change in vegetation is apparent: beech and white ash amid a rich undergrowth and herbaceous layer. As Fort Stanton is approached, the topography, and consequently the vegetation, change. The slopes become steep, reflecting the heavy dissection in that area. Due to an increase in moisture and improved drainage, tulip trees reappear. In small, protected pockets with high moisture and rich soil, beech, ash, and sour gum grow. From Forts Chapin and Dupont there are exceptional views of the city.

The section from Fort Mahan to the National Training School for Boys strongly contrasts with the previous section of the drive. From a very undulating land form, the topography changes abruptly as the open Anacostia River flats are crossed. The flood plain vegetation consists of river birch, cottonwood, and alders, along with marshes and wild rice. Across the river, the terrain becomes hilly again.

The drive continues past Fort Stevens and crosses the fall line. The geology and topography change dramatically, revealing ravinelike valleys and igneous outcroppings in contrast to the flat valley of the Anacostia. Accordingly, the vegetation varies from the rich mesophytic association on the valley floor to an oak and pine association on Tenley Ridge, and elsewhere a mixed oak-tulip poplar association.

The final event of the drive occurs at the Potomac Palisades, a principal feature of physiography and natural identity of Washington. This particular feature contrasts with both the Anacostia River and Rock Creek and presents a visible definition of the fall line, the division between the piedmont and the coastal plain. A notable change in the vegetation occurs. The sassafras becomes the dominant species, and the rich collection of the flood plain association of river birch, white elm, and cottonwood reappears on a scale not previously experienced on the drive.

The significant components of identity, the genius loci, both natural and man-made, are revealed and in turn suggest policies for preservation, enhancement, and development—the essential components of a comprehensive plan. It seems advantageous to extend the boundaries of the study to include the whole national capital region. Yet the fact that the boundaries of the District have no physiographic or ecological importance should not serve as a reason to arrest action now. The possibilities for action within the national capital present a great and immediate challenge. The prospective fruits of this method of planning justify an early and energetic program.[3]

Clearly the task is not one of providing a decorative background for the human play, or even ameliorating the grim city; it is the necessity of sustaining nature as source of life, whole milieu, teacher, sanctum, and challenge. But today nature is often seen to be merely sites for our momentous acts of transformation, which proceed without perception of natural process—blind to its operation, its values, and its array of inherent opportunities, scarcely modified by appeals for conservation or further study.

Those who are engaged in changing the land—especially professional planners, landscape architects, architects, and engineers among many others—have a critical role to play. In that circumstance where they are comfortable with the prevailing views of society, they may be willing and effective servants, giving form to its values and processes. When, however, these values are so alien to the creative instincts of these professionals that they are unable to fill creative roles, today, they must enter the arena of values, seeking to change them to better correspond to their idea of the creative fit.

The natural scientists have been pointing out the interdependence which characterizes all relationships, organic and inorganic, in nature. Ecologists stress that an ecological community survives as a result of the interdependent activity of all the species within it. This single lesson of interdependence common to all nature—common to systems—is in my own view the final refutation of man's assumptions of independence and exploitation.

Man understanding this will have learned that when he degrades nature in the countryside at large, or within the enlarging cities, he degrades himself, as a natural being; that when he creates, he adds to his life. He may be able to participate in the environment in a way appropriate for survival, and emerge as a fit agent in evolution.

Notes
This essay is an excerpt from Ian McHarg, "Ecology, for the Evolution of Planning and Design," *VIA* 1 (1968): pp. 44-66.

Endnotes
[1] Aldo Leopold, *A Sand County Almanac* (Oxford: Oxford University Press, 1949); pp. 202-203.
[2] "Metropolitan Open Space From Natural Processes" is a research project directed by Dr. David A. Wallace. Mr. McHarg is principal investigator, studying natural processes as determinants for open space selection and proposing ways to incorporate this method in the planning process. Further investigations are being made by Nohad A. Toulan on land values, by Ann Louise Strong on existing and potential acquisition and control devices, by William G. Grigsby on market demand for recreation. by Anthony R. Tomazinis on the relationships of transportation to recreation, and by William H. Roberts on design implications. This study is to be published in 1968, and was made possible by funds received through the Urban Renewal Administration, the Housing and Home Financing Agency (under the provision of Section 314 of the Housing Act of 1954), and the States of Pennsylvania and New Jersey. In the spring of 1968 further implications of the study were taken up in a comprehensive regional planning studio at the University of Pennsylvania.
[3] "Toward a Comprehensive Landscape Plan for Washington, D.C.," a report prepared for the National Capital Planning Commission by Wallace, McHarg, Roberts and Todd, under the direction of the author and with the assistance of Narendra Juneja and Lindsay Robertson (United States Government Printing Office, 1967).

A New Systemic Nature
For Mussolini's Landscape Urbanism
Alan Berger and Case Brown

The Pontine Plain of the Italian Latina Province, historically home to the notorious Pontine Marshes, has reached a critical environmental tipping point. Natural systems are so stressed that a total landscape system collapse—including devastation of the agricultural economy—may be less than a decade away, depending on variables such as climate change, precipitation patterns, and sea-level rise. These conditions exemplify a much larger problem, a global scale crisis involving all low-lying agricultural zones with the same inputs and outputs as Latina.

Working closely with the Province's planning and environmental agencies, the Project for Reclamation Excellence (P-REX) at MIT, conducted research and design testing that led to a Protocol Agreement signed between the Province of Latina and P-REX. The protocol sets terms for P-REX and Latina to collaborate on planning and design for a new constructed wetland park within Mussolini's Pontine Marshes.

Murky Past

Benito Mussolini was a fascist and landscape urbanist. From 1928 to 1934, the Italian leader designed, approved, and built five cities in a malaria-ridden territory known as the Pontine Marshes. Through top-down government control and an iron regulatory grip, Mussolini summoned his military advisors to relocate some 80,000 citizens of the northern Italian provinces to a mostly uninhabited, marshy area located 40 miles south of Rome. The Pontine Marshes sits within the Pontine Plain, measuring 378 square miles. Today the Pontine Marshes and Plain remains Rome's

Pontine Marshes
The Pontine Marshes naturally formed thousands of years ago in a depression along the base of the limestone rich Lepini Mountains. Today, agriculture, canal drainage, and irrigation fill in the area known as the Pontine Plain.

Latina
City of Latina, the largest in the Province at 120,000 inhabitants. Of the 378 square miles studied in this project, only 11% of surface area is considered urban, with 8 cities or towns having any notable density.

major food producing region, with a huge agricultural economy, including vegetables, flowers, fruits, and wine. First settled by Etruscans some 2,500 years ago, the Pontine Plain has a well-documented history. Attempts to drain the marshes began as early as 312 B.C., when the Via Appia was constructed through them linking Rome to Terracina as a strategic military and goods port. The Via Appia needed to stay dry and accessible, and by the early twentieth century there had been twenty-three attempts to drain the low-lying "lagoon" marsh areas whose wide open plains also offered a valuable resource to the capital Rome. All of these attempts failed to reclaim the area.

Soon after coming to power, Mussolini strove to do what his predecessors couldn't—to engineer and drain the entire malarial marshes and thus win prestige for his regime. In December 1928, the Italian government approved a blueprint for the area's reclamation, handing responsibility to the Consorzio della Bonifica di Agro Pontino. Within a few short years the marsh morphed into a complex network of canals and drainage ditches. From 1928 to 1935, eighty thousand people were brought in, mostly from the north of Italy, to drain 600 square miles of the Agro Pontino. They suffered greatly under miserable working and living conditions, many contracting malaria themselves. By 1934, the water engineering was done and the Agro Pontino's settlement was under way. The new land was divided into 5,000 plots by the Opera Nazionale Combattenti— the military veterans who Mussolini placed in charge of land management. It was a systemic, holistic approach

Bonifiche Agro Pontino, 1928
By 1934, The new land was divided into 5,000 plots. It was a systemic, holistic approach to landscape design, planning, development, and environmental engineering, or what was termed the "Bonifica Integrale," or integrated reclamation, for a new ruralism based on fascist ideals

Rich Ground

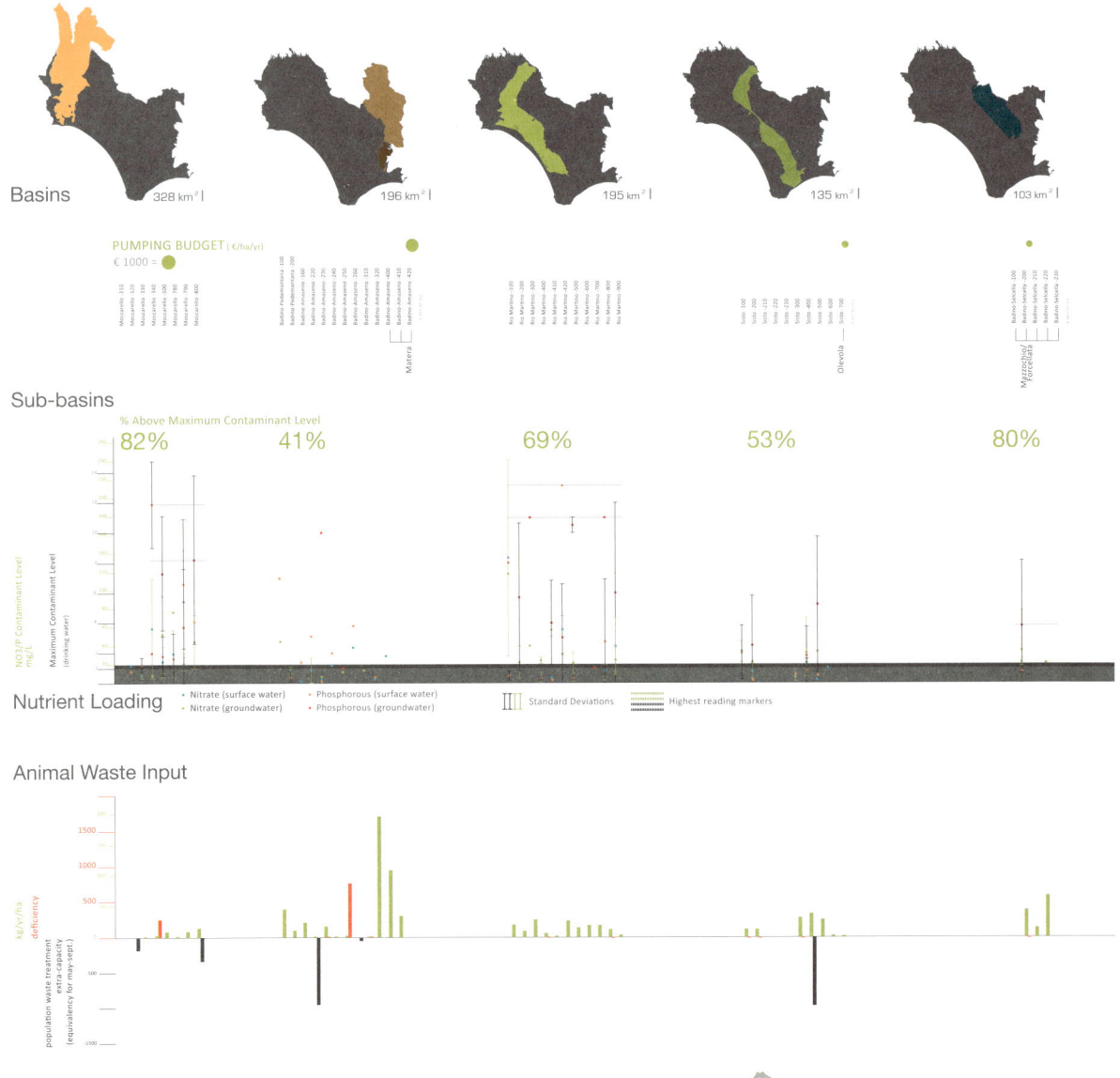

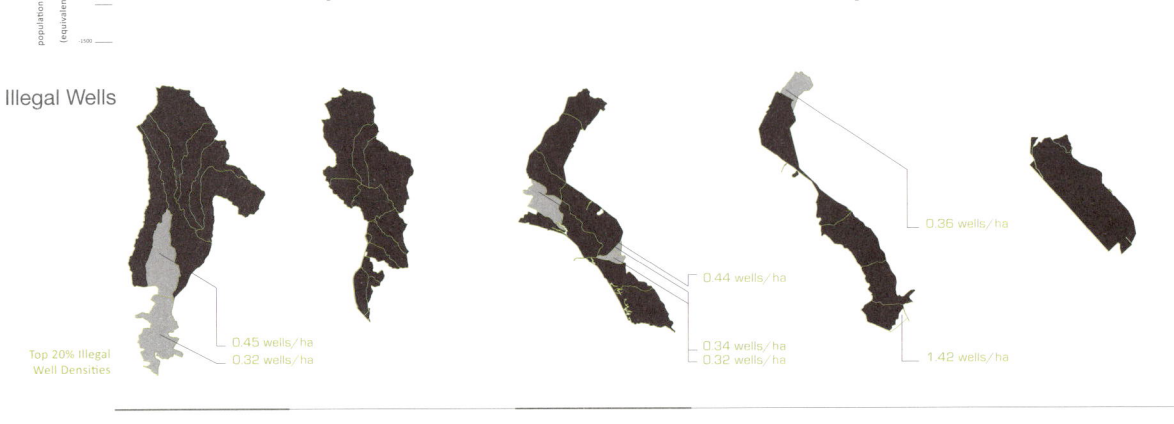

Basins

328 km² | 196 km² | 195 km² | 135 km² | 103 km²

PUMPING BUDGET (€/ha/yr)
€ 1000 =

Sub-basins

% Above Maximum Contaminant Level

82% **41%** **69%** **53%** **80%**

NO3/P Contaminant Level mg/l
Maximum Contaminant Level (drinking water)

Nutrient Loading

- Nitrate (surface water)
- Nitrate (groundwater)
- Phosphorous (surface water)
- Phosphorous (groundwater)
- Standard Deviations
- Highest reading markers

Animal Waste Input

kg/y/ha deficiency
population waste treatment extra-capacity (equivalency for may-sept.)

Illegal Wells

0.45 wells/ha
0.32 wells/ha

0.44 wells/ha
0.34 wells/ha
0.32 wells/ha

0.36 wells/ha
1.42 wells/ha

Top 20% Illegal Well Densities

Pollution Matrix

The mapping by P-REX recombines all of the Province's data for more than 119 hydrological sub-basins. These are nutrient loading readings taken in the groundwater and surface test-water wells in the sub-basins. The percentages (in yellow) are cumulative readings of nutrient loading above safe water levels. Safe level is the grey/green areas at the bottom of the graph's x-axis. For example, for phosphorus the maximum contaminant level for drinking water is 1mg/l, and for nitrates is 20mg/l based on the U.S. Environmental Protection Agency's standards, which are internationally recognized.

Greater than 20mg/l leads to an anaerobic aquatic zone deficient of the oxygen to support fish or plant life. Causes of high nitrate levels in water include shallow wells contaminated with surface water, water containing animal wastes, and surface runoff from heavy rain after fertilization with ammonium nitrate, an industrial chemical fertilizer used ubiquitously in farming.

A New Systemic Nature Alan Berger and Case Brown

50% 67% 50% 77% 75%

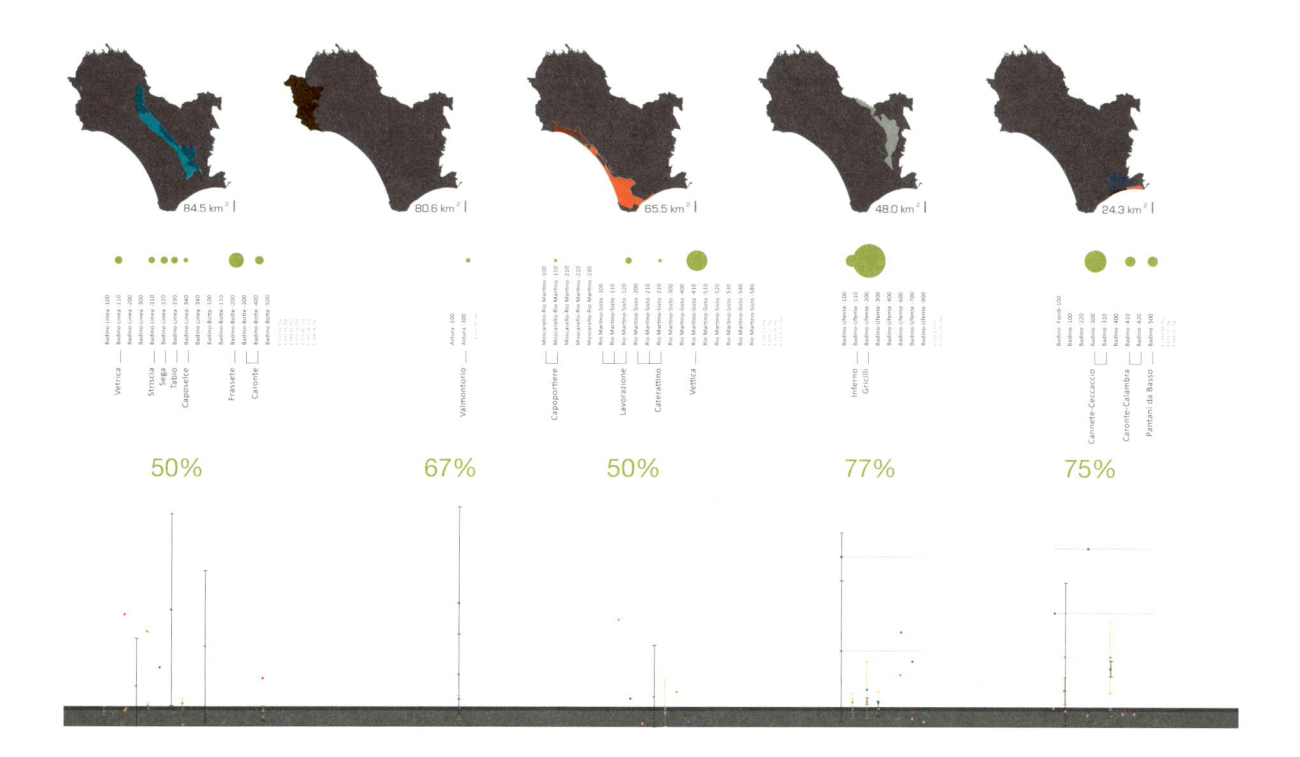

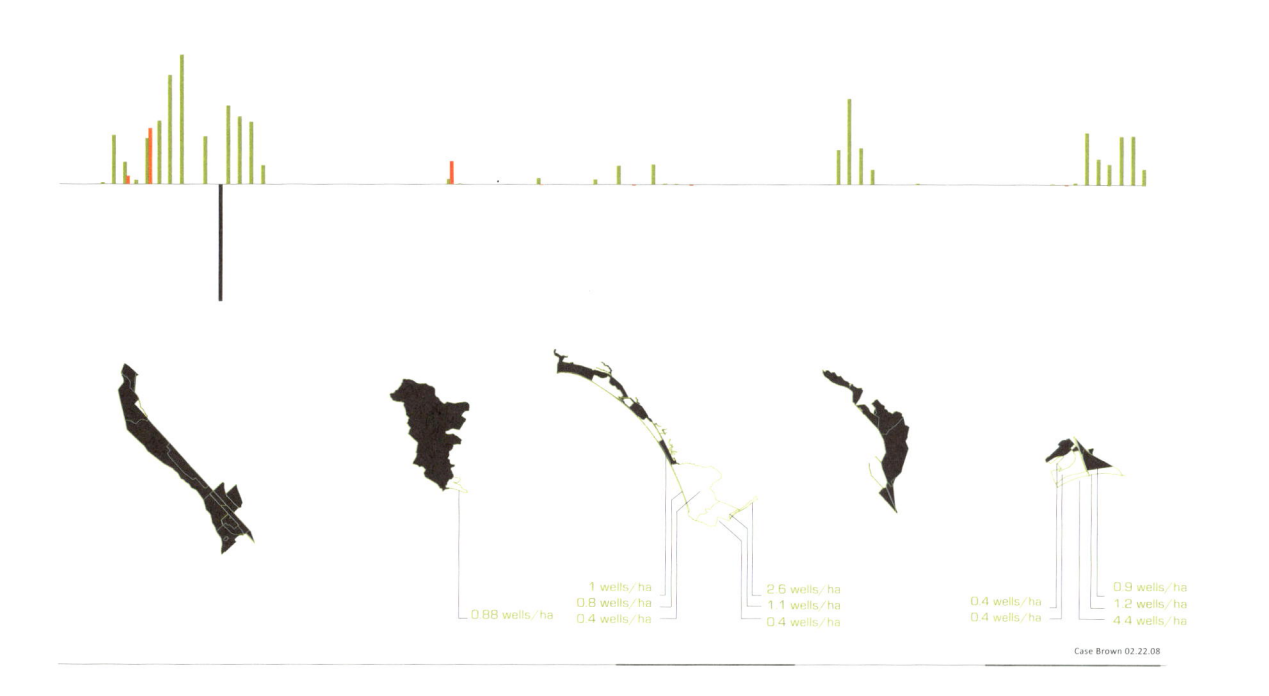

Rich Ground

to landscape design, planning, development, and environmental engineering, or what was termed the "Bonifica Integrale"—integrated reclamation—for a new ruralism based on fascist ideals.

Mechanized Marshes

Today the total population of the Latina Province is around 450,000 with the largest city being Latina (previously Littoria). In the Pontine Plain there are 2.7 times more man-made drainages than natural ones, with all major drainages being artificial/engineered. As the rivers come out of the mountains they are channelized, controlled, and output to the Mediterranean Sea. The elaborate system to drain the low areas, and keep rivers from naturally meandering and forming marshes, is managed by the Consorzio della Agro Pontino. Their mandate is to get the water out of the Pontine Plain and into the sea as quickly as possible, while supplying farmers with irrigation water through the canal network. If the pumps were to be shut off, severe flooding would occur in the plain within twenty-four hours, a tactic already utilized by the Germans to slow the allied landing advance here during World War II.

All of this drainage engineering has made way for a vast agricultural machine. The Consorzio has an annual budget of about seven million euros to pump and maintain over 200 pumping structures and the vast canal network. They remain the governing body of all canal water in the province and are controlled by a board of directors consisting of many large-scale farmers. Today, over eighty percent of the province's surface area is arable land cover that is drained by the Consorzio's network of rivers, canals, and pumps. Engineered systems are so ubiquitous here that less than five percent of the territory is not farmed or urbanized, excluding national parks.

To manage the water flow and removal, the hydrological system is segmented into over 100 water-draining micro-basins, which collect into ten macro-basins. Mapping the Province's own pollution data, P-REX found that only one of the ten macro-basins has relatively clean drinking water from surface or groundwater sources.

Water and soil contamination in the region has been attributed to many factors over the decades including poor land use policy and regulation, and relatively few environmental standards for development compared to other European Union countries. Human assaults on the marshland have included DDT and diesel coating of standing water for malarial eradication by the allied troops during World War II, and severe

Porto Bandino
Nutrient plume of untreated agricultural fertilizer and sediment dumping directly into the Tyrannian Sea at Porto Bandino.

Mazzochio Pumphouse
The famous Mazzochio Pumphouse with six pumps put in place in 1934 by Mussolini. There are over 1,615 miles of canals in the plain, 1,336 miles of man-made canals and 500 miles of natural drainages in territory. Each day they drain up to 9,500 gallons per second from the Pontine Plain.

Public Riparian Corridor

Throughout Latina, the roads are clogged with truck and car traffic making it difficult and dangerous for bicycles and pedestrians to circulate between villages and cities. The remaining fragmented riparian corridors and associated vegetation could provide the only opportunity for a new public connective circulation infrastructure. The reclamation site is a treatment/filtration system. With trails, diverse habitats, sporting fields, and undulating topography, the site could generate a new recreation-based economy for the Province. Vast new habitat could be managed by a new division of the water consortium to assist filtering of water, nesting of aquatic and terrestrial life, and storing of genetic heritage from the Mediterranean costal environs. All of this could be achieved while maintaining the basic integrity of the historic landscape interior.

WETLAND MACHINE SITE LOCATION
- Drainage Area
- Site

PONTINE MARSHES

- Drainage Basin – Canale Acque
- Urbanized
- Parks / Riparian
- Drainages
- Filtration Landscape

The Wetland Machine
The Wetland Machine systemic regional strategy.

Rich Ground

under-capacity of sewage treatment for the urbanized areas in the plain. Nutrient loading of nitrogen and phosphorus through agricultural fertilizers, however, is the largest contemporary environmental problem. These compounds are used in abundance to grow myriad vegetables and kiwi fruit. Italy is the world's largest producer and exporter of kiwi, accounting for thirty-five percent of the global market. Lazio, the jurisdictional region where Latina is located, contains the highest concentration of Italy's kiwi production farms.

A New Systemic Nature

Based on the combined regional analyses and local fieldwork, P-REX is testing design strategies developed to simultaneously maximize new public realms, remediate the environmental impacts of the large-scale agricultural economy, limit urbanization and groundwater extraction near the sea's edge, and create much needed recreational open-space for the citizens of the region. These strategies focus on reclamation over restoration. Given the historically synthetic, engineered nature of the Province's landscape systems, it was deemed unfeasible to go back in time to recover a version of landscape that no longer could exist without massively expensive inputs and maintenance regimes.

1: The Wetland Machine

The first design imperative is to artificially re-introduce ecological functions normally performed by wetlands, (which were all drained in the 1920s) by creating a gigantic new "wetland machine" for filtering, habitat, and biological exchange. This operates at two scales: regional and local. The regional strategy stems from P-REX's research on environmental toxicity. The greatest amount of pollution in the agricultural-filled plain is flowing down the Acque Alte macro-basin, past the largest city of Latina, from distributed non-point sources. Locating a design intervention near this basin's outlet to the Sea will intercept the most pollution. Furthermore, the coastal areas suffer from saltwater intrusion, so a water storing/cleaning intervention near the coast maximizes the buffering effect of groundwater recharge. The site best suited for these functions is at the edge of the ancient dune system, where the soil is relatively unproductive, and farming is of less value.

From a planning perspective, choosing a large, single consolidated wetland site offers a more viable local, site-scale strategy within the Province's complex patchwork of land ownership. Given the Province's governance and each city's independent land control mechanisms, smaller

The Wetland Machine
The Wetland Machine will feature large open vegetative landscapes with edge habitat and programmed use diversity that the region currently lacks.

Hydrological Flows

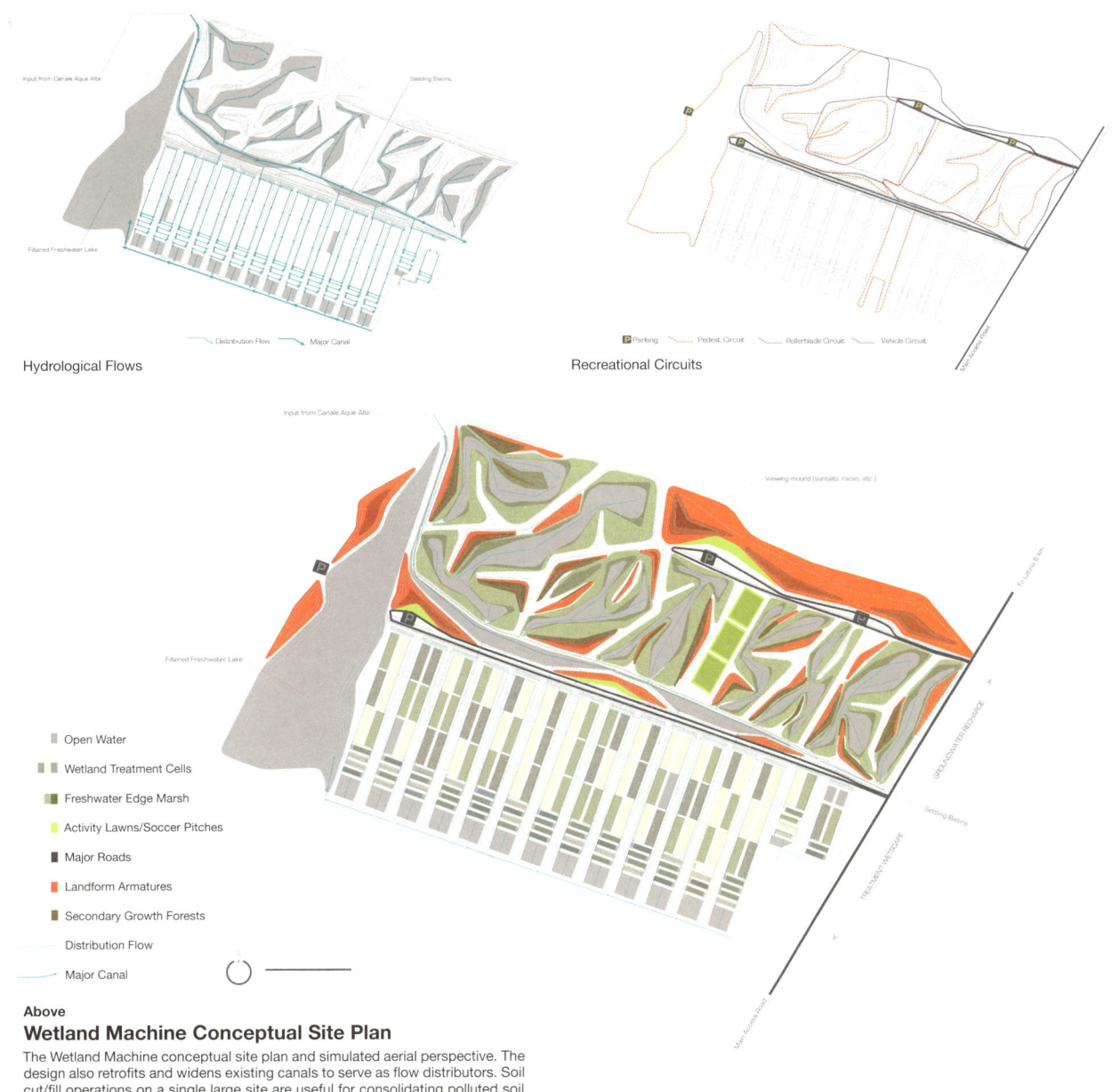

Recreational Circuits

- Open Water
- Wetland Treatment Cells
- Freshwater Edge Marsh
- Activity Lawns/Soccer Pitches
- Major Roads
- Landform Armatures
- Secondary Growth Forests
- Distribution Flow
- Major Canal

Above
Wetland Machine Conceptual Site Plan
The Wetland Machine conceptual site plan and simulated aerial perspective. The design also retrofits and widens existing canals to serve as flow distributors. Soil cut/fill operations on a single large site are useful for consolidating polluted soil, and terraforming depressions to hold/treat water and cleansed areas for new public space and program.

Below
Simulated Aerial Perspective
The Wetland Machine simulated ground perspective.

Rich Ground

distributed treatment areas are both enormously complex to purchase and likely ineffective for treating the amount of water flowing through the canal network. The *Wetland Machine's* dimensions are directly related to the amount of wetland area needed to treat the amount of water in the Canale Acque Alte—the major collector for this highly polluted zone. At 0.8 square miles, the new wetland machine is a tiny intervention relative to the entire plain. But given its strategic location and systemic intelligence, vast improvements to the regional landscape are possible.

At only 3.7 miles from Latina, the site will host programs and environments almost completely lacking in the region: large open landscapes with complex vegetative assemblages. It will open extensive edge habitat diversity and programmed use diversity, including shallow shoals for juvenile fish and swimming, and starker edges for fishing and water storage.

2: The Dune Machine

In addition to agriculture, tourism is a big economic generator in this region, especially near the beaches and sea. The Province has data showing massive increases of waste, water pollution, and traffic during peak summer months. After analyzing a twelve month cycle of Latina's permanent versus temporary population trends, and their respective waste flows, P-REX proposed an alternative tourism for the area: a lower impact version to standard Mediterranean Sea edge development with direct vehicular access to the sea/land interface.

A shallow dune environment currently exists along the entire coastline, sliced on top by a road—the worst possible place to prevent dune erosion. The road serves vacation houses built into the dune's southern end. The northern end of the dune, however, is not densely developed and would naturally widen if the road was decommissioned. Allowing the northern dune to grow in certain places would redirect annual costs away from dune removal from roadways and towards dune maintenance instead. Moreover, establishing the conditions for an enlarged and renewed northern dune to grow would help protect the city of Latina from rising sea levels, while allowing the backsides of the dunes to be activated for a low-impact recreational and tourist economy.

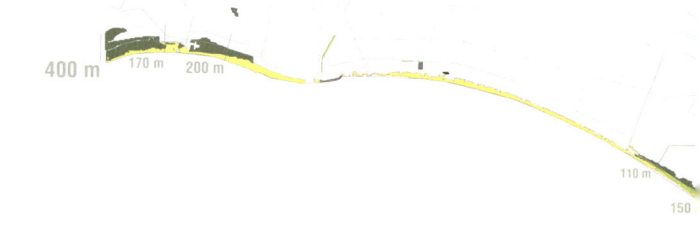

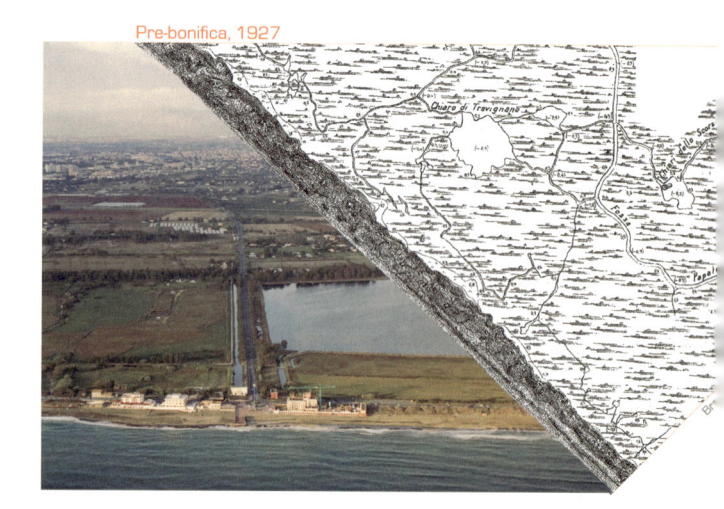

The Dune Machine
The southern portion of the dune encroached with roads and housing along the near the city of Sabaudia. Circeo National Park is the hill in the background.

To generate a viable dune ecology, zonation—the subdivision of biomes into unique habitats—is critical to achieve a full vegetative assemblage across gradients: salt to fresh water, windy zones to calm, and so forth. The site subsequently chosen for the dune machine lies along the thinnest sections of the dune, where the existing road has greatest relative impact. The dune would ideally grow north to Anzio and qualify for national park status and Eurpoean Union regulatory protection and funding.

A New Systemic Nature Alan Berger and Case Brown

PONTINE PLAIN

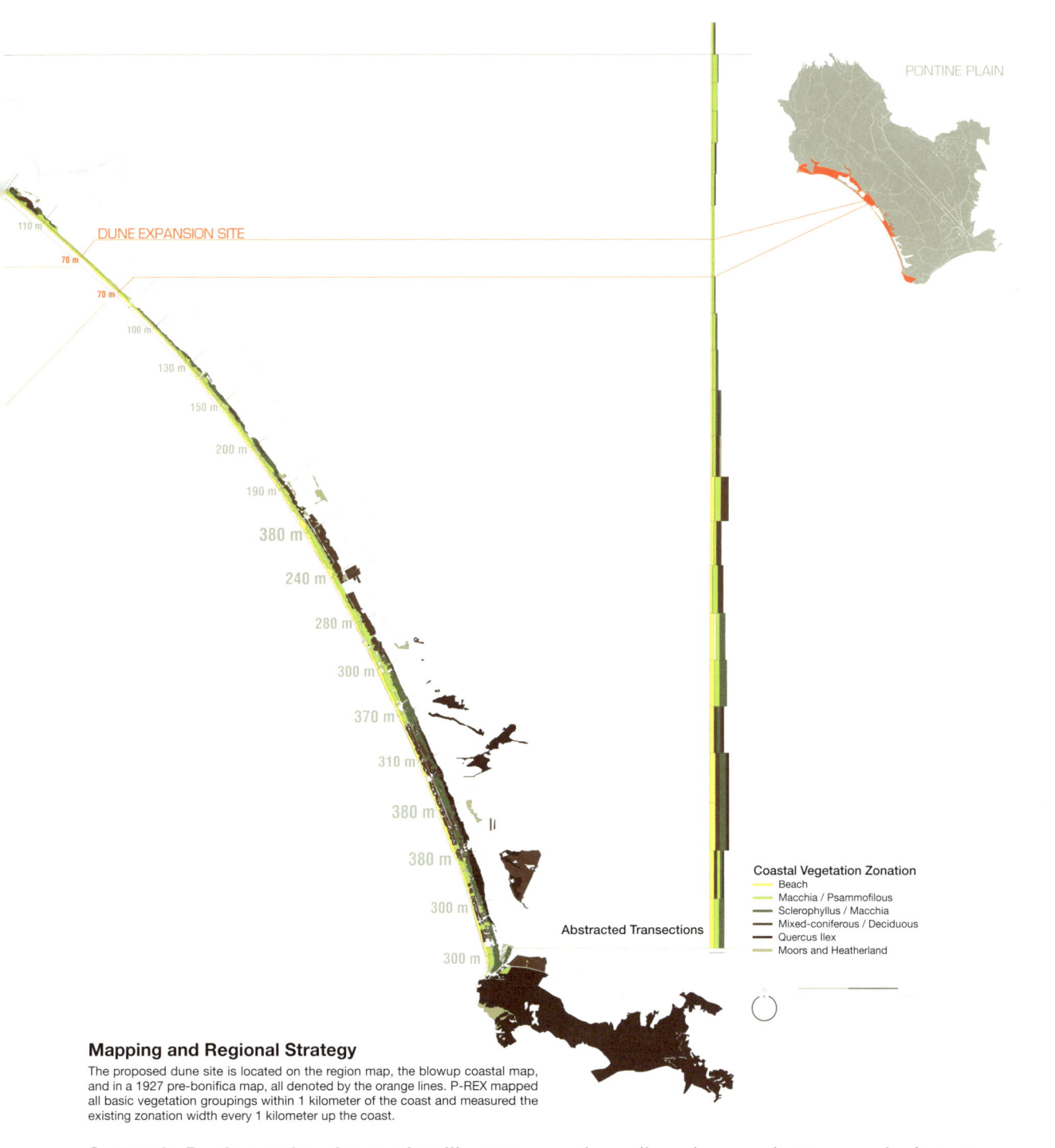

DUNE EXPANSION SITE

Coastal Vegetation Zonation
- Beach
- Macchia / Psammofilous
- Sclerophyllus / Macchia
- Mixed-coniferous / Deciduous
- Quercus Ilex
- Moors and Heatherland

Abstracted Transections

Mapping and Regional Strategy
The proposed dune site is located on the region map, the blowup coastal map, and in a 1927 pre-bonifica map, all denoted by the orange lines. P-REX mapped all basic vegetation groupings within 1 kilometer of the coast and measured the existing zonation width every 1 kilometer up the coast.

Systemic Design as Landscape Intelligence

The *Wetland* and *Dune Machines* are samples of P-REX's Systemic Design research and practice. Our methodology seeks to expand program and strategy outward, adjusting and feeding-back small-scale issues based on large-scale logic all the way through the project-scale design process. The resulting landscape design becomes demonstrably more sustainable—and thus able to live without expensive, infinite inputs—only if a larger scale logic is encoded in the smaller scale proposals. Moreover, the design is more intelligent if the landscape systems are retrofitted with a robust plasticity rather than with a delicate balance of elements in need of constant preservation. In short, we seek to design with Darwinian landscape survival—not maintenance—in mind.

Rich Ground

Surface In-Depth
Between Landscape and Architecture

Surface In-Depth brought together six practitioners from landscape architecture and architecture to discuss the concept and construction of 'surface.' The topic was chosen for the ways in which it straddles both disciplines, though each views it in different ways.

Variation, density, diversity, indeterminacy, and complexity; these are buzzwords current in each discipline that are intimately tied to surface. Our question: how do these terms circulate within each field, and how do they connect, or, indeed, separate them?

The debate was organized around three questions:

1. What is surface?
How is a surface in landscape different from a surface in architecture? How are they the same? Surface is critical to contemporary theories and practices in both architecture and landscape. Variation, diversity, indeterminacy, complexity, fluidity, and continuity are themes in both contemporary disciplines, and surface has been used as a design tool to engage these issues.

2. How is a surface made?
Moving from the digital environment to the physical world a surface will inevitably thicken with layers and material. Surfaces are also made through the layering of both natural and artificial process over time. When and why does a surface become thick? What is gained and what is lost in the thickening of a surface?

3. What can a surface do?
How does surface operate as plane of potential program and performance? The flatness and continuity of a surface enable diverse and unexpected events to take place. Surfaces establish boundaries between internal and external spaces as well as filter activity, process, and information. Does the performance of a surface change when oriented horizontally versus vertical?

Question 1
What is surface?

William Braham
I would question the distinction between what is surface and what is boundary. Performative surfaces are boundaries that are exchanges between different domains. The boundary is thus a separation between two zones of great depth and potential.

James Corner
If we had this conversation twenty years ago there would be discussion of the formal properties of surface. We might be looking at the paintings of Malevich or Kandinsky, or the photography of Gursky. Perhaps we would be having a serious conversation about the formal and aesthetic properties of flatness, depth, opacity, transparency, and the implied depth of a picture plane with Robert Slutzky.

In architecture, you would think of Mies van der Rohe, or more recently, Herzog & de Meuron, as having an interest in this kind of surface. In landscape architecture, Peter

Alumnae Valley
Michael Van Valkenburgh Associates. Material cross section

Walker, for instance, has an expressed interest in flatness, in *taut surfaces*. They do not photograph well at all, but when you see them they are extraordinary because of that taut, flat quality.

Architects and landscape architects make drawings on a surface. Plan dominates early on, later venturing into section, axonometric, or even perspective, but it is always on the flat. The act of making a drawing is somehow analogous to the production of the built work; particularly in modernist architecture, which has a very clear relationship between the act of drawing and the work. In landscape architecture the relationship is particularly clear in planning and mapping.

The computer allows for a much more fluid form of surface imaging. What we are talking about today is the performative aspects of surface. Robert Rauschenberg, for instance, was interested not in the aesthetic product of a flat surface, but rather what a flat surface enabled him to do as an artist. By using a canvas horizontally, he was able to push things around, collate, and view the surface more as an operational table than an aesthetic plane of reception. I am less interested in a surface's aesthetic reception or its aesthetic properties, than in how a surface actually supports things. Buckminster Fuller's unfolding of the surface of the earth, for instance, is interesting because it avoids the problem of scalar distortion when you take a spherical surface and make it flat. It also gets

Rich Ground

Olympic Sculpture Park
Weiss/Manfredi. Subsurface construction.

around many of the geopolitical and cultural issues surrounding how the content of the surface is arrayed. In other words, with each iteration he is setting up nations, trade, and economics in a very different way. A surface as drawing, in the manner of a Carlo Scarpa, or as map, in the manner of a Buckminster Fuller, has the potential to construct different realities and allow work to be performed in a different way.

The fascination with surface in architecture and the appropriation of landscape as a typology began in the 1990s with young architects who were very excited about the single surface effects of the digital milieu. They could create fantastic topographic things that could then become buildings. In many ways they resembled landscapes because they had topographic properties and it was not always clear what was inside and what was outside. That ran its course by the end of the 1990s. More recently, perhaps because of the sustainability agenda, there has been interest in the ability of these single surface skins to do more than just shape space. They can also have performative properties: they can have solar arrays; they can shape and channel water; they can help collect water; they can filter and store water; they can do things with wind. If the shaping of these surfaces can perform then it would be even more valid than a purely formal concern.

Marion Weiss
Surface is a connective tissue. The landscape surface introduces the idea of continuities, flows, systemic connections, urban connections, longer connections to things that architects typically do not control. Landscape is also an embracing of temporal effects. Architecture can be about resisting change, resisting weathering, resisting water, while landscape is about taking it in, being nourished by it, and moving it along.

During the competition for the *Olympic Sculpture Park* in Seattle, we were preoccupied with the question of how surface in landscape differs from surface in architecture. If there are three separate sites that need to be connected across highways and train tracks, it is no longer possible to do architecture. Even landscape is impossible. Thus the question became, "What is the subsurface?" In this case the subsurface had to be infrastructural engineering.

Beneath the depth of what we see as architecture and landscape was the general strategy of movement and the creation of the subsurface condition: contaminated; compacted; mechanically stabilized; vertical; diagonal; no more than a one-in-three slope for mowing; no more than a one-in-eight slope for stabilization; no more than a void of a quarter of a meter wide for salmon habitat degradation. The techniques that we needed to learn as a vocabulary went well beneath the surface of architecture or landscape.

Phu Hoang
A surface, in its most basic form, delineates a territory. In architecture, surfaces can delineate between wet and dry

Olympic Sculpture Park
Weiss/Manfredi. Opening Day.

territories. This follows architecture's basic function of providing shelter from the environment by eliminating water in its various forms whether precipitation, condensation, humidity, or ice. In landscape, surfaces have a much more varied relationship with water. They can funnel, hold, absorb, or release water. Landscape surfaces and water are not in opposition as they are in architecture.

Anita Berrizbeitia

A surface is a living system with its own structure and cycles of production. It is a performative medium that conveys water and supports organisms like bacteria, fungi, plants, and animal life. It is the result of processes that take place under it such as the decomposition of rocks and their migration upwards from the depth of the ground. It is also the result of processes that take place over it like erosion caused by wind, water, and human activity. It responds to external systems like climactic patterns that evolve in their own composition.

In its biological sense, the surface in landscape architecture is less a boundary and more a zone of connectivity. It is a place where vegetational, hydrological, and soil systems interact. The structure and biology of surfaces support the establishment and future development of systems on the site. Alexandre Chemetoff's *Jardin des Bambous* in *Parc de la Villette*, for instance, speaks of the surface as an index of its underlying condition, as a layer that produces information about its host environment, and as a dialectic between thick ground and thin surface in urban sites.

Keith Kaseman

I'm wondering if, as a test, we could all get by without using the word surface for a time. Because of the recent historical developments of the term, it is quite loaded. The mere use of that term brings so much baggage and so much pressure. The term cannot hold information without qualifiers. In the design phase for the *Pentagon Memorial*, for instance, surfaces were intensely focused on as a means of understanding how we were going to build the project.

But once it left our hands and we broke up the model, made changes, and sent different file formats all around the country to different fabricators, we did not have to utter the word 'surface' anymore; we talked about the upper lip, the side belly, the finishes, and so on. You can strictly hold that term inside the digital realm, but when you pull out of that realm the vocabulary has to change; it becomes more about thicknesses, membranes, and material properties.

Question 2
How is a surface made?

Anita Berrizbeitia

I would like to draw the distinction between surface and ground. At *Burnett Park*—a post-structuralist surface if you allow me that term—Peter Walker addresses the subject of flatness. Unlike in architecture, the flat surface in landscape architecture is never a given. Horizontal

Rich Ground 265

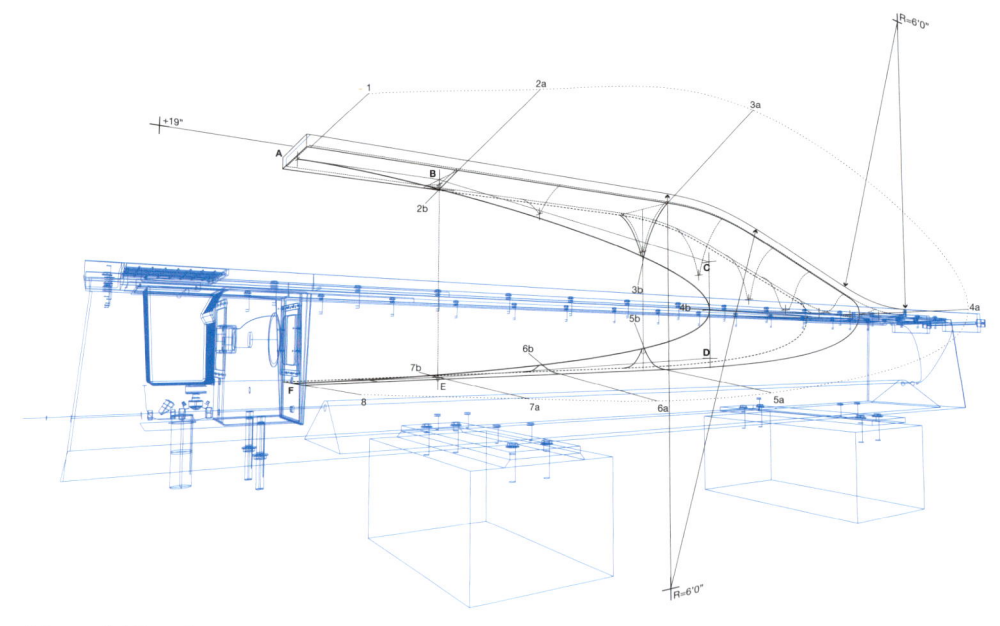

Pentagon Memorial Bench
KBAS. Fabrication drawing.

surfaces are never flat to begin with. They are constructed and they need to be maintained in order for that condition to persist.

Walker constructed the park to speak of a 'made' flatness. In a classic post-structuralist move, the appearance of a traditional park lawn is made new through displacement. Here the lawn is placed in an unexpected relationship with the path and is thus transformed into a figure. The lowering of the grass in relation to the path not only objectifies the lawn, it transforms it from its traditional sense of a soft background surface to a taut, fragmented plane not unlike those of paved plazas. In a simple project, Walker isolates the typical components of a landscape surface, pulls them apart, and reassembles them in a new way, thus reconstituting the surface to comment on the processes of its making.

The transformation of a surface from a service parking lot to a naturalized landscape in Michael Van Valkenburgh's *Alumnae Valley Landscape Restoration* on the campus of Wellesley College entailed the construction of many layers of surfaces with varied structural and biological properties each with a different function to perform. Some layers permanently encapsulate toxic soils, while others contain surface flows, or release them slowly into the ground. Other layers maintain more typical functions as planting medium. This is a ground designed with built-in differentiation that will promote the establishment of ecological complexity on the surface.

Phu Hoang

Our *Water Wrapper* is a research project for a responsive building envelope that attempts to take the surface of water, rotate it to a vertical plane, and wrap it around a building. We ask the question, "Can a building envelope behave like the Earth's oceans by absorbing solar heat and air pollutants, refracting light, and mitigating climate?" The surface of the wrapper is not made in a conventional tectonic sense. Instead, the surface is manipulated by environmental factors, building controls, or users. The technology consists of two rows of water nozzles that are digitally controlled and attached to sensors to create a water zone around a building. The digital sensors detect solar heat, air pollution, building control systems, and users, literally images made out of water. The density of water controls solar heat mitigation: the more water droplets that you have, the more heat or pollutants are absorbed.

There are two sets of arrays: one for global impact, which is environmental, and the other for local impact, which is programmatic or performative. There is a constant global input that is detected by the sensors, and the local one can be controlled either by the users or by specific program allocations—in this case, living rooms, bedrooms, dining

Pentagon Memorial
KBAS. Bench detail and opening day.

rooms, and their relationship to the amount of water that is required in each of those programs.

James Corner

In a close up micro-photograph of skin you can actually see sweat globules. Obviously the hotter the skin, the bigger those globules will become in an effort to cool the skin. As the skin cools the globules will diminish. It is an extremely interactive form of work occurring upon a surface to warm and cool. In a similar way, a moss garden breeds the surface through a complex installation of foggers, misters, and irrigators that are there to allow that surface to breed, grow, or transform in a very pliant and flexible way: a surface is being cultivated with an extraordinary flexibility and, at the same time, extraordinarily tactile properties. There is an aesthetic receptiveness to it, but it is deeper than just the visual.

This is the effect that we wanted to achieve on the *High Line* by breeding growth that had a certain indeterminacy and wildness to it. There is an awful lot of work that goes into how exactly that surface system is built to allow water life, bacterial life, and fungal life to produce the organic life to that will come through the folds and the cracks. Most smart projects, whether architectural or landscape-architectural projects, are responsive to their site. That site might be a physical location. It might be the brief that the client wants. It might be the political or the planning milieu. Really interesting projects are responsive to those conditions in clever ways.

Marion Weiss

For the *Olympic Sculpture Park*, we had to become experts in aquatic engineering, geotechnical engineering, civil engineering, environmental encapsulation, BNSF train railways and clearances for Amtrak, and aerial street vacations that create bridges over federally mandated high- and wide-bodied trucking routes. This subsurface agenda generated the potential and the obligations for the surface possibilities. Once those were fully understood, the park could be a performative surface. What you see is the urban infrastructure; water collection becomes visible because the water run-off has to be able to nourish the newly created beach for the salmon habitat. Each component sends up layers to create the surface that are then seen as the landscape.

There is a thirty-foot grade change from the city edge to the water's edge at the site, which leveraged the possibility to create the twenty-foot clearance of the federal trucking requirement while still having a total gradient from top to bottom. The site allowed us to have a topographic continuity—calibrated for us by the bluff that is the water's edge—that allowed us to show the strength of the infrastructure rather than conceal it.

Hotel Tower
Phu Hoang Office. Exterior "Water Wrapper."

The site's geometries are all about showing an intensification of high-speed forces while giving the pretense of a slow meander, a pedestrian infrastructure if you will.

Keith Kaseman
The surface of the *Pentagon Memorial* unit was made through an intricate and prolonged game of geometric chess: research and development adjustments, as well as expert input, over the course of several years informed the construction of the curves that in turn control the bench's surface. The surface then controls and provisionally ties together approximately eighty-five other surfaces in a complex and very precise model. Ultimately, the polysurface is cut in half: the bottom is concrete, while the top steel. This model drove a dozen large CNC machines around the country.

The project was a collaboration between academic, industrial and construction experts, metallurgists and scientists, federal government employees, and family members of the victims. We took the insight gained and embedded it in the intelligence of the geometry.

Cathrine Veikos
The question of how a surface is made brought to mind Oscar Wilde's famous rhetoric, "It is only shallow people who do not judge by appearances." At the *New Museum*, designed by SANAA, the seamless, perceptually evanescent and resilient surface is an architectural example of material ingenuity.

The desire to establish an appearance for the building as a series of stacked solid boxes, coupled with the technical performance requirements, called for a particular effect of the building's material surface. The challenge was met with an inquiry into matter and perception that implemented seamlessness and dynamism.

Florian Idenburg, a senior associate at SANAA, described the trajectory of the research for the *New Museum*:

> We began with full scale models which tested the material at the level of the detail. Which material required the fewest seams? Which seams were the most invisible? The long story, which ends with the invention of a series of layers of corrugated and expanded metal panels and anodized aluminum, takes turns through the hundred year history of expanded metal through to the identification of a factory at least that old which had saved the dies required to punch the large holes and the creation of countless, representational, and experimental or simulated models.[1]

Question 3
What can a surface do?

Keith Kaseman
Is it enough to consider surfaces as merely thickness generators?

Anita Berrizbeitia
Peter Eisenman and Laurie Olin's project for *Rebstock Park* in Frankfurt and Michel Desvigne's garden at the

Centraal Museum Utrecht represent two projects that have a very different scale; one a large housing site, and the other a tiny museum garden. Both engage the surface as a continuous layer, but one that is modulated by difference and variation to become planes of potential program and performance. At *Rebstock Park*, Olin and Eisenman used the concept of the fold to generate the varied surface conditions for different programs. They superimposed two grids of different sizes, and by connecting the equivalent points they deformed the surface, causing folds to occur. In these folds, there is a new logic for the otherwise flat and nondescript site. Zones of difference, areas of linear water and vegetation, forests, and zones of recreation are redistributed, which creates a logic to tie architecture and landscape together.

The *Centraal Museum Utrecht* garden is a beautiful project made with only two materials, brick and grass. The surface ties together the disparate and broken-up spaces between the buildings that make the site. The bricks are laid in a gradient from very tight with a very narrow joint, to very far apart. The varying widths of the joints allow different grass species to grow and their different heights define spaces for different activities in the garden. The garden achieves maximum effects with minimum means. When in that landscape, approaching Utrecht, pastureland is all one sees. Then the passage shifts into the city, through the museum, and out to the garden, to the same material, grass. This time it is modulated between these joints: the wider the joints the higher the grass. It is a space of extraordinary richness and poetry that is created just by varying those two conditions. It is about the culture of landscape that is outside of that building, yet it is a complete invention, a complete manufacturing of these two systems of brick and grass in a very creative way.

Cathrine Veikos

In my seminar, *Surface and Effects*, I posit surface as a site for perceptual and performative effects, a site of architectural innovation. Sheer opacity refers to the continuous thickness of a building enclosure and brings into question the clarity of surface as a representation of internal spaces. Increasingly the presence of a building is constituted less by the display of its interior function than by the material effects of its multilayered and multivalent building surface. In the complex thickness that constitutes these enclosures, the material surface forms and mediates an inconstant image of the interior, rather than the interior itself. This notion of sheer opacity, in which solid and void become perceptions of surface conditions, challenges an aesthetic condition of disembodied contemplation and problematizes the binary reading of interior and exterior as simply being continuous or discontinuous.

At what point on the spectrum from thinness to depth does surface begin to challenge tectonics and received notions of space? The spatial and tectonic qualities of surface are particularly defined by their relationship to structure and frame. In contrast, the creation of a perceptual field transforms space through a surface condition. Rather than render surface insubstantial or superficial, sheer opacity situates surface as a primary constituent in the creation of space. The idea of responsive skins in our seminar comes from a framework that promotes a design methodology driven by investigations in dynamic relationships between the building's surface and its sensorial performance. The question of the architectural surface and its relation to both production and representation form the basis for this research.

Phu Hoang

In the hotel prototype, instead of the kind of one-to-one relationship demonstrated in the housing example, we create a waterscape: as the occupancy changes the waterscape changes throughout the day. We are trying to achieve a strategy for a building envelope that allows us to speak about the vertical surface of building envelopes in terms of microclimates. You can adjust the microclimate of a zone of the building envelope according to differences in programmatic needs or differences in what particular people want. We are trying to demonstrate performance: not only what the system can do, but also what it can look likenot only environmental performance, but also the programmatic performance of its users.

James Corner

The recent work of Herzog & de Meuron is exploring a new aesthetic potential of performative surfaces. We now build landscapes and buildings that have surface skins, and building skins that have more pliant relationships in

The High Line
James Corner Field Operations and Diller Scofidio + Renfro. 10th Avenue Square.

space, which are enabled by the digital milieu, because we could never imagine these things before. We should push technology to allow these surfaces to deal with sun, wind, water, environmental conditions, programmatic conditions, as well as the psychological effects and temporal effects these surfaces afford.

In schools of architecture and landscape architecture over the past ten or twenty years, the rise of the single surface afforded by new digital software techniques allowed for a merging of architecture and landscape, initially formally, then later in performance terms, and in new forms of aesthetic potential. In architecture, in particular, new technologies are being developed around the thickness of that surface. Not just the surface as a skin that sweats, but the surface as a thickness that allows for water, energy, plant life, or occupational program to become embedded in the thickness of the surface.

Our project for *Governors Island* in New York is about re-sculpting the surface of the island so that tidal flows and weather patterns can engage with the land over time. In our competition entry for the *Rio Manzanares Park*, Madrid, a perforated land or skin over a running river, the river is allowed to ebb and flow to crreate pools rather than lines. There enormous technicality behind these surfaces, but there is also an effort to create extraordinary aesthetic effect. In recent years, the functionality of the surface has trumped formal properties. We are attempt to merge the two to work together so that extraordinarily functional surfaces also have extraordinarily tactile effects.

Conclusion

Surface In-Depth: Between Landscape and Architecture examined surfaces operating as performative, infrastructural, thick, and fertile fields; as ecologies, living mediums that in turn produce life; as layered, effective, atmospheric constructs; in short, as anything except static, two-dimensional planes. From the "thick 2-D" (James Corner and Stan Allen) to the "synthetic carpet" (Rem Koolhaas), to a "thick atmosphere" (Helene Furján), the surface in both architecture and landscape architecture is both a term to be interrogated and a terrain of invention and innovation.

But above all, *Surface In-Depth: Between Landscape and Architecture* demonstrated that conversations across disciplinary lines are always fertile—a space in which disciplinarity is both asserted and set aside, and in which our differences feed unexpected emergences in our commonalities, the noise in the system that is most productive of invention and creativity.

Endnotes
1 Personal conversation with author.

Facing Page
The High Line
James Corner Field Operations and Diller Scofidio + Renfro. View of the Chelsea Thicket and 23rd street Lawn beyond.

Rich Ground 271

Waste and Dirt
Notes on the Architecture of Compost
William W. Braham

> What makes composting such a useful template for an ecotechnic society is precisely that it highlights the ways such a society would have to differ from the way things are done in today's industrial civilization.
>
> John Michael Greer, *Archdruid Report* (2008)

Eating is messy. It is a fact of life—and even of not-quite-life—that every act of consumption produces waste. Even the most thoroughgoing vegan consuming raw food right from the plant can only extract so much value from food and will later leave a little pile of waste, somewhere. It is even messier when we consider the parts of the plant that can not be eaten, especially if it has to be harvested, and the messiness only increases when we imagine the long chain of discarded waste involved in transforming that raw plant into say, a warm hamburger delivered in a wrapper through the drive-in window while you sit idling in your car.

As for dirtiness, the location of all that waste will determine whether it is "dirty" or not. It is no accident that our active senses—sight, smell, hearing, taste—all point in the same direction as our mouths, where they can help locate and evaluate food, while the organs for depositing waste are literally at the rear. Buildings, too, have a front- and back-of-the-house, dictating where the dumpster goes. Waste is something to be voided, avoided, and left behind, once its value has been extracted. Dirtiness, on the other hand, is more symbolic, more a question of where waste should go. As Mary Douglas observed, dirt is "matter out of place," meaning that cleanliness is a particular order, specific to the society in which the waste is produced.[1]

With all the anxieties about waste, about resource scarcity and about hygiene, it is the transformation of dirtiness that makes compost so interesting. Sim van der Ryn, the architect who wrote *Ecological Design*, cites his development of an easy-to-build composting toilet for the back-to-the-land generation as the turning point in his own development as an ecologically minded designer.[2] For the first generation of the "hippie-garde," a composting toilet took the dirtiest waste, the one invoking the most anxieties and requiring the most euphemisms, and not only rendered it clean, but also made it into productive food for the garden. That organic transformation came to represent a broad criticism of the industrial civilization of the 1970s, of the post-war boom of disposable pens, super highways, and plastic diapers.

Perhaps the most immediate architectural contrast to the composting toilet would be the "sanitary" tiles developed for American bathrooms in the 1920s. They were called sanitary because the edges and inside corners were smoothed and rounded to allow easier cleaning and to eliminate the sharp corners in which dirt could lodge. The smooth shiny surfaces of the tiles facilitated and made visible the removal of dirt, and still form part of the palette of architectural finishes that accompany indoor plumbing and the porcelain flush toilet. In that symbolic system, waste is removed as instantaneously as possible, as are any smells or traces of its deposit.

The composting toilet offers a different aesthetic code altogether, a code of transformation in which composting has become wholly theological, from the pagan ethos of the Archdruid, cited at the beginning of this essay, to essays on the "Tao of Compost," and even Unitarian process theology.[3] The central point made by Mary Douglas is that pre-modern religions regulated dirt and dirtiness, not because of hygiene, but as a source of power invoked in rituals to maintain and advance social codes. In modern, open societies religious strictures are largely matters of choice and identity, but dirtiness itself has lost little of its power and is still used to describe and maintain cultural identities of many kinds. Privies and outhouses have existed for millennia—what choice was there—but the introduction of running water and the flush toilet heralded a wholly modern ethos of cleanliness. It was an ethos given particular force by the successes of germ theory in the late nineteenth century, empowering sanitary engineers as the regulators of public health and order.

The counter culture of the 1970s attacked that system of cleanliness at many levels, ridiculing materials that resisted aging and smoothly shaved armpits alike. The elegance of the compost critique is that "germs" make compost work. Their many tiny acts of consumption transform our waste into something cleaner, which gives the composting toilet

Compost Pile

Rich Ground

Living Machine
Water treatment facility at Ethel M. Botanical Cactus Garden, Las Vegas, Nevada.

Green Roof
"Green roof" in E.V.A. Lanxmeer district (a "green district" named Lanxmeer, built at Culemborg, The Netherlands).

moral force as a cleaning technology that works with natural processes. It is worth remembering that at the heart of conventional sewage treatment plants, where all the flush toilets secretly deliver their waste, there are also "germs" at work, forced microbial laborers engaged in the serious business of waste transformation, though their bodies are "settled out" and a final dose of chlorine is used to ensure that nothing is left alive before the water is returned to the ecosystem. At the end of the day, compost offers a different kind of cleanliness, one that makes the organic processes visible.

It is tempting to see the compost critique of sewage treatment and sanitary tiles carried over to the smooth forms of contemporary architecture. To place the now commercialized Living Machines, with their neatly packaged, wetland composting system in opposition to the clean forms of Gehry or Zaha, or even the smooth glass and cleanly caulked joints of commercial construction. Green roofs, too, make visible the ecological processes involved in water flow as a rebuke against conventional stormwater management, whose smooth pipes offer a similar kind of cleanliness as the sanitary tiles. That easy opposition misses the deeper critique offered by the composting toilet, not the hazy theology of transformation, but the importance of cleanliness in regulating waste.

In the biosphere there really is no "away," wastes are simply left behind or moved elsewhere, ultimately into one of the active environmental reservoirs—the air, the sea, or the ground—where they eventually become food for other creatures and processes. Like the composting toilet, the environmental slogans "there is no away" and "eliminate the concept of waste" are meant to raise awareness of ecological connections. They help make human consumption more efficient by turning more waste into food for some other process. But even in the healthiest ecosystem, eating is still messy. There are no perfect processes. The second law of thermodynamics argues that every act of consumption will leave some residue that can not be used for anything else, mostly low-grade heat, that we can only call waste.

The second law has led to its share of nihilistic theologies, but the striking fact has been that the relentless production of waste, the running down of the universe, seems also to produce increasingly complex arrangements, from galaxies to ecosystems to the rich variety of organic life itself. Those arrangements evolved over millennia, through myriad trials and errors, developing intricate feed-back loops and indirect reinforcements as they arrived at ever more productive arrangements despite the steady production of degraded energy.

The enduring challenge for designers of the modern period has been to understand what to do with these natural examples of complex order? In the design fields, we have had over a century of experimentation with biological and organic analogies of one kind or another.[4] Both composting toilets and green roofs continue one route of that exploration, presenting arguments for more direct integration of human and natural systems. But human society has been navigating—and exceeding—its ecological conditions long before the question of environmental design became overt. In traditional societies, the ideas of dirtiness and cleanliness helped establish and organize quite precise ecological arrangements well before the concept of an eco-system existed. Those traditional arrangements were not perfect and were slow to change even in the face of ecological disasters, but they served to preserve and make intelligible complex systems of consumption and interaction.[5]

In those terms, architecture is part of a rich social system that helps regulate the messiness of eating. The opposition between the composting toilet and the sanitary tile, or the green roof and the storm drain, is an argument about different social and ecological orders. For environmentalists, cleanliness may seem a soft and subjective measure for design, but it involves an extremely powerful, even biological, understanding of the world. Put more directly, environmental design can not succeed if ecological imperatives are only formulated in technical terms presented to avoid impending disasters. It succeeds when it offers a compelling vision of a prosperous future, supported and made intelligible by the distinctions between dirtiness and cleanliness.

The success of the compost critique may be to have transformed the hippie-garde's retreat from industrial civilization into persuasive proposals that link more effective, ecological arrangements with new understandings of cleanliness. The green roof and the living machine may be the two most emblematic elements, but it is only a start. Success occurs when environmental designs offer items as desirable as the well-appointed bath or the carefully prepared meal. Both provide full-bodied kinds of luxury and leave a mess after they are done.

Endnotes

1 Mary Douglas, *Purity and Danger: An Analysis of Concepts of Pollution and Taboo* (New York: Frederick Praeger, 1966); p. 35.
2 See Sim van der Ryn and Stuart Cowen, *Ecological Design* (Washington, DC: Island Press, 2005). Sim van der Ryn, *The toilet papers: designs to recycle human waste and water: dry toilets, greywater systems & urban sewage* (Santa Barbara: Capra Press, 1978).
3 See John Michael Greer, "Theology of Compost," in The Archdruid Report: Druid perspectives on nature, culture, and the future of industrial society, February 21, 2008, accessed on 16 Apr. 2010 at <http://thearchdruidreport.blogspot.com/2008/02/theology-of-compost.html>. See also Joseph Jenkins, "The Tao of Compost," in *The Humanure Handbook: A Guide to Composting Human Manure*, 3rd ed. (Grove City, Pa: Joseph Jenkins, 2005); and Chris Hillman, "Theology of Compost," in 2000 Summer Minister, July 23, 2000, accessed on 16 Apr. 2010 at <http://www.rochesterunitarian.org/1999-2000/20000723.html>.
4 See Phillip Steadman, *The Evolution of Designs: Biological analogy in architecture and the applied arts* (Cambridge; New York: Cambridge University Press, 1979).
5 See Jared Diamond, *Collapse: How Societies Choose to Fail or Succeed* (New York: Viking, 2004).

Hydrophile
Hydrodynamic Green Roof
Marcelyn Gow and Ulrika Karlsson, Servo

"Grass above, glass around" was Reyner Banham's glib characterization, in a 1977 article of the same name, of the binary aesthetic he observed in Norman Foster's building for the *Willis Faber and Dumas Headquarters* in Ipswich, England.[1] The "inscrutability" of the building, discussed by Banham in the context of both aesthetics and performance, owes in part to the apparent energy-wastefulness of curtain wall construction of the time juxtaposed with the presence of growing turf on the roof of the building: "[T]urf on top of a high-technology building full of air-conditioning, escalators, computers, and stuff? Once again, separated expectations, different architectural languages have been shotgun-married without apology or regard for the niceties of academic discourse, where turf is perfectly acceptable as long as it is on small-windowed, irregular technologically low-profile buildings."[2]

The apparently conflicting performance value of these materials is resolved in the surprising fact that the building performs relatively well as an energy-efficient structure due to its deep plan that produces a low ratio of glass to internal volume, and to the presence of a vernacular and time-tested insulating material on the roof—turf. The binary aesthetic of *Willis Faber* derives from an apparent lack of what Banham refers to as "craftsmanship, detail, decoration, and incident" in the curtain wall construction—a blank affect, impervious to accident—combined with the unruliness of vegetal matter.

The separation of the biotic and abiotic can be, and has historically been, considered in terms of entropy. "*Construction* = minus entropy" was the equation formulated by Kisho Kurokawa in his 1970 *Capsule Declaration*, the same year Robert Smithson demonstrated the extreme entropic consequences of the coexistence of dirt, a backhoe, and an empty shed in his *Partially Buried Woodshed*.[3] Recent discussions centering on a more conscious and sustainable administration of energetic, material, and ecological resources in the production of habitable environments suggest a radical rethinking of the equation. A potential *imbalance* in the equation on an *energetic* level plays a critical role in the contemporary architectural discussion.

The construction of environments that have the capacity to embrace entropic tendencies, breeds a new strain of architecture. This architecture exploits the latent responsiveness of energetic exchanges—specifically the transfer of heat, moisture, sound, and light through an architectural medium and their effects on more extensive ecologies—and ecosystems' alternative stable states.[4] Balance is relevant in this work not only in terms of the statics of bodies in space but more importantly in an ecological sense. Imbalances become the impetus of design innovation. A composite approach to material and environmental architectural systems emerges in this work.

The *Hydrophile Hydrodynamic Green Roof* considers the entropic potentials of the interaction between biotic and abiotic matter in architecture. This proposal for a

Facing Page
The Roof Meadow
View from west heath area of roof looking east toward meadow areas.

Rich Ground

Interior View
Roof seen from interior public space.

4,000 square meter bioscience innovation center with a hydrodynamic vegetated roof, located in the Albano region of Stockholm, operates at a building scale as well as at an urban scale. The project reconsiders the green roof typology in terms of architectural design and urban biodiversity enhancement. Departing from a standardized extensive green roof, usually comprised of a thin horizontal substrate for growing vegetation and limiting stormwater runoff with limited importance for the urban biodiversity, this project investigates the production of a non-standardized, variegated, semi-intensive green roof—an occupiable zone characterized by immersive depth, responding to the design and differentiation of roof morphology. The section of the building incorporates a series of depressions and swells, instances where the vegetated roof permeates the interior exposing the tectonic and biotic qualities of the roofscape.

The green roof is designed to be experienced from several vantage points: from above—walking amidst a dense landscape of indigenous vegetation intertwined with protuberant forms that emit water, air, or light; from below—as a suspended ceiling system that pulls down to close proximity with the floor; or from within—viewed through large apertures in the roof.

The *Hydrophile* derives its name from the hydrodynamic properties found in the shell of the Namib Desert beetle. A coalescence between formal and material performance occurs at a micro scale in the shell of the beetle where hydrophilic—water attracting—and hydrophobic—water repelling—regions are interspersed to collect and direct the flow of water. In the *Hydrophile* prototype, this principle is applied on an architectural scale for the design of a *hydrodynamic* green roof system. The hydrodynamic properties of a building system are exploited in this project for the cultivation of biotopes on and through a variegated roofscape augmented with systems for percolating water through soil substrates. The material properties of ceramics with varying degrees of porosity are coupled with the protuberant roof morphology in order to perform as hydrophilic and hydrophobic agents, directing the flow of water for soil irrigation.

The factors most critical to the design of the *Hydrophile* building and its plant communities are the substrate thicknesses, substrate design, and the roof topography and geometry. The articulation of morphological and material properties generates structural and environmental performances, producing a gradient diversity of inhabitable wet, dry, and intermediate microclimates. The roof topography is designed to direct water to depressions where large amounts can be stored to support wet meadows or fens. Substrate thickness is used to create vegetational gradients ranging from shrub-lands and meadows on thicker substrates, to dry meadows and heathland in thin zones. The plant material for the green roof is established through seeding, planting, and hay

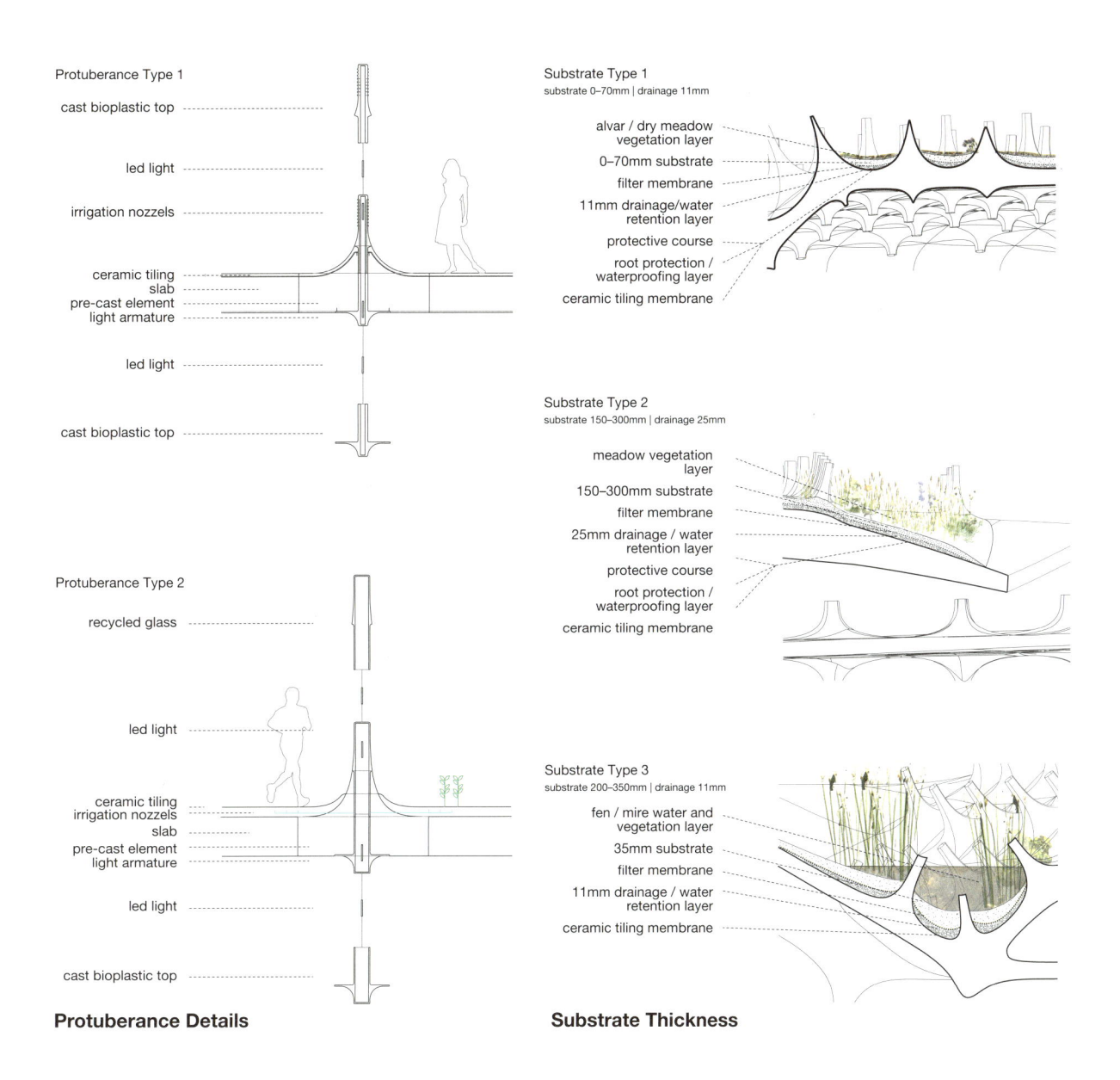

Protuberance Type 1

- cast bioplastic top
- led light
- irrigation nozzels
- ceramic tiling
- slab
- pre-cast element
- light armature
- led light
- cast bioplastic top

Protuberance Type 2

- recycled glass
- led light
- ceramic tiling
- irrigation nozzels
- slab
- pre-cast element
- light armature
- led light
- cast bioplastic top

Protuberance Details

Substrate Type 1
substrate 0–70mm | drainage 11mm

- alvar / dry meadow vegetation layer
- 0–70mm substrate
- filter membrane
- 11mm drainage/water retention layer
- protective course
- root protection / waterproofing layer
- ceramic tiling membrane

Substrate Type 2
substrate 150–300mm | drainage 25mm

- meadow vegetation layer
- 150–300mm substrate
- filter membrane
- 25mm drainage / water retention layer
- protective course
- root protection / waterproofing layer
- ceramic tiling membrane

Substrate Type 3
substrate 200–350mm | drainage 11mm

- fen / mire water and vegetation layer
- 35mm substrate
- filter membrane
- 11mm drainage / water retention layer
- ceramic tiling membrane

Substrate Thickness

Rich Ground

Dry Systems
substrate 0–70mm / drainage 11mm

The thinnest vegetation systems will be dominated by drought tolerant grasses, herbs, and succulents on the thicker sections, and by bryophytes/moss and lichen on thinner sites and on edges towards bare roofing material. These thin vegetation systems will in many cases look similar to traditionally constructed green roof systems or mimic more naturally occurring alvar systems. The substrate layers will have a neutral to alkaline reaction and range from 0–7cm in depth.

The vegetation will be established using cuttings (succulents) and seeds (grasses and herbs). Planting will be made in certain spots. Bryophytes will be left for spontaneous colonization.

Alvar
Allium schoenoprasum, Arenaria serpyllifolia, Erophila verna, Geranium pusillum, Melica ciliata, Satureja acinos, Sedum acre, and Sedum album.

Dry meadow on bedrock
Allium schoenoprasum, Artemisia campestris, Festuca ovina, Festuca rubra, Sedum album, and Thymus serpyllum.

Dry meadow rich in herbs on bedrock
Allium oleraceum, Allium schoenoprasum, Anthyllis vulneraria, Artemisia campestris, Briza media, Centaurea jacea, Centaurea scabiosa, Festuca ovina, Filipendula vulgaris, Fragaria viridis, Galium verum, Helictotrichon pratense, Helictotrichon pubescens, Plantago media, Plantago lanceolata, Poa compressa, Potentilla argentea, Potentilla tabernaemotani, Primula veris, Pulsatilla vulgaris, Thymus serphyllum, Trifolium montanum, Verbascum thapsus, and Veronica spicata.

Meadow Vegetation
substrate 150–300mm / drainage 25mm

Increasing substrate layers will allow higher and more dominant vegetation as compared to the drier areas. This will allow a larger range of plants. These systems will have supplementary irrigation with recycled water.

False Oatgrass meadow
Anthriscus sylvestris, Arrhenatherum elatills, Artemisia vulgaris, Centaurea jacea, Cerastium fontanum sp vulg., Cirsium vulgare, Dactylis glomerata, Festuca pratensis, Festuca rubra, Heracleum sphondylium, Holcus lanatus, Knautia arvensis, Leucanthemum vulgare, Plantago lanceolata, Rumex acetosa, and Veronica chamaedrys.

Flower meadow*
Agrostis capillaris, Ajuga pyramidalis, Anthoxanthum odoratum, Campanula patula, Campanula persicifolia, Festuca rubra, Helictotrichon pubescens, Hieracium aurantiacum, Hypochoeris maculata, Knautia arvensis, Leontodon autumnalis, Leontodon hispidus, Leontodon hispidus, Leucanthemum vulgare, Lotus corniculatus, Plantago media, Poa pratensis, Potentilla crantzii, Primula veris, Rhinanthus minor, Scorzonera humilis, andVerbascum nigrum.

Intermediate rich meadow
Alchemilla spp., Anthoxanthum odoratum, Briza media, Deschampsia cespitosa, Festuca ovina, Filipendula ulmaria, Galium boreale, Geranium sylvaticum, Geum rivale, Hypericum maculatum, Hypochoeris maculata, Knautia arvensis, Luzula multiflora, Potentilla erecta, Prunella vulgaris, Ranunculus auricomus, Rhinanthus minor, Rumex acetosa, Solidago virgaurea, Veronica chamaedrys, Viola canina, and Viola riviniana.

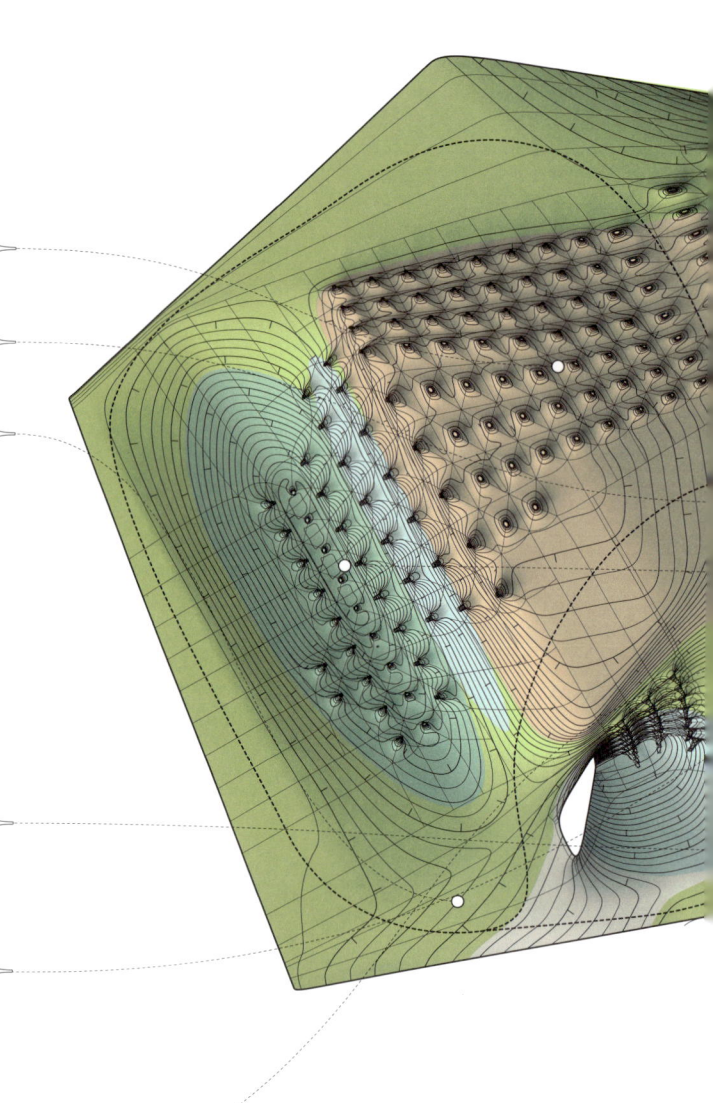

Wet Systems
substrate 200–350mm | drainage 11mm

Water is a key element in the roof design of the Albano building. The building is located on the western fringe of the Nationalstadspark, a short distance from the Brunnsviken Bay in the east. A thoughtful design of the water system on the roof and on the lot would increase available wet habitats in the area and support movement of amphibians from the wet areas in the west and towards the protected areas in east.

Wet Deschampsia (Tall grass meadow)
Achillea millefolium, Agrostis capillaris, Anthriscus sylvestris, Carex nigra, Deschampsia cespitosa, Festuca pratensis, Festuca rubra, Filipendula ulmaria, Leueanthemum vulgare, Phleum pratense, Poa pratensis, Potentilla anserina, Ranunculus acris, Ranunculus repens, Rumex acetosa, and Succisa pratensis.

Tall sedge mire
Agrostis canina, Caltha palustris, Carex paniculata, Carex pseudocyperus, Cirsium palustre, Cladium mariscus, Deschampsia caespitosa, Equisetum fluviatile, Equisetum palustre, Eriophorum angustifolium, Filipendula ulmaria, Iris pseudocorus, Lysimachia nummularia, Lysimachia thyrsiflora, Lysimachia vulgaris, Lythrum salicaria, Phalaris arundinacea, Phragmites australis, Schoenoplectus lacustris, Solanum dulcamara, Thelypteris palustris, Typha angustifolia, Typha latifolia, Viola epipsila, and Viola palustris.

Fen
Carex diandra, Carex elata, Carex flacca, Carex panicea, Eriophorum angustifolium, Eriophorum latifolium, Filipendula ulmaria, Menyanthes trifoliata, Parnassia palustrisPedicularis palustris (halvparasit), Primula farinosa, Succisa pratensis, and Trichophorum alpinum.

This vegetation system is comprised of a rather low meadow type with high herb diversity. It is maintained through cutting but also through careful plant selection. This vegetation type will also include hemiparasitic plants that have been shown to influence plant dynamics and dominance between species.

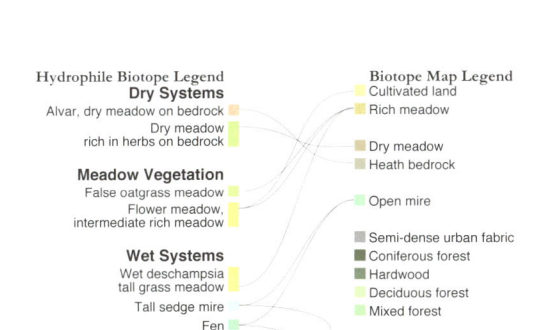

Path

Hydrophile Biotope Legend
Dry Systems
Alvar, dry meadow on bedrock
Dry meadow rich in herbs on bedrock

Meadow Vegetation
False oatgrass meadow
Flower meadow, intermediate rich meadow

Wet Systems
Wet deschampsia tall grass meadow
Tall sedge mire
Fen
planned wet ground

Biotope Map Legend
Cultivated land
Rich meadow
Dry meadow
Heath bedrock
Open mire
Semi-dense urban fabric
Coniferous forest
Hardwood
Deciduous forest
Mixed forest

Biotope Map
Stockholm, Albano Region

Rich Ground 281

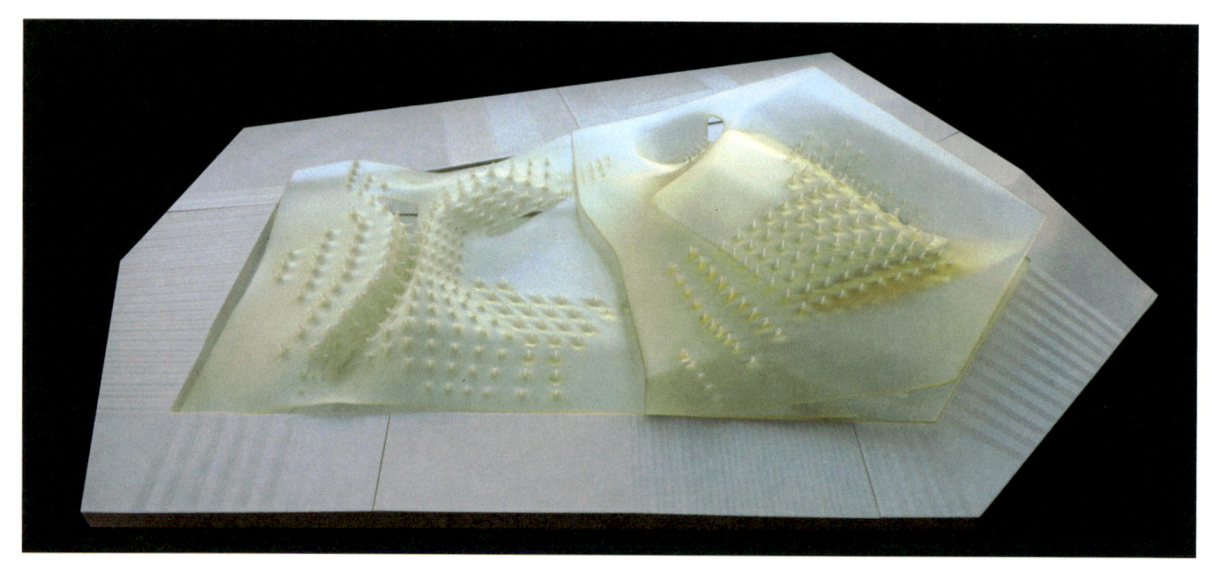

Hydrophile Physical Model

transfer from similar local habitats. Adaptive maintenance techniques including soil disturbance, haymaking, and water flow management are used to intentionally increase the production of entropy thereby supporting the biodiversity of indigenous plant and animal species. This stimulates changes in the texture, color, density, moisture levels, and other material properties of the vegetated roof, informing and augmenting its tectonic qualities and architectural affect.

Vernacular sod roof construction instigates varying degrees of imbalance between vegetal matter and the "detail, decoration, and incident" of the building type. The entropic tendencies of landscape partially obliterate the features of the architecture. Imbalance between biotic and abiotic properties is calibrated to produce specific qualities in the *Hydrophile* project. The relationship between high and low resolution in the architecture is played out through the emergence and disappearance of articulations such as edge, contour, and ridge in the slabs and apertures, producing varying degrees of definition and ambiguity across several scales in the project. Likewise the difference in resolution between the *Willis Faber* building and its immediate context is resolved to some extent for Banham by the "surprise, truncation, concealment, and confrontation" produced by the reflection of adjacent buildings in its glass envelope.[5] This constitutes a certain form of contextualism related to the material performance of the glass. The *Hydrophile* project addresses contextualism through the growth of indigenous vegetation from the cultivated grounds in the region. The roofscape is incorporated into a system of urban green surfaces that provide important links for the migration of species, possibly supporting existing ecosystems, biotope structures, and habitat networks while promoting biodiversity in the local environment.

The *Hydrophile Hydrodynamic Green Roof* is an architectural environment that actively embraces entropic tendencies. Energetic exchanges are activated on an environmental and urban scale in *Hydrophile* through its role as a constituent of an urban infrastructure and ecosystem that enables new patterns of occupancy (the migration of species) to emerge on and through its site. Vegetal matter performs as an integrated architectural material reshaping the architectural atmosphere.

Endnotes

1 Reyner Banham, "Grass Above, Glass Around," in *A Critic Writes: Selected Essays by Reyner Banham*, eds. Reyner Banham and Mary Banham (Berkeley: University of California Press, 1999); pp. 208-211. Originally published in *New Society* 42, 783 (6 October 1977): pp. 22-23.
2 Banham, "Grass Above, Glass Around," pp. 210.
3 Kurokawa asserted that, "The basic kinetic form in which space develops is metabolism, and its process is expressed as an increasing entropy. 'Construction' (minus-entropy) which is repeatedly put in during the development of space metamorphoses the 'organization' of the space. Modern architecture needs a methodology of metabolism and metamorphosis." Kisho Kurokawa, "Capsule Declaration," in *Metabolism in Architecture*, ed. Kisho Kurokawa (London: Studio Vista, 1977), p. 85.
4 B.E. Beisner, D.T. Haydon and K. Cuddington, "Alternative Stable States in Ecology," *Frontiers in Ecology and the Environment* 1 (July 2003): pp. 376-382. See also C.S. Holling, "Resilience and Stability of Ecological Systems," *Annual Review of Ecological Systems* 4 (1973): pp. 1-24, and R.C. Lewontin, "The Meaning of Stability," *Brookhaven Symposia in Biology* 22 (1969): pp. 13-23.
5 Banham, "Grass Above, Glass Around," p. 211.

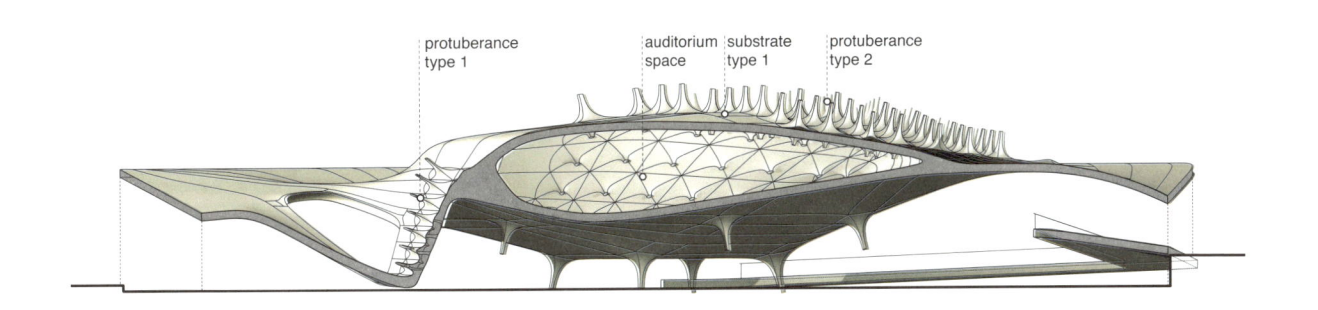

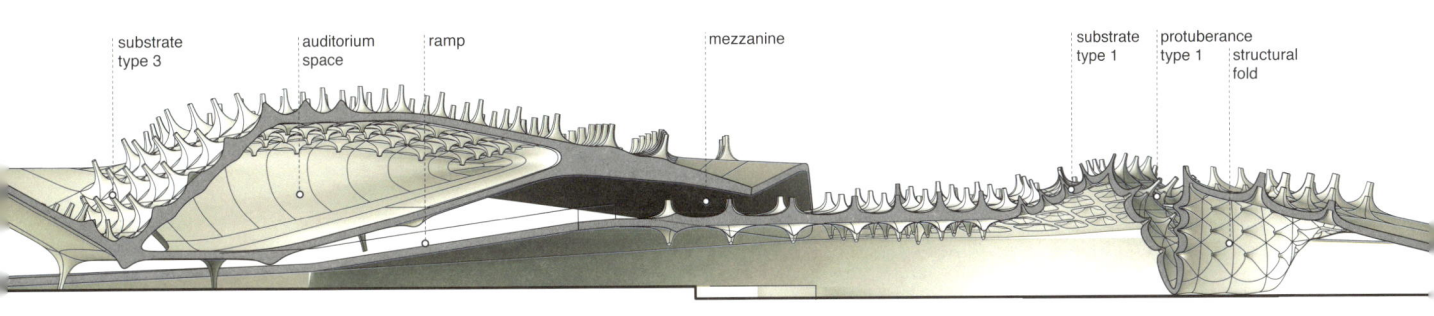

Sections

Above
Long section looking north showing auditorium space, ramp to mezzanine, exhibition area, and office area.

Below
Short section looking into auditorium space from east.

Not Garden

Karen M'Closkey and Keith VanDerSys

In western cultures, ornament was exiled for a large part of the twentieth century, rejected by many modernists as an outmoded means of expression, irrelevant and wasteful in light of emerging technologies of mass-production and the social needs of the general population. When Christopher Tunnard, James Rose, and Garrett Eckbo jointly pummeled the Beaux Arts preoccupation with scenography, ornament in landscape lost its agency; it became associated with elitist taste culture and social correctness (décor, decorum, decoration). Instead, these mid-century modern landscape architects constructed a doctrine of practicality that relied on the analysis of site and program as the basis for shaping space. Hence, the masks of ornament were replaced by the supposed transparency of utility.

In *Gardens in the Modern Landscape*, Tunnard opens the section on "Art and Ornament" with a familiar quote from architect Adolf Loos: "Progress in taste goes hand in hand with the elimination of ornament in everyday things."[1] While Tunnard would not go so far as Loos in associating ornament with degeneracy, they both saw the use of ornament as a gesture to past ages and claimed that it was "natural" that it should fall away with a proper emphasis on function and efficiency.[2] This emphasis on economy of means is echoed by landscape architect James Rose, who states that massing plants together is inefficient and "unscientific." Rather, he argues that the use of individual specimens is a more resourceful delineator of space because, by using all sides of the plant, fewer plants are needed.[3] In another essay, Rose banishes ornament to the annals of history: "ornamentation with plants in landscape design to create 'pictures' or picturesque effect means what ornamentation has always meant: the fate call of an outworn system of aesthetics."[4] Similarly, Garret Eckbo notes:

> The naïveté of the pictorial approach to landscape design has been its persistent clinging to vertical picture planes: the terminal feature, the focal point—and the horizontal picture planes: the garden pattern.[5]

Thus, these designers denigrate pattern and ornament for privileging static vision and surface rather than inhabitable volume and space: landscapes for viewing rather than "landscapes for living." This is not to say that surface effects were dismissed outright; rather, they were desirable so long as they expressed *inherent* qualities (truth to materials). Tunnard uses the example of concrete whose appealing sparkling effect is achieved because it was treated with a sealant to prevent slipperiness and therefore came about as a result of necessity.[6]

Some of these criticisms were not new. Seventeenth century garden designer André Le Nôtre, who took no issue with the axial focal point, is said to have disliked parterres for the same reasons, namely that one can only "walk through them with their eyes" and that they were best suited for nannies who could view them from the

Facing Page
Not Garden (detail of surface)

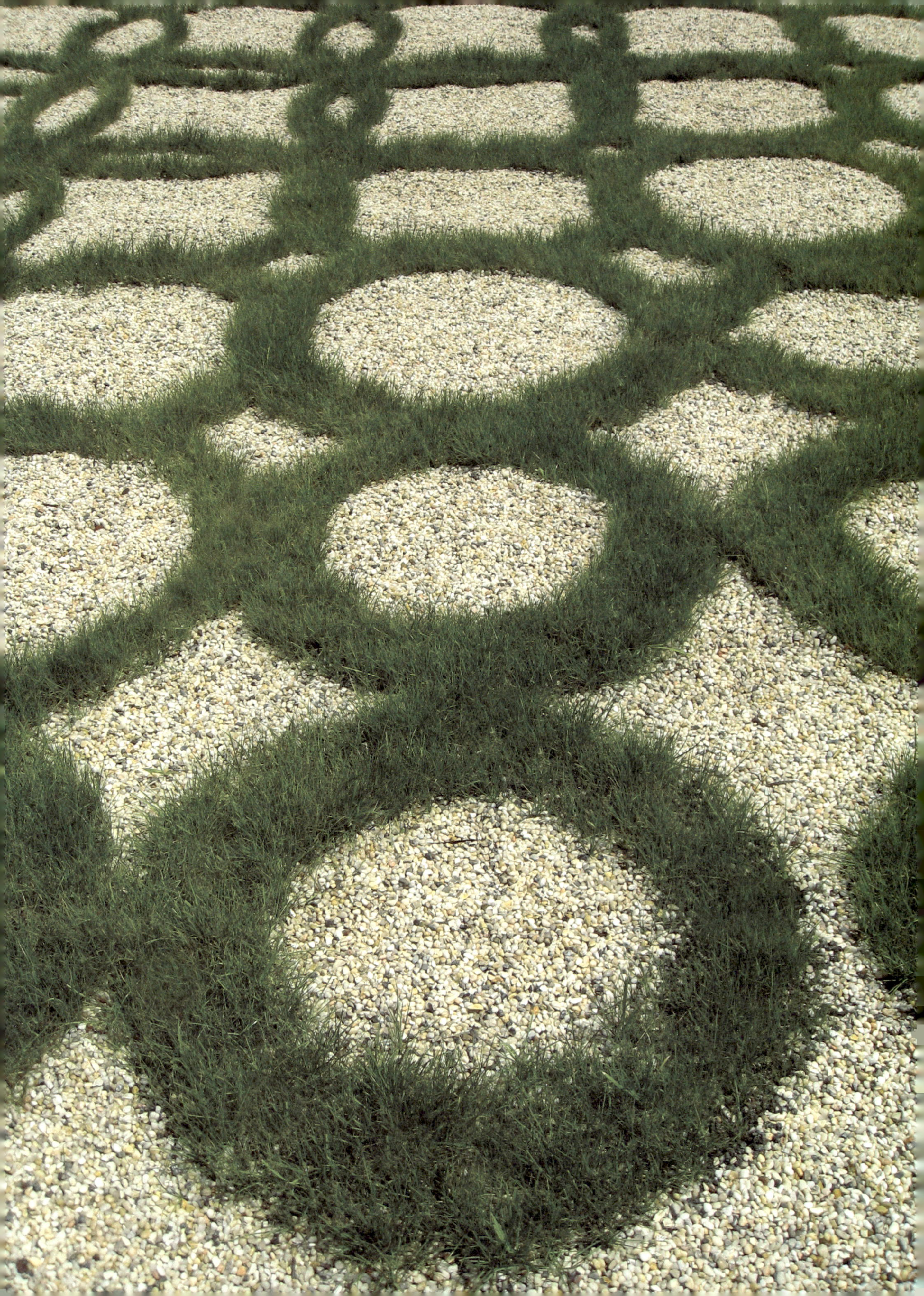

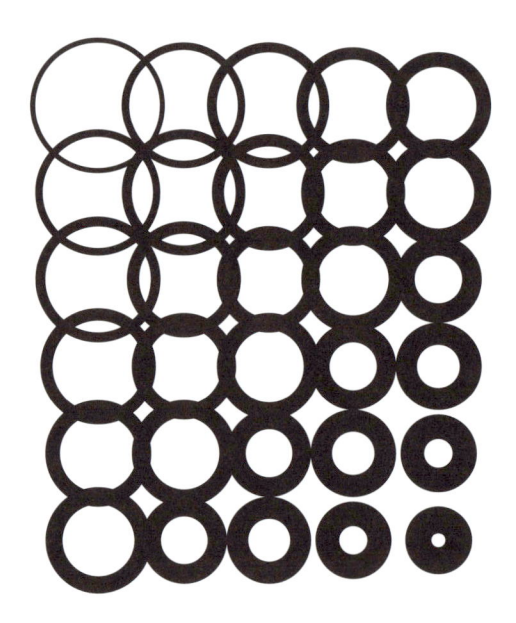

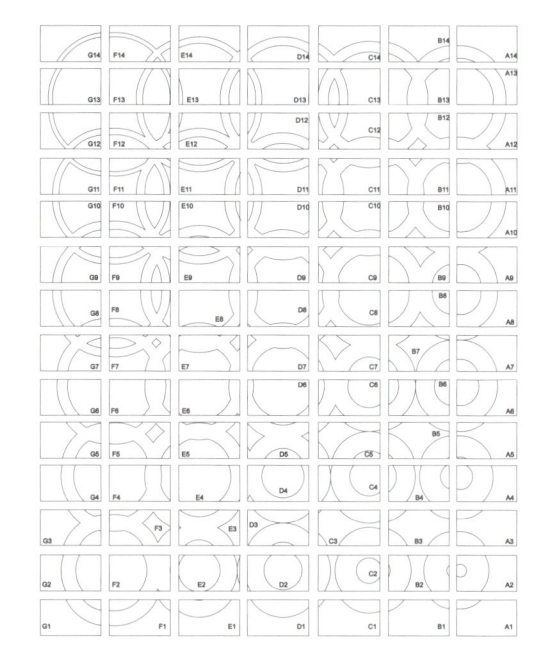

Not (pattern)

Not (template)

Not Garden (installation)

286   **Not Garden** Karen M'Closkey & Keith VanDerSys

second floor.[7] However, Tunnard and his colleagues went a step further. The problem for them was not simply that such garden patterns were visually biased—since these designers were certainly interested in color, light, form, etc.—but that their geometry was pre-determined, and inflexible, and thus presumably failed to take advantage of the particulars of place or program. Tunnard notes that "the present-day rule is to adapt the site to fit the designer's technique, and not the technique to fit the site, as should surely be the case."[8]

The rigor of a site-based, program-based design process still predominates today. Organization is typically "found" through various procedures of mapping and measure, or based on programmatic or ecological function. Though today's adherents to logistical, operational, or infrastructural approaches to landscape would not position their work under a functionalist paradigm, there are similarities with the modernist position: projects emphasizing ornament or pattern are met with suspicion. They are considered too reminiscent of pictorial approaches that landscape architects have tried to squelch since the middle of the last century.[9] In this view, ornament is seen in opposition to site and program; it is something *applied to* the site rather than *derived from* it. But if there is anything we have learned from process-based methods, it is that context matters and, in some contexts, a pictorial approach is in fact a site-specific response.

Vacancy offers one such example. It is a condition that has received much attention given that our shrinking cities are full of formerly inhabited sites that now lie abandoned. Certainly these sites must be re-imagined in logistical or infrastructural terms, where the patchwork of holes is considered in aggregate for future rehabilitation and development, stormwater infrastructure, food production, etc. But with an abundance of vacant land, there is ample room for localized responses that are not systemic, administratively complex, or dependent on being filled with a specific program. Philadelphia is a perfect laboratory for experimenting with such approaches given its immense stock of vacant land (over 60,000 properties). Approximately 3,000 abandoned lots have been cleaned and planted over the past seven years through the *Neighborhood Transformation Initiative* (2002). This interim land-management program has provided neighborhoods with relatively low-cost ways to lessen unsanitary conditions and garbage dumping on abandoned sites.

The current 'cleaning and greening' strategy involves re-grading, planting several trees, and installing a lawn with a perimeter picket fence. This is a justifiable approach for handling the vast acreages of un-taxable properties; however, the response is limited by the default towards abstraction via the uniform, unarticulated lawn surface. To look at an alternative, we built a test-plot in West Philadelphia in order to evaluate the versatility and performance of geo-textiles (weed-control barrier) as a subsurface design and maintenance strategy. Our goal was to derive an efficient way to achieve the same *aesthetics of care* that the lawn typifies yet with potentially more visual richness and lower maintenance. We found this was achievable by custom-cutting patterns out of the geotextile. Working to promote imageability, our proposed strategy for addressing vacant lots is unapologetically graphic; its function is simply to *get noticed*.

Playing off of the traditional knot-garden's intricate geometric patterns, we enlisted ornament as an approach to address vacancy. Knot-gardens, which became widespread in the sixteenth century, were comprised of repetitive, overlapping figures contained within a square plan. Our first proposal, *Not Garden,* is a low-maintenance interpretation of the traditional knot. In a twenty-foot by twenty-foot square plot, we applied a pattern of circles that align in a grid along their center-points but incrementally change size and thickness. The overall pattern transitions from independent to overlapping figures. While there are various debates about the distinction between pattern and ornament, our project stays near to the definition that characterizes the traditional knot garden, which is an ornamental garden whose pattern is based on figural repetition and adherence to geometric rules.[10] Within this definition, a distinction between a simple pattern—a gridded surface—and an ornamental pattern is that the latter has the added characteristic of a repetition that either undergoes a transformation—scaling, rotation, reflection—or is based on a recognizable motif or figure—for example, a flower.[11] *Not Garden* uses the former approach, and the second test, *Not Again,* uses both strategies as a means of display.

Pattern 01 Pattern 02 Pattern 03 Pattern 04

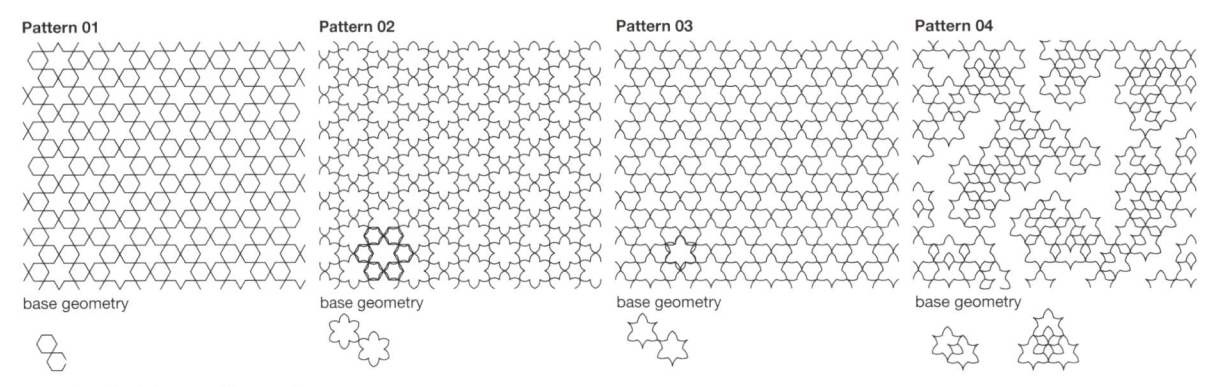

base geometry base geometry base geometry base geometry

Not Again (cluster diagram)

Not Again (bloom pattern)

Not Again (surface detail)

288　**Not Garden** Karen M'Closkey & Keith VanDerSys

Using laser-cutter fabrication, we made templates to precisely cut the patterns out of the geotextile. After the site was cleaned and prepped, the precut fabric was laid on the soil, seeded, and the fabric—the un-seeded area—was covered with gravel. After several weeks, the lawn circles of *Not Garden* began to fill in. (*Not Again* will fill in spring 2010.) Using a common, though typically invisible, material in such a manner has the potential to produce diverse configurations with very low-investment, effort, installation expertise, or long-term care; therefore, the *Not Gardens* combine new technology, efficiency, utility and truth to materials, all expressed in a surface pattern. In the context of an abandoned site, form is the function—a more visible and controlled space appears more cared for.

The mid-century modernists cited earlier suggested that ornament was the fetish of surface. While it is true that ornament resides in, is indeed inseparable from, surface, it can be more than skin deep. Ornament is a technique for making spatial and functional order more visible and, therefore, more receptive. Ornament transforms utility into something beyond mere necessity.[12] Once denigrated and dismissed, ornament's reconstitution can shape new forms of expression and engagement arising out of today's mediums.

Endnotes

1 Christopher Tunnard, *Gardens in the Modern Landscape* (London: The Architectural Press, 1948 [1938]); p. 96.
2 Tunnard, *Gardens*, p. 96.
3 James Rose, "Why Not Try Science?" (1939), reprinted in Marc Treib, ed. *Modern Landscape Architecture: A Critical Review* (Cambridge: MIT Press, 1993); p. 77.
4 James Rose, "Plants Dictate Garden Forms" (1938), reprinted in Marc Treib, ed. *Modern Landscape Architecture: A Critical Review* (Cambridge: MIT Press, 1993); p. 72.
5 Garrett Eckbo, *Landscape for Living* (Santa Monica: Hennessey + Ingalls, 2002; Originally published by New York: Architectural Record, 1950); p. 68.
6 Tunnard, *Gardens*, p. 102.
7 As reported by Saint-Simon on Le Nôtre. See Thierry Mariage, *The World of André Le Nôtre* (Philadelphia: University of Pennsylvania Press, 1999); p. 85.
8 Tunnard, *Gardens*, p. 94. Obviously, they were not against composition per se, but they preferred cubist-inspired, collage-based overlays that were a technique believed to be more responsive to site conditions and program.
9 Of course not all American landscape architects since then have felt this way. Beginning in the late 1970s and early 1980s, most notably in the work of landscape architects Peter Walker, Martha Schwartz, and Ken Smith, the graphic emphasis of landscape was, and is, critical. They all use a key technique of traditional ornament—repetition—and Schwartz and Smith also use garden ornaments (frogs, plastic flowers, etc.). However, they all frame their work as being from minimalist or pop art lineages rather than an attempt to reframe ornament per se.
10 In the texts by Tunnard et al., the terms are used somewhat interchangeably in the authors' criticisms of the Beaux-Arts style. More recent debates in architecture state that pattern is "one of ornament's chief incarnations" [Robert Levitt, "Contemporary Ornament: the Return of the Symbolic Repressed," in *Harvard Design Magazine* 28 (Spring/Summer 2008): 1]; and that in the "history of ornament there is an abundance of figural repetition, almost to the point that repetition seems thematic to the very essence of ornament..." in Kent Bloomer, *The Nature of Ornament: Rhythm and Metamorphosis in Architecture*, (New York, London: W.W. Norton & Co, 2000); p.37. Others argue that ornament resides in surface but is not necessarily expressed as pattern (Jeffrey Kipnis, "The Cunning of the Cosmetics" *Du* 5 (706)(May 2000); pp. 6-9.
11 This in line with some of the examples by Bloomer (see citation above) and also Thomas Beeby, "The Grammar of Ornament, Ornament as Grammar," *VIA* 3 (1977); pp. 10 – 29.
12 Bloomer, *The Nature of Ornament*, p. 33. "Utility authorizes and fuels ornament, which, in turn, awakens mundane objects from the necessity of their everyday work."

An Ornament of Sustainability,
or, How Do I Keep This Damn Orchid Alive?
Lily Jencks

An edifice becomes a kind of spectacle whose scenes seem to change...A series of animated nature.

Quatrémere de Quincy, *Dictionnaire d'Architecture* (1788-1825)

A suitable structure may keep a man cool in summer, but no structure will make him warmer in sub-zero temperatures. A suitable structure may defend him from the effects of glaring sunlight, but there is no structure that can help him to see after dark... Power has always had to be consumed for some part of every year, some part of every day. Fires have had to be burned in winter, lamps lit in the evening, muscle power for fans, water power for fountains used in the heat of the day.

Reyner Banham, *The Architecture of the Well-Tempered Environment* (1969)

We live in an era in which sustainability has become *the* global value driving rhetoric, politics, and architecture.[1] In this period of optimization, where efficiencies dictate design, what is the place of architectural ornament? Ornament's excesses seem contrary to sustainability's principles of efficiency. Ornament crystallizes social dreams and communicates ideals not explicit in expressions of function or utility. I am going to argue for an unlikely proposition: that architectural ornament can make a difference to sustainability. In this era of optimized design, architects must insist on the appreciation of that which cannot be measured by quantifiable standards alone. Quantifiable standards of high-tech sustainability can be complemented by the humanist goals of architectural ornament. Moreover, ornament has the power to ensure that sustainable architecture becomes an enduring movement by appealing to all human instincts and desires.

In this search for an "ornament of sustainability," we must be careful to distance ourselves from an instrumentalization of either art or ecology. This sustainability mandate must not turn ornament into a political ideology. It is true that the ability of ornament to quantatively lessen human induced-climate change is infinitesimal, but its efficacy in the cultural shift that sustainability requires to be successful makes it a potent territory for contemporary architects. *Orskid-in* is my proposal for an architectural ornament of the sustainable age.

Situated on the façade of a building, *Orskid-in* performs as the climate-modulating interface between interior and exterior, and as the public face of the building. Borrowing the tripartite argument of Felix Guattari's sustainable philosophy as described in *The Three Ecologies*, these performances are designed on three scales: from the experience of a visiting subject (the subjective experience), the relations between those subjects (social relations), and the building in the environment (the environment).[2] Guattari argues that only "an ethico-political articulation—which I call *ecosophy*—between the three ecological registers (the environment, social relations and human subjectivity) would be likely to clarify [the ecological disasters of the twenty-first century]."[3] Articulating sustainable principles through these three

Facing page
Orskid-in
Cloud forest interior view

291

Figure 1
Reyner Banham's Standard of Living Pack
A transparent blob with an excess of high-tech appliances to enable human habitation; this is architecture-stripped-bare to its engineered essentials. Banham's focus on architecture experienced as an environment focuses on the thermo-dynamics of the building, the haptic experience of visitors, and denies the power of the augmented surface of a facade.

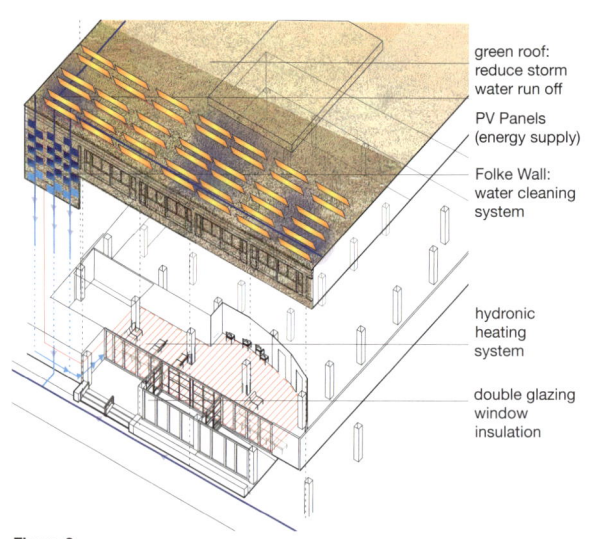

Figure 2
Presbyterian Hospital LEED-Certified Add-Ons
Radiant temperature modulation in the form of hydronic tubing decreases the energy used by the existing convection systems. This hydronic tubing creates the chairs in which people now sit. The lighting system is replaced by low voltage LED lights color-calibrated for human occupation that varies through out the day, and powered by new solar panels positioned on the roof. This technological solution quantifiably reduces energy use, but does not address the experience of the visitor.

criteria, I believe *Orskid-in* would create an affective appeal to a visitor's understanding of their place in nature, while also acting upon a more global notion of ecology, just like species evolution within an environment, where both organism and environment mutually modify and 'co-evolve' one with the other.

Ornament's action upon the realm of human subjectivity, through the senses of a creative individual is Guattari's first register. A visitor's subjective experience is acted upon through perceptual senses—eyes, ears, nose especially—and through the body, and this experience can be modulated to create affects in the visitor that highlight the interaction of body and environment. Social relations, Guattari's second register, are those ties that bind humans together, most often through different forms of communication. Ornament gains meaning through interaction and communication within the many social relations that make up public space. Due to ornament's specific historical role as a possible medium for communicating meaning, the design of sustainable ornament would communicate the interaction of a species within their environment. To complete Guattari's sustainable registers, sustainable ornament also acts on the environment, to re-relate building and environment. This means engaging architecture's energy-using processes over time, to lessen the carbon-footprint of a building. Designing *Orskid-in* through its engagement with this trio of registers achieves an architecture that appeals to the sum of human desires, becoming sustaining and sustainable for generations to come.

Orskid-in proposes the re-design of a hospital facade. The site for healing humans is the site for addressing the 'sick' relationship between planet and mankind. I chose the hospital as space of precise climatic modulation with a sterile purity because it typifies technologically-advanced Modern architecture. *Orskid-in* dirties this high-tech space with the humanist impulses that are the domain of ornament.

The existing north facing façade of the Presbyterian Hospital in Northwest Philadelphia was chosen as a site with a desperate need to be reconsidered for its occupants. The interior program is a waiting room: a place where people sit for hours with little to do but wait and think. Waiting conditions are dire. The concrete and glass façade faces a busy polluted street, the interior temperature fluctuates with seasonal extremes, the television blares, and one plant languishes in the corner. The embodied energy in an existing building is worth saving, as we know the environmentalist's maxim that the most sustainable building is the one already built. However, the interaction between that building, the surrounding environment, and the people who wait, is worth reconsidering.

An Architecture of Ornamented Climate

For Reyner Banham, architecture is concerned with the manipulation of climate to enable habitation. In *The Architecture of the Well-Tempered Environment*, Banham posits the campfire as a model of architecture in which gradients of microclimates allow for different programs. The gradient model "dissolves what architecture has been made of to date: customary forms," there are no formal barriers delineating space, but rather modulations of heat, light, and humidity.[4]

Banham's systems-driven and anti-iconic agenda could seem antagonistic to ornamental explorations. His own answer was "the standard of living pack": a transparent glass blob of engineered essentials, decidedly high-tech, minimal and bare. (Fig. 1) Banham's model treated architecture as a thermodynamic system that uses energy management to enable habitation. Since 48% of U.S. greenhouse gas emissions are generated by commercial and industrial buildings, sustainable architecture also focuses on energy use, aiming to limit energy consumption of a building, by using energy saving mechanisms and stripping away anything superfluous to climatic equilibrium.[5] This is architecture as engineered thermo-dynamics, driven by efficiencies.

Any architecture that engages in the sustainability debate must seriously address and reduce the energy used by buildings. But it must also address how buildings interact with the environment, working to restructure how buildings and environments interact. It is also important to recognize that this high-tech, quantifiably sustainable approach of LEED-certified add-ons has lost significant power by not exciting the experience of a feeling and thinking visitor. Sustainable architecture must not only be about a building's interaction with an environment, but also the interactive registers of a visiting subject, and the relationships between those subjects.

To address the environmental register, *Orskid-in* reduces the energy used by the Presbyterian Hospital by reengineering the climate control system into a new ornamental façade of the building. (Fig. 2) These add-ons realize a quantifiable reduction in energy use, but acting alone they are not sustainable. Banham's idea of architecture dematerialized into climate modulation provides a richer potential than his own transparent "standard pack." His work marks a shift explained by theorist Helene Furján as "'a transition from imagining space as an abstract thing, which is framed, to imagining space as matter itself' a shift in which atmosphere becomes the very matter of architecture."[6] This shift from architecture as a formalizing element towards an architecture of atmospheres turns the debate back towards our first register of sustainable ornament, the haptic experience of the human subject. Architecture becomes a 'cloud,' a climate experienced by all of a visitor's senses. The creation of architectural atmosphere is thus a material that can be put to ornamental—that is to say multi-faceted, meaningful and affective—effect.

Orskid-in uses the network of hydronic piping, which provides the new low-energy climate control system, to blur the façade into a thick atmosphere with different environmental qualities. The effects of climate controls such as misting/dehumidifying, heating/cooling, lighting modulations, etc., create specific atmospheric affects experienced by the visitor. The formal barrier between interior and exterior is thickened into a series of modulated climate zones that envelope the visitor. The hydronic piping that creates these climate modulations is bent to become the new seating areas of the waiting room, creating pockets of seating within the façade with variable degrees of atmospheric effect. For example, the cloud forest climate area is a lightly-misted seating area with a cool atmosphere of dappled light. The piped seats lower the temperature, while light-misting adds moisture to the air and the lighting is modulated to a variously dark green-blue, providing a seating area ideal for use in the summer heat, or perhaps those patients with high temperatures who desire to sleep while they wait.

An additional system of pipes siphons water off the roof (decreasing storm water run-off), which is used as irrigation for growing plants within the thickened atmospheric facade. The climate modulations not only create atmospheric effect, they have been put to productive use to create climatic-gardens.

Rich Ground   293

Figure 3
Patrick Blanc's Vertical Garden
Musée Quai Branly, Paris. Vertical garden technology provides the vision of a more sustainable and green future. However, the excessive infrastructure required to keep these plants alive and the resultant puddles on the side walk reveal a different attitude to nature's resources.

Figure 4
Arid Climate Seating of *Orskid-in*
Orskid-in uses an adaptation to the hospital's existing climate control systems to create climate-gardens. These gardens are inhabited by patients who are waiting for appointments as the hydronic tubing creates new seats within the thick atmosphere of the new ornamented facade.

Green Walls: All Metaphor No Matter

The use of living matter in architectural facades has become a strong trend in recent years as issues of 'green' living and sustainability have become fashionable. Recent living wall technologies have fulfilled the public's desire for a vision of building 'green.' To the layman, they easily communicate the idea of a more sustainable future where humans live closely with nature. This technique of 'greening walls' enters the realm of social relations as a sustainable icon. By directly using living matter, green walls do not rely on elitist modes of representation, but on a seeming hybridization of the easily recognizable eighteenth-century dialectic of nature and culture.

However, while communication is a meaningful goal, operating in the category of ecology Guattari identified as social relations, these façades are not meaningfully sustainable. Like 'lipstick on a pig,' green walls are the ultimate in 'green-wash,' superficial eco-cosmetics: a quick visual that politicians can point to as a sign that we are moving towards a culture that lives more closely with nature. Their visual melding of grey and green creates an easy and obvious meaning that popular culture has quickly identified. But the 'green' neither challenges nor merges with the 'grey', but sits meekly on its surface. The reality, then, is that the infection of the natural elements into the architecture is superficial. Appliqué green-walls maintain the dichotomy of 'nature' and 'culture.' They also suck resources away from the building, requiring an infrastructure of irrigation and drainage. Actually increasing the carbon footprint of the building, they insist on a future where nature is exploited to further political goals. (Fig. 3) We might understand the plants used in these types of green walls as decoration rather than ornamentation. The plants, like medals or badges worn as decorations of honor, portray status and credibility. Designed to be seen from the street, they are symbols privileging the gaze of passers-by. Maintaining the flat picture plane of the façade, in privileging the gaze of the viewer over the bodily experience of a visitor, these green walls do not exploit a visitor's sensory subjective experience.

The living wall is a story that our sustainable-minded society longs for: the hybridization of landscape and architecture, living and artificial, interior and exterior, subject and experience, sustainable ornament and ornamented sustainability. By reworking the green wall through Banham's consideration of the façade as a zone of climate modulation and the building as climate

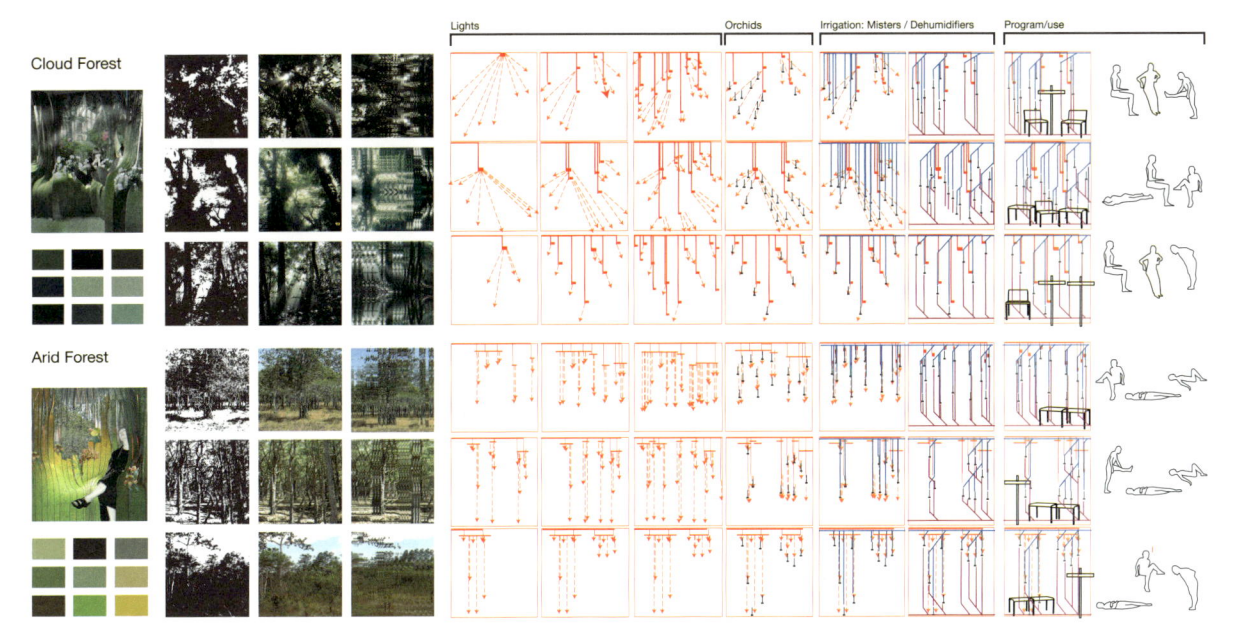

Figure 5
Hydronic Piping, LED, and Planting Diagrams for *Orskid-in*
The climate gardens are simulations of existing climates. These existing forests are quantatively analysed for light levels, air humidity, and temperature. Experiential effects were also analysed, such as the different qualities of dabbled light due to varied foliage in an arid versus a cloud forest, the varieties of color tones in each climate, and the striation effect of the different tree girths in each forest. The hydronic piping, lighting, and planting plan are designed to simulate the experience in each climate. The resulting layout provides dimensions for different activities in the waiting room such as sleeping, sitting, stretching, etc.

modulating system, the 'green' of *Orskid-in* infects the flat elements of the façade, and grows from the systems that control the building's climate. (Fig. 4) *Orskid-in*'s 'grey' becomes fertile ground for the 'green.' The building's systems that provide light and temperature modulation—the energy-processes of the building—are simultaneously the dynamic system for the living matter. Capitalizing on and elaborating existing micro-climates within a room, *Orskid-in*'s new gardens are simulations of existing environments around the world: a Moroccan arid forest, a Pennsylvanian temperate forest, and an Argentinean cloud forest. The three different climates chosen for simulation also have potential to lessen a patient's symptoms with the modulations of humidity, heat, and light. (Fig. 5) Unlike typical green wall technology, *Orskid-in* emphasizes the haptic experience of the climatic interaction between nature and architecture, while using the actual climate control mechanisms of the building, rather than its own infrastructure. (Fig. 6) As the hydronic and irrigation piping provide new seating arrangements within the waiting room, the visitors sit enveloped within the new climates. In the cloud forest seating area the damp earth smells fertile, in the arid forest the dry air and white-light increase the intensity of the heated seats. While using the green wall's obvious visual icon for a more sustainable future where humans live within nature's cycles, *Orskid-in* intensifies the atmospheric and climatic experience of that interaction, fully engaging all of the senses of a visiting human subject.

Brief Notes on Ornament

Ornament is often confused with surface-augmentation techniques such as geometry, pattern, and decoration. (Figs. 7-9) While ornament may be composed of any combination of these, its potent—and controversial—role in design is as a mode to communicate meaning. An abridged history of ornamental design reveals the lineage that *Orskid-in* inhabits. Architectural ornament is understood as that which is additional to primary function and creates affects through surface modulation, thereby creating a contemporary and narrativistic engagement between matter and culture.

Ornament's ability to communicate once relied on a lineage of signs and signifiers that were recognizable to an elite public well versed in Western art history. Owen Jones' comprehensive survey of ornament highlighted an understanding of the grammatical use of specific motifs designed through stylization.[7] Gottfried Semper's ornamental forms were tied to value and meaning in

Rich Ground

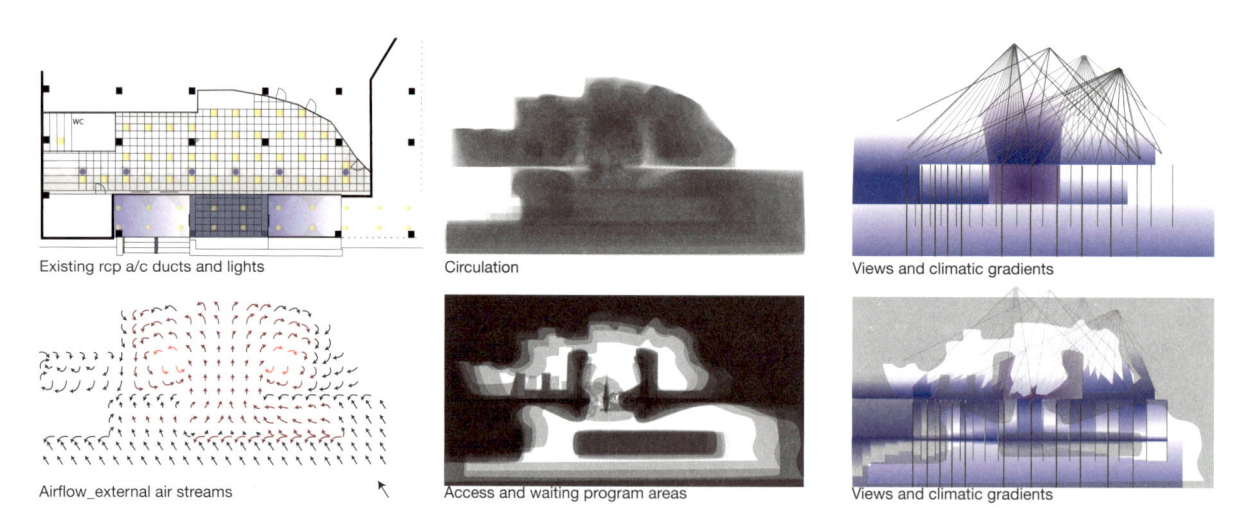

Figure 6
Analysis of Existing Building Conditions of *Orskid-in*
The places for interaction with the thermodynamic systems of the waiting room were mapped. The existing climatic gradients within the room were measured to find conditions that could be elaborated on, or would have to be balanced.

The circulation and view corridors were established to ensure the waiting room functions would not be compromised. This provided a massing study for the new seating arrangements and points of contact with the existing services.

a significance accumulated through use over time.[8] It was partly the Modernist desire for democratization that tried to strip architecture of referential ornament. However, even its white walls, with their overtones of truth and purity, were themselves a meaningful style with a worrying lack of self-awareness.[9] Venturi, Scott-Brown's application of ornament, as decoration on the shed, again showed architects falling back on an model of semantics that priviledged the visual experience.[10] This brief history shows the privileging of visual symbolism in ornament's history, with a de-emphasis of other non-visual modes of communication. It is no surprise that we know this story of ornament through many textbooks of history. But while we can recognize this lineage as important, we must also realize what it is lacking, or even repressing.

In a reaction against the desire to communicate through symbolic or representational means, contemporary architect Farshid Moussavi, asks that ornament be justified by its form and affective function.[11] Moussavi states that the functional roles for ornament are "affects that seem to grow directly from matter itself. They build expressions out of an internal order."[12] However illuminating and powerful her argument, Moussavi here limits ornament to 'affective' pattern making, an art of internal logics with complex and emergent effects that make an impression upon a visitors senses. These impressions are affects that are interpreted by each individual visitor in particular ways according to their subjective state.[13] Moussavi goes on to explain that these affects "overcome the need to communicate through a common language, the terms of which may no longer be available. It is paradoxically in this way that building expressions remain resilient in time."[14]

For Moussavi, the resulting 'affect' of ornament is free from socially constructed symbolic languages. This is necessary because Moussavi believes our globalized culture does not share a common language, and cannot rely on future generations to understand the intended meaning. But affect is not only stimulation. Affect can also become meaningful, inviting judgment and understanding, whether it is part of the design intent or not, particularly as it enters into the public realm of political and social relations. The fashion for the green wall reveals this power. The tabloid alter-egos of iconic buildings, where Gherkins, Bird's Nests, and Cheese Graters compete for attention, plays directly to this social phenomena. The meaning that is created is occasionally haphazard and never the result of a pure or singular reading, but it does occur. As architect and theorist Robert Levitt argues in his essay, "Contemporary Ornament: The Return of the Symbolic Repressed," ornament is, and historically has been, a particular category of design that can engage in the recognition of form as symbolic and meaningful.[15]

Figure 7
Yokohama Ferry Terminal
Foreign Office Architect's *Yokohama Ferry Terminal*, 2002. FOA uses geometric surface modulation to enable the programming of the surface, from structure to playspace etc. This is not ornamental.

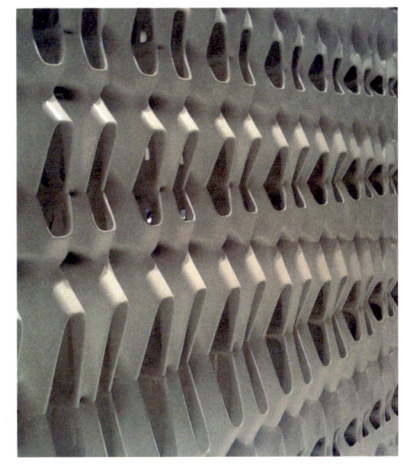

Figure 8
Migrating Formations
Contemporary Architecture Practice's wall exhibited at the Museum of Modern Art's exhibition *Home Delivery* uses a morphing pattern derived from structural and construction logics to create surface modulation. The resulting pattern is not ornament.

Figure 9
Eberswalde Library
Herzog and de Meuron's *Eberswalde Technical School Library*, 1999, creates surface iconography using images screen-printed on concrete. This is ornament as image, privileging the gaze of passers-by.

While Moussavi's argument is strong in readdressing the balance of ornament's history away from purely cognitive and symbolic uses of ornament, her denial of representational meaning, among the strategies employed by ornament, represses one of the strengths particular to this mode of design. This is not a return to the crisis of historical post-modernism, where only visual symbolic interpretation created ornamental meaning, but rather to create a celebration of multivalent meanings using forms that have a high degree of impact on both affect-driven perception, and cognition. It is important for designers to use the communicative potentials existing in both the visual and the affective experience of architecture over time, as fertile territory for ornamental meaning.

Orskid-in's ornament is that which is additional to primary function and creates affects and representational meaning. The affects and meanings are dependent on the interaction of the human subject, and gain potency in the discussion and communication between visitors. Meaning in architectural ornament is a social exercise. *Orskid-in* is not an ornamentation of symbolic form but an ornament of simulated and stimulating place. The climate gardens of *Orskid-in* are designed for meaningful ornamental effect: rather than creating arbitrary climates, these gardens simulate environments that exist around the world. The cloud forest is near Tafi del Valle in Argentina, the temperate forest is Woodbourne Forest in Pennsylvania, and a semi-arid forest in Southern Morocco. The system of piping, lighting, surface texture, colors, and living plant species recreates the forms and phenomenological experience of each type of climate. The environments chosen for simulation reveal the extreme climates where orchids, the most discerning of plant species, have adapted to flourish. The precise calibration of the climatic conditions necessary to keep orchids alive exaggerates the requirement for the precisely engineered performance of *Orskid-in*, while the simulation of the extreme climates show the marvelous adaptation possible in the evolution of a species with its environment. This process of ecology, revealed in the interaction and evolution of species plus environment, is the meaning of *Orskid-in*'s sustainable ornament.

Me-skin

Gilles Deleuze and Felix Guattari write about the processes of 'deterritorialization' and 'reterritorialization' that happen when a wasp lands on an orchid. They write, "The orchid deterritorializes by forming an image, a tracing of the wasp," in a process that causes the orchid flower to be displaced from its botanical 'territory' as defined by conceptual human language.[16] As the wasp lands on the flower it becomes part of the orchid's reproductive technique and tools, and takes on a different role and meaning from that originally assigned to it. Deleuze and Guattari explain this process

Section through Cloud Forest to Temperate Forest Section

- 2" felt (acoustics)
- LED light panel
- Water feed pipe
- Mister
- Orchid opening
- Structural pipe
- louver
- 2" felt (comfort)
- Drain pipe hydronic cooling
- Structural ribs

Interior | Exterior

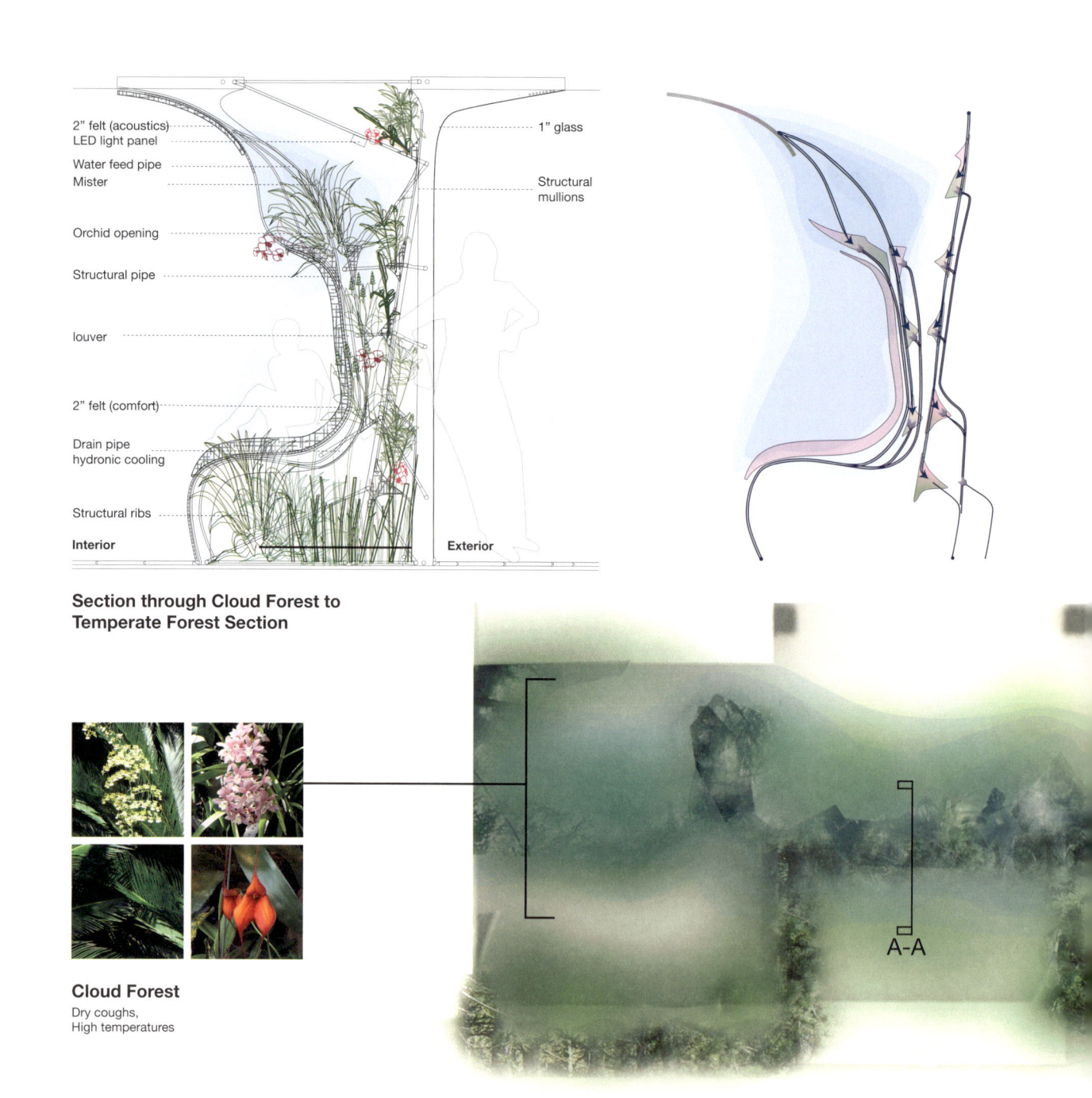

1" glass
Structural mullions

Cloud Forest
Dry coughs,
High temperatures

A-A

External Facade Elevation (Temperate Forest)

298 **An Ornament of Sustainability** Lily Jencks

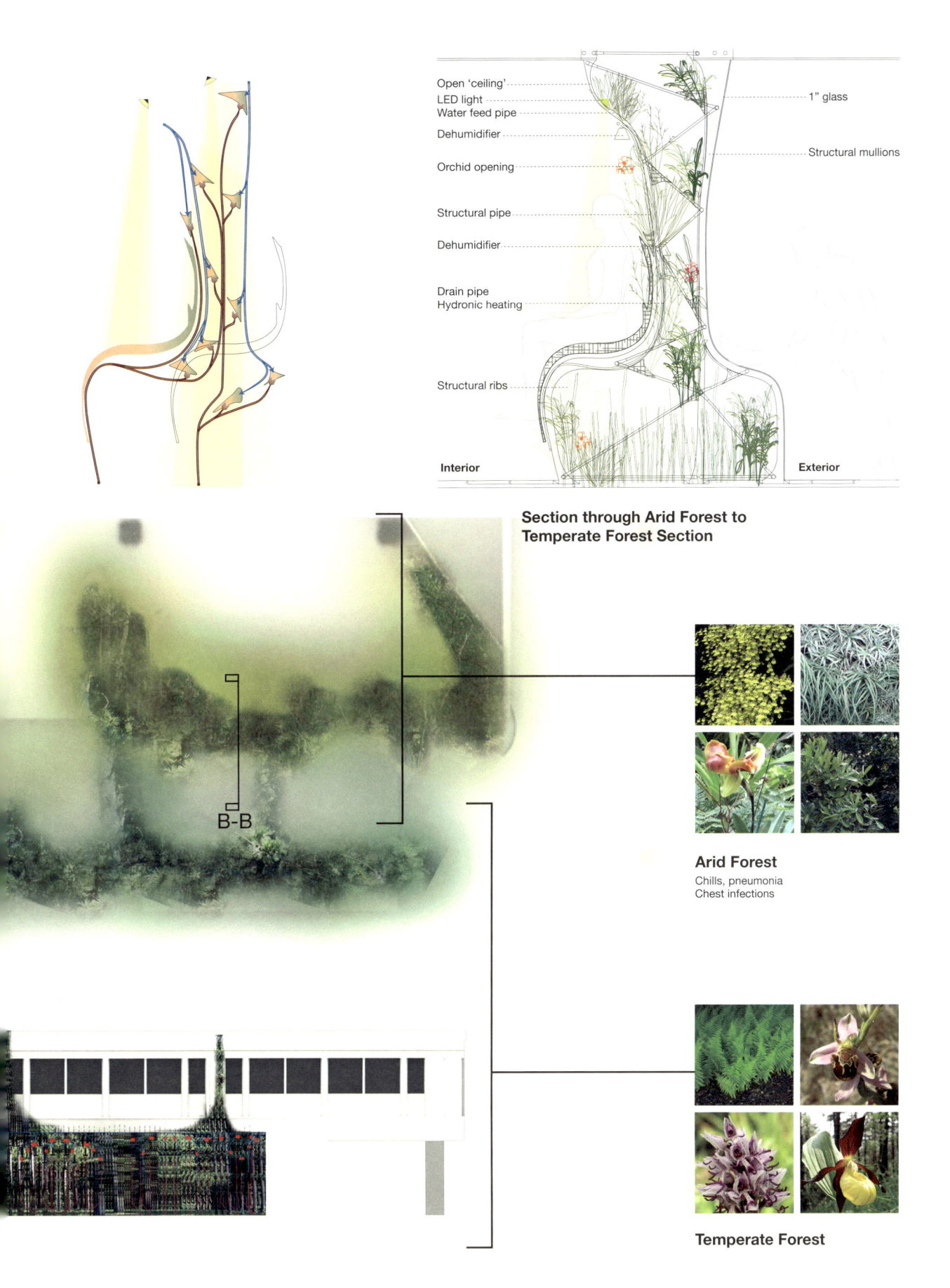

Open 'ceiling'
LED light
Water feed pipe
Dehumidifier

Orchid opening

Structural pipe

Dehumidifier

Drain pipe
Hydronic heating

Structural ribs

1" glass

Structural mullions

Interior　　　　　　　　　　　　　　　　　　Exterior

Section through Arid Forest to Temperate Forest Section

B-B

Arid Forest
Chills, pneumonia
Chest infections

Temperate Forest

Rich Ground　　299

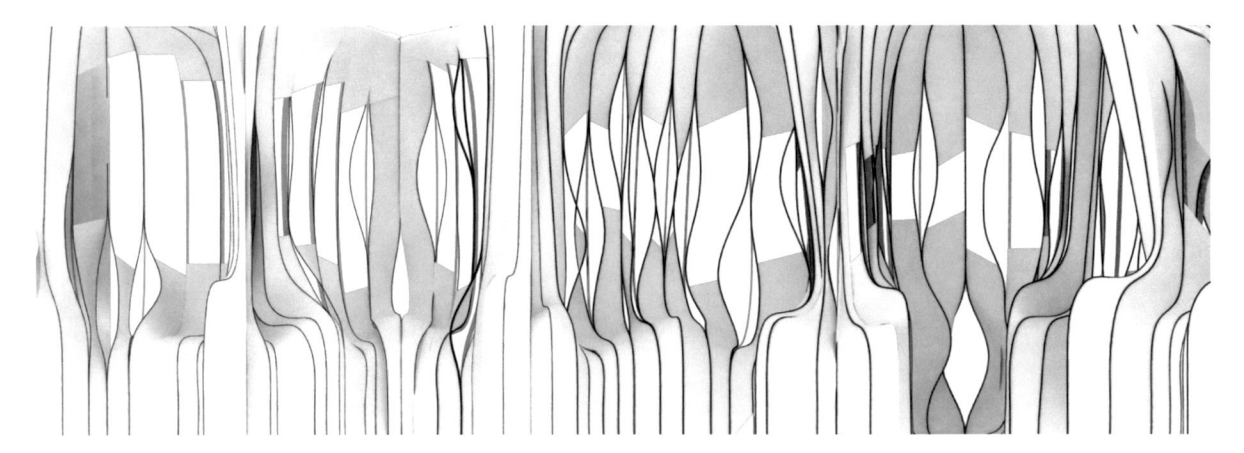

Interior Elevation for Cloud Forest Seats
Interior elevation showing seating for cloud forest. The dimensions of the vertical striations are taken from the girth of trees growing in Tafí del Valle in Argentina. The diagonal cuts through the chairs are quite large to simulate the large holes in the cloud forest canopy as trees, overladen with epiphytes and heavy with moisture tend to fall creating large gaps where light pours onto the forest floor.

as 'rhizomatic,' since it occurs from the multitude of possibilities inherent to different functions and flows of matter-energy, rather than emerging from a structural arrangement of functions essential to each organism. This discussion of the orchid and wasp is important here to emphasize both the fluidity of the material definitions between organisms and environments in the living world, as well as the multivalent meanings that flow through our thought processes by using one potent reference.

The use of an orchid is evasive of one politically and symbolic meaning, but full and open to many readings. The fluidity between organism and environment, as well as the multivalent meanings of the design, were explored in the design process with a narrative story to describe the experience of *Orskid-in*. *Me-skin* illustrates and makes obvious the experience of *Orskid-in* in lessening the boundaries that define organism and environment, allowing the subject to slip into the environment and vice versa. The effect is a fully immersive environment that vacillates between an insistence upon recognition, and being lost in the blurring with the visitor.

Sustainable Ornament Conclusion

Orskid-in blurs architectural form into atmospheric ornament through the performance of its climate-control systems. The first concern with creating a sustainable architecture emphasizes not what the Presbyterian facade looks like, but rather what it does. Banham is used to bring the subject and the environment into a calibrated relationship. How that façade is experienced is central: both what it looks like and how it feels, and eventually, what it means. The experience of *Orskid-in* puts the human body back into the dirty environment. It highlights the overlap between outside-body and inside-body and the cycle between an ecology, a human subject, and architecture as a mediating mechanism of climate control. The final effect is one in which the distinctions between man-made and natural, useful and superfluous, performance and ornament, subject and environment, interior and exterior, are not repressed as beyond the realm of architectural ornament, but constantly renegotiated and held in oscillation.

Orskid-in recognizes the realm of human subjectivity and creativity as the visiting individual's embodied experience is engaged. It also asks to be understood, to have meaning and cultural efficacy through simulation, the communicative potential of ornament. By insisting on the dynamic reciprocity between interior and exterior, and the performance of the human subject, the meaning of *Orskid-in* is not stagnant, nor based on a recognition of forms, but becomes embodied in the performance and engagement of the visiting subject. Humans are not machines, nor are we only ecologies; we are also sentient, cognitive beings. For sustainable architecture to become loved and cared for, to be sustained and sustaining throughout history, it must appeal to each of these modes of human interaction with the environment for centuries of use and pleasure.

Interior Elevation for Arid Forest

Interior elevation showing seating for arid forest. The dimensions of the vertical striations are taken from the girth of trees growing in Southern Morocco. The trees of this region tend to grow fast and have narrow trunks. The foliage here is consistent and fine allowing a constant light to reach the forest floor. This is simulated by allowing the top of the seats to be transparent.

Endnotes

1 Sustainable development was usefully defined by the Brundtland Commission as development that "meets the needs of the present without compromising the ability of future generations to meet their own needs." "Report of the World Commission on Environment and Development," United Nations General Assembly, Resolution 42/187, 11 December 1987. Retrieved: 2007-04-12.

2 See Félix Guattari, *The Three Ecologies* (London/New Brunswick: Athlone Press, 2000).

3 Guattari, *The Three Ecologies*, p. 23.

4 Reyner Banham, *The Architecture of the Well-Tempered Environment* (London: The Architectural Press, 1969), p. 312. "The greatest of all environmental powers is through, and the usefulness of thought, the very reason for applying radical intelligence to our problems, is precisely that it dissolves what architecture has been made of to date: customary forms."

5 Richard Moe, president of the National Trust for Historic Preservation, in a speech following his receipt of the National Building Museum's prestigious 2007 Vincent Scully Prize. See http://vimeo.com/6723601.

6 Helene Furján, "Eco-Logics," in *Softspace: From a Representation of Form to a Simulation of Space*, eds. Sean Lally and Jessica Young (London: Routledge, 2006), p.116. She is quoting Jesse Reiser, in *Crib Sheets: Notes on the Contemporary Architectural Conversation* (New York: Monacelli, 2005), p. 18.

7 See Owen Jones, *The Grammar of Ornament* (CITY: A & C Black Publishers Ltd, 2008).

8 See Gottfried Semper, *Style in the Technical and Tectonic Arts: Or, Practical Aesthetics*, trans. H. F. Mallgrave and M. Robinson (Santa Monica: The Getty Center for the History of Art and the Humanities, 2004).

9 See Mark Wigley, *White Walls, Designer Dresses: The Fashioning Of Modern Architecture* (Cambridge, Mass: MIT Press, 1995). In the denial of symbolism in modernism the white wall was able to stand in for overcoming a fashion while becoming a fashion itself.

10 See Robert Venturi, *Complexity and Contradiction in Architecture* (New York: The Museum of Modern Art Press, 1966).

11 See Farshid Moussavi: *The Function of Ornament* (Actar, Barcelona, 2008); and *Pattern: Ornament, Structure and Behavior*, eds. Andrea Gleiniger and Georg Vrachliotis (Basel: Birkhauser 2008).

12 Moussavi, *The Function of Ornament*, p. 4.

13 See Farshid Moussavi, "The Return of Nature: Organicism Contra Ornament," lecture presented Sept. 2009 at the GSD, Harvard University. A video recording of the lecture can be accessed at <http://sorcerer.design.harvard.edu/gsdlectures/f2009/nature6.mov>.

14 Moussavi, *The Function of Ornament*, p. 4.

15 See Robert Levitt, "Contemporary Ornament: The Return of the Symbolic Repressed," *Harvard Design Magazine* 28 (Spring/Summer 2008); pp. 70-85.

16 Gilles Deleuze and Felix Guattari, *A Thousand Plateaus, Capitalism and Schizophrenia* (Minneapolis, University of Minnesota Press, 1987); p. 10.

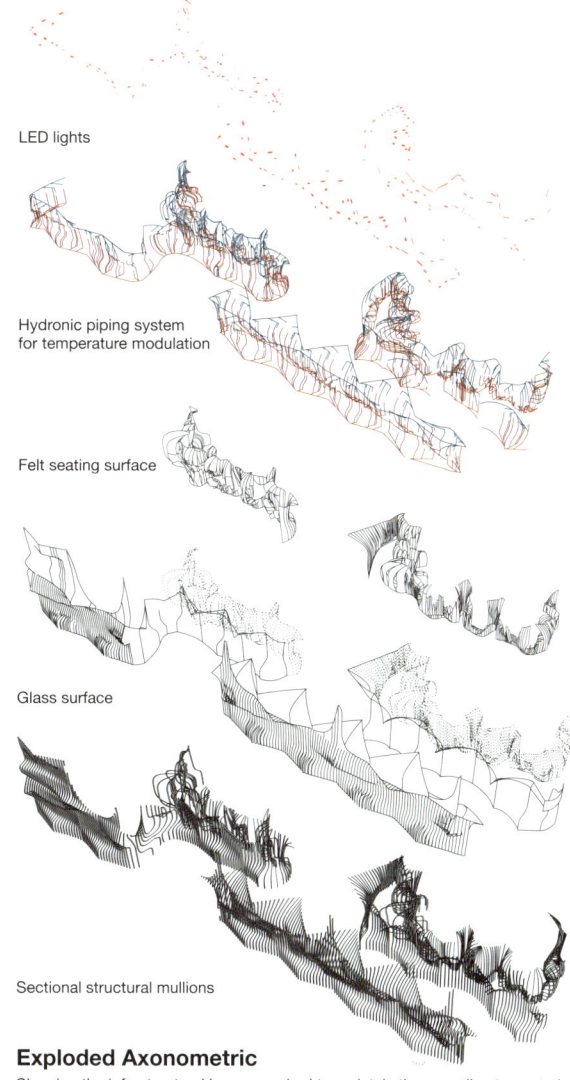

LED lights

Hydronic piping system for temperature modulation

Felt seating surface

Glass surface

Sectional structural mullions

Exploded Axonometric

Showing the infrastructural layers required to maintain the new climate control system, with rendered axonometric showing full system and environmental effects of *Orskid-in*.

Rich Ground

Contributors

Barry Bergdoll is the Philip Johnson Chief Curator of Architecture and Design at the Museum of Modern Art (MoMA), a position he has held since 2007. He was formerly Chair of the Department of Art History at Columbia University, where he taught nineteenth- and twentieth-century architectural history. He has organized, curated, and consulted on many exhibitions, including *Rising Currents: Projects for New York's Waterfront* (2010), *Home Delivery: Fabricating the Modern Dwelling* (2008), *Lost Vanguard: Soviet Modernist Architecture, 1922-32* (2007), and *Mies in Berlin* (with Terence Riley, 2001) at MoMA.

Alan Berger is an Associate Professor of Urban Design and Landscape Architecture at MIT, and the founder and director of the multi-disciplinary research unit Project for Reclamation Excellence (P-REX, www.theprex.net) at MIT, which focuses on the design and reuse of deindustrialized landscapes worldwide.

Anita Berrizbeitia is Professor of Landscape Architecture at the Graduate School of Design, Harvard University. Her research focuses on design theories of modern and contemporary landscape architecture, the productive aspects of landscapes, and Latin American cities and landscapes. She was awarded the 2005/2006 Prince Charitable Trusts Rome Prize Fellowship in Landscape Architecture. A native of Caracas, Venezuela, she studied architecture at the Universidad Simon Bolivar before receiving a BA from Wellesley College and an MLA from the GSD.

Megan Born is a landscape and architectural designer at James Corner Field Operations, and teaches at Yale University and the School of Design, University of Pennsylvania. A graduate of the University of Pennsylvania, she holds a dual M.Arch and MLA.

William W. Braham is an Associate Professor of Architecture in the School of Design, University of Pennsylvania, where he is Director of the Master of Environmental Building Design. He received an engineering degree from Princeton University and an M.Arch and Ph.D. Arch from the University of Pennsylvania, where he has taught graduate courses on ecology, technology, and design since 1988. He practices with the *TC Chan Center* and as a design consultant for *Ivalo Lighting* and *Lutron Electronics*. At the Chan Center, his most recent projects have been the Sustainability Plan, the Carbon Footprint, and Carbon Reduction Action Plan for the University of Pennsylvania. In 2006 he published a book called *Rethinking Technology: A Reader in Architectural Theory*, and in 2002 published a book called *Modern Color/Modern Architecture: Amédée Ozenfant and the genealogy of color in modern architecture* (www.modcolor.com). He is working on another book project, *Ecology, Technology, and Design,* and blogs at www.williambraham.net.

Lindsay Bremner was the chair of architecture in the School of Architecture and Planning at the University of the Witwatersrand in Johannesburg, South Africa and is currently a Professor of Architecture at Temple University in Philadelphia. She was a member of the Johannesburg Transitional Metropolitan Council between 1993 and 1997, and has lectured and published widely on Johannesburg, including the book *Johannesburg: One City, Colliding Worlds* (2004). She is an award-winning architect, most recently for her project for the rebuilding of the Sans Souci Cinema in Kliptown Soweto (with 26'10 South Architects). She contributed to the Rotterdam Architecture Biennale in 2005, the Venice Architecture Biennale in 2006 and was co-curator of exhibition *Johannesburg Emerging / Diverging Metropolis* at the Universita della Svizzera Italiana in Mendrisio in 2007.

Kim Brickley is an artist whose interest lies in the tension between the natural and the unnatural, drawn from her work on farms at a young age. She attended Carnegie Mellon University, Pittsburgh, where she focused on video and sound installations. After a series of family members and friends fell ill, her work focused on chemical or biological anatomical invasion. Her current work investigates daily pollutants in the human body. In 2009, she received her MFA from the Universtiy of Pennsylvania with a certificate in media design and a concentration in painting.

Case Brown is Senior Research Associate at P-REX, and an Assistant Professor at Clemson University.

Mark Campbell teaches at the Architectural Association and practices as an architect. He previously taught at the Cooper Union and worked as the Managing Editor of *Grey Room*. He is completing his PhD at Princeton University.

K.T. Anthony Chan is an architectural designer working at the Solomon R. Guggenheim Museum in the architectural management department for the BMW Guggenheim Lab (Cycle 1). He holds a M.Arch degree from the School of Design, University of Pennsylvania.

James Corner is Chair of the Department of Landscape Architecture at School of Design, University of Pennsylvania and principal of James Corner Field Operations, a landscape architectural and urban design practice based in New York City. His design projects, which include the *High Line* in New York and *Fresh Kills Park* in Staten Island, have won numerous awards and have been exhibited internationally. He received a B.A. in architecture and landscape architecture from Manchester Metropolitan University (1983) and a MLA and Urban Design Certificate from the University of Pennsylvania (1986). He is the author, with photographer Alex MacLean, of *Taking Measures Across the American Landscape* (1996), which received the AIA International Book of the Year Award and the ASLA Award of Honor.

He is also the editor of *Recovering Landscape: Essays in Contemporary Landscape Architecture* (1999).

Phillip M. Crosby is a registered architect and an Adjunct Assistant Professor of Architecture in the Tyler School of Art at Temple University. He is currently pursuing a Ph.D. in the history and theory of architecture and urbanism at the University of Pennsylvania where his research focuses on twentieth-century and contemporary urbanisms. He is writing a dissertation on the urban discourse of Team 10. In addition to his academic research in 2007 he founded the award-winning interdisciplinary design practice DUAL:workshop. He holds architectural degrees from the University of Florida and the Georgia Institute of Technology.`

Keller Easterling is an American architect, urbanist, writer, and teacher. She earned both her B.A. and M.Arch from Princeton University and has taught architectural design and history at Parsons The New School for Design, Pratt Institute, and Columbia University. She is currently Associate Professor of Architecture at Yale University. Easterling is one of the most important contemporary writers working on the issues of urbanism, architecture, and organization in relation to the phenomena commonly defined as globalization.

Ruth Erickson is currently pursuing a doctoral degree in the history of art at the University of Pennsylvania. Her research focuses on modern and contemporary art, with specific interest in video, film, institutional critique, and collectivity. She is completing a dissertation on political art collectives that emerged in Paris after May 1968 and received a Fulbright fellowship to support her research for the 2010-11 academic year. She has published in *Framework* and organized an interdisciplinary conference on animal studies in the humanities. From 2004-2007, she was Curator at the Firehouse Gallery, Burlington, VT, where she organized over two-dozen exhibitions.

Larissa Fassler is a Canadian visual artist based in Berlin, Germany. She completed her MFA at Goldsmiths College, University of London in 2003 and BFA at Concordia University in 1999. She has lived and worked in Berlin since 1999. In her work she examines the construct of public space and explores the impact of these complex built environments on those who move and inhabit the city.

Annette Fiero is an Associate Professor in Architecture at the School of Design, University of Pennsylvania. Her current research traces the radical technological speculation of the 1960s to present-day London. Fierro published *The Glass State: The Technology of the Spectacle, Paris 1981–1998* with the MIT Press in 2003.

Helene Furján is an Assistant Professor in the Department of Architecture at the School of Design, University of Pennsylvania, where she is Series Editor of viaBooks, Director of the *Conversations Series* of interdisciplinary debates, and Chair of the Architecture Lecture Committee. Her book, *'Glorious Visions': John Soane's Spectacular Theater*, was released by Routledge in 2011, and she has had essays and reviews published in journals including *Grey Room, AAFiles, Assemblage, Casabella, Journal of Architecture, JAE, Art Forum,* and *Interstices*. She published *Crib Sheets: Notes on the Contemporary Architectural Conversation* with Sylvia Lavin (2005), and has chapters in *Intimate Metropolis* (2008), *306090: Models* (2008), *Softspace* (2006), *Gen(H)ome* (2006), and *Performalism: Form and Function in Digital Architecture* (2008). She is working on a new book with Linda Taalman and Orkan Telhan investigating the history, theory, and design of "diagram thinking" in design fields; and Fine Fabling, a book examining differing British "Gothicisms" in the eigtheenth century.

Future Cities Lab is an interdisciplinary design and research collaborative bridging architecture and urbanism with material sciences, robotics and engineering. FCL was initiated in 2004 by architects Jason Kelly Johnson and Nataly Gattegno. They were most recently the 2009 New York Prize Fellows at the Van Alen Institute in New York City, and also served as the 2008-9 Oberdick and Muschenheim Architecture Research Fellows at the University of Michigan. Both Johnson and Gattegno graduated from Princeton University. They hold full-time faculty positions at the California College of the Arts and have taught at the University of Virginia, the University of Pennsylvania and UC Berkeley, leading studios and research seminars in design, ecology, landscape urbanism, and advanced technologies. They have exhibited and published their work world-wide, most recently in Subnature*: Architecture's Other Environments*, by David Gissen and *Interactive Architecture*, by Michael Fox and Miles Kemp, and a forthcoming AD entitled *Territories*.

Andrea Hansen is a Lecturer in Landscape Architecture at the GSD, Harvard University. She graduated from the University of Pennsylvania a dual M.Arch and MLA. She is continuing to develop *FLUXscape,* and her research interests include issues and methodologies of representation.

Phu Hoang is a Lecturer in Architecture at the School of Design, University of Pennsylvania and the founder and principal of Phu Hoang Office, a New York-based architecture practice with projects in architecture, interiors, and exhibition design. Phu Hoang Office has received awards and competition prizes both nationally and internationally. The practice was awarded the Architectural League Prize in 2009. In 2010, Phu Hoang Office won (with Rachely Rotem Studio) the Oceantfront competition organized by Art Basel Miami Beach and Creative Time.

Mark Alan Hughes is a Distinguished Senior Fellow in Architecture at the University of Pennsylvania and an opinion columnist at the Philadelphia Daily News. Hughes was previously Chief Policy Adviser to Philadelphia's Mayor Michael A. Nutter and the founding Director of Sustainability for the City of Philadelphia. As a cabinet member in the Administration of Mayor Nutter, Hughes established the City's first Office of Sustainability, created a distinguished 20-member Sustainability Advisory Board, and designed and produced the City's 2015 policy framework, Greenworks Philadelphia. He also designed and led the City's strategy for maximizing the value and impact of federal resources under the Recovery Act. He graduated from Swarthmore College in 1981 and received a Ph.D. in Regional Science from the University of Pennsylvania in 1986. Hughes joined the standing faculty at Princeton's Woodrow Wilson School at the age of 25, teaching land use planning, public management, and antipoverty policy. He has held non-resident senior fellow appointments at Brookings and the Urban Institute; served as a senior consultant to the Urban Poverty Program at The Ford Foundation; and served as the first Vice President for Policy Development at Public/Private Ventures in Philadelphia. Hughes is the leader of the Policy, Markets, and Behavior Team for the Greater Philadelphia Innovation Cluster (GPIC) for Energy Efficient Buildings, a $122 million project funded by the Department of Energy.

Tetsugo Hyakutake is a photographer who has worked for Fujifilm in Tokyo, and holds a Master's Degree of Fine Arts from the University of Pennsylvania where he was awarded a Toby Devan Lewis Fellowship. He also holds a Bachelor of Fine Arts in Photography from the University of the Arts, receiving the Promising Artist Award and Society for Photographic Education Mid-Atlantic Region Scholarship Award. His work has been exhibited in Tokyo, Philadelphia, New York, Madrid, Venice, and he is currently represented by Gallery339 in Philadelphia and Alan Klotz Gallery in New York.

Lily Jencks is a landscape and architectural designer, working on projects as LJA+Land in Glasgow and Hong Kong for Maggies Cancer Caring Centers. She is currently collaborating with JencksSquared on a landscape project at CERN in Geneva and with Nathaniel Dorent Architects on Ruins studio in Dumfries, Scotland. She recently collaborated on an award winning design for Safe Trestles with Co-Lab. Her work has been published in Landscape Journal and viaOccupation. She holds a dual M.Arch and MLA degree from the School of Design, University of Pennsylvania.

Peter Lloyd Jones is an Associate Professor of Pathology & Laboratory Medicine, Lecturer in Architecture, and Director of the Penn-CMREF Center for Pulmonary Hypertension Research at The Institute for Medicine & Engineering (IME) at the University of Pennsylvania. In 2006, he co-founded the Sabin+Jones LabStudio with Jenny E. Sabin. His research investigates the role of 3-D tissue architecture in the lung vasculature and breast cancer.

Keith Kaseman is a Lecturer in Landscape Architecture at the School of Design, University of Pennsylvania, an Adjunct Associate Professor of Architecture at Columbia University's GSAPP, and a founding partner of KBAS, LLC, the Philadelphia-based firm selected for the Pentagon Memorial to the victims of September 11th. He received a BSD in Architecture from Arizona State University and a Master of Architecture from GSAPP. A Leopold Schepp Scholar, he graduated from Columbia with Honors for Excellence in Design and was a recipient of the Lucille Smyser Lowenfish Memorial Prize.

Ferda Kolatan is a founding partner of su11 architecture+design in New York City and a Senior Lecturer at the School of Design, University of Pennsylvania. su11's work has been exhibited nationally and internationally in such venues as the Walker Art Center, Documenta, Archilab, Vitra Design Museum, Art Basel, SIGGRAPH, PS1 and MoMA. Publications featuring su11's work include Archilab's *Futurehouse, Space, Monitor, L'Arca, Arch+, New-New York, PreFAb Modern, Digital Real, The Metapolis Dictionary of Advanced Architecture, AD, Dwell, Le Monde, NY Times, LA Times* and *Washington Post*. su11 was named a finalist for the Chernikhov Price in 2007 and the MoMA/PS1 YAP competition in 2008. The firm received the Swiss National Culture Award for Art and Design and the ICFF Editors Award for 'Best New Designer' in 2001.

John D. Landis is Crossways Professor of City and Regional Planning at the University of Pennsylvania, where he is currently Department Chair and Urban Spatial Analytics Academic Director of the Department of City and Regional Planning. Prof. Landis' research interests span a variety of urban development topics; his recent research and publications focus on growth management, infill housing, and the geography of urban employment centers. Together with several generations of Ph.D. students, Prof. Landis developed the California Urban Futures series of urban growth models. He is currently engaged in a National Science Foundation-funded project to model, forecast, and develop alternative spatial scenarios of U.S. population and employment patterns and their impacts on travel demand, habitat loss, and water use through 2050.

Sylvia Lavin is the Chair of the Ph.D. in Architecture program and Professor of Architectural History and Theory at UCLA, where she was Chairperson of the department of Architecture and Urban Design from 1996 to 2006. Lavin is also a frequent visitor at Harvard University's GSD and was a Visiting Professor of Architectural Theory at Princeton University's School of Architecture. A leading figure in current debates, Lavin is known both for her scholarship and for her criticism in contemporary architecture and design.

Andrew Lucia holds an Associate Research and Design position within the Sabin+Jones LabStudio and also teaches courses in Visual Studies in the Department of Architecture at the School of Design, University of Pennsylvania. His current research and design explores aspects of rhythm and difference as they relate to the generation and perception of matter. He holds a M.Arch degree from the School of Design, University of Pennsylvania.

Ian McHarg (1920-2001) was the Founder and Chair of the Department of Landscape Architecture at the University of Pennsylvania. His writings, teaching, and design career have inspired subsequent generations of landscape architects, city planners and environmentalists. In 1969 he wrote *Design with Nature*, the seminal text in environmental architecture. His mapping strategies have evolved into the Geographic Information System (GIS), now an industry standard. He is thought to be the most important landscape architect since Frederick Law Olmsted.

Frank Matero is Professor of Architecture, Graduate Program in Historic Preservation and Founder and Director of The Architectural Conservation Laboratory, School of Design, University of Pennsylvania.

Karen M'Closkey and **Keith VanDerSys** co-founded PEG office of landscape + architecture in 2004. The firm has been published internationally and won numerous design awards, including First Place in the Emerging New York Architects HB:BX design competition in 2010, an Honorable Mention for their entry into the *Buzzard's Bay Bridge: Park* international design competition, three AIA awards and an I.D. Magazine award. PEG's work was among six firms awarded the 2010 Architectural League Prize for Young Architects and Designers. PEG has been featured in *Architectural Record and Urban Spaces: Squares & Plazas, 1000x Architecture of the Americas,* and *ELA environment & landscape architecture of Korea*, the book series *Advanced Public Design, Advanced Interior Design,* and *Public Landscape*.

Rhett Russo is an Associate Professor and the Graduate Curriculum Coordinator in the College of Architecture and Design at the New Jersey Institute of Technology where he teaches courses in architectural design. He previously served as the 501 Design Studio Coordinator at the School of Design, University of Pennsylvania and also taught elective seminar courses on design and drawing. He has taught previously at Pratt Institute, where he served as the first year design coordinator in the undergraduate program from 2000 – 2001, Cornell University, and Columbia University's Graduate School of Planning and Preservation. Russo is a graduate of Columbia University's Master's of Architecture program, where he received the McKim Award for Design Excellence. He has lectured nationally and internationally on his design work and was a panel member of the *NsO* conference in 2005 where he first presented the *Orbigraphia*.

Jenny E. Sabin is Principal of Jenny Sabin LLC and is Co-Director of the Sabin+Jones LabStudio, and Assistant Professor of Emerging Technologies at Cornell University. Her research, teaching and design practice focus on the contextual, material and formal intersections between architecture, textiles, tectonics, and biology. Her trans-disciplinary approach to design computation has generated a body of creative and applied work that sits at the nexus of the arts, science, technology and society.

Gabriela Carmen Sarhos is a designer and writer and the founder of the design practice GSA&D. She holds a M.Arch degree from the School of Design, University of Pennsylvania.

servo, principals Marcelyn Gow and Ulrika Karlsson, is an architectural design collaborative. *servo* adopts the organizing principles of a network, integrating geographically discrete nodes of operation through various forms of telecommunication. The group's work focuses on the development of architectural *environments*, active design systems comprised of temporal conditions, shifting material states, the proliferation of electronic and digital equipment and interfaces, and the ebb and flow of information in real-time. *servo*'s work has been exhibited at the Venice Architecture Biennale, the Centre Pompidou, SFMoMA, the Cooper-Hewitt National Design Museum, the Wexner Center for the Arts, MoMA/QNS, Artists Space, the MAK Center for Art and Architecture, and the Storefront for Art and Architecture in New York. Recent publications include a monograph, *Networks and Environments*. Marcelyn Gow is currently Visiting Professor in Architecture Technology at the Royal Institute of Technology in Stockholm. Ulrika Karlsson is currently the Director of Academic Program and Visiting Professor at the Royal Institute of Technology in Stockholm.

Cathrine Veikos is Assistant Professor of Architecture at the School of Design, University of Pennsylvania where she coordinates the Visual Studies sequence and teaches design studios and advanced seminars. Her research addresses the relation between drawing and building, materials, and media-based techniques in art and architectural practice. Her current book, forthcoming from Routledge, examines these themes in the work of Lina Bo Bardi framed around the first translation into English of a key essay by Bo Bardi.

Phoebe Washburn received an MFA in 2002 from the School of Visual Arts. Washburn has had solo exhibitions at the Kestnergesellschaft, Hannover; Deutsche Guggenheim, Berlin; Institute of Contemporary Art, Philadelphia and UCLA Hammer Museum, Los Angeles. Her work has been featured in group exhibitions at the Guggenheim Museum, the Whitney Museum of American Art, and P.S. 1.

Marion Weiss is the Graham Chair Professor of Architecture at the University of Pennsylvania and is a partner at *Weiss/Manfredi* with Michael Manfredi. Her firm is at the forefront of design practices that are redefining the relationships between architecture, landscape, infrastructure, and art. Weiss/Manfredi won the American Academy of Arts and Letters Award for Architecture, AIA New York's Gold Medal, the Architectural League of New York's "Emerging Voices" award, and numerous international design competitions. Her firm's *Olympic Sculpture Park*, winner of an international competition, received the Nature Award at the World Architecture Festival and the VR Green Prize, an international award given to one project in the world every two years. *The Diana Center* at Barnard College, winner of a national competition and a Progressive Architecture Award, opened to students and the public in January 2010.

Richard Wesley is adjunct professor of architecture at the School of Design, University of Pennsylvania, where he teaches undergraduate design and a theory course on modern architecture, and is Chair of the Undergraduate Program in Architecture in the College of Arts and Sciences and a member of the Visual Studies Program. Wesley is author of essays in Harvard Design Magazine, RES, and Rassegna.

Credits

Flashes of Brilliance
Interview transcribed by Phillip M. Crosby.

Rumor
Images are taken from the exhibition "Some True Stories: Researches in the Field of Flexible Truth," curated by Keller Easterling with graphic design by Neil Donnelly, Storefront for Art and Architecture, 2008. Thanks to the New York State Council on the Arts and Yale School of Architecture. The designers and researchers included: Keller Easterling, Rustam-Marc Mehta, Thom Moran, Mustapha Jundi, Ashima Chitre, Gaby Brainard, Jacob Reidel, Carol Ruiz, Santiago del Hierro, and Mwangi Gathinji. All images are courtesy of Storefront for Art and Architecture, New York.

Things Themselves Are Lying
This essay is excerpted from an essay originally published in *VIA 2: Structures Implicit and Explicit*, James Bryan and Rolf Sauer, eds. (Philadelphia: Graduate School of Fine Arts, University of Pennsylvania, 1973): pp. 80-109.

Branching Morphogenesis
Design Team: Jenny E. Sabin, Andrew Lucia, Christopher Lee, Jonathan Asher. Science Team: Peter Lloyd Jones and members of the Jones Laboratory. Design Critic: Annette Fierro. Assembly Team: Dwight Engel, Matthew Lake, Austin McInerny, Marta Moran, Misako Murata.

Secret Pact of Parts
CHROMAZON—Partners in Charge: Ferda Kolatan and Erich Schoenenberger. Project Team: Andrew Ruggles, Matt Lake, Andrew Lucia, and Kyu Chun. Structural Consultant: Matthew Clark, Ove Arup & Partners, New York. Graphic Design Consultants: Erin Bazos and Gabriela Lazcarro. Animation: GMD THREE studio. PS_Canopy—Partners in Charge: Ferda Kolatan and Erich Schoenenberger. Project Team: Richard Baxley and Hart Marlow. Photography: Ferda Kolatan. Models printed and sponsored by ZCorp. Special thanks to Bentley Systems and Makai Smith.

Live Models
Partners in Charge: Jason Kelly Johnson and Nataly Gattegno. Design and Fabrication Collaborators: Carrie Norman and Thomas Kelley. Project Assistants: Troy Rogers, Noah Keating, Kezia Ofiesh, Paul Fromm, Sarah Fugate, Hank Byron, Taylor Burgess, Ed Yung, Ben Fey, Dayoung Shin. Additional Assistance: Kyle Kugler, Jim Staddon, Gin Harr, Yukin Staddon, Matt Young, Brad DeVries, David Kwon, Christo Logan, Nicole Seekely, and Philip Anzalone. Institutional Support: The Van Alen Institute (NY Prize in Systems and Ecology), Taubman College at the University of Michigan (Research Through Making Grant), Dean Monica Ponce de Leon, The University of Michigan Map Library, Graham Foundation for Advanced Studies in the Fine Arts Grant, Columbia University Avery CNC Fabrication Lab, NYC College of Technology – CityTech CUNY Fab Lab.

Tickle the Shitstem
Interview conducted by Debs Hoy and Megan Born. Transcription by Phillip M. Crosby.

Between Line and Shadow
Interview transcribed by Morgan Martinson.

Rising Currents
This essay was adapted from a commencement address delivered at the University of Pennsylvania School of Design, 2010. The exhibition "Rising Currents: Projects for New York's Waterfront," on view at The Museum of Modern Art from March 24 to October 11, 2010, was organized by Barry Bergdoll. The exhibition installation was designed by Lana Hum, Production Manager, Department of Exhibitions and Production. The installation graphics were designed by Ingrid Chou, Assistant Director, Graphics and Inva Cota, Designer, Department of Graphic Design.

Dirty Cities, Dirtier Policies
Interview conducted by Megan Born, Lily Jencks, and Helene Furján. Transcription by Gabriela Sarhos.

Ecology, for the Evolution of Planning and Design

This essay is excerpted from an essay originally published in *VIA 1: Ecology in Design*, James Bryan, Rolf Sauer, and Thomas Gilmore, eds. (Philadelphia: Graduate School of Fine Arts, University of Pennsylvania, 1968): 44-66.

A New Systemic Nature

This project is the result of research conducted at the American Academy of Rome during Alan Berger's 2007-08 Prince Charitable Trusts Rome Prize Fellowship in Landscape Architecture. This essay is part of a forthcoming book on global environmental challenges and systemic thinking in design and planning.

Surface In-Depth

This event was moderated by Helene Furján and Karen M'Closkey. Transcription by Morgan Martinson and Phillip M. Crosby.

Hydrophile

This project was commissioned for the exhibition "Envelopes," curated by Christopher Hight and exhibited at the Pratt Manhattan Gallery, New York, from March 4-May 5, 2010. Architectural Proposal: Marcelyn Gow, Ulrika Karlsson, and Chris Perry. Design Team: Marcelyn Gow, Ulrika Karlsson, and Jonah Fritzell. Green Roof/Ecology Consultant: Tobias Emilsson, PhD. Funding: Vetenskapsrådet (Swedish Research Council). Special Thanks: KTH School of Architecture, Hanna Erixon, Sara Grahn, Lars Marcus, KIT, Stockholm Resilience Center, and William Mohline.

Not Garden

This installation was made possible with the assistance of School of Design, University of Pennsylvania students and financial support from the Dean's Office and the Department of Landscape Architecture. This work was made possible with the assistance of the Urban Tree Connection, a non-profit group that has a long-established community garden initiative that provided us with an in-place community network for oversight of the project after installation. Also, the Redevelopment Authority provided us with a vacant lot, from its stock of approximately 5,000 properties, for the second installation, *Not Again*. *Not Garden*—Garden Design: PEG office of landscape + architecture (Karen M'Closkey and Keith VanDerSys). Installation Team: PEG, Marisa Bernstein, Aron Cohen, Marguerite Graham, Sahar Moin, Tiffany Marston, Steven Tucker, and Amy Wickner. *Not Again*—Garden Design: PEG office of landscape + architecture (Karen M'Closkey and Keith VanDerSys). Installation Team: PEG, Marisa Bernstein, Sahar Moin, Steven Tucker, and Sean Williams.

Image Credits

All reasonable efforts to secure permissions for the visual material reproduced herein have been made by the authors of each essay. The publisher and authors apologize to anyone who has not been reached.

The location of the image on a page is indicated by the following key:
(L) Left, (C) Center, (R) Right,
(T) Top, (M) Middle, (B) Bottom.

Story Lines
10-17, All images used courtesy of Eric Fischer from Flickr.com. Freely used as in the public domain in accordance with a Creative Commons License. All base maps © OpenStreetMap, CC-BY-SA.

Flashes of Brilliance
19, Lily Jencks. 22, Mcginnly, November 2006, from Wikimedia Commons used under a Creative Commons License.

Autonomous Worlds
25-29, All images courtesy of Larissa Fassler.

Rumor
30, Storefront for Art and Architecture. 32 (T), Storefront for Art and Architecture, Carol Ruiz, and Santiago del Hierro. 32 (M), Storefront for Art and Architecture, Rustam Mehta, and Thom Moran. 32 (B), Storefront for Art and Architecture, Rustam Mehta, and Thom Moran. 34 (T), Storefront for Art and Architecture, Ashima Chitre, and Mustapha Jundi. 34 (M), Storefront for Art and Architecture, Keller Easterling, and Mwangi Gathinji. 34 (B), Storefront for Art and Architecture, Gaby Brainard, and Jacob Reidel. 35, Storefront for Art and Architecture and Keller Easterling.

6 Ways of Being a Stranger
41, Intelligence Branch of the War Office, *Narrative of the Field operations connected with the Zulu War of 1879* (London: Greenhill Books, 1989). Permission granted by Greenhill Books. 42 (T), Culen Africa Library, University of Witwatersrand, Johannesburg. Copyright expired. 42 (M), Barlow Rand archive. 44, South African Democracy Education Trust, *The Road to Democracy in South Africa, vi* (Cape Town: Zebra Press, 2004), p. 456. Permission requested, no reply. 45 (T), Image by Dimitar Pouchnikov from Twala, M. and Bernard, E., *Mbokodo Inside MK: Mwezi Twala – A Soldier's Story* (Parklands: Jonathan Ball, 1994), pp. 80-81. Every effort has been made to contact the copyright holders by the publishers with no success. 45 (B), How To Master Secret Work (Fourth Quarter, 1989), p. 14. Permission granted by the South African Communist Party. 46 (T), Lindsay Bremner from "South African Border War," *Nation Master* website, accessed 9 Dec. 2008 at <http://www.nationmaster.com/encyclopedia/South-African-Border-War>. 47 (T), Author's collection. 47 (B), Image by Dimitar Prouchnikov. Sources accessed 26 Dec. 2007, African Hut <http://africanhut.com>, South Africa Shop <http://www.southafricashop.co.uk>, Beer Store <http://www.beerstore.com.an/detail.asp?beerID-536>, Beer Trash <http://www.beer.trash.net/beerpage.php(beernum-756>.

Fertile Minds
48-49, Image used courtesy of NASA/JPL/Caltech. Freely used as in the public domain in accordance with the National Aeronautics and Space Administration's contract. Credit: NASA, ESA, and The Hubble Heritage Team (STScI/AURA). Acknowledgement: NASA, ESA, M. Robberto (Space Telescope Science Institute) and the Hubble Space Telescope Orion Treasury Project Team. 50-51, Image used courtesy of NASA/JPL/Caltech. Freely used as in the public domain in accordance with the National Aeronautics and Space Administration's contract. Credit: NASA, ESA, and The Hubble Heritage Team (STScI/AURA)-ESA/Hubble Collaboration. Acknowledgement: B. Whitmore (Space Telescope Science Institute). 52-53, Image used courtesy of NASA/JPL/Caltech. Freely used as in the public domain in accordance with the National Aeronautics and Space Administration's contract. Credit: NASA, ESA, SSC,

CXC, and STScI. **54-55**, Image used courtesy of NASA/JPL/Caltech. Freely used as in the public domain in accordance with the National Aeronautics and Space Administration's contract. Credit: NASA, ESA, N. Smith (University of California, Berkeley), and The Hubble Heritage Team (STScI/AURA).

Robert Le Ricolais

56-63, All images courtesy of the Architectural Archives of the University of Pennsylvania.

Things Themselves Are Lying

66-73, All images courtesy of the Architectural Archives of the University of Pennsylvania.

At the Boundaries of Practice

75, Estate of Robert Smithson, licensed by VAGA, New York, NY. **77**, Vik Muniz, licensed by VAGA, New York, NY.

Skull/Kidney/Skin

78-83, Kim Brickley.

On Duration

85, Jason Santa Maria (Architect: Philip Johnson). **86**, Frank Matero. **87**, Author's collection (Artist: William Hogarth). **88 (L)**, Frank Matero. **88(R)**, Frank Matero (Architect: McKim, Mead and White). **89**, Author's collection. Source: John Ruskin, *The Seven Lamps of Architecture* (1855 edition). **90**, Author's collection. Drawing by I.F. Sullivan. Source: *Fun Magazine*, 1877. **91**, K. Fong. **92**, Frank Matero.

So Close You Can Touch It

95, Image courtesy of Kevin Burkett, used under a Creative Commons License (source: Flickr.com). **96 (L)**, Helene Furján. **95 (R)**, Helene Furján. **97 (L)**, Helene Furján and The Museum of Modern Art, New York. **97 (R)**, Helene Furján (Architects: Office dA and Johnston Marklee). **98 (L)**, Image courtesy Dave Kliman, used under a Creative Commons License (source: Flickr.com). **98 (R)**, Helene Furján (Architect: OMA, Graphic Design: Michael Rock). **99 (L)**, Helene Furján (Architect: OMA, Graphic Design: Michael Rock). **99 (R)**, K.T. Anthony Chan (Artist: Anish Kapoor). **100**, Image captured by GeoEye Satellite, courtesy of Earth Observatory, NASA, Image of the Day program. **101**, Helene Furján (Artist: James Turrell). **102** Helene Furján (Artist: Olafur Eliasson). **103**, Jeremy Leman. **104**, Helene Furján (Architect: Peter Zumthor).

Process Work

106-113, Megan Born and K.T. Anthony Chan.

Orbigraphia

114-129, Rhett Russo.

Branching Morphogenesis

130-135, Sabin + Jones LabStudio. **131 (L)**, JonesLab, University of Pennsylvania.

Secret Pact of Parts

136-141, su11 architecture + design.

Live Models

142-147, Future Cities Lab.

Tickle the Shitstem

148-153, Phoebe Washburn and Tom Powel Imaging, courtesy of Zach Feuer Gallery, New York.

Between Line and Shadow

All drawings produced under the guidance and direction of Marion Weiss in her elective seminars titled *Between Line and Shadow*. **154-155**, Michael Filsky (Spring 2005). **156-157**, Gavin Riggall (Spring 2005). **158-159**, Megan Born (Spring 2007). **160-161**, Jackie Wong (Spring 2007). **162-163**, Peter Rae (Spring 2007). **164-165**, Ashley Wendela (Spring 2007).

Active Agents

166-167, Image used courtesy of NASA Earth

Observatory. Freely used as in the public domain in accordance with the National Aeronautics and Space Administration's contract. Image created by Robert Simmon, based on Landsat 5 data. 168-171, Images used courtesy of NASA Earth Observatory. Freely used as in the public domain in accordance with the National Aeronautics and Space Administration's contract. Images created by Jesse Allen, using data provided courtesy of NASA/GSFC/METI/ERSDAC/JAROS, and the U.S./Japan ASTER Science Team. 172-173, Image used courtesy of NASA Earth Observatory. Freely used as in the public domain in accordance with the National Aeronautics and Space Administration's contract. Image created by Jesse Allen, using Landsat data provided by the United States Geological Survey and ASTER data provided courtesy of NASA/GSFCMETI/ERSDAC/JAROS, and the U.S./Japan ASTER Science Team.

Rising Currents
175, The Museum of Modern Art, New York. 176 (L), The Museum of Modern Art, New York. 176 (R), The Museum of Modern Art, New York, ARO, and dlandstudio. 177, The Museum of Modern Art, New York and LTL Architects. 178, The Museum of Modern Art, New York and Matthew Baird Architects. 179 (L), The Museum of Modern Art, New York and nArchitects. 179 (R), The Museum of Modern Art, New York and SCAPE.

The Suburbs are Dead
184, IDuke, November 2005, from Wikimedia Commons used under a Creative Commons License.

Pathos and Irony
186-193, Tetsugo Hyakutake.

Dirty Cities, Dirtier Policies
195 (T), Philadelphia City Center District. 195 (B), Peter Tobia for Philadelphia City Paper. 196, Mark Alan Hughes. 199 (T), Eli Pousson from Flickr.com, used under a Creative Commons License. 199 (B), David Barrie from Flickr.com, used under a Creative Commons License. 201, Philadelphia Water Department. 204, Helene Furján.

FLUXscape
207-217, Andrea Hansen. 212 (L), PhillyHistory.org, a project of the Philadelphia Department of Records. 212 (R), "verplanck" from Flickr.com, used under a Creative Commons License. 214 (L), Janis Jade. 214 (R), Antonio Navarez from Flickr.com, used under a Creative Commons License. 216 (L), PhillyHistory.org, a project of the Philadelphia Department of Records.

Holey Urbanisms
221-222, Phillip Crosby, sketches by the author after originals by Alison Smithson.

Rich Ground
224-231, K.T. Anthony Chan.

Root Words
234, James Corner Field Operations. 235-237, PORT Architecture + Urbanism.

Ecology
238-251, All images courtesy of the Architectural Archives of the University of Pennsylvania.

A New Systemic Nature
252-261, All photos courtesy Alan Berger/P-REX. All maps and drawings courtesy Alan Berger and Case Brown/P-REX.

Surface In-Depth
263, Michael Van Valkenburgh Associates. 264-265, Weiss/Manfredi. 266-267, KBAS. 268, Phu Hoang Office. 270-271, James Corner Field Operations and Diller Scofidio + Renfro.

Waste and Dirt
273, Andrew Dunn from Wikimedia Commons, used under a Creative Commons License. 274 (T), Lamiot from Wikimedia Commons, used under a Creative Commons License. 274 (B), Stan Shebs from Wikimedia Commons, used under a Creative Commons License.

Hydrophile
276-283, All renderings and drawings courtesy of servo. 280 (T), Dry Systems from top: Galium Verum-Image courtesy of Tobias Emilsson. Pulsatilla Vulgaris-Image courtesy of David Castor from Wikimedia Commons, used under a Creative Commons License. Centaurea Scabiosa-Image courtesy of Kristian Peters from

Wikimedia Commons, used under a Creative Commons License. 280 (**B**), Meadow Vegetation from top: Antrhiscus Sylvestris-Image courtesy of Kristian Peters from Wikimedia Commons, used under a Creative Commons License. Dactylis Glomerata Bluete-Image courtesy of Kristian Peters from Wikimedia Commons, used under a Creative Commons License. Rhinanthus Minor-Image courtesy of Guido Gerding from Wikimedia Commons, used under a Creative Commons License. Leucanthemum Vulgar-Image courtesy of Magnus Manske from Wikimedia Commons, used under a Creative Commons License. Campanula Patula-Image courtesy of Miika Silfverberg from Wikimedia Commons, used under a Creative Commons License. 282, Wet Systems from top: Deschampsia Cespitosa-Image courtesy of Christian Fischer from Wikimedia Commons, used under a Creative Commons License. Cirsium Palustre-Image courtesy of Kristian Peters from Wikimedia Commons, used under a Creative Commons License. Cladium Mariscus-Image courtesy Kristian Peters from Wikimedia Commons, used under a Creative Commons License. Eriophorum Angustifolium-Image courtesy of Kenraiz from Wikimedia Commons, used under a Creative Commons License. Caltha Palustris-Image courtesy of Wildfeuer from Wikimedia Commons, used under a Creative Commons License.

Not Garden
284-289, PEG office of landscape + architecture.

An Ornament of Sustainability
290-303, Lily Jencks. 292 (**L**), Reyner Banham Archive, no response from copyright holder. 294 (**L**), Megan Born. 297 (**L**), Brandon Shigeta from Flickr.com, used under a Creative Commons License. 297 (**C**), Helene Furján. 297 (**R**), Joshua Mings from Flickr.com, used under a Creative Commons License.

Gimme the Skinny
318-323, Jake Levine.

VIA Journals
1968 to 2000

Via 1: Ecology in Design (1968)
Editors: Rolf Sauer, James Bryan, Thomas Gilmore
Publisher: Graduate School of Fine Arts, University of Pennsylvania

Via 2: Structures Implicit and Explicit (1973)
Editors: James Bryan and Rolf Sauer
Publisher: Graduate School of Fine Arts, University of Pennsylvania

Via 3: Ornament (1977)
Editor: Stephen Kieran
Publisher: Graduate School of Fine Arts, University of Pennsylvania

Via 4: Culture and the Social Vision (1980)
Editors: Mark A. Hewitt, Benjamin Kracauer, John Massengale, Michael McDonough
Publisher: The MIT Press and the Graduate School of Fine Arts, University of Pennsylvania

Via 5: Determinants of Form (1982)
Editors: Darl Rastorfer (Editor in Chief), Deborah Allen, Christine Albright, Outerbridge Horsey, Jr., Jill Stoner, Merle Thorpe
Publisher: The MIT Press and the Graduate School of Fine Arts, University of Pennsylvania

Via 6: Architecture and Visual Perception (1983)
Editors: Alice Gray Read, Peter C. Doo with Joseph Burton
Publisher: The MIT Press and the Graduate School of Fine Arts, University of Pennsylvania

Via 7: The Building of Architecture (1984)
Editors: Paula Behrens, Anthony Fisher
Publisher: The MIT Press and the Graduate School of Fine Arts, University of Pennsylvania

Via 8: Architecture and Literature (1986)
Editors: Muscoe Martin, Patreese Martin, Jennifer Pearson, Suzannah Reid, Neil Sandvold
Publisher: Rizzoli International Publications and the Graduate School of Fine Arts, University of Pennsylvania

Via 9: Re-Presentation (1988)
Editors: Charles Hay, Peter Wong, Bryan Fleenor, Alex Gotthelf
Publisher: Rizzoli International Publications and the Graduate School of Fine Arts, University of Pennsylvania

Via 10: Ethics and Architecture (1990)
Editors: John Capelli, Paul Naprstek, Bruce Prescott
Publisher: Rizzoli International Publications and the Graduate School of Fine Arts, University of Pennsylvania

Via 11: Architecture and Shadow (1990)
Editor: David Murray
Publisher: Rizzoli International Publications and the Graduate School of Fine Arts, University of Pennsylvania

viaBooks
from 2008

viaOccupation (2008)
Investigates the macro- and micro-scales that inform how we read, claim, and intervene in our evolving territories.
Editors: Morgan Martinson, Tonya Markiewicz, and Helene Furján

Words from the Pages of *Dirt*
Illustration by Jake Levine

"Benito Mussolini was a fascist and landscape urbanist."

"To perceive space through dust is to render space-time literally visible. Such perception is an indicator of the internal dynamics of space. Dust in space is an index of four-dimensional reality."

"Gossip never started anywhere. It cannot be attributed to anyone... Rumor is perhaps considered to be witchcraft because it can be invisible, venomously destructive and impossible to contain. Moreover, gossip and rumor are universal tools.

"Benito Mussolini was a fascist and landscape urbanist."

"Informality, in the context of Mexico City has become a way of life, changing the city in both its social and economic dynamics as well as in urban space and everyday experiences."

"To perceive space through dust is to render space-time literally visible. Such perception is an indicator of the internal dynamics of space. Dust in space is an index of four-dimensional reality."

"When I set out to do work I had little sense of what would transpire. What I wanted it to be was purely part of bringing together a set of facts that were unrelated; topologies, bodies, and colors. In this respect it was a dirty process; clouded by the presence of interests in other disciplines – mathematics, biology, optics – that I had no formal training in, and a desire to intermingle their traits."

"Gossip never started anywhere. It cannot be attributed to anyone... Rumor is perhaps considered to be witchcraft because it can be invisible, venomously destructive and impossible to contain. Moreover, gossip and rumor are universal tools..."

Epilogue

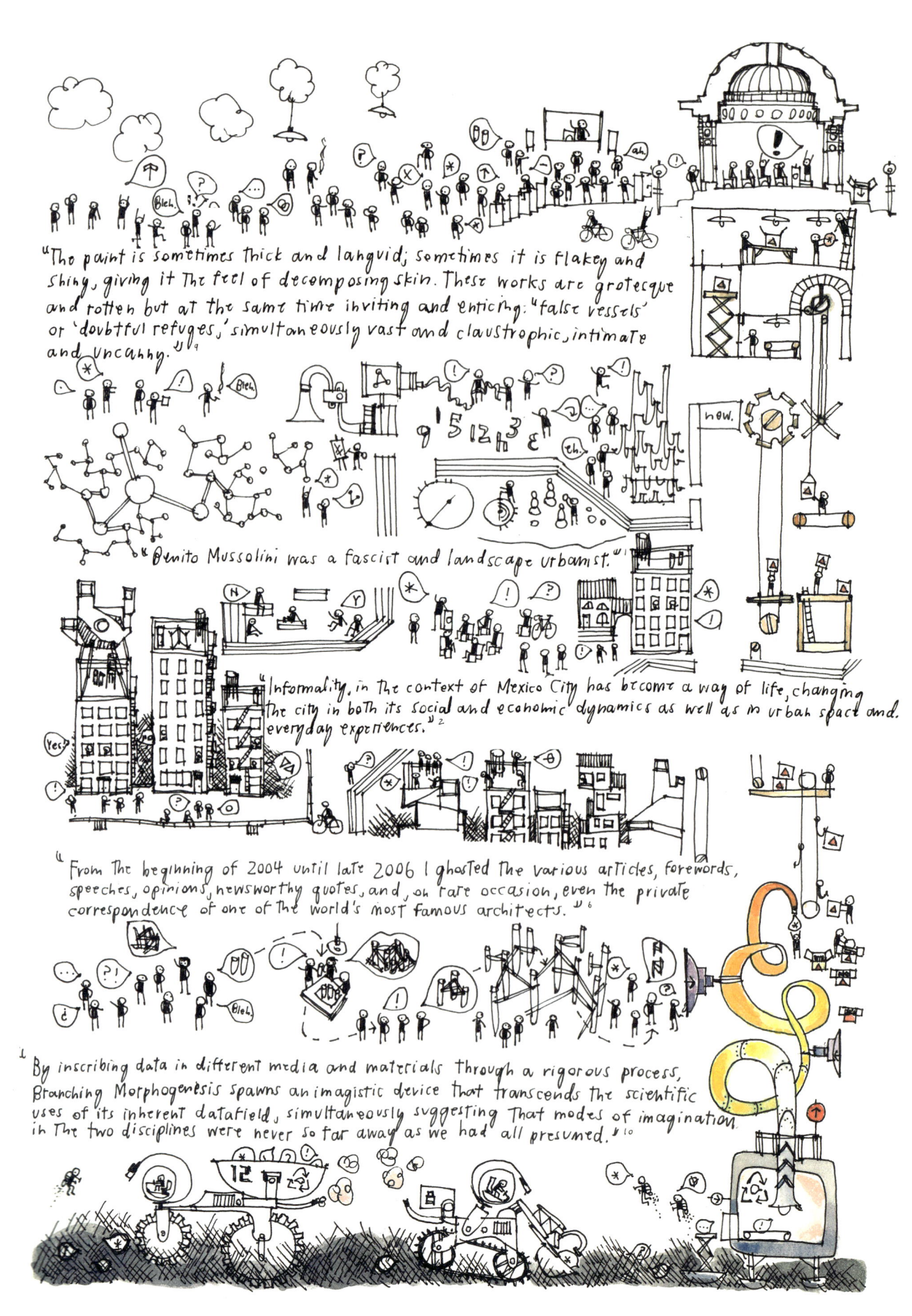

"The paint is sometimes thick and languid; sometimes it is flakey and shiny, giving it the feel of decomposing skin. These works are grotesque and rotten but at the same time inviting and enticing: 'false vessels' or 'doubtful refuges,' simultaneously vast and claustrophic, intimate and uncanny."9

"Benito Mussolini was a fascist and landscape urbanist."1

"Informality, in the context of Mexico City has become a way of life, changing the city in both its social and economic dynamics as well as in urban space and everyday experiences."2

"From the beginning of 2004 until late 2006 I ghosted the various articles, forewords, speeches, opinions, newsworthy quotes, and, on rare occasion, even the private correspondence of one of the world's most famous architects."6

"By inscribing data in different media and materials through a rigorous process, Branching Morphogenesis spawns an imagistic device that transcends the scientific uses of its inherent datafield, simultaneously suggesting that modes of imagination in the two disciplines were never so far away as we had all presumed."10

Words from the Pages of *Dirt* Jake Levine

"Waste is something to be voided, avoided, and left behind, once its value has been extracted. Dirtiness, on the other hand, is more symbolic, more a question of where waste should go."[7]

"It's important to discover that mistakes are often far more compelling than the things you set out to do. You need to defer to the discoveries that happen along the way. Often there's an idea that's robust enough to make it through to the end, but sometimes a radical mistake takes ownership of the direction you're moving in."[3]

"To perceive space through dust is to render space-time literally visible. Such perception is an indicator of the internal dynamics of space. Dust in space is an index of four-dimensional reality."[8]

"When I set out to do work I had little sense of what would transpire. What I wanted it to be was purely part of bringing together a set of facts that were unrelated; topologies, bodies, and colors. In this respect it was a dirty process; clouded by the presence of interests in other disciplines — mathematics, biology, optics — that I had no formal training in, and a desire to intermingle their traits."[4]

"Gossip never started anywhere. It cannot be attributed to anyone... Rumor is perhaps considered to be witchcraft because it can be invisible, venomously destructive and impossible to contain. Moreover, gossip and rumor are universal tools."[5]

J. Levine 2009